OXFORD STUDIES IN EUROPEAN LAW

*Series Editors*



# The Jurisprudence of Constitutional Conflict in the European Union

# OXFORD STUDIES IN EUROPEAN LAW

*Series Editors*



The aim of this series is to publish important and original research on EU law. The focus is on scholarly monographs, with a particular emphasis on those which are interdisciplinary in nature. Edited collections of essays will also be included where they are appropriate. The series is wide in scope and aims to cover studies of particular areas of substantive and of institutional law, historical works, theoretical studies, and analyses of current debates, as well as questions of perennial interest such as the relationship between national and EU law and the novel forms of governance emerging in and beyond Europe. The fact that many of the works are interdisciplinary will make the series of interest to all those concerned with the governance and operation of the EU.

OTHER TITLES IN THIS SERIES

**Reflexive Governance in EU Equality Law**
Emma Lantschner

**Enhanced Cooperation and European Tax Law**
Caroline Heber

**Legal Pluralism in European Contract Law**
Vanessa Mak

**Europe's Passive Virtues**
*Deference to National Authorities in EU Free Movement Law*
Jan Zglinski

**Accountability in EU Security and Defence**
*The Law and Practice of Peacebuilding*
Carolyn Moser

**Accountability in the Economic and Monetary Union**
*Foundations, Policy, and Governance*
Menelaos Markakis

**Official Secrets and Oversight in the EU**
*Law and Practices of Classified Information*
Vigjilenca Abazi

**Risk Regulation in the Internal Market**
*Lessons from Agricultural Biotechnology*
Maria Weimer

**EU Health Law & Policy**
*The Expansion of EU Power in Public Health and Health Care*
Anniek de Ruijter

**The Horizontal Effect of Fundamental Rights in the European Union**
*A Constitutional Analysis*
Eleni Frantziou

**EU Powers Under External Pressure**
*How the EU's External Actions Alter its Internal Structures*
Christina Eckes

**Frontex and Human Rights**
*Responsibility in 'Multi-Actor Situations' under the ECHR and EU Public Liability Law*
Melanie Fink

**EU Equality Law**
*The First Fundamental Rights Policy of the EU*
Elise Muir

**Subnational Authorities in EU Law**
Michèle Finck

**Accessing Asylum in Europe**
Violeta Moreno-Lax

**National Parliaments after the Lisbon Treaty & the Euro Crisis**
Davor Jančić

**Environmental Integration in Competition and Free-Movement Laws**
Julian Nowag

**EU Agencies**
*Legal and Political Limits to the Transformation of the EU Administration*
Merijn Chamon

# The Jurisprudence of Constitutional Conflict in the European Union

ANA BOBIĆ
Référendaire at the Court of Justice of the European Union

OXFORD
UNIVERSITY PRESS

OXFORD
UNIVERSITY PRESS

Great Clarendon Street, Oxford, OX2 6DP,
United Kingdom

Oxford University Press is a department of the University of Oxford.
It furthers the University's objective of excellence in research, scholarship,
and education by publishing worldwide. Oxford is a registered trade mark of
Oxford University Press in the UK and in certain other countries



First Edition published in 2022

Impression: 2



Published in the United States of America by Oxford University Press
198 Madison Avenue, New York, NY 10016, United States of America

British Library Cataloguing in Publication Data

Data available

Library of Congress Control Number: 2022931398

ISBN 978–0–19–284703–4

DOI: 10.1093/oso/9780192847034.001.0001

Printed and bound by
CPI Group (UK) Ltd, Croydon, CR0 4YY

*Za Brunu i Grgu*

# Series Editors' Preface

The interplay between national courts and the Court of Justice of the European Union (CJEU) has been a key issue ever since the inception of the European Economic Community (EEC). This is equally true now, as it was in the early years of the Community legal order. The CJEU established the foundational precepts of EEC law, notably direct effect and supremacy, and generations of scholars have debated their meaning, import, and boundaries. This is more especially so in relation to the supremacy of EU law over national law, which is the subject matter of Ana Bobić's book.

The issue is of relevance to all Member States, and this is so irrespective of whether they have sought to push back from the demands of EU law imposed by the EU institutions including the Court of Justice. The intellectual terrain is rich and varied. Scholars have debated the meaning of the case law at both national and EU level. There has been normative discourse as to whether national courts should be able to question the ambit and application of EU law, with the ultimate possibility that they could refuse to apply it. These debates have played out across multiple topics, the most prominent being fundamental rights, *ultra vires* review, and identity review.

Ana Bobić provides insight and analysis of this intellectual terrain. It is impossible to engage in this discourse without taking a normative position and the author makes clear that her preferred view is that of constitutional pluralism and heterarchy. She does, however, distinguish between constructive and destructive versions thereof, with recent jurisprudence of the Polish Constitutional Tribunal exemplifying the latter. The analysis is framed by what are termed triangular relationships: that between the CJEU and national constitutional courts; that between the CJEU and ordinary national courts; and that between national constitutional courts and ordinary national courts. This provides a helpful window through which to view the prevalent tensions and power relations at play in this area.

The centrality of the issues addressed in this book means that it will be of interest to all those concerned with EU law and to those from other disciplines who study the inter-relationship between the EU and the Member States.

Paul Craig
Gráinne de Búrca

# Acknowledgements

On this day four years ago, I handed in the manuscript of my doctoral thesis and took a flight to Berlin to start my post-doctoral programme. This book is based on that doctoral thesis, extended by all of the events in EU constitutional jurisprudence that unfolded in the next four years. This book has been written in Oxford (before and after Brexit), Zagreb, Luxembourg, Amsterdam, Berlin, and in Bourg-Saint-Maurice. In that sense, it is truly a living proof of what a wonderful project the borderless European Union is. The writing journey that is now coming to an end would not have been possible had it not been for the incredible support and beautiful friendships that I made along the way. I would like to use this opportunity to say thank you.

I am grateful to my supervisors Angus Johnston and Josephine van Zeben, who took over reading my work in the most crucial periods. I would like to thank Josephine for being available beyond what anyone would expect and taking up quite a sizeable amount of reading, while also preparing for the birth of her first son. But her help and support with my work is only the tip of the iceberg. She has during these years become my academic mentor in every sense of the word, and my dear friend whose kindness, care, and sense of humour can hardly be matched. After Oxford, my work was read and constructively criticized by Mark Dawson, Petra Weingerl, Stephen Weatherill, Jan Komárek, Julian Nowag, Gareth Davies, Orla Lynskey, and a number of anonymous reviewers, as well as participants of various conferences where I presented different parts of this book. Finalizing the manuscript has been made less stressful thanks to the trust and support of Oxford University Press and in particular Paulina Dos Santos Major and Alex Flach. This book would not have been finished without the brilliant research support of Kristina Hatas, who also made my time at the Hertie School in Berlin such a unique and enjoyable experience. I am extremely happy to be part of the EU law academic community and hope to be able to pay the same favour forward in the decades to come.

My thanks also go to the Oxford Law Faculty and the great amount of effort the faculty, staff, and the research community put into making it a thriving academic environment. Even more so, I am lucky that already during my undergraduate studies I was taught by Siniša Rodin, Tamara Ćapeta, Tamara Perišin, and the EU Law Chair of Zagreb's Law Faculty, who were the ones to introduce me to and spark an ever-growing interest in EU law. I am especially grateful to Siniša for having me as a *stagiaire* in his Chambers at the Court of Justice and to the judges and Advocates General of the Court for taking the time to talk to me about the issues discussed in this book. Afterwards, working at the Hertie School enriched the way I think about legal scholarship, research methods, interdisciplinary research, and making my work understandable not only to lawyers ... it's quite a special place. The final stages of writing this book were also supported by the Modern Law Review Fellowship.

My friends have been an incredible support and I can only scratch the surface of thanking them for making Oxford and Berlin such happy places. Petra, my Oxford sister, has been with me on this journey since day one of our MJur, both as a friend and the toughest reviewer of my work. You are so funny and smart and it's incredible to me that you are my friend! I am also grateful to Lilas for her crucial long hugs, her warmth and compassion, the writing sprints, and the French Alps ... everyone needs a Lilas in their lives. The beautiful times I've spent with Michael, Miguel, Giovanni, and Poorna made the often gloomy and grey Oxford the sunniest place. In Berlin, it was yet another Michael, Toni, Mark, Pierre, Adina, Tom, and Nina who gave me that delicate mix of distraction and support, something anyone writing a book needs. Jelena, Milan, Lucija, Mislav, Miran, Maja, Bruno, and Grga—my family—have certainly learned more about EU law than they wanted to during these years. Their constant calls, messages, funny photos, and videos filled with love, support, and cheerfulness are a must-have for anyone stuck in the academic writer's block.

And then there is Ole. It's highly unlikely that these few lines will do justice to the ways in which he has made my life happier and just better since that house-warming party in Neukölln, but here's a poor attempt. His irreplaceable friendship; the dark smoky bars in Berlin; Sameheads; his patience; Tempelhof and Tiergarten; the book club; the cave (with special thanks to the CFC for making the lockdown such a great experience!); the office; the castle; Garth and Quentin and Chekhov; the days of the week; the German grammar; checking whether I am changing the law; the flights booked and changed and taken and all those yet to come; das Baby: this book is because of you. I love you.

Bourg-Saint-Maurice, France
21 August 2021

# Contents

## PART II THE JURISPRUDENCE

# List of Figures

# Table of Cases

## EUROPEAN UNION

### Court of Justice

**Opinions of Advocates General**

### General Court



## COUNCIL OF EUROPE

### European Court of Human Rights



## NATIONAL CONSTITUTIONAL JURISPRUDENCE

### Austrian Constitutional Court (Verfassungsgerichtshof)



### Belgian Constitutional Court (Cour constitutionnelle)



### Belgian Cour d'Arbitrage



### Bulgarian Constitutional Court (Конституционен съд)



### Bulgarian Supreme Administrative Court



### The Supreme Court of Cyprus (Ανώτατο Δικαστήριο)



### Czech Constitutional Court (Ústavní Soud)



### Danish Supreme Court (Højesteret)

**French Constitutional Council (Conseil constitutionnel)**



**French Conseil d'État**



**German Federal Constitutional Court (Bundesverfassungsgericht)**



**Hungarian Constitutional Court (Magyarország Alkotmánybírósága)**

**Italian Constitutional Court (Corte Costituzionale)**



**Latvian Constitutional Court (Satversmes tiesa)**



**Polish Constitutional Tribunal (Trybunał Konstytucyjny)**



**Polish Supreme Court**



**Portuguese Constitutional Tribunal (Tribunal Constitucional)**



**Romanian Constitutional Court (Curtea Constituţională)**



**Slovak Constitutional Court (Ústavný súd)**



**Slovenian Constitutional Court (Ustavno sodišče)**

### Spanish Constitutional Tribunal (Tribunal Constitucional)



## UNITED KINGDOM

### House of Lords/Supreme Court



### Lower courts

# Table of Legislation

## SECONDARY EU LAW

## OTHER EU DOCUMENTS



## INTERNATIONAL TREATIES

# List of Abbreviations

| | |
|---|---|
| AFSJ | Area of Freedom, Security and Justice |
| CC | Constitutional Court |
| CFSP | Common, Foreign and Security Policy |
| CJEU | Court of Justice of the European Union |
| EAW | European Arrest Warrant |
| ECB | European Central Bank |
| ECHR | European Convention on Human Rights |
| ECtHR | European Court of Human Rights |
| EFTA | European Free Trade Agreement |
| EEA | European Economic Area |
| OMT | Outright Monetary Transactions Mechanism |
| ONC | ordinary national courts |
| PSPP | public sector purchase programme |
| SEA | Single European Act |
| TEU | Treaty on the European Union |
| TFEU | Treaty on the Functioning of the European Union |
| UN | United Nations |

# List of Abbreviations

# PART I
# THEORIZING CONSTITUTIONAL CONFLICT

# 1
# Introduction

The European Union[1] can be characterized as one of the most significant political creations in recent history, bringing together nearly half a billion people in an economic project, which has since developed into an increasingly political project. Equally, the European legal landscape has evolved into a system that has empowered the individual, national administrations, and the judiciary through legal principles such as primacy[2] and direct effect; the creation of the internal market; the introduction of EU citizenship; the establishment of the Euro; and the protection of fundamental rights.

Despite the benefits of EU membership, Member States have not always been entirely ready or willing to embrace this political and legal 'revolution'.[3] This reluctance is exemplified through the behaviour of national courts performing constitutional review, who have traditionally been and still are considered to be the ultimate guardians of national constitutions. These institutions have not always shared the Court of Justice's enthusiasm in expanding the self-referential system of the Treaties.[4] There are two specific dynamics driving this reluctance: first, the principles of direct effect and primacy have called into question the previously undisputed supremacy of constitutions in the national hierarchy of legal norms; and, secondly, these same principles combined with the preliminary reference procedure have undermined the position and influence of national courts performing constitutional review and safeguarding the constitution's supremacy.

For example, in the wake of the Euro crisis, the German Bundesverfassungsgericht and the Court of Justice engaged in a back and forth exchange concerning the limits that the Treaties impose on the mandate of the European Central Bank.[5]

[1] I will use the term European Union throughout the book, except when a reference to the European Community is due to the particular point in time or a direct citation. Equally, I will use EU law as a general term encompassing the entirety of the European Union legal order, save for when a difference between EC and EU law is of relevance for the analysis.

[2] It suffices to remember that it was the vigilant individual, Flaminio Costa, unsatisfied with a slightly overpriced electricity bill due to the nationalization of the electricity company (the relevant amount was 1925 lire, which can be translated into today's worth of approximately €17.51) and the assiduousness of a Milan giudice conciliatore (a first instance single judge) that we have to thank for one of the most important cases in the history of EU law (Case 6/64 *Costa v ENEL* [1964] EU:C:1964:66).

[3] To borrow the phrasing from Joseph Weiler. See J H H Weiler, 'A Quiet Revolution: The European Court of Justice and Its Interlocutors' (1994) 26(4) *Comparative Political Studies* 510.

[4] See ch 5, ss 4, 5, and 7 for a detailed analysis of this development.

[5] German Bundesverfassungsgericht Case 2 BvR 2728/13 *Gauweiler and Others* Order of 14 January 2014 (German reference); Case C-62/14 *Gauweiler and Others* [2015] EU:C:2015:400 (Court of Justice's response); Case 2 BvR 2728/13 *Gauweiler*, Judgment of 21 June 2016 (German acceptance of the response); Cases 2 BvR 859/15, 2 BvR 980/16, 2 BvR 2006/15, 2 BvR 1651/15 *Weiss* Order of 18 July 2017

*The Jurisprudence of Constitutional Conflict in the European Union*. Ana Bobić, Oxford University Press. © Ana Bobić 2022.
DOI: 10.1093/oso/9780192847034.003.0001

During the same period, in reviewing austerity measures demanded as part of bailout conditionality, the Portuguese Constitutional Court chose instead to safeguard the high level of social protection enshrined in the Portuguese Constitution.[6] In parallel, when reviewing the reductions of salaries in the Portuguese public sector, the Court of Justice declared judicial independence the cornerstone of the rule of law and expanded its application to all Member State actions regardless of the applicability of EU law in the specific case.[7] This in turn had the consequence of obliging the Polish government to refrain from intruding in the nomination of and disciplinary procedures against judges.[8] The developments in Poland resulted in the Commission initiating numerous rule of law infringement proceedings before the Court of Justice.

All these cases involve a conflict between demands of EU law on the one hand and national constitutions on the other. Accordingly, they most commonly materialize before the Court of Justice and national constitutional courts. However, these incidents do not stand in isolation, but rather form part of a long-standing pattern, which has captured the attention of both EU legal scholars and the wider public. In addition, not all constitutional conflicts that take place within this framework are equally conducive to the development of the EU's constitution broadly understood. As will become evident in the course of analysis throughout this book, it is possible to distinguish between constructive and destructive conflicts. So long as the national level interprets the 'constitutional', expressed through the values in Article 2 TEU,[9] coherently within the limits of mutual respect and sincere cooperation by an independent judiciary, we can speak of constructive conflict, conducive to the dynamic development of the EU's constitutional sphere. This means that the conflict is contained within the scope of the 'constitutional', thus respecting the existence of the basic values shared by the EU and its Member States. Constructive conflict allows for varying interpretations within the scope of reasonable disagreement and remains 'pluralist'.[10] Destructive constitutional conflicts conversely deny

(second German reference); Case C-493/17 *Weiss and Others* [2018] EU:C:2018:1000 (Court of Justice's response); Cases 2 BvR 859/15, 2 BvR 980/16, 2 BvR 2006/15, 2 BvR 1651/15 *Weiss II* Judgment of 5 May 2020 (German rejection of the response).

[6] R De Brito Gião Hanek and D Gallo, *Constitutional Change through Euro Crisis Law: Report of Portugal* Annex I https://eurocrisislaw.eui.eu/wp-content/uploads/sites/44/2019/05/Portugal.pdf. All links in this book were last accessed on 15 July 2021.

[7] Case C-64/16 *Juízes Portugueses* [2018] EU:C:2018:117.

[8] M Bonelli and M Claes, 'Judicial Serendipity: How Portuguese Judges Came to the Rescue of the Polish Judiciary ECJ 27 February 2018, Case C-64/16, *Associação Sindical dos Juízes Portugueses*' (2018) 14 *European Constitutional Law Review* 622.

[9] The provision reads: 'The Union is founded on the values of respect for human dignity, freedom, democracy, equality, the rule of law and respect for human rights, including the rights of persons belonging to minorities. These values are common to the Member States in a society in which pluralism, non-discrimination, tolerance, justice, solidarity and equality between women and men prevail.'

[10] A Bobić, 'Constructive Versus Destructive Conflict: Taking Stock of the Recent Constitutional Jurisprudence in the EU' (2020) 22 *Cambridge Yearbook of European Legal Studies* 60, 70.

the very existence of these shared values, presenting themselves as an extreme exception that cannot be resolved through judicial accommodation, but demands collective action in both the political and legal realm.

Against this backdrop, the present book addresses the incidences of, and reasons for, constitutional clashes between the European Court of Justice and national constitutional courts in the application and enforcement of EU law. It seeks to determine how the principle of primacy of EU law works in reality and whether national constitutional jurisprudence supports this concept. In so doing, the book is based on the contributions of the theory of constitutional pluralism and seeks to reinforce its normative prescriptions in the management and resolution of constitutional conflict in the EU.

## 1 Setting the Stage

Starting from *van Gend en Loos* and *Costa v ENEL*, the Court of Justice made it clear that for the purposes of achieving effectiveness and uniformity of EU law,[11] individuals can invoke their EU law rights directly before national courts and national law cannot be applied if it contradicts an EU law obligation.[12] In *Internationale Handelsgesellschaft*, the Court of Justice explicitly stated that even provisions of national constitutions ('rules of national law, however framed')[13] cannot override obligations stemming from EU law. Four years later, the Court of Justice stated that EU law obliges national courts to disregard diverging jurisprudence of superior courts,[14] subsequently explicitly confirming that this also applies to decisions of constitutional courts.[15] An obligation of an ordinary national court to refer a question of constitutionality to the constitutional court equally cannot relieve it from the obligation of referring a preliminary reference to the Court of Justice.[16]

This jurisprudence of the Court of Justice established the so-called '*Simmenthal* mandate', according to which each national court must apply EU law to cases within their jurisdiction and protect the rights that it accords to citizens in their entirety.[17] These foundational cases placed the individual and her EU rights at the forefront unlike any international organization founded on public international

[11] Case 106/77 *Simmenthal* [1978] EU:C:1978:49 [18]–[22].

[12] Case 6/64 *Costa v ENEL* (n 3).

[13] Case 11/70 *Internationale Handelsgesellschaft* [1970] EU:C:1970:4 [3].

[14] Case 166/73 *Rheinmühlen* [1974] EU:C:1974:3 [4].

[15] Case C-348/89 *Mecanarte* [1991] EU:C:1991:278 [46]; Case C-399/09 *Landtová* [2011] EU:C:2011:415 [49]. See also Opinion of Advocate General Cruz Villalón in Case C-173/09 *Elchinov* [2010] EU:C:2010:336 [21]; and Case C-416/10 *Križan* [2013] EU:C:2013:8 [73].

[16] Case C-188/10 *Melki and Abdeli* [2010] EU:C:2010:363 [51]–[56].

[17] M Claes, *The National Courts' Mandate in the European Constitution* (Hart Publishing 2006) 108.

law has ever done before.[18] This consequently had the effect of dismantling some of the traditional principles of national legal systems: a clear hierarchy of norms with the national constitution on top, as well as the principles of *lex posterior derogat legi prior* and *lex specialis derogat legi generali*.[19] This created conditions for the emergence of constitutional conflict.

The introduction of the preliminary reference procedure presents a separate, although closely linked, procedural issue. The preliminary reference procedure was established as a cooperative mechanism between national courts and the Court of Justice,[20] which empowered ordinary national courts[21] who then took up an additional identity as EU courts.[22] This new relationship between ordinary national courts and the Court of Justice, in particular when regarded jointly with the case law presented above, undermined the classic national judicial hierarchical structure, where the highest courts' legal reasoning represented an undisputable final authority.

In addition, the preliminary reference procedure had two important implications. First, it placed a strong emphasis on judicial review as a method of ensuring the effectiveness of EU law.[23] This, in turn, shaped the second consequence: a more general decentralization of constitutional review in the Member States.[24] Unsurprisingly, both have marginalized the role of national courts with constitutional jurisdiction.[25] The structure and coherence of national constitutional orders and judiciaries appears to have been sacrificed to ensure the uniformity and effectiveness of EU law.

Going even further, the Court of Justice has disregarded the higher level of protection of fundamental rights offered by the Spanish Constitution in *Melloni*,[26]

[18] S Rodin, 'Back to Square One: The Past, the Present and the Future of the *Simmenthal* Mandate' in J M Beneyto and I Pernice (eds), *Europe's Constitutional Challenges in the Light of the Recent Case Law of National Constitutional Courts: Lisbon And Beyond* (Nomos 2011) 298.

[19] Although it may well be concluded that now the latter of the two principles is central for the uniform and effective application of EU law. As put by Weatherill, any directly effective provision of EU law, however minor and technical, has priority in application over any provision of national law, however weighty and fundamental. S Weatherill, *Law and Integration in the European Union* (OUP 1995) 106.

[20] G Martinico and O Pollicino, 'Between Constitutional Tolerance and Judicial Activism: The Specificity of European Judicial Law' (2008) 10(1) *European Journal of Law Reform* 97, 108.

[21] The argument of empowerment of ordinary national courts has most famously been put forward in A-M Burley and W Mattli, 'Europe Before the Court: A Political Theory of Legal Integration' (1993) 47 *International Organization* 41; and further elaborated in W Mattli and A-M Slaughter, 'Revisiting the European Court of Justice' (1998) 52 *International Organization* 177. See also Claes (n 17) 387.

[22] J Temple Lang, 'The Duties of National Courts under Community Constitutional Law' (1997) 22 *European Law Review* 3.

[23] See eg J E Rytter and M Wind, 'In Need of Juristocracy? The Silence of Denmark in the Development of European Legal Norms' (2011) 9(2) *International Journal of Constitutional Law* 470, 471. For a comprehensive list of what is entailed in the duty of national courts to review national law see Claes (n 17) 67–68.

[24] Rodin (n 18) 315; J Komárek, 'The Place of Constitutional Courts in the EU' (2013) 9(3) *European Constitutional Law Review* 420, 421.

[25] Rodin (n 18) 315; Claes (n 17) 387.

[26] Case C-399/11 *Melloni* [2013] EU:C:2013:107 [58].

prioritizing uniformity, effectiveness, and primacy of Union law. In this particular instance, the Spanish Constitutional Tribunal accepted the Court's interpretation, in a result that placed primacy of Union law above a higher standard of protection of a fundamental right. However, the Tribunal Constitucional also stated that, should it be necessary for the preservation of the basic sovereignty of the Spanish people, it would have the final say.[27] These developments are a good illustration of how the Court of Justice has marginalized national courts performing constitutional review in favour of primacy and effectiveness of Union law.

The penetration of Union law and its peculiarities into national constitutional orders has created a relationship of unease between the Court of Justice and national courts with constitutional jurisdiction. The Court of Justice, on the one hand, is convinced in the utmost value of effectiveness of Union law and is expecting all national courts to share its zeal. On the other hand, national courts performing constitutional review tend to prioritize their respective constitutions. Consequently, they have employed different methods of adhering to the requirements of EU law while at the same time fulfilling their original role of safeguarding the supremacy of the national constitution. Some rejected particular findings of the Court of Justice by declaring them *ultra vires*,[28] whereas others joined ordinary national courts in submitting preliminary questions to the Court of Justice.[29] With the aim of analysing and corroborating the descriptive and normative side of constitutional pluralism, in the following section I present the judicial triangle that I will use as an analytical tool aimed at capturing the changes in judicial power relations as the result of the jurisprudence of constitutional conflict.

## 2 The Judicial Triangle as an Analytical Tool

The conundrum faced by national courts performing constitutional review is multi-faceted and depends on the national constitutional setting in which they operate. Crucially, the Court of Justice has by way of cooperation with ordinary national courts dismantled the concept of a state as a homogeneous actor in the EU.[30] This intra-state layering was in large part attributable to the preliminary reference

[27] Spanish Tribunal Constitucional Case 26/2014 *Melloni* Judgment of 13 February 2014 ground 3. For a more detailed analysis on the identity review aspects of the case see ch 6, s 2.2.3. For fundamental rights review aspects of the case see ch 7, s 4.2.

[28] Czech Ústavní Soud Case Pl. ÚS 5/12 *Slovak Pensions* 31 December 2012 https://www.usoud.cz/fileadmin/user_upload/ustavni_soud_www/Decisions/pdf/Pl%20US%205-12.pdf. See ch 5, s 6.2 for further analysis.

[29] With the Belgian Cour Constitutionnelle leading in the number of submitted references with 44. Court of Justice, Annual Report [2020] 231 https://curia.europa.eu/jcms/upload/docs/application/pdf/2021-04/ra_jud_2020_en.pdf.

[30] J H H Weiler, *The Constitution of Europe: 'Do the New Clothes Have an Emperor?' and Other Essays on European Integration* (CUP 1999) 37.

procedure as a novel enforcement mechanism.[31] The judicial triangle will thus be used as a visual representation describing the changes in power relations between courts over time: the darker the arrow, the stronger the influence of specific courts in the triangle, and vice versa. It will depict the balance of powers between national constitutional courts and the Court of Justice, as well as their authority towards ordinary national courts.

Building on the scholarship on judicial dialogue[32] and inter-court competition,[33] the triangle will follow the horizontal relationship between the Court of Justice and national constitutional courts. This relationship, despite its supranational/national nature, is horizontal due to the contested nature of primacy and the nature of EU constitutional sphere as necessarily comprised of contributions from the national and EU levels of constitutional authority. In line with the main arguments of the book, their relationship is therefore not hierarchical.

Grounded in the literature on judicial empowerment,[34] the judicial triangle also captures the resulting vertical power relations between the Court of Justice and ordinary national courts on the one hand and between national constitutional courts and ordinary national courts on the other. The first relationship is vertical due to the mandate that the Court of Justice has in interpreting EU law based on Article 19(1) TEU and the binding nature of preliminary references, placing it in a hierarchical position towards ordinary national courts. Ordinary national courts have, under the empowerment thesis, accepted this new hierarchy towards the Court of Justice, in order to reposition themselves in the national constitutional structure.[35] The second relationship is vertical due to the hierarchical position that constitutional/supreme courts traditionally have towards ordinary national courts in their respective constitutional settings.

In order to demonstrate the way the judicial triangle operates, I will briefly address the introduction of constitutional doctrines of direct effect and primacy of

[31] ibid 27.

[32] M Cartabia, 'Taking Dialogue Seriously: The Renewed Need for a Judicial Dialogue at the Time of Constitutional Activism in the European Union' (2007) Jean Monnet Working Paper 12/07 https://jeanmonnetprogram.org/wp-content/uploads/2014/12/071201.pdf; F Fontanelli, G Martinico, and P Carrozza (eds), *Shaping Rule of Law through Dialogue: International and Supranational Experiences* (Europa Law Publishing 2009); G Martinico, 'Judging in the Multilevel Legal Order: Exploring the Techniques of "Hidden Dialogue"' (2010) 21 *King's College Law Journal* 257; C Guarnieri and D Piana, 'Bringing the Outside Inside: Macro and Micro Factors to Put the Dialogue among the Highest Courts into Its Rights Context' (2012) 8 *Utrecht Law Review* 139; G Martinico and O Pollicino *The Interaction between Europe's Legal Systems: Judicial Dialogue and the Creation of Supranational Laws* (Edward Elgar Publishing 2012).

[33] H Rasmussen, *On Law and Policy in the European Court of Justice: A Comparative Study in Judicial Policymaking* (M Nijhoff 1986); Burley and Mattli (n 1); R Dehousse, *The European Court of Justice: The Politics of Judicial Integration* (Macmillan St Martin's Press 1998); S K Schmidt, *The European Court of Justice and the Policy Process: The Shadow of Case Law* (OUP 2018).

[34] K Alter, 'Explaining National Court Acceptance of European Court Jurisprudence: A Critical Evaluation of Theories of Legal Integration' in A-M Slaughter, A Stone Sweet, and J H H Weiler (eds), *European Court and National Courts—Doctrine and Jurisprudence: Legal Change in Its Social Context* (Hart Publishing 1998); K Alter, *Establishing the Supremacy of European Law: The Making of an International Rule of Law in Europe* (OUP 2003).

[35] Alter (n 34) 241.

EU law by the Court of Justice and the ensuing contestation from the national level in respect of protection of fundamental rights. This famous development of EU constitutional law demonstrates that the EU's constitutional space is distinctly characterized by a mutual feedback loop between the judiciary at the EU and national level through constitutional conflict. This tells us that vertical judicial interactions hold a decisive position in configuring and transforming the division of powers in the horizontal judicial relationship. The conceptualization of the judicial triangle is based on the assumption that, under conditions of contested primacy, the power relations in the triangle will always be imbalanced at individual points of conflict; at times in favour of the Court of Justice and its relation with ordinary national courts, at others in favour of national constitutional courts over ordinary national courts. Thus, the judicial triangle demonstrates that heterarchy is the guiding scheme of judicial interactions, which becomes visible when all the imbalanced judicial triangles are regarded in aggregate and over time.

The creation of EU constitutional doctrines took place with the introduction of the principles of direct effect and primacy of EU law. Based on these characteristics of the Treaties, the Court of Justice was able to extend their application into new areas of Member State action. Accordingly, ordinary national courts were now able to bypass their constitutional courts' decisions through the preliminary reference procedure or else by applying interpretations by the Court of Justice. National courts performing constitutional review and the Court of Justice have in consequence found themselves in a relationship of 'interpretative competition'[36] and have in diverse ways contested the expansions created by the Court of Justice.[37] We can therefore observe an imbalance in favour of the Court of Justice in Figure 1.1, depicted by the thick arrow 1.

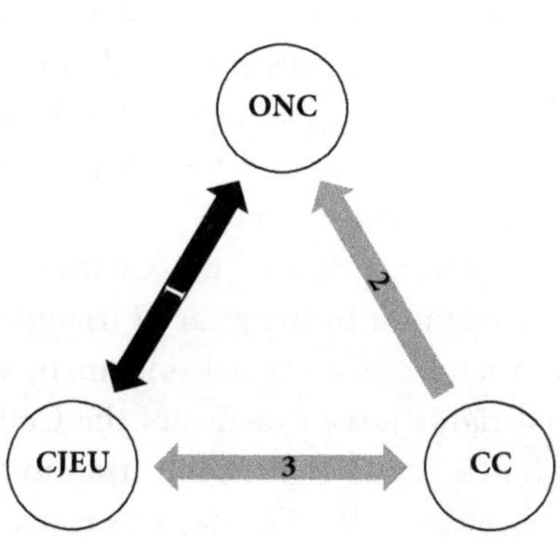


**Figure 1.1** Power relations in the judicial triangle after direct effect and primacy

[36] G Martinico, 'Multiple Loyalties and Dual Preliminarity: The Pains of Being a Judge in a Multilevel Legal Order' (2012) 10(3) *International Journal of Constitutional Law* 871, 885.

[37] Italian Corte Costituzionale Case 183/1973 *Frontini* judgment of 27 December 1973; German Bundesverfassungsgericht Case 37 BVerfGE 271 *Internationale Handelsgesellschaft (Solange I)* Judgment of 29 May 1974.

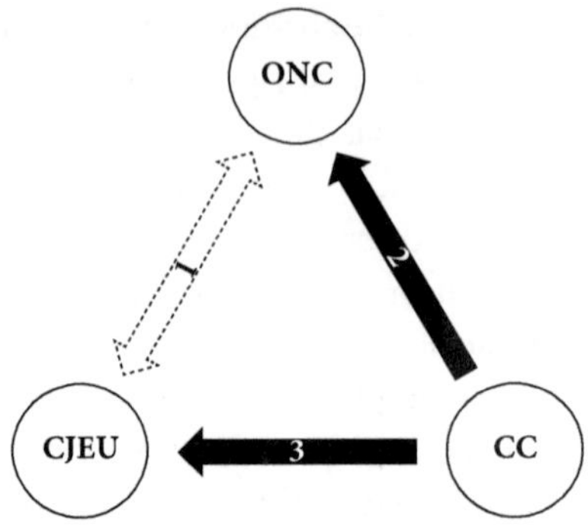


**Figure 1.2** Power relations in the judicial triangle after national decisions to review EU law against fundamental rights

In response to this jurisprudence, a number of constitutional courts established limits to the application of the principle of primacy of EU law in the area of fundamental rights.[38] More specifically, until the EU acquires a proper fundamental rights catalogue and ensures the protection on a par with that of national constitutions, constitutional courts retain the right to review EU law. The power relations in the triangle thus shifted in favour of constitutional courts, as in Figure 1.2. Unlike in the first triangle, not only do constitutional courts exhibit authority vis-à-vis ordinary courts through the mandatory interpretations of fundamental rights protection, but they also do so in relation to the Court of Justice, given that it no longer has unfettered power to interpret EU law. Rather, arrow 3 denotes the power reserved by constitutional courts to review EU law as well, in situations when it possibly breaches constitutionally protected fundamental rights. The vertical relationship between the Court of Justice and ordinary national courts thus remains the weakest side of the triangle (arrow 1), given the due regard that the latter now owe to their constitutional courts.

Subsequently, the EU's introduction of the Charter of Fundamental Rights again changed the power relations in the judicial triangle. One of the rationales behind introducing the Charter as a formal document was the codification of the existing fundamental rights jurisprudence of the Court of Justice,[39] without producing novelties in fundamental rights protection in the EU more generally. Originally, thus, the application of the Charter was restricted in its Article 51(1) to situations where Member States are implementing EU law. However, the Court of Justice expanded[40] the scope of the Charter to all situations within the scope of

[38] This development is analysed in detail in ch 7, s 2.2.

[39] G de Búrca, 'The Drafting of the European Union Charter of Fundamental Rights' (2001) 26(2) *European Law Review* 126, 130.

[40] L Besselink, 'The Protection of Fundamental Rights Post-Lisbon: The Interaction between the EU Charter of Fundamental Rights, the European Convention on Human Rights (ECHR) and National

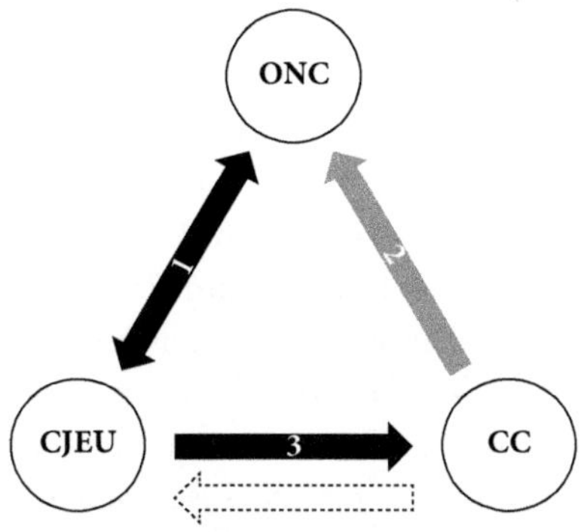


**Figure 1.3** Power relations in the judicial triangle after the expanded scope of the Charter

EU law,[41] regardless of the existence of Member State discretion.[42] This development further diminished the role of constitutional courts, as they were now restricted in applying their own constitutionally entrenched fundamental rights standards solely to situations without any connection to EU law. The changed power relations in the triangle are visible in Figure 1.3. Horizontally, the Court of Justice displaced the constitutional court given the wide breadth[43] of areas of law that can be shown to have any connection to EU law. The remaining influence of the constitutional court can be found in some constitutional courts' decisions, where they insisted on the persistent application of their own constitutional standards of fundamental rights protection,[44] resulting in a somewhat hybrid approach to fundamental rights protection in the EU's constitutional order.[45] The authority of the constitutional court is also diminished in relation to ordinary national courts, which will be the fora more likely applying EU law and by extension the Charter.

The different judicial triangles were therefore not able to provide us with a conclusive answer as to the final arbiter in the EU in the area of fundamental rights protection. Individual points of conflict necessarily display imbalances in power relations, as the pluralist framework operates by way of incremental accommodation through the auto-correct function.[46] It will also become visible that destructive

Constitutions' (2012) FIDE General Report; S Weatherill, *Law and Values in the European Union* (OUP 2016) 211. See also ch 7, s 3.2.

[41] Order C-339/10 *Estov* [2010] EU:C:2010:680; Case C-617/10 *Fransson* [2013] EU:C:2013:105.

[42] Joined Cases C-411/10 and C-493/10 *NS* [2011] EU:C:2011:865.

[43] Weatherill (n 40) 30.

[44] French Constitutional Council Case 2013-314 QPC *Mr Jeremy F (II)* Decision of 14 June 2013; German Bundesverfassungsgericht Case 2 BvR 2735/14 *Mr R* Order of 15 December 2015.

[45] A Bobić, 'Developments in the EU-German Judicial Love Story: The Right to Be Forgotten II' (2020) 21(S1) *German Law Journal* 31.

[46] On these concepts see ch 3, s 3.

conflicts distort the triangle itself, as the captured constitutional courts no longer operate on the basis of sincere cooperation within the judicial system, but are under the decisive influence from the executive.[47] The example for this situation concerns the constitutional entrenchment of judicial independence as the cornerstone of the rule of law, shared by all Member States and expressed in Article 2 TEU. The national identity clause in the Lisbon Treaty (Article 4(2) TEU) placed an obligation on the EU to ensure diversity and protect national 'fundamental structures, political and constitutional', which opened new space for contestation of EU law at the national level. However, national executives in a number of Member States have been introducing reforms aimed at disempowering national courts in their use of the preliminary reference procedure and the application and enforcement of EU law more generally.[48] In response, the Court of Justice[49] declared judicial independence the cornerstone of the rule of law, expanding its application to all Member State action, regardless of the applicability of EU law in a specific case.

In complete disregard of sincere cooperation and mutual respect in the EU's judicial space, the Polish Disciplinary Chamber of the Supreme Court declared a judgment of the Court of Justice concerning judicial independence in Poland void.[50] This shift is the latest example of a transformation of the EU constitutional space resulting from destructive constitutional conflict. As Figure 1.4 shows, the relationship between the Court of Justice and the constitutional court on the occasion of a destructive conflict is broken by the lack of sincere cooperation and mutual respect. In addition, the disciplinary proceedings in Poland target ordinary national

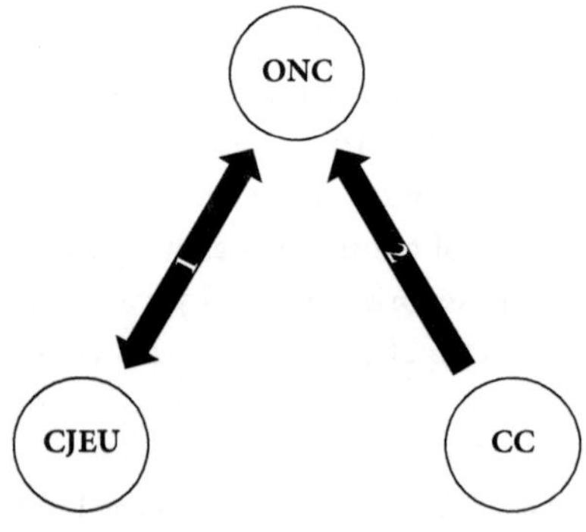


**Figure 1.4** Power relations in a situation of a destructive constitutional conflict

[47] More detailed attention is given to these destructive developments in ch 4, s 3 and ch 5, s 7.

[48] L Pech and K L Scheppele, 'Illiberalism Within: Rule of Law Backsliding in the EU' (2017) 19 *Cambridge Yearbook of European Legal Studies* 3.

[49] Case C-64/16 *Juízes Portugueses* (n 8).

[50] Polish Disciplinary Chamber of the Supreme Court Decision DO 52/20 of 23 September 2020 http://www.sn.pl/sites/orzecznictwo/OrzeczeniaHTML/ii%20do%2052-20.docx.html.

courts submitting preliminary references to the Court of Justice.[51] We therefore cannot speak of constitutional conflict here that can be remedied through judicial accommodation and cooperation. Rather, the deficiencies in judicial independence are of such degree that they require political and legal action as a response.[52]

In constitutional pluralism, the judicial triangle will always be unbalanced: at times in favour of the Court of Justice and its relationship to ordinary national courts and at other times in favour of national constitutional courts. Thus, the normative argument of constitutional pluralism and heterarchy as the guiding scheme of judicial interactions will only become visible when all the imbalanced judicial triangles are regarded in aggregate.[53] For this purpose, this book will offer an in-depth analysis of constitutional conflict, whereas the resulting judicial triangles from all case studies will be analysed jointly in chapter 8.

## 3 Methods

This section will explain, first, the choice of sources and, secondly, the choice of the Member State courts under analysis. I will also underline some limitations of the book.

### 3.1 Sources

In order to capture the nuances of judicial interactions between the national and the EU level beyond the existing contributions in the literature, I have combined both theoretical and empirical sources on three levels. The first level of analysis has been theoretical, through the use of secondary sources from the literature to establish the doctrinal groundwork for the remainder of the analysis.

The second level of analysis used the following primary legal sources: (1) judgments of the Court of Justice and courts with constitutional jurisdiction; and (2) national reports composed by national constitutional courts for the 26th Congress of Constitutional Courts of the Conference of European Constitutional Courts.[54] The advantage of the reports is that all the courts under analysis answered the same questionnaire, thereby ensuring that the responses comparably covered the same issues. In addition, the reports shed light on how national courts understand

[51] For example, an ordinary court has, through legislative changes (which the Constitutional Tribunal did not oppose) lost jurisdiction over the case while the reference was pending. The Court of Justice found such changes contrary to judicial independence and found that primacy of EU law and judicial independence require that the national court reassume jurisdiction by applying the national rule prior to the amendment. Case C-824/18 *AB and Others* [2021] EU:C:2021:153.

[52] For more on this point see ch 4, s 3.

[53] See ch 4, s 1.

[54] All reports are available at https://www.confeuconstco.org/en/common/home.html.

and regard the issues surrounding the relationship between national and EU law, of particular relevance for constitutional pluralism. However, unlike previous studies, the present analysis looks not only at the outcome of individual judgments or conclusions found in the reports, but also at the vocabulary used in those documents. The vocabulary of *obiter dicta* often paints a more detailed image of how the courts under analysis understand and conceive relationships in the European judicial space, but also more generally the EU's constitutional constellation.

The third level of analysis aims to triangulate the findings from the previous analysis by including semi-structured interviews conducted with Judges and Advocates General of the Court of Justice. The interviews were conducted as part of the research visit to the Court of Justice between February and May 2015, with seven Judges and Advocates General. The questions in the interviews broadly corresponded to the questionnaire of the 26th Congress of Constitutional Courts as part of the Conference of European Constitutional Courts, to ensure the comparability of results. To safeguard the anonymity of the interviewees, they will be referred to as 'Interviewee 1', 'Interviewee 2', etc. In addition, I have analysed public statements of all the judicial actors involved by way of academic writings, talks, seminars, and public interviews.

While the last group of sources does not represent the official stance of the institution(s) for which the interviewees work, Grainger pointed out, in relation to the Court of Justice in particular, that it is not a homogeneous actor, but is rather a 'complex social entity'.[55] Similarly, Weiler stated that any analysis of the Court of Justice cannot be complete if the Court is regarded simply as a 'homogeneous institution'.[56] Consequently, personal opinions of decision-makers at the Court of Justice and other national constitutional courts bear significance as regards the work and position of their institution(s). The Irish Supreme Court similarly confirmed the influence of the jurisprudence of both the Court of Justice and the European Court of Human Rights (ECtHR) in Strasbourg on the case law of the Supreme Court, underlining how inevitable this is given the work experience of current Supreme Court judges as judges at European courts.[57] The study of the mentioned sources resulted in a finding of a widespread use of several common expressions[58] that are used by both national courts with constitutional jurisdiction and the members of the Court of Justice.

Finally, a limitation of this methodology lies in the problem of comparing identical expressions that come from different legal systems and might have different contextual meaning. This certainly holds true in comparing, for example, the notion of 'openness to European law' in the jurisprudence of the

[55] M-P Grainger, 'The Future of Europe: Judicial Interference and Preferences' (2005) 3 *Comparative European Politics* 155, 175.

[56] J H Weiler, 'The Reform of European Constitutionalism' (1997) 35 *Journal of Common Market Studies* 95, 106.

[57] National Report, The Supreme Court of Ireland (2014) 3.

[58] I will refer to them as keywords throughout the book.

Bundesverfassungsgericht and a statement of a Judge or Advocate General at the Court of Justice given in an anonymous interview. For this purpose, particular care was taken to ensure that keywords were only included in the analysis when used in the same context. Where necessary, additional doctrinal support was consulted when use was made of vocabulary from national constitutional jurisprudence or that of the Court of Justice.

## 3.2 Definitions and Scope

In order to offer a comprehensive analysis of the jurisprudence of constitutional conflict, this book will address it by topic rather than by Member State. There are two main reasons behind this choice. First, rather than scattering different topics across Member States, a targeted analysis will provide a richer illustration of the relevant area of constitutional review to make more general conclusions on the jurisprudence of constitutional conflict throughout the EU. Secondly, such an approach will give a clearer idea not only on the relationship between national constitutional jurisprudence and EU law, but will also render the analysis comparative in relation to different Member States and how they influence each other.

The book analyses interactions between the Court of Justice and national courts performing constitutional interpretation and review. For this purpose, I will use de Visser's definition of constitutional interpretation: '[the] process of constructing, establishing the meaning of and explaining a country's written constitution (if there is one), other constitutional texts and other (unwritten) norms and principles that are of constitutional quality'.[59] Constitutional review will refer to what de Visser calls 'constitutional review in a narrow sense':

> [The] actor conducting the assessment of constitutional conformity is empowered to attach consequences to a finding that the acts of other State organs do not comport with the relevant constitutional yardsticks; and is thus legally able to impose its position on a constitutional issue on other State organs.[60]

However, while de Visser's definition is potentially inclusive of any type of state institution,[61] this book will look exclusively at judicial bodies atop the national hierarchy with the power of constitutional interpretation and review, including countries with centralized and decentralized constitutional review.[62] The

[59] M de Visser, *Constitutional Review in Europe. A Comparative Analysis* (Hart Publishing 2014) 2.
[60] ibid.
[61] ibid.
[62] H Kelsen, 'Judicial Review of Legislation: A Comparative Study of the Austrian and the American Constitution' (1942) 4 *The Journal of Politics* 183.

centralized model of constitutional review presupposes a specialized constitutional court whose jurisdiction is limited to issues of constitutional interpretation and review (for example, Austria), while a decentralized model enables all courts in the national judiciary to perform constitutional review, and the supreme court on top of the national hierarchy has the ultimate say (for example, Denmark).[63]

In the remainder of this section, I will present the position and powers of each of the national courts under analysis.[64] Secondly, I will discuss the four countries that are excluded from the analysis—Finland, Greece, the Netherlands, and Sweden—with specific reference to the reasons for their exclusion.

### 3.2.1 United Kingdom

The United Kingdom Supreme Court will be included in the analysis as an example of a decentralized system of constitutional review.[65] However, the situation in the United Kingdom is more nuanced when it comes to powers of courts to review legislation, thus warranting some further attention to its organization. The principle of parliamentary sovereignty emphasizes the exclusive power of the Parliament to enact legislation and gives the Parliament the power to repeal any previous legislation, be it expressly or by implied repeal.[66] In this reading of the principle, all statutes are considered equal and courts are not allowed to review them. Nevertheless, Lord Justice Laws in his decision in *Thoburn*[67] made a distinction between ordinary and constitutional statutes. The latter, he claims, have a higher level of entrenchment and may not be repealed by implication. Constitutional statutes are, among others, the European Communities Act 1972 and the Human Rights Act 1998.

This exception is relevant for the position of constitutional review in the United Kingdom, as section 4 of the Human Rights Act allows the courts to review all acts of Parliament against its standards and declare their incompatibility. The

[63] For a more detailed overview of the two models see V Ferreres Comella, 'The European Model of Constitutional Review of legislation: Toward Decentralization?'(2004) 3(2) *International Journal of Constitutional Law* 461. See also de Visser (n 59) 54.

[64] It will at times be inevitable to include the jurisprudence of supreme or supreme administrative courts. When this is the case, the relationship to the constitutional court will be additionally addressed.

[65] The United Kingdom was included in the analysis regardless of the subsequent decision of the British voters to leave the European Union. This was done primarily as the Supreme Court has been part of the European judicial space, contributing to the development of the relationship between United Kingdom and EU constitutional law. The decision of the United Kingdom to leave the EU does not do away with the role of the Supreme Court in relation to EU law, nor would the analysis be complete without it. The jurisprudence and contributions of the United Kingdom Supreme Court are included up to the Brexit date on 31 January 2020.

[66] J Laws, 'Constitutional Guarantees' (2008) 29(1) *Statute Law Review* 1, 3.

[67] United Kingdom High Court Case *Thoburn* [2002] EWHC 195 (Admin) [62]–[63].

**Table 1.1** National courts under analysis

| Court | System of constitutional review | Abstract and/ or concrete review | *Ex ante* and/ or *ex post* review |
|---|---|---|---|
| Austrian Constitutional Court (*Verfassungsgerichtshof*) | Centralized | Both | Both |
| Constitutional Court of the Kingdom of Belgium (*Cour constitutionnelle*) | Centralized | Both | Both |
| Bulgarian Constitutional Court (*Конституционният съд*) | Centralized | Abstract | *Ex post*[a] |
| Croatian Constitutional Court (*Ustavni Sud*) | Centralized | Both | *Ex post* |
| The Supreme Court of Cyprus (*Ανώτατο Δικαστήριο*) | Decentralized | Both | *Ex post* |
| Czech Constitutional Court (*Ústavní Soud*) | Centralized | Both | *Ex post* |
| Danish Supreme Court (*Højesteret*) | Decentralized | Concrete | *Ex post* |
| Estonian Supreme Court (*Riigikohus*) | Mixed system[b] | Both | *Ex post* |
| French Constitutional Council (*Conseil constitutionnel*) | Centralized | Both | Both[c] |
| German Federal Constitutional Court (*Bundesverfassungsgericht*) | Centralized | Both | Both |
| Hungarian Constitutional Court (*Magyarország Alkotmánybírósága*) | Centralized | Both | Both |
| Irish Supreme Court (*Cúirt Uachtarach na hÉireann*) | Decentralized | Both | Both |
| Italian Constitutional Court (*Corte Costituzionale*) | Centralized | Both | *Ex post* |
| Latvian Constitutional Court (*Satversmes tiesa*) | Centralized | Both | Both |
| Lithuanian Constitutional Court (*Konstitucinis Teismas*) | Centralized | Abstract | *Ex post* |
| Luxembourgish Constitutional Court (*Cour constitutionnelle*) | Centralized | Concrete | *Ex post* |
| The Constitutional Court of Malta | Mixed system[d] | Concrete | *Ex post* |

*Continued*

**Table 1.1** *Continued*

| Court | System of constitutional review | Abstract and/or concrete review | *Ex ante* and/or *ex post* review |
|---|---|---|---|
| Polish Constitutional Tribunal (*Trybunał Konstytucyjny*) | Centralized | Both | Both |
| Portuguese Constitutional Court (*Tribunal Constitucional*) | Hybrid[e] | Both | Both |
| The Constitutional Court of Romania (*Curtea Constituțională*) | Centralized | Both | Both |
| The Constitutional Court of the Slovak Republic (*Ústavný súd*) | Centralized | Both | *Ex post* |
| Slovenian Constitutional Court (*Ustavno sodišče*) | Centralized | Both | Both[f] |
| Spanish Constitutional Tribunal (*Tribunal Constitucional*) | Centralized | Both | Both[g] |

[a] *Ex ante* review is only possible for treaties pending ratification.

[b] A constitutional chamber forms part of the decentralized Supreme Court.

[c] *Ex ante* review by the Constitutional Council is mandatory for the basic laws and regulations of Houses of Parliament, as well as international treaties prior to their ratification, while it is optional for ordinary legislation. *Ex post* review was introduced by the constitutional amendment in 2008 and can be initiated by way of a preliminary ruling on the compatibility of a valid piece of legislation with constitutionally guaranteed rights and freedoms.

[d] It operates as a separate court specialized for issues of constitutional interpretation and constitutional review, but it is also the superior court on top of the Maltese judiciary hearing appeals connected to constitutional interpretation and review.

[e] All courts in Portugal are entitled to carry out constitutional review and the Constitutional Tribunal operates as a concentrated appeal instance.

[f] The only *ex ante* review the Constitutional Court can undertake is that of treaties pending ratification.

[g] *Ex ante* review is reserved solely for Statutes of Autonomy, prior to their receipt of the royal assent.

Parliament has so far repealed all statutes where the courts found an incompatibility[68] but the one concerning the prisoners' voting rights,[69] resulting in a new role for judicial review in the United Kingdom. In addition, the courts have also been torn between the requirements of EU law and national law. In the controversial *Factortame*[70] decision, the House of Lords granted interim relief in relation to an

[68] K Malleson, 'The Evolving Role of the Supreme Court' [2011] *Public Law* 754, 760.

[69] House of Lords and House of Commons Joint Committee on Human Rights, 'Human Rights Judgments' (2015) 19 https://www.publications.parliament.uk/pa/jt201415/jtselect/jtrights/130/130.pdf.

[70] *Factortame (No 2)* [1991] 1 AC 603 (HL).

act of Parliament, relying on the response received by the Court of Justice,[71] creating a precedent for constitutional review.[72]

Finally, the role of the reformed Supreme Court, in opposition to a clearly defined political *ex ante* review of legislation as can be found in the Netherlands and Finland,[73] holds additional importance for including it in the analysis.[74] Malleson presents an array of opinions on the role the Supreme Court might assume and concludes there is a wide consensus that it took up the position of more actively policing the boundaries of Parliament action.[75] It can therefore be concluded that the United Kingdom Supreme Court can be regarded as a court with the competence to perform constitutional review, albeit to a limited extent,[76] thus warranting its inclusion in the analysis. The position of the Supreme Court is additionally relevant due to its interpretations of the British constitution, which place it in interinstitutional dialogue with the Court of Justice.

### 3.2.2 Excluded Member States: Finland, Greece, the Netherlands, and Sweden

These four countries are difficult to include in the analysis as none of them has a permanent court performing constitutional interpretation and review of legislative acts against the constitution. The Greek system of constitutional review may be one of the most complicated in the EU, where no single court has the status of a centralized constitutional court. However, since 1897, Greek courts have regularly checked the constitutionality of laws and the Constitution explicitly empowered them to do so since 1927.[77] In addition, Greece has three supreme courts (the Council of State, the Supreme Civil Court, and the Auditor's Court), who are at the top of the judicial hierarchy in their specific areas of law. Moreover, Greece has a special, non-permanent Special Supreme Court (Ανώτατο Ειδικό Δικαστήριο), which has the power to annul an entire piece of legislation as well as settle disputes that usually fall into the jurisdiction of a centralized constitutional court, such as

[71] Case C-213/98 *Factortame* [1990] EU:C:1990:257.

[72] Political and Constitutional Reform Committee of the House of Commons, 'Constitutional Role of the Judiciary if There Were a Codified Constitution' (2014) 22 http://www.publications.parliament.uk/pa/cm201314/cmselect/cmpolcon/802/802.pdf.

[73] ibid 21.

[74] See de Visser (n 59) 83–86.

[75] Malleson (n 68) 763.

[76] See Lord Neuberger's response to the Political and Constitutional Reform Committee of the House of Commons (n 79) 24. For a comprehensive analysis of the influence that the introduction of the Human Rights Act has had on constitutional review and an argument supporting the existence of constitutional review in the United Kingdom see Malleson (n 75); A Kavanagh, *Constitutional Review under the Human Rights Act* (CUP 2009).

[77] A Kaltsa, 'The Review of Constitutionality of Laws in Greece' (1998) 4(3) *European Public Law* 292, 293.

competence disputes. However, since it is non-permanent and is only set up in exceptional situations where the case law of the three supreme courts is divergent, there is no single judicial institution that may come into conflict with the Court of Justice.

Sweden's Supreme Court and Supreme Administrative Court combine to form a Council that performs non-binding review of legislative drafts, whereas Finland's draft legislation is reviewed by the Constitutional Committee of the Parliament.[78] In the Netherlands, judicial constitutional review is prohibited by the Constitution[79] and is instead performed by the Council of State (Raad van State), an independent adviser to the government, Parliament, and the Dutch Senate. Such a situation removes the point of comparison for these three Member States, as there is no national jurisdiction performing constitutional review against the Constitution.[80] Consequently, no judicial interactions are taking place in the context of a conflict of constitutional interpretation with the interpretation of EU law.

The status of parliamentary sovereignty in the United Kingdom and the Netherlands[81] prima facie suggests that both jurisdictions should be excluded from analysis. However, at closer inspection, the principle is interpreted and applied differently in the two jurisdictions, leading to the inclusion of the United Kingdom Supreme Court. First, the Dutch Constitution prohibits constitutional review by the courts against the Constitution, but allows them to review acts of Parliament against treaty law.[82] This means that courts are allowed to appraise acts of Parliament solely in relation to 'external' sources of law, but not the Constitution.[83] Substantively, therefore, it is almost impossible for Dutch courts to find themselves in conflict with the Court of Justice, as it is EU law (among other sources of treaty law), rather than national constitutional law that is the standard of review envisaged in Article 94 of the Dutch Constitution. This addition removes the possibility to analyse judicial interactions, as there is no supreme jurisdiction in the Netherlands able to interpret the Constitution contrary to EU law. Finally, given the powers of constitutional review of the Dutch Council of State and the

[78] F Mayer, 'The European Constitution and the Courts Adjudicating European Constitutional Law in a Multilevel System' (2003) Jean Monnet Working Paper 9/03 1, 4.

[79] Article 120 of the Constitution http://www.parliament.am/library/sahmanadrutyunner/niderland.pdf. The prohibition includes *ex ante* and *ex post* review, as well as substantive and procedural review. See G van der Schyff, 'Constitutional Review by the Judiciary in the Netherlands: A Bridge Too Far?' (2010) 11 *German Law Journal* 175, 277.

[80] Claes (n 17) 253–54.

[81] For a comparative analysis of the two systems see G Yein Ng, 'Judicialisation and the End of Parliamentary Supremacy: Shifting Paradigms in the Protection of the Rule of Law and Human Rights in the UK, France and the Netherlands' (2014) 3 *Global Journal of Comparative Law* 50.

[82] Article 94 of the Dutch Constitution: Statutory regulations in force within the Kingdom shall not be applicable if such application is in conflict with provisions of treaties or of resolutions by international institutions that are binding on all persons. See also van der Schyff (n 86) 280.

[83] As a result of the monist approach to the incorporation of international law, the Dutch courts have a peculiar role in interpreting directly applicable international law and using it as a standard of review against national statutes. Yein Ng (n 81) 88.

Dutch Senate, both non-judicial bodies, the Supreme Court of Netherlands was excluded from the analysis.[84]

## 3.3 Limitations

This book is subject to two main limitations. First, by focusing exclusively on the Court of Justice and national courts performing constitutional interpretation and review, the book does not capture the contributions of political institutions on both the EU and the national level. The book therefore does not avoid the criticism directed towards court-centred research,[85] which is particularly present in accounts of constitutional pluralism.[86] Whenever possible, therefore, I will refer to the national constitutional setting and how it has influenced a specific development through the judicial triangle.[87]

However, there are two reasons for attention to be confined to courts. First, the Court of Justice has been the dominant institution to expand the self-referential system of the Treaties[88] and has consequently attracted considerable attention not only for itself, but also for the judicial branch more generally. Secondly, and relatedly, the prominence of judicialization as the dominant method of constitutionalization of EU law has placed most constitutional conflicts in the judicial arena. In that respect, studying constitutional conflict in the EU is inherently linked to studying courts. Ultimately, I argue there is still more to learn from exploring the courts and their relationship in the EU from new perspectives.

The second limitation of the book is the exclusion of the ECtHR from the analysis.[89] There are three reasons for this exclusion. First, the relationship between the ECtHR and national courts performing constitutional review is one of hierarchy and has therefore not significantly influenced the position of constitutional courts in their national constitutional constellation. The relationship between the Court of Justice and the ECtHR is more complicated, but it has not (yet) led to instances of disagreement that would contribute to the existing jurisprudence of constitutional conflict between the national level and the EU. For matters of analytical and normative precision, the theoretical framework presented in Chapters 3

[84] Yein Ng also concludes that the Netherlands, in comparison with the United Kingdom and France, has the weakest form of judicial review. Yein Ng (n 81) 93.

[85] J Komárek, 'Institutional Dimension of Constitutional Pluralism' (2010) Eric Stein Working Paper 3/2010, 4–5https://csesp.files.wordpress.com/2015/05/eswp-2010-03-komarek.pdf.

[86] N Walker, 'The Idea of Constitutional Pluralism' (2002) 65(3) *Modern Law Review* 317, 336.

[87] For example, when analysing the jurisprudence of the Danish Supreme Court in relation to *ultra vires* review, the role and influence of the Danish parliament was explicitly addressed, owing to the strong principle of judicial self-restraint to the legislature in Denmark. See ch 5, s 6.3.

[88] As will become visible throughout ch 5.

[89] For an analysis of the national, EU, and ECtHR relationship in the context of constitutional pluralism see T Flynn, *The Triangular Constitution: Constitutional Pluralism in Ireland, the EU and the ECHR* (Hart Publishing 2019).

and 4 cannot be used as a Procrustean bed to accommodate these conceptually and structurally different relationships. The second reason for the exclusion of the ECtHR is its reduced influence within the EU legal order since the adoption of the Charter of Fundamental Rights and the activity of the Court of Justice in the interpretation of its scope. Relatedly, the third reason for exclusion is the rejection of the EU's accession to the European Convention on Human Rights by the Court of Justice,[90] which would otherwise inherently include the ECtHR into the pluralist network of judicial interactions in the European Union.

## 4 Aims and Outline of the Book

Against the background described in the preceding sections, this book has three aims. First, it seeks to determine how the principle of primacy of EU law works in reality and whether the jurisprudence of the courts under analysis supports this concept. It does so by providing a comprehensive map of the jurisprudence of constitutional conflict between the Court of Justice and national courts with the power of constitutional review.

Secondly, the book substantiates the descriptive and strengthens the normative contributions of the theory of constitutional pluralism in relation to the web of relations in the European judicial space. I first present the theoretical framework for this analysis in the remainder of Part I, in Chapters 2, 3, and 4. The theory is based largely on the idea that the lines between national and supranational law are becoming increasingly blurred, in particular in the European Union context, where the doctrines of direct effect and primacy of EU law have significantly changed the position of constitutional courts in Member States. In particular, the theory rests on the premise that the question of who is the final arbiter among the courts under analysis is futile as they co-exist in a multi-level, heterarchical setting. The analysis of the jurisprudence in Part II of the book across the case studies demonstrates the existence of such constellation—the potential of all the courts involved for being ranked in a number of different ways at different times—grounded in mutual respect and self-restraint through the incremental application of the auto-correct function. In addition, the analysis demonstrates the normative power of value pluralism, grounded in Article 2 TEU, and exemplified in the still emerging case law concerning the rule of law. The normative contribution of this book is a distinction between constructive and destructive constitutional conflict and an analysis of each in its respective context.

The book then takes a targeted approach by focusing on specific topics where constitutional conflict takes place in Part II: (i) *ultra vires* review (Chapter 5);

[90] Opinion of the Court of Justice 2/13 [2014] EU:C:2014:2454.

(ii) identity review (Chapter 6); and (iii) fundamental rights review (Chapter 7). These areas have been selected based on their proneness to generate clashes in interpretations provided by the Court of Justice and national constitutional courts. Certainly, this categorization stems from the German jurisprudence on matters of European integration and their response on the EU level. However, the three heads of review are more broadly connected to the main *material* components of constitutionalism: the division of competences in a polity, the constitutional core reflecting the main values of a polity, and the protection of fundamental rights. Accordingly, they also reflect the main roles of constitutional adjudication, thus resulting in collisions between the courts under analysis.[91]

*Ultra vires* review addresses the structural view of the relationship between the EU and the national level and may be seen as representing the underlying struggle in the relationship between the Court of Justice and national courts with constitutional jurisdiction. *Ultra vires* review is also content-neutral, as it can result in both more and less integration.

Furthermore, the concept of national identity is inherently different in every Member State and works as a dividing element in the evolution of EU and national constitutional law. The national identity clause, first introduced in the Maastricht Treaty and further expanded in the Lisbon Treaty, served as a basis for national courts performing constitutional review to place more emphasis on their constitution. As a result, identity review has become a prominent area for constitutional courts to preserve its fundamental role as guardians of the constitutional core untouchable by European integration.

Finally, the protection of fundamental rights has been one of the first areas of constitutional conflict between the Court of Justice and national courts performing constitutional review. One of the basic reasons behind the establishment of constitutional review was precisely the protection of fundamental rights of minorities against the 'majority of the day',[92] which is one of the reasons why national constitutional courts attempted to reserve this role for themselves in the face of the requirements of the principle of primacy. While fundamental rights protection has been subject of an ever-growing unification in the European Union, most recently by the elevation of the Charter of Fundamental Rights to the status of primary law, tension and constitutional discord continues to take place concerning the appropriate level of protection of fundamental rights.

The final aim of the book is to map the changes that occur in power relations between the Court of Justice, national constitutional courts, and ordinary national courts, done in Part III. The book developed the judicial triangle which serves as

[91] My argument is that every instance of constitutional conflict falls within one of these three areas of review. For an argument that democracy represents an additional, fourth, area of constitutional conflict see M Claes, 'Luxembourg, Here We Come? Constitutional Courts and the Preliminary Reference Procedure' (2015) 16(6) *German Law Journal* 1331, 1335.

[92] Claes (n 17) 392.

an analytical tool to follow the changes in said power relations over time and in relation to each of the case studies presented below. By examining the influence that the jurisprudence of constitutional conflict has on the balance of powers between the Court of Justice and constitutional courts, the judicial triangle depicts the consequences for the horizontal (constitutional courts vis-à-vis the Court of Justice) and vertical judicial relationships (Court of Justice vis-à-vis ordinary national courts; constitutional courts vis-à-vis ordinary national courts). Importantly for its theoretical contribution to constitutional pluralism, the judicial triangle will always display imbalances in power at individual points of constitutional conflict; at times the triangle will shift to the side of the Court of Justice and at others to the side of national constitutional courts. In consequence, it is possible to observe patterns in relation to specific areas of law under review as well as across different systems of constitutional review. In addition, this analysis demonstrates the existence of heterarchy rather than hierarchy among the courts under analysis, when their interactions are regarded in their entirety and over time.

# 2

# Theoretical Framework

## Constitutional Pluralism

### 1 Introduction

> If an alien were to land on earth and (let us assume the impossible ...) were to be interested in the relationship between European law and national law, his perception of reality would vary considerably depending on whether he would land on the European Court of Justice or some national constitutional courts. One thing would not change however: he or she (in case aliens have gender differences) would not question the source of ultimate authority.[1]

As Maduro tells us, the European Union's constitutional setup is to an outsider as puzzling as it is unique. The main constitutional actors operate in a setting where it seems they are permanently talking past, instead of to, each other. Equally, the question of the final arbiter in the European Union appears to be unsettled to everyone except to the courts under analysis. In an attempt to deconstruct this ostensibly chaotic conundrum, MacCormick[2] paved the way for and Walker[3] ultimately developed the theory of constitutional pluralism. In short, the theory tells us that the EU's constitutional setup is comprised of multiple constitutional sites of discourse and authority;[4] these claims are characterized by their incommensurability;[5] and the mutual recognition and respect between these multiple sites of constitutional authority is 'the only acceptable ethic of political responsibility for the new Europe'.[6]

The theory has been extensively praised and criticized in the literature,[7] and scholars have developed a number of its different strands. This chapter clarifies

[1] M P Maduro, 'Contrapunctual Law: Europe's Constitutional Pluralism in Action' in N Walker (ed), *Sovereignty in Transition* (Hart Publishing 2003) 502–503.

[2] N MacCormick, 'The Maastricht Urteil: Sovereignty Now' (1995) 1 *European Law Journal* 259; N MacCormick, *Questioning Sovereignty: Law, State and Nation in the European Commonwealth* (OUP 1999).

[3] N Walker, 'The Idea of Constitutional Pluralism' (2002) 65(3) *MLR* 317.

[4] ibid 337.

[5] ibid 338. See also N Walker, 'Constitutional Pluralism Revisited' (2016) 22(3) *European Law Journal* 333, 333–34; K Tuori, *European Constitutionalism* (CUP 2015)355.

[6] Walker (n 5).

[7] See also N Barber, 'Legal Pluralism in the European Union' (2006) 12(3) *European Law Journal* 306; N Krisch, *Beyond Constitutionalism: The Pluralist Structure of Postnational Law* (OUP 2013) 71–78; M

*The Jurisprudence of Constitutional Conflict in the European Union.* Ana Bobić, Oxford University Press. © Ana Bobić 2022.
DOI: 10.1093/oso/9780192847034.003.0002

my own understanding of the theory and argues that it is not only relevant in describing the judicial interactions that are the object of this book, but its normative argument holds value in guiding these interactions moving forward. In that sense, section 1 introduces the debates surrounding legal pluralism more generally, and the creation and development of constitutional pluralism in the EU's idiosyncratic context. Against this background, section 2 outlines the main descriptive features of the theory and offers a broad brush empirical demonstration thereof. The analysis shows the recurring use of a shared judicial vocabulary which points to the existence of a common understanding of the division of obligations among the participants of the European judicial space.

After establishing that constitutional pluralism indeed properly describes the state of play and dispels any confusion to Maduro's alien, this chapter then shows that such a constellation is the desirable way for judicial interactions to operate in the future. More specifically, I argue in section 3 that constitutional pluralism has a strong normative core, ensuring the essential values shared by all Member States and the European Union itself are preserved in the pluralist framework. In addition, constitutional pluralism as a theory embraces constitutional conflict, which is not a bug, but an important feature contributing to the system's functioning and incremental development.[8] I therefore further distinguish between two types of constitutional conflicts taking place in the EU's constitutional space: constructive and destructive ones. The former take place as long as they remain within the possible interpretation of values contained in Article 2 TEU. This creates a situation where the conflict is contained within the 'constitutional', respecting the existence of its basic values, but the interpretation varies within the scope of reasonable disagreement and remains 'pluralist'.[9] It is important to note that the preponderance of constitutional conflicts are constructive and are accommodated in an incremental fashion through the operation of the auto-correct function within the realm of judicial interactions. Importantly, this does not mean that the system is immune to bugs: by way of an exception, destructive constitutional conflict takes place when the site claiming ultimate constitutional authority is questioning the very existence of values of Article 2 TEU, and by extension the foundations of the system. In the concluding section I briefly reflect upon the way in which this theoretical frame will guide the analysis throughout the book.

Avbelj, 'The EU and the Many Faces of Legal Pluralism' (2006) 2 *Croatian Yearbook of European Law and Policy* 377; R Michaels, 'Global Legal Pluralism' (2009) 5 *Annual Review of Law and Social Science* 243; M Avbelj and J Komárek (eds), *Constitutional Pluralism in the European Union and Beyond* (Hart Publishing 2012).

[8] A Bobić, 'Constructive Versus Destructive Conflict: Taking Stock of the Recent Constitutional Jurisprudence in the EU' (2020) 22 *Cambridge Yearbook of European Legal Studies* 60.

[9] ibid 70.

## 2 The Plurality of Pluralisms

Generally, pluralism represents one 'common, overarching legal framework that would integrate postnational governance, distribute powers, and provide for means of solving disputes between the various layers of law and politics'.[10] Michaels traces the origins of legal pluralism in legal, sociological, and anthropological studies from the 1970s and 1980s, researching the co-existence of normative orders within societies.[11] In legal research, the definition that seems to be the common denominator in the different readings of pluralism is that of a multitude of legal systems operating in one political unit.[12] It has further developed into different versions that may be surmised into what Griffiths calls 'weak' and 'strong' pluralism: the former describes the plurality of sources of law within a system with a *Grundnorm* (thus essentially falling into monism), whereas the latter imagines a situation in which not all law is state-sourced, or state-administered.[13] In its sociological form, Griffiths' 'strong' pluralism provides the theoretical groundwork[14] for MacCormick's concept of an institutional normative order that is not limited to states. While the present work focuses exclusively on the contributions of constitutional pluralism as developed by MacCormick and Walker, I will briefly address radical and global legal pluralism that are crucial for understanding their work.

Radical pluralism, which is relevant as it corresponds to MacCormick's early work on pluralism in the European Union, finds that the relationship between constitutional sites is not guided by any means of reconciliation or coordination. Rather, it is characterized by a complete lack of any *Grundnorm* that would ultimately guide contestation and conflict between different institutional normative orders.[15] Radical pluralism in this sense attempts to avoid the trap of becoming the 'new monism', as Walker explains:

> [It] may well be that in the EU context, even though we talk about a brave new world of pluralism, that actually what we are doing is just inventing a new vocabulary which in the final analysis will end up pushing us in that federal-but-centralising direction . . .[16]

[10] Krisch (n 7) 69.

[11] Michaels (n 7) 245. See also Barber (n 7) 307.

[12] B de Sousa Santos, *Towards a New Legal Common Sense* (Butterworths 2002) 89; Michaels (n 7) 245.

[13] J Griffiths, 'What Is Legal Pluralism?' (1986) 24 *Journal of Legal Pluralism and Unofficial Law* 1, 5.

[14] But also a shift from the anthropological methodology whose object of inquiry was the relationship between state law and other less formal or 'self-styled' normative orders within the territory of that state. N Walker, 'Reconciling MacCormick: Constitutional Pluralism and the Unity of Practical Reason' (2011) 24(4) *Ratio Juris* 369, 374.

[15] N Krisch, 'Who Is Afraid of Radical Pluralism? Legal Order and Political Stability in the Postnational Space' (2011) 24(4) *Ratio Juris* 386, 388.

[16] M Avbelj and J Komárek, 'Symposium: Four Visions of Constitutional Pluralism (Symposium Transcript)' (2008) 2(1) *European Journal of Legal Studies* 325, 344.

Kumm's account of constitutionalism beyond the state aims to address this gap: the *Grundnorm* is not possible to discern either in EU or in national constitutional law, but is rather normatively rooted in political morality, also characterized as pertaining to the radical side of pluralism.[17] Kumm argues that, when faced with a constitutional conflict, the national judge should apply the 'principle of best fit'.[18]

In his later work, MacCormick softened his radical approach[19] and argued that, while EU and national law are on an equal footing as a matter of principle, the *Grundnorm* is to be found in international law, what he calls 'pluralism under international law'.[20] Viewed in this way, it is international law that validates both national and EU legal systems, rather than looking at them from either a state-centrist (states are masters of the treaties and thus validate EU law) or an EU-centrist (the EU is a new legal order hierarchically superior to national law and thus validates national law) perspective. For MacCormick, thus, there is no 'all-purpose superiority of one system over another'.[21] The relationship between EU and national legal systems in 'pluralism under international law' does not represent a third approach—a new non-hierarchical interpretative system (as radical pluralism suggests)—but is a framework for relationships between these non-hierarchically interacting systems.[22]

Global legal pluralism, as developed by Teubner,[23] argues that 'law is not generated by the state but instead creates itself (*autopoiesis*), and that the centre of law-making has moved away from the state and into the periphery of transnational actors'.[24] Teubner's work looks further away from jurisprudential instances of pluralism and includes other sectors of society which, more or less spontaneously, engage in 'self-constitutionalisation and constitutional fragmentation'.[25] Teubner's work was a sound basis for research into different sources of non-state law in a transnational environment caused by globalization,[26] but what diminishes its

[17] M Kumm, 'The Jurisprudence of Constitutional Conflict: Constitutional Supremacy in Europe before and after the Constitutional Treaty' (2005) 11(3) *European Law Journal* 262, 286.

[18] Defined as an optimal interpretation and balancing of values sourced in the applicable constitutional orders. Kumm (n 17). See also G Davies, 'Interpretative Pluralism and the Constitutionalisation of the EU Legal Order' in M Dawson and M Jachtenfuchs (eds), *Autonomy without Collapse in a Better European Union* (OUP forthcoming 2022).

[19] Krisch (n 7) 73.

[20] N MacCormick, 'Risking Constitutional Collision in Europe?' (1998) 18(3) *Oxford Journal of Legal Studies* 517, 527.

[21] ibid 529.

[22] ibid. See also H Birkenkötter, 'International Law as a Common Language across Spheres of Authority?' (2020) 9(2) *Global Constitutionalism* 318.

[23] G Teubner, 'The Two Faces of Janus: Rethinking Legal Pluralism' (1992) 5 *Cardozo Law Review* 1443.

[24] Michaels (n 7) 247.

[25] J Priban, 'Asking the Sovereignty Question in Global Legal Pluralism: From "Weak" Jurisprudence to "Strong" Socio-legal Theories of Constitutional Power Operations' (2015) 28(1) *Ratio Juris* 31, 38. The way Teubner describes the process of fragmentation and self-constitutionalization can also be connected to studies of polycentric theory, with the difference that the latter analyses these developments as they emerge in a bottom-up fashion. See J van Zeben and A Bobić, *Polycentricity in the European Union* (CUP 2019)12 ff.

[26] Michaels (n 7) 247.

usefulness for the purposes of the present work is its predominantly top-down approach, attempting to analyse different variations in global law.[27] As a consequence, global legal pluralism appears too broad to help capture the subtleties of interactions between the EU and national legal orders, as it denounces any institutionalized form of interaction between the different systems.[28]

This brings us to constitutional pluralism that Walker developed from MacCormick's ideas. In his ground-breaking piece[29] he makes three claims: (1) the EU's constitutional setup is comprised of multiple constitutional sites of discourse and authority (explanatory claim);[30] (2) the mutual recognition and respect between these multiple sites of constitutional authority is 'the only acceptable ethic of political responsibility for the new Europe' (normative claim);[31] and (3) pluralism revolves around the notion of incommensurability of different claims to authority (epistemic claim).[32]

Since, in the understanding of epistemic pluralism, the different sites of authority speak a different language, they lack a common denominator that might provide them with a 'monist' solution to possible conflicts. However, Walker claims that heterarchy and horizontality are underlying the relationship between the different sites of constitutional authority,[33] where conflicts are addressed through meta-constitutionalism: a process of mutual negotiation, learning, open dialogue, and cross-examination.[34]

The initial success of Walker's theory was followed by criticism,[35] most vehemently expressed by Loughlin[36] who called it an 'oxymoron'. His critique is premised on unlimited state sovereignty, which can either be complete or it no longer exists.[37] He further strongly disagrees with MacCormick's claim that any institutional normative order is 'deserving of acknowledgement and even respect'.[38] For Loughlin, it is impossible for a constitution to be treated as a category able to transcend the confines of a state into any normative order, nor for these normative orders to be treated as equal counterparts.[39] He concludes that any acceptance by

[27] ibid.
[28] Krisch (n 7) 76–77; Avbelj (n 7) 3. Such a conclusion is rather disappointing given Teubner's own criticism of classical legal pluralism as vague and ambiguous. See Teubner (n 23) 3.
[29] Walker (n 3).
[30] ibid 337.
[31] ibid.
[32] ibid 338. See also N Walker, 'Constitutional Pluralism Revisited' (2016) 22(3) *European Law Journal* 333, 333–34; K Tuori, *European Constitutionalism* (CUP 2015)355.
[33] Walker (n 3) 337.
[34] ibid 358–59.
[35] See eg J Baquero Cruz, 'The Legacy of the Maastricht-Urteil and the Pluralist Movement' (2008) 14 *European Law Journal* 389. See also Avbelj and Komárek (n 7).
[36] M Loughlin, 'Constitutional Pluralism: An Oxymoron?' (2014) 3(1) *Global Constitutionalism* 9.
[37] ibid 13.
[38] ibid 16.
[39] ibid 17.

pluralists of a conflict resolution mechanism necessarily draws them back into monism—otherwise, they are near-anarchists eroding any normative stance.

Such classic theories denying sovereign features to polities beyond the state can, in my view, no longer accommodate and explain the legal nature of European integration and the EU's legal system,[40] nor its relationship to national law.[41] This inability results from the problem of using and translating state-centred constitutionalist terms with the aim of explaining and legitimizing non-state settings, such as the EU. As Walker explains it:

> Just because the 'state constitutionalism' is the default determinant, and because the destination language of 'non-state constitutionalism' is under-developed, there is a danger that both scholars and actors in the integration process presume an isomorphism between the EU and their respective national polities.[42]

Therefore, the EU and its institutions should not be judged against the 'state' vocabulary and standards, but should be regarded as having its own idiosyncratic nature.[43]

What is then left of constitutional pluralism and is it still a theory worth exploring and developing? Krisch emphasized the need for 'more empirical work and deeper inquiries into the institutional dynamics of pluralist orders in the varied contexts of postnational governance'.[44] Taking Walker's theoretical groundwork as the premise for my own understanding of constitutional pluralism, in this book

[40] J Shaw, 'Process and Constitutional Discourse in the European Union' (2000) 27 *Journal of Law & Society* 4, 21.

[41] The Polish Trybunał Konstytucyjny recognized this important momentum in its decision on the Accession Treaty:

> The concept and model of European law created a new situation, wherein, within each Member State, autonomous legal orders co-exist and are simultaneously operative. Their interaction may not be completely described by the traditional concepts of monism and dualism regarding the relationship between domestic law and international law.

Polish Trybunał Konstytucyjny Case K 18/04 *Accession Treaty* Judgment of 11 May 2005 [12] http://trybunal.gov.pl/fileadmin/content/omowienia/K_18_04_GB.pdf. See also Czech Ústavní Soud Case Pl. ÚS 19/08 *Lisbon Treaty I* Judgment of 26 November 2008 [101], [104]–[105] http://www.usoud.cz/en/decisions/20081126-pl-us-1908-treaty-of-lisbon-i-1/.

[42] N Walker, 'Late Sovereignty in the European Union' in N Walker (ed), *Sovereignty in Transition* (Hart Publishing 2003) 40. See also Shaw (n 40) 20; R Dehousse, 'Beyond Representative Democracy: Constitutionalism in a Polycentric Polity' in J H H Weiler and M Wind (eds), *European Constitutionalism Beyond the State* (CUP 2003) 136; Krisch (n 7) 35 ff. In the political science literature see also I Bache and M Flinders (eds), *Multi-level Governance* (OUP 2004)78.

[43] The same was underlined by Siniša Rodin, Judge at the Court of Justice, in a talk at the Bingham Centre in London on 2 November 2015. He put forward the argument that the criticism addressed to the Court of Justice should be confined to those internal characteristics of the Court—not in comparison to a preferred, ideal type of a court, or even in comparison to a certain national constitutional or supreme court, but having in mind the specific context in which it operates as an institution of the EU. In the same vein, see also Czech Ústavní Soud Case Pl. ÚS 29/09 *Lisbon Treaty II* Judgment of 3 November 2009, [137]–[140] http://www.usoud.cz/en/decisions/20091103-pl-us-2909-treaty-of-lisbon-ii-1/.

[44] Krisch (n 7) 70.

I will delve into an in-depth inquiry of the European Union as one institutional (or, more precisely, constitutional) normative order forming part of a pluralist system. As a starting point of this endeavour, the following section will present its determinative descriptive features that will serve as the framework for analysis of the jurisprudence of constitutional conflict in the EU in the case studies pertaining to chapters 5 to 7.

# 3

# Constitutional Pluralism as a Descriptive Theory

Constitutional pluralism is a theory that both describes the current constellation in the EU's constitutional, and specifically judicial, space; it further provides normative guidance as to the future operation of the system. This chapter will address its descriptive elements, first theoretically, and subsequently, offering a broad brush prima facie substantiation of their operation. The operation of judicial interactions between the EU and its Member States follows three broad patterns pertaining to the pluralist understanding of the EU's constitutional space.

First, the decisive determinants for defining and differentiating among diverse legal systems are no longer based on spatial boundaries[1] but, instead, on an idea that the EU and national constitutional orders inherently overlap within the same geographical space.[2] The demands of each of the claims to ultimate authority are, under Walker's epistemic pluralism, incommensurate and we can thus observe their parallel, competing operation in the same supranational political unit of the EU. This leads us to the second pattern in judicial interactions: the reading of interactions between the national and the EU constitutional systems cannot be conducted in hierarchical terms.[3] Such an understanding does not disregard the existence of hierarchy in national constitutional settings, as the constitutional jurisdictions remain ultimate interpreters and arbiters in their respective areas of jurisdiction. However, constitutional pluralism emphasizes heterarchy as the framework for the interaction of a plurality of constitutional orders co-existing and claiming sovereignty in the same geographical space.

[1] J Shaw, 'Process and Constitutional Discourse in the European Union' (2000) 27 *Journal of Law & Society* 4, 7. See also I Pernice, 'Introduction: Achievements and Challenges: The European Union, Its Constitutional Courts and the Perspectives after Lisbon' in J M Beneyto and I Pernice (eds), *Europe's Constitutional Challenges in the Light of the Recent Case Law of National Constitutional Courts—Lisbon and Beyond* (Nomos 2011) 9–10. In the political science literature see L Hooghe and G Marks, 'Unraveling the Central State, but How? Types of Multi-Level Governance' (2003) 97 *American Political Science Review* 233, 237; N Chowdhury and R A Wessel, 'Conceptualising Multilevel Regulation in the EU: A Legal Translation of Multilevel Governance?' (2012) 18 *European Law Journal* 335, 340.

[2] W Twining, *Globalization and Legal Theory* (Butterworths 2000) 83. See also M de Visser, *Constitutional Review in Europe: A Comparative Analysis* (Hart Publishing 2014) 3; J H H Weiler, 'Journey to an Unknown Destination: A Retrospective and Prospective of the European Court of Justice in the Arena of Political Integration' (1993) 31(4) *Journal of Common Market Studies* 417, 422.

[3] N Krisch, *Beyond Constitutionalism: The Pluralist Structure of Postnational Law* (OUP 2013) 69.

*The Jurisprudence of Constitutional Conflict in the European Union.* Ana Bobić, Oxford University Press. © Ana Bobić 2022.
DOI: 10.1093/oso/9780192847034.003.0003

Heterarchy can be defined as 'the relation of elements to one another when they are unranked or when they possess the potential for being ranked in a number of different ways'.[4] It thus captures the relations between different units claiming authority without defining their relationships in advance and statically. Understood in this sense, constitutional pluralism has the aim of overcoming 'the almost unconscious assumption of hierarchy-as-order'[5] that I find to be an inherent fallacy of monist views on the EU.

A final, third, pattern that we can observe is the manner in which conflicts that necessarily occur between different sites of constitutional authority are resolved. In this respect, I will demonstrate that the system has an in-built auto-correct function that serves to accommodate points of conflict in an incremental fashion, which operates as a check and balance among constitutional jurisdictions on the national and EU level. Such an understanding waters down the importance of competition for the final say in the EU,[6] because judicial interactions are taking place in a setting of mutual respect and are based on the principle of sincere cooperation.[7] In the final part of this chapter, I will present the shared judicial vocabulary that serves as a broad-brush demonstration of these three patterns.

## 1 Competing Claims to Ultimate Authority

Constitutional pluralism as a theory presupposes the existence of parallel claims to ultimate authority in the same geographical space, exemplified in the European Union context by the claims to the ultimate say by Member States, as well as the EU itself. On behalf of the Member States, national courts with a constitutional mandate have consistently claimed final authority in their territory, in particular in relation to their role of protecting the national constitution as hierarchically the highest act applicable in a Member State,[8] and underlining sovereignty as the

[4] C L Crumley, 'Heterarchy and the Analysis of Complex Societies' (1995) 6 *Archaeological Papers of the American Anthropological Association* 1, 3.

[5] ibid.

[6] A Stone Sweet, 'A Cosmopolitan Legal Order: Constitutional Pluralism and Rights Adjudication in Europe' (2012) 1(1) *Global Constitutionalism* 53, 55.

[7] Different versions of the same principle are also in place at the national level. For an analysis of the principle of friendliness towards European integration in constitutional jurisprudence of Member States see section 4 below, and in particular n 120. On this point see also de Visser (n 2) 3, fn 14.

[8] See eg Czech Ústavní Soud Case Pl. ÚS 19/08 *Lisbon Treaty I* Judgment of 26 November 2008 [216] http://www.usoud.cz/en/decisions/20081126-pl-us-1908-treaty-of-lisbon-i-1/; Danish Højesteret Case I 361/1997 *Carlsen* Judgment of 6 April 1998; German Bundesverfassungsgericht Case 2BvR 2661/06 *Honeywell* Order of 06 July 2010 [68] http://www.bundesverfassungsgericht.de/SharedDocs/Entscheidungen/EN/2010/07/rs20100706_2bvr266106en.html; National Report: The Constitutional Court of the Republic of Lithuania (2014) 5; Polish Trybunał Konstytucyjny Case K 18/04 *Accession Treaty* Judgment of 11 May 2005 [11] http://trybunal.gov.pl/fileadmin/content/omowienia/K_18_04_GB.pdf; *Pham* [2015] UKSC 19 [90].

ultimate limit for European integration and the reach of the principle of primacy.[9] National constitutional courts have also put forward identity-based limits to the primacy of EU law,[10] reasserting the untouchable character of the constitutional core.[11] Sovereignty claims on the national level are consistently put forward by constitutional adjudicators, in particular in situations of possible clashes in interpretation with EU law demands.[12]

On behalf of the EU, the debate concerning its claim to sovereignty is complex.[13] Legal academics have long faced the challenge of describing and assessing the nature of the European Union as a polity, specifically in relation to the well-established[14] categories of states and international organizations. The struggle of calling the EU legal order a constitutional one stemmed from an almost natural assumption of states as constitutional orders, as opposed to international organizations based on public international law and created by the authority of participating states. Nevertheless, taking into account direct effect and primacy (ultimately constructing state responsibility beyond what the public international law sphere ever entailed),[15] constitutional features of the European Union are no longer disputed,[16]

[9] For example, Czech Ústavní Soud Case Pl. ÚS 50/04 *Sugar Quotas III* Judgment of 8 March 2006 headnote [8] http://www.usoud.cz/en/decisions/20060308-pl-us-5004-sugar-quotas-iii-1/; German Bundesverfassungsgericht Cases 2 BvR 2134/92 and 2 BvR 2159/92 *Maastricht Treaty* Judgment of 12 October 1993 [C.II.1.a] http://www.judicialstudies.unr.edu/JS_Summer09/JSP_Week_1/German%20ConstCourt%20Maastricht.pdf; Spanish Tribunal Constitucional Case DTC 1/2004 *Constitutional Treaty* Declaration of 13 December 2004 [II-2].

[10] Most recently referring to constitutional identity see the Portuguese Constitutional Tribunal Case 422/2020 Decision of 15 July 2020 [2.6.2.2.]http://www.tribunalconstitucional.pt/tc/acordaos/20200422.html.

[11] Czech Ústavní Soud Case Pl. ÚS 29/09 *Lisbon Treaty II* Judgment of 3 November 2009 [150] http://www.usoud.cz/en/decisions/20091103-pl-us-2909-treaty-of-lisbon-ii-1/; French Conseil Constitutionnel Case 2006–540 DC *Information Society* Decision of 27 July 2006 [19]; German Bundesverfassungsgericht Case 2 BVerfG 2/08 *Lisbon Treaty* Judgment of 30 June 2009 [240] ff http://www.bverfg.de/e/es20090630_2bve000208en.html; German Bundesverfassungsgericht Case 9/2014 *Gauweiler* Press release of 7 February 2014 [2.a] https://www.bundesverfassungsgericht.de/SharedDocs/Pressemitteilungen/EN/2014/bvg14-009.html; Italian Corte costituzionale Case 183/1973 *Frontini* Judgment of 27 December 1973; Latvian Satversmes tiesa Case 2008-35-01 *Treaty of Lisbon* Decision of 7 April 2009 paras [16.3], [17]; Polish Trybunał Konstytucyjny Case K 32/09 *Treaty of Lisbon*, Judgment of 24 November 2010 [1.1.2] http://trybunal.gov.pl/fileadmin/content/omowienia/K_32_09_EN.pdf; Belgian Cour Constitutionnelle Case 62/2016 *Stability Pact* Judgment of 28 April 2016, summary http://www.const-court.be/cgi/judgments_popup.php?lang=en&ArrestID=4097.

[12] For an analysis of the increasing frequency of state-centred claims by the Bundesverfassungsgericht see J E K Murkens, '"We Want Our Identity Back": The Revival of National Sovereignty in the German Federal Constitutional Court's Decision on the Lisbon Treaty' (2010) 25 *Public Law* 530.

[13] For a summary of the debate see also S Rehling Larsen, *The Constitutional Theory of the Federation and the European Union* (OUP 2021) 11–12.

[14] N Walker, 'Late Sovereignty in the European Union' in N Walker (ed), *Sovereignty in Transition* (Hart Publishing 2003) 9.

[15] J H H Weiler, 'Prologue: Global and Pluralist Constitutionalism—Some Doubts' in G de Búrca and J H H Weiler (eds), *The Worlds of European Constitutionalism* (CUP 2012) 11–12. See also N MacCormick, *Questioning Sovereignty: Law, State and Nation in the European Commonwealth* (OUP 1999) 97–98.

[16] The Court of Justice called the system of the Treaties the EU's 'constitutional charter' in Case 294/83 *Les Verts* [1986] EU:C:1986:166 [23]. For Lenaerts, this was an undisputed fact back in 1990. K Lenaerts, 'Constitutionalism and the Many Faces of Federalism' (1990) 38(2) *American Journal*

despite a more general reluctance in the literature to ascribe constitutionalist characteristics to entities beyond the state.[17] Taking into account that the EU's claim to ultimate authority is incommensurate to that of Member States, in what follows I further explore the nature of its sovereignty claim.

The major transformative momentum in this debate was the Maastricht Treaty, more precisely, the sharp decline in public support that was taken for granted in respect of all previous integration benchmarks.[18] The public outrage translated into important judicial challenges to the ratification of the Treaty,[19] where national courts asserted their right to review the transfer of competences to the EU and remained firmly of the view that they are the Masters of the Treaties.[20] In that respect, MacCormick concluded that law is an institutional normative order, the 'principal example'[21] being found in nation states, but not restricted solely to them[22]—they are only a species of a *genus*.[23] For a normative order to be an institutional one (regardless of whether we are dealing with the nation state or another type of polity), it needs to possess the ability for the norms of the order to be applied to the situation they govern, which results in the self-referential quality of the system.[24] Decades of development of the European Union and the self-referential nature of the *acquis communautaire* make it impossible to reach any other conclusion than to recognize it as a 'full-blown instance of an institutional normative order'.[25]

The debate on the possible existence of sovereignty beyond the state aroused a great deal of scepticism, connected mainly to the problem of defining any non-state system as constitutional.[26] The fear sparked by the Maastricht Treaty revolved strongly around the threat to the democratic form of self-government by the people.[27] The argument, in short, goes: only 'We the People' are able to create the constitutional framework claiming ultimate authority in a given space and no unit beyond the state can satisfy this requirement.[28] While the EU certainly does

*of Comparative Law* 205, 210. See also E Stein, 'Lawyers, Judges, and the Making of a Transnational Constitution' (1981) 75(1) *American Journal of International Law* 1.

[17] M Kumm, 'The Cosmopolitan Turn in Constitutionalism: An Integrated Conception of Public Law' (2013) 20(2) *Indiana Journal of Global Legal Studies* 605, 606.

[18] J H H Weiler, *The Constitution of Europe: 'Do the New Clothes Have an Emperor?' and Other Essays on European Integration* (CUP 1999) 4. See also MacCormick (n 15) 98.

[19] MacCormick (n 15) 98–99.

[20] For example, reiterated in German Bundesverfassungsgericht Case 2 BVerfG 2/08 *Lisbon Treaty* (n 11) [231].

[21] MacCormick (n 15) 1.

[22] He concludes that the European Union is one such institutional normative order. See MacCormick (n 15) 102–103.

[23] ibid 1. See also K Tuori, *European Constitutionalism* (CUP 2015) 87 ff.

[24] MacCormick (n 15) 7.

[25] ibid 131. For a detailed presentation and analysis of the expansion of the self-referential system of the Treaties by the Court of Justice see ch 5, ss 4, 5, and 7.

[26] Kumm (n 17) 608. See also Krisch (n 3) 27.

[27] MacCormick (n 15) 125.

[28] Kumm (n 17) 608. See German Bundesverfassungsgericht Cases 2 BvR 2134/92 and 2159/92 *Maastricht Treaty* (n 9) 94. For a fierce critique of this reasoning see J H H Weiler, 'Does Europe

not establish its ultimate authority in the same manner as states do, the Court of Justice's development of the self-referential system of the Treaties, grounded in the doctrines of primacy and direct effect,[29] not only restricts Member States' sovereignty[30] in the classic sense, but also renders the EU legal order 'independent, autonomous and non-derivative'.[31] The EU's sovereignty is thus rooted in the creation of the autonomous, independent, and self-referential nature of the system of Treaties.[32] In Opinion 1/91, the Court finds primacy and direct effect to have resulted in constitutionalizing the Treaties, based on the rule of law:

> In contrast, the EEC Treaty, albeit concluded in the form of an international agreement, none the less constitutes the constitutional charter of a Community based on the rule of law. As the Court of Justice has consistently held, the Community treaties established a new legal order for the benefit of which the States have limited their sovereign rights, in ever wider fields, and the subjects of which comprise not only Member States but also their nationals.[33]

But does this mean that we can equate the EU's constitutional frame to that of a federation, as part of the legal scholarship argues? Such a view would in fact make the EU's claim to ultimate authority commensurate to those of Member States and position it atop a federal hierarchy. Lenaerts defines the common denominator of federalism to be 'the appropriate balance between the federation and its component entities'.[34] He further explains that integrative federalism, as a mode of constitutionalism that strives to unite diverse entities, can be applied to the model of the (then) supranational European Community.[35] The Treaty provisions setting out the vertical division of competences between the EU and the Member States, as well as the manner of exercise of these competences by the Union institutions (including a strong Court of Justice)[36] have been interpreted as clear indicators of

Need a Constitution? Demos, Telos and the German Maastricht Decision' (1995) 1(3) *European Law Journal* 219.

[29] G de Búrca, 'Sovereignty and the Supremacy Doctrine of the European Court of Justice' in N Walker (ed), *Sovereignty in Transition* (Hart Publishing 2003) 452–53, 12.

[30] Stated explicitly by the Court of Justice as early as Case 26/62 *Van Gend en Loos* [1963] EU:C:1963:1 at 12; and Case 6/64 *Costa v ENEL* [1964] EU:C:1964 at 593.

[31] de Búrca (n 29) 453.

[32] See also H Lindahl, 'Sovereignty and Representation in the European Union' in N Walker (ed), *Sovereignty in Transition* (Hart Publishing 2003) 107; J Komárek, 'It's a Stupid Autonomy ...' *Verfassungsblog* (14 March 2015) http://verfassungsblog.de/its-a-stupid-autonomy-2/.

[33] Opinion 1/91 [1991] EU:C:1991:490 [21].

[34] Lenaerts (n 16) 205. Similarly, Kelemen provides the following, as he terms it, minimalist definition of federalism: 'Federalism is an institutional arrangement in which (a) public authority is divided between state governments and a central government, (b) each level of government has some issues on which it makes final decisions, and (c) a high federal court adjudicates disputes concerning federalism.' R D Kelemen, 'The Structure and Dynamics of EU Federalism' (2003) 36(1–2) *Comparative Political Studies* 184, 185.

[35] Lenaerts (n 16) 206–207.

[36] ibid 216.

a federalist structure.[37] In addition, federalism is praised owing to its applicability to any system of divided powers, whereas any *sui generis* approach is discarded as methodologically flawed.[38] Finally, the development of EU citizenship has been extensively addressed from the perspective of federalism, given its clear connection to multiple vertical levels of government and political association.[39]

The crucial reason why federalism as a theory holds insufficient explanatory and normative power for the EU is because it fails to take into account national contributions to the EU constitutional landscape, which deprive the primacy of EU law of its unconditional character.[40] For example, Lenaerts denies that the Lisbon Treaty diminishes any of the EU's federal features, since EU law retained a pervasiveness into national law, both through the obligation of national regulators not to legislate contrary to EU law, as well as due to a spill-over effect that EU law may have in the area of exclusive competences of Member States.[41] However, the position of the Court of Justice as the 'high federal court'[42] in the EU is but one reality; national courts performing constitutional review have developed a reality of their own, supported by jurisprudence that at times outright contradicts that of the Court of Justice. Thus, federalism cannot capture the nature of the EU's constitutional frame without being stretched beyond recognition.[43] Federalism is thus, in my view, unable to account for the complex relationship of contestation between the EU and the national level and in particular the incommensurability of their claims to ultimate authority.

We are then left with one final question: if Member States retain their sovereignty claim to the ultimate say, as does the EU in areas of its functional sovereignty, is there a way to redress the incommensurability of claims by these two levels of constitutional authority? Maduro argues that state constitutionalism is but a 'contextual representation of constitutionalism'.[44] In other words, how far can each of the levels of authority go in contestation before the constitutional frame

[37] ibid. See also Stein (n 16) 1.

[38] F Fabbrini, *Fundamental Rights in Europe: Challenges and Transformations in Comparative Perspective* (OUP 2014) 24–25.

[39] For a comprehensive contribution see D Kochenov (ed), *EU Citizenship and Federalism: The Role of Rights* (CUP 2017).

[40] See also M Fichera, 'Solidarity, Heterarchy, and Political Morality' (2020) *Jus Cogens* 2.

[41] He defines spill-over as the voluntary 'application by national authorities of EU norms (e.g., rules, principles, concepts) to situations governed entirely and exclusively by national law'. K Lenaerts, 'Federalism and the Rule of Law: Perspectives from the European Court of Justice' (2010) 13 *Fordham International Law Journal* 1338, 1340–41.

[42] Kelemen (n 34) 185.

[43] Tuori (n 23) 345. See also P Eeckhout, 'The EU Charter of Fundamental Rights and the Federal Question' (2002) 39(5) *Common Market Law Review* 945, 946; D Halberstam, '"It's the Autonomy, Stupid!" A Modest Defense of *Opinion 2/13* on EU accession to the ECHR, and the Way Forward' (2015) 16(1) *German Law Journal* 105, 114.

[44] M P Maduro, 'Europe and the Constitution: What if This Is as Good as it Gets?' in J H H Weiler and M Wind (eds), *European Constitutionalism Beyond the State* (CUP 2003) 74. On the debate on different views on constitutionalism as regards the EU see N Walker, 'European Constitutionalism in the State Constitutional Tradition' (2006) 59 *Current Legal Problems* 51, 51–56.

is broken? For this, it is necessary to answer Jessica Lawrence's question posed to scholars of constitutional pluralism: 'what the "common project" is, what types of conflicts can be resolved within it, and/or which metaconstitutional principles apply'.[45] Constitutionalism can be defined as 'a normatively ambitious project of establishing legitimate authority over persons that are ultimately conceived as free and equals';[46] as 'having an overarching normative structure', where fundamental rights represent the normative expression of a constitutional system.[47] In the EU context, Shaw's four pillars of constitutionalism determine: (1) the nature of the polity; (2) the rule of law and its systemic properties;[48] (3) key values, principles, and norms;[49] and (4) the exercise and limitation of power of the polity.[50] Ultimately, thus, constitutionalism is a quality capable of existing in the EU as an institutional normative order claiming ultimate authority. In the next section, I explore in more depth the heterarchical relationships in the EU's constitutional space.

## 2 Heterarchy and the Question of the Final Arbiter

As mentioned above, the theory of constitutional pluralism rests upon the assumption that the question of the final judicial instance in the EU as we know it is immaterial. On the contrary, the basis for the inter-institutional relationship of national courts with a constitutional mandate and the Court of Justice is not that of hierarchy, but instead an interactive[51] heterarchy. Consequently, the pluralist theory asserts, there is no final arbiter, and there need not be one.[52]

How does heterarchy work? As mentioned above, heterarchy is defined as the relationship of elements to one another when they are unranked or they possess the ability to be ranked in a number of different ways.[53] In practice, this means that

[45] J C Lawrence, 'Constitutional Pluralism's Unspoken Normative Core' (2019) 21 *Cambridge Yearbook of European Legal Studies* 24, 28.

[46] Kumm (n 17) 609. Similarly, Tuori sets out a functional definition of the European legal order as constitutional. However, he openly uses state-rooted terminology, finding that the European 'constitution' deviates from it. Tuori (n 23) 28–30, 257.

[47] A Stone Sweet, 'The Structure of Constitutional Pluralism: Review of Nico Krisch, *Beyond Constitutionalism: The Pluralist Structure of Post-National Law*' (2013) 11(2) *International Journal of Constitutional Law* 491, 493.

[48] See also Krisch (n 3) 27.

[49] Including fundamental rights, non-discrimination, and the institutionalization of Union citizenship as foundations of the delivery of fairness and justice. Shaw (n 1) 16.

[50] ibid 15–18. Similarly, according to Priban, '[the] modern notion of democratic constitutionalism draw[s] on constituent power, ultimate sovereignty and the self-constitution of the people'. J Priban, 'Asking the Sovereignty Question in Global Legal Pluralism: From "Weak" Jurisprudence to "Strong" Socio-legal Theories of Constitutional Power Operations' (2015) 28(1) *Ratio Juris* 31, 33.

[51] N MacCormick, 'The Maastricht Urteil: Sovereignty Now' (1995) 1 *European Law Journal* 259, 264.

[52] M Kumm, 'Who Is the Final Arbiter of Constitutionality in Europe: Three Conceptions of the Relationship between the German Federal Constitutional Court and the European Court of Justice' (1999) 36 *Common Market Law Review* 351, 384.

[53] Crumley (n 4) 3.

we cannot ascribe superiority neither to the national nor the EU claim to ultimate authority. Rather, as will become evident through the operation of the auto-correct function explained below, both levels of constitutional authority possess the potential of prevailing in single points of conflict, whereas incrementally we are able to see the balancing of these claims through the application of mutual respect and sincere cooperation. This ultimately renders the question of the final arbiter immaterial, as there are no predetermined winners and losers, but rather, different courts will have the final say at different times.

Kelemen has been particularly critical of how easily the pluralist theory has accepted that it is not problematic, but rather preferable, to leave out an answer to the question of the final arbiter.[54] In his view, reluctance to make an attempt to resolve this issue is a sign of immaturity of a legal system, and he called for a resolution of this question in order for the EU legal system to be able to call itself a constitutional order.[55] His proposition is that, in order for the EU constitutional order to be considered 'mature', a decision on the final arbiter is necessary and this should be the Court of Justice in line with the primacy of EU law.[56] Should a national court with constitutional jurisdiction disagree, he added, it should declare the continuing membership of its Member State in the EU as unconstitutional, thus urging their governments to approach the resolution of constitutional conflict, if necessary, by recourse to Article 50 TEU and withdrawing their membership in the Union.[57]

Such an approach seems extreme and resembles the Cold War logic: the question of the final arbiter will seemingly be settled, solely because anything else would result in ending the relevant Member State's EU membership. In fact, it seems much more *im*mature than the status quo, as it is proposing a shift from mutually assured trust to mutually assured destruction.[58] While both might yield the same result, cooperation between courts is far more fruitful when they operate in the context of a self-imposed restraint,[59] where none actually considers using the heavy weapons that are theoretically available.[60]

[54] R D Kelemen, 'On the Unsustainability of Constitutional Pluralism: European Supremacy and the Survival of the Eurozone' (2016) 23(1) *Maastricht Journal of European and Comparative Law* 136, 139.

[55] ibid 140.

[56] ibid 141.

[57] ibid 141, 148–49.

[58] Mutually assured destruction is a doctrine of military strategy and national security policy in which a full-scale use of nuclear weapons by two or more opposing sides would cause the complete annihilation of both the attacker and the defender. It is based on the theory of deterrence, which holds that the threat of using strong weapons against the enemy prevents the enemy's use of those same weapons. The strategy is a form of Nash equilibrium in which, once armed, neither side has any incentive to initiate a conflict or to disarm. See https://en.wikipedia.org/wiki/Mutual_assured_destruction.

[59] See also M Claes and M de Visser, 'Are You Networked Yet? On Dialogues in European Judicial Networks' (2012) 8(2) *Utrecht Law Review* 100, 106.

[60] Prior to its political capture, the Polish Trybunał Konstytucyjny proposed several possible solutions in the event of a constitutional conflict before leaving the EU:

> 'In such an event [of a collision between provisions of EU law and the Constitution] the Nation as the sovereign, or a State authority organ authorised by the Constitution to represent the Nation, would need to decide on: amending the Constitution; or causing modifications within

The difference is clearly reflected in the EU's national identity clause, whose importance appears to be overlooked by both Kelemen and Fabbrini. While Kelemen entertains the idea of respect for national (constitutional) identity,[61] it results from his proposition that a proper safeguard of the inviolable core of a national constitution can only take place in the ultimate withdrawal of the Member State from the EU.[62] The doomsday device[63] activates, and everyone loses. Fabbrini, as will be discussed below, subordinates the national identity clause entirely to the principle of equality of Member States, thereby leaving the reader in doubt as to the reasons for its very existence.[64]

Applying these arguments to interactions between the Court of Justice and a national court with constitutional jurisdiction demonstrates the weaknesses of these arguments. If Kelemen's reasoning is applied to the case of the Outright Monetary Transactions Mechanism (OMT) of the European Central Bank (ECB),[65] it would not have been necessary at all for the Bundesverfassungsgericht to submit the preliminary reference to the Court of Justice. According to his arguments, all the doubts the Bundesverfassungsgericht had concerning the boundaries of the ECB's monetary policy competence are easily resolved in two ways: (1) by unconditionally accepting the OMT as it is; or (2) by requiring withdrawal from the EU if it found it to be in breach of Germany's constitutional identity. In a pluralist context, however, the Bundesverfassungsgericht was able to express its own view of constitutional identity, how it might be affected by the introduction of the OMT, and continue with its pattern of EU-friendly reasoning.[66] The Court of Justice entered the discussion, focusing solely on the analysis of the mechanism, but deferring to the Bundesverfassungsgericht on questions of national constitutional identity.[67]

Community provisions; or, ultimately, on Poland's withdrawal from the European Union.' Polish Trybunał Konstytucyjny Case *Accession Treaty* (n 8) [13]. See also S Weatherill, *Law and Values in the European Union* (OUP 2016) 243, 251.

61 Kelemen (n 54) 148.

62 ibid.

63 A doomsday device is a hypothetical construction—usually a weapon, or a collection of weapons—which could destroy all life on a planet, particularly Earth, or destroy the planet itself, bringing 'doomsday', a term used for the end of planet Earth. See https://en.wikipedia.org/wiki/Doomsday_device.

64 F Fabbrini, 'After the *OMT* Case: The Supremacy of EU Law as the Guarantee of the Equality of the Member States' (2015) 16(4) *German Law Journal* 1003, 1018.

65 German Bundesverfassungsgericht Case 2 BvR 2728/13 *Gauweiler and Others* Order of 14 January 2014.

66 On this matter see A Voßkuhle, 'Multilevel Cooperation of the European Constitutional Courts: Der Europäische Verfassungsgerichtsverbund' (2010) 6(2) *European Constitutional Law Review* 175, 188; M Wendel, 'Judicial Restraint and the Return to Openness: The Decision of the German Federal Constitutional Court on the ESM and the Fiscal Treaty of 12 September 2012' (2013) 14 *German Law Journal* 21, 41 ff.

67 The Court only inserted a reference to the mention of national identity in the preliminary points of the judgment, omitting any further analysis in the remainder of the judgment. Case C-62/14 *Gauweiler and Others* [2015] EU:C:2015:400 [17].

From the perspective of constitutional conflict, the two courts have been discussing the appropriate level of control of the ECB as an idiosyncratically independent institution for some time now.[68] The decision of the German court in *Weiss II* is the last instance of conversation. This reference revolved around three issues: whether the ECB had complied with its obligation to state reasons in devising the Public Sector Purchase Programme (PSPP), whether the said programme falls within the monetary policy mandate of the ECB, and whether it is contrary to the Treaty prohibition of monetary financing. The principle of proportionality was mentioned by the Bundesverfassungsgericht only in relation to the first two issues. After receiving the response from the Court of Justice, the Bundesverfassungsgericht found that the proportionality test as applied by the Court of Justice deprives the said principle of its ability to protect Member State competence[69] and declared the judgment of the Court of Justice[70] and the PSPP[71] of the ECB *ultra vires*.

Regrettably, the Bundesverfassungsgericht failed to emphasize the centrality of proportionality (in particular its *stricto sensu* step) in its preliminary reference, therefore not engaging in a genuinely open dialogue with the Court of Justice.[72] This runs counter to its statement in *Gauweiler* that there is an obligation to 'respect judicial development of the law by the Court of Justice even when the Court of Justice adopts a view against which weighty arguments could be made'.[73] The Bundesverfassungsgericht placed great emphasis on the Court of Justice maintaining consistency with the standards concerning the ECB's mandate in *Gauweiler*,[74] as well as in the Order for reference in *Weiss*.[75] And yet, the German court itself behaved entirely inconsistently: the *stricto sensu* step of the proportionality test touted as central to the review of the PSPP was only introduced in the response to the decision of the Court of Justice, whereas no such expectation was hinted at in the order for preliminary reference itself, and even less so in the *Gauweiler* litigation.

In the structure of constitutional pluralism, mutual respect and sincere cooperation play a central role in incrementally managing interpretative differences and the possible constitutional conflict ensuing.[76] The way in which proportionality was

68 See also D Grimm, 'A Long Time Coming' (2020) 21 *German Law Journal* 944.

69 German Bundesverfassungsgericht Cases 2 BvR 859/15, 2 BvR 980/16, 2 BvR 2006/15, 2 BvR 1651/15 *Weiss II* Judgment of 5 May 2020 [123].

70 ibid [116], [163].

71 ibid [117], [178].

72 M Wendel, 'Paradoxes of Ultra-Vires Review: A Critical Review of the PSPP Decision and Its Initial Reception' (2020) 21 *German Law Journal* 979, 987.

73 German Bundesverfassungsgericht Case 2 BvR 2728/13 *Gauweiler* Judgment of 21 June 2016 [161].

74 ibid [180], [193], [205].

75 German Bundesverfassungsgericht Cases 2 BvR 859/15, 2 BvR 980/16, 2 BvR 2006/15, 2 BvR 1651/15 *Weiss* Order of 18 July 2017 [79].

76 M Goldmann, 'Constitutional Pluralism as Mutually Assured Discretion: The Court of Justice, the German Federal Constitutional Court, and the ECB' (2016) 23(1) *Maastricht Journal of European and Comparative Law* 119, 128; L D Spieker, 'Framing and Managing Constitutional Identity Conflicts: How

introduced in *Weiss II* can hardly be referred to as a role model for this approach. Language and expressions used by constitutional courts and the Court of Justice are of importance in the way constitutional conflict and its resolution is managed, and as will be seen in section 4, there is a coherence in this sense among different constitutional courts in the EU. The allegation of the Bundesverfassungsgericht that the judgment of the Court of Justice is 'simply not comprehensible'[77] is in that sense not the sort of language that should be employed between courts that have for so long interacted in a constructive manner, enhancing the EU's constitutional sphere. It departs from the need for mutual respect and sincere cooperation, and unnecessarily distracts from the issues that can constructively be addressed through constitutional conflict.

Nevertheless, the advantage of constitutional pluralism has in large part been precisely addressing issues such as the competence control carried out by the Court of Justice, dynamically and incrementally developing EU's constitutional sphere and preventing outright domination of one constitutional order over the other. Under conditions of heterarchy, constitutional conflicts over the meaning and interpretation of values contained in Article 2 TEU form part of the pluralist constellation. Demanding an increased standard of accountability for the ECB in that sense promotes democracy and the rule of law and is a feature of the system that brings about its enhancement. In other words, the conversation concerning the accountability of the ECB will continue and develop further either in the judicial or political sphere (or both).

A further criticism against a heterarchical view of the EU's constitutional space is that such an understanding diminishes the importance of primacy of EU law,[78] as it is expressed by the Court of Justice in its long-standing jurisprudence.[79] Fabbrini (correctly) underlines that the principle of primacy surpasses bilateral disagreements between the EU and individual Member States and their constitutional/supreme courts and serves to provide a guarantee of equality of all Member States in a multilateral manner.[80] Yet, he questions the usefulness of the pluralist theory in relation to the principle of primacy in cases of a potential conflict in interpretation between EU law and national constitutions.[81]

This approach disregards the nature of the EU's constitutional frame as explained in the previous section: national and EU constitutional claims will at times necessarily find themselves in opposition, owing to their parallel operation

to Stabilize the Modus Vivendi between the Court of Justice and National Constitutional Courts' (2020) 57(2) *Common Market Law Review* 361, 381.

77 German Bundesverfassungsgericht Cases *Weiss II* (n 69) [116], [153].
78 Kelemen (n 54) 144.
79 Introduced in Case 6/64 *Costa v ENEL* (n 30).
80 Fabbrini (n 64) 1014–16.
81 ibid 1014.

in the same political space. Moreover, two counter-claims reconcile primacy with the pluralist approach: (1) primacy should not be regarded as subordination; and (2) the respect for the principle of primacy in ensuring the equality of Member States is as important as the obligation of the EU to respect national identity. In relation to the first claim, it is important to distinguish primacy from subordination. MacCormick explains this as follows:

> [t]he doctrine of supremacy of Community law is not to be confused with any kind of all-purpose subordination of Member State law to Community law. Rather, the case is that these are interacting systems, one of which constitutes in its own context and over the relevant range of topics a source of valid law superior to other sources recognized in each of the Member State systems.[82]

To understand this position better, it is useful to reflect upon the distinction between supremacy and primacy made by the Spanish Tribunal Constitucional in its decision on the Constitutional Treaty:

> Supremacy is sustained in the higher hierarchical character of a regulation and, therefore, is a source of validity of the lower regulations, leading to the consequent invalidity of the latter if they contravene the provisions set forth imperatively in the former. Primacy, however, is not necessarily sustained on hierarchy, but rather on the distinction between the scopes of application of different regulations, principally valid, of which, however, one or more of them have the capacity for displacing others by virtue of their preferential or prevalent application due to various reasons.[83]

Both statements underline the principle of primacy as a trigger for the application of EU law in areas of EU competence in the event there is a conflicting provision on the national level. This outright rejects the absolute primacy of EU legal order as a whole over national legal orders. Dougan further explains such a view through what he calls 'trigger primacy': in a situation of conflict between national and EU law, the latter has primacy when it satisfies the criteria for direct effect.[84] In essence, Dougan is right to note that the trigger model accommodates constitutional

[82] MacCormick (n 51) 264.

[83] Spanish Tribunal Constitucional Case DTC 1/2004 *Constitutional Treaty* (n 9) [II-4]. Significantly, the Court of Justice has consistently been using the term 'primacy' and not 'supremacy'. See also J Kokott, 'Report on Germany' in A-M Slaughter, A Stone Sweet, and J H H Weiler (eds), *The European Court and National Courts, Doctrine & Jurisprudence: Legal Change in its Social Context* (Hart Publishing, 1998) 83; Czech Ústavní Soud Case Pl. ÚS 50/04 *Sugar Quotas III* (n 9) [VI.A]; National Report: The Constitutional Court of the Republic of Lithuania (n 8) 5; P M Huber, 'The Federal Constitutional Court and European Integration' (2015) 21(1) *European Public Law* 83, 87.

[84] M Dougan, 'When Worlds Collide! Competing Visions of the Relationship between Direct Effect and Supremacy' (2007) 44 *Common Market Law Review* 931, 934.

requirements of national legal systems, while at the same time respecting the primacy of Union law under the condition of direct effect.[85] It is also important to point out that national constitutions of Member States have all, to a certain extent, gone through a process of amendments with the aim of accommodating the requirements and specificities of EU law.[86] Mutual respect and judicial self-restraint do not deny the primacy of EU law in its particular context, but a pluralist account does reject the outright subordination of national legal orders in their entirety to the EU legal order.

In close connection with the previous point, I now turn to claim (2), which underlines the importance of respect for national identity and its effect on the equality of Member States. If unconditional primacy of EU law is to be accepted, the national identity clause in Article 4(2) TEU would become redundant. To understand this dynamic, it is useful briefly to recall Fabbrini's argument on the importance of primacy in ensuring the equality of Member States. Looking at the EU not through a series of bilateral relations, but rather as a multilateral entity in which actions of particular members affect all other Member States, he identifies the principle of primacy as the ultimate insurance of equality of all Member States in the EU.[87] He dismisses the possibility for each Member State to renegotiate the terms of their membership and concludes that EU law should be applied in all Member States in an equal manner.[88]

When faced with the counter-claim of the importance of the national identity clause in the EU setting, Fabbrini's response does not seem convincing, as he uses a literal interpretation of Article 4(2) TEU, stating that the respect for national identity of Member States is located after, i.e. is subordinate to, the declaration of equality of Member States.[89] His dismissal of the role of the national identity clause in ensuring equality of Member States seems too quick and has the following important shortcoming: the national identity clause was agreed upon by all Member States and, when applied under the same conditions, in fact it contributes to the equality of Member States, while also respecting the plurality of legal systems in the EU. In other words, all Member States are able to protect their national particularities and constitutional specificities under equal conditions. In addition, neither

85 ibid 942.

86 Millet points to different constitutional amendments that several Member States undertook in order to accommodate the implementation of the European Arrest Warrant (EAW). See F-X Millet, 'How Much Lenience for How Much Cooperation? On the First Preliminary Reference of the French Constitutional Council to the Court of Justice' (2014) 51 *Common Market Law Review* 195, 196. Moreover, the Spanish Constitutional Tribunal accepted the necessary changes in its *Melloni* decision (Judgment 26/2014 *Melloni* of 13 February 2014), after receiving a response to the preliminary reference submitted to the Court of Justice in Case C-399/11 *Melloni* [2013] EU:C:2013:107. In addition, this demonstrates that national courts performing constitutional review are but one among many of the relevant constitutional actors at the national level, and while their jurisprudence might be seen as central to the prospect of constitutional conflict, the overall national constitutional structure will also serve as a break in conflict control.

87 Fabbrini (n 64) 1019.

88 ibid 1015.

89 ibid 1019.

the case law of the Court of Justice nor any other international document[90] supports the literal interpretation suggested by Fabbrini. Quite to the contrary, cases such as *Omega*,[91] *Sayn-Wittgenstein*,[92] and *Runevič-Vardyn*[93] serve as excellent examples of how the Court of Justice itself found that national particularities are to be protected at the cost of primacy of EU law, but without any effect on the equality of Member States.[94]

It is true that Member States where we can observe serious rule of law backsliding have increasingly relied on constitutional identity to reject the rule of law and judicial independence demands introduced in the case law of the Court of Justice.[95] This has in turn resulted in additional critique of the ease with which theorists of constitutional pluralism support the role of the national identity clause. However, as I will show in more detail in chapter 4, section 3, the auto-correct function of constitutional pluralism does not stretch to accommodate destructive conflict, relying on any of the judicial techniques previously used in good faith (including national identity), to deny the very essence of the normative core of the EU's constitutional space.

The national identity clause aims to accommodate national particularities in the application of EU law on the national level, while the role of the Court of Justice is to determine the limits to this exception through the application of the principle of proportionality. The pluralist nature of the proposed interpretation of Article 4(2) TEU stems from its intrinsically heterarchical nature, as it does not impose an overarching European value over specific national values.[96] On the contrary, it endorses an equal position of a variety of national specificity claims that are all subject to the same process of assessing such claims through the proportionality test. Consequently, respect for national specificities, subject to the principle of proportionality, reinforces the role of the Court of Justice in ensuring the coherent application of Union law through providing an essentially common limit to the exception of Article 4(2) TEU and ensuring the equality of Member States.[97] At

[90] Article 31(1) of the Vienna Convention on the Law of Treaties states that treaties shall be interpreted: 'in good faith in accordance with the ordinary meaning to be given to the terms of the treaty in their context and in the light of its object and purpose'. No mention can be found of the literal interpretation which would result in a subordinate relationship of two clauses within the same provision. Vienna Convention on the Law of Treaties (adopted 23 May 1969, entered into force 27 January 1980) 1155 UNTS 331.

[91] Case C-36/02 *Omega* [2004] EU:C:2004:614.

[92] Case C-208/09 *Sayn-Wittgenstein* [2010] EU:C:2010:806.

[93] Case C-391/09 *Runevič-Vardyn* [2011] EU:C:2011:291. Recently see also Case C-673/16 *Coman* [2018] EU:C:2018:385.

[94] K Lenaerts and J A Gutiérez-Fons, 'The Constitutional Allocation of Powers and General Principles of EU Law' (2010) 47(6) *Common Market Law Review* 1629, 1663.

[95] For example in Case 64/16 *Juizes Portugueses* [2018] EU:C:2018:117 and Case C-824/18 *AB and Others* [2021] EU:C:2021:153.

[96] For a similar pluralist reading of the national identity clause see A von Bogdandy and S Schill, 'Overcoming Absolute Primacy: Respect for National Identity under the Lisbon Treaty' (2011) 48 *Common Market Law Review* 1417, 1452.

[97] The Polish Trybunał Konstytucyjny made an excellent point concerning the manner of using the national identity clause: 'confirming one's national identity in solidarity with other nations, and not

the same time, its wording allows for a variety of interpretations by national sites of constitutional authority without demanding a uniform, monist solution in every single case.[98] This means that it is possible to sustain the primacy of EU law on the one hand and the supremacy of national constitutions on the other through a heterarchical understanding of the relationships in the EU's constitutional space. I now turn to the last descriptive feature of constitutional pluralism that remains to be explored: the auto-correct function.

## 3 The Auto-correct Function

We have so far concluded that Member States' courts performing constitutional review and the Court of Justice all hold claims to ultimate authority and these operate in a heterarchical fashion where no single site of authority is given the right to the final say. I further argue that the pluralist system contains within itself an auto-correct function, which serves as a check and balance among constitutional jurisdictions on the national and on the EU level.[99]

In order to understand the auto-correct function fully, it is first necessary to address another feature of a pluralist legal order—incrementalism. In particular, incrementalism accentuates the gradual development of institutional interactions, but also substantively the creation of rules and principles.[100] Incrementalism may be regarded as stemming from an understanding of law as process, where the lines between *lex lata* and *lex ferenda* are becoming increasingly blurred, as the use of analogy and contextual interpretation take centre stage.[101] With these premises in mind, the lack of legal norms concerning the resolution of constitutional conflict cannot be considered a defect of the system.

Let us recall briefly the *Solange* saga to depict how incrementalism influences intra-EU judicial interactions and contributes more broadly to the development of EU constitutional law.[102] In its first *Solange* judgment,[103] the

against them'. K 32/09 *Treaty of Lisbon*, Judgment of 24 November 2010 [2.1] http://trybunal.gov.pl/fileadmin/content/omowienia/K_32_09_EN.pdf.

[98] This will be further explored in the analysis of the normative side of constitutional pluralism in ch 4.

[99] Weiler similarly talks about the 'persuasion pull' and 'compliance pull' as the drivers behind the implementation of the case law of the Court of Justice. Weiler (n 2) 419.

[100] L Helfer and A-M Slaughter, 'Toward a Theory of Effective Supranational Adjudication' (1997) 107 *Yale Law Journal* 273, 314; Krisch (n 3) 247.

[101] R Higgins, *Problems and Process: International Law and How We Use It* (Clarendon Press 1995) 10. See also M Claes, *The National Courts' Mandate in the European Constitution* (Hart Publishing 2006) 713.

[102] See also Shaw (n 1) 14, 19, 24; Z Bańkowski and E Christodoulidis, 'The European Union as an Essentially Contested Project' (1998) 4(4) *European Law Journal* 341, 342.

[103] German Bundesverfassungsgericht Case 37 BVerfGE 271 *Internationale Handelsgesellschaft (Solange I)* Judgment of 29 May 1974.

Bundesverfassungsgericht retained the right to exercise judicial review in matters of fundamental rights protection as long as the European integration process did not reach a satisfactory level of protection. If we were to use the arguments of those criticizing pluralism today and apply them to the *Solange* situation, this judgment would probably signify the demise of the entire European project, while judicial interactions would be touted at their absolute low. Conversely, subsequent events[104] demonstrated the gradual, step-by-step[105] development of the fundamental rights protection on the EU level,[106] but also the contribution to the relationship between national constitutional jurisdictions and the Court of Justice.[107] It has also demonstrated how such a gradual development helped avoid an outburst of conflict or the activation of Kelemen's doomsday device.[108] Therefore, in order to conclude on the applicability of constitutional pluralism to the EU constitutional setting, one needs to take a step back from individual judgments and analyse the relevant jurisprudence as a process.[109] It is precisely due to incrementalism that a broader examination of the relevant case law confirms the main premises of the pluralist theory. Furthermore, it prevents future conflicts from taking place through the auto-correct function.

The auto-correct functions in the following context: issues prone to constitutional conflict arise regularly in the EU,[110] and both the Court of Justice and national constitutional jurisdictions are able, through their respective procedural avenues and interpretative tools, to control the extent of the conflict. There are also two legal imperatives driving this dynamic in two opposite directions: the principle of primacy of Union law on the one hand and the obligation to respect national identities of Member States on the other. An explicit primacy clause that would serve as a resolution to this inherent conflict failed to come into force as part of the Constitutional Treaty after its signature in 2004, implying that the sentiment among Member States was and is against any such a conclusive provision.[111] In the

[104] For a detailed analysis of this interaction until its resolution see ch 7, s 2.

[105] Krisch (n 3) 247 ff. See also Czech Ústavní Soud Case *Sugar Quotas III* (n 9) [VI.A-3], where the Constitutional Court stated that both the case law of the Court of Justice and national constitutional courts has undergone a dynamic development in the area of fundamental rights.

[106] The area of fundamental rights is an excellent example of how the EU has evolved as a constitutional legal order not comparable to nation states. See eg G de Búrca, 'After the EU Charter of Fundamental Rights: The Court of Justice as a Human Rights Adjudicator?' (2013) 20(2) *Maastricht Journal of European and Comparative Law* 168, 169.

[107] See also Stone Sweet (n 47) 500.

[108] Kelemen (n 54) 141, 148–49.

[109] Similarly, Rodin differentiates among the immediate and the future impact of the case law of the Court, arguing that the latter is based on the changed societal context, gradually transforming a judgment into a landmark. See S Rodin, 'Dumb and No More Here', presented on the conference: Central and Eastern European Judges under the EU Influence: The Transformative Power of Europe Revisited on the 10th Anniversary of the Enlargement, 12–13 May 2014, European University Institute, Florence, Italy (cited with the author's permission) 10, 14 ff.

[110] Stone Sweet argues that the possibility of a conflict is a 'manifestation, probably permanent, of a pluralist structure of EU law'. Stone Sweet (n 6) 65.

[111] This is not to diminish the importance of the principle of primacy in the case law of the Court of Justice, but rather to emphasize the importance of the 'political' in relation to the 'legal'. Moreover, it also

following Treaty amendment in 2007, the provision on the obligation of the EU to respect national identities of Member States was expanded in its wording, but it also henceforth fell under the jurisdiction of the Court of Justice.[112]

Support for the auto-correct function can be found in the Bundesverfassungsgericht's decision in *Mr R*. The German court denied the application of a European Arrest Warrant (EAW) to an American citizen who was to be extradited to Italy where he was sentenced *in absentia*.[113] In particular, the Bundesverfassungsgericht emphasized that any conflict that may arise would be an exception without harming the uniform application of Union law, as each individual case will be handled with restraint and in a manner open to European integration, thus confirming that individual judgments do not prejudice the relationship between the two legal orders.[114] The auto-correct function does not call into question or undermine the parallel sovereign claims of the twenty-seven national constitutional systems, as well as the primacy claim of the Court of Justice. It is precisely in the acknowledgement of these claims that the auto-correct takes centre stage.

As the analysis of judicial vocabulary will show, a clash between parallel sovereignty claims is avoided through the application of self-restraint and mutual accommodation. More particularly, each of the systems has in-built conditions for the application of the auto-correct function, such as the principle of EU-friendly interpretation, or the national identity clause. However, it is only through interactions between the systems that the auto-correct function takes place and brings about a balance among the different individual systems claiming sovereignty. Thus, while the conditions for the utilization of the auto-correct function are contained within each of the systems, its consequences have an effect on the balance of the system as a whole.

In such a setting, the auto-correct has the function of preventing long-term conflict between either of the constitutional jurisdictions involved. In the EU judicial architecture, an awareness on the part of all the actors involved of the benefits of a pluralist setting results in conflict management and control. The result of a particular case will sometimes be on the side of national concerns[115] and other

serves to reiterate the importance of the national constitutional setting and its ability to constrain national constitutional jurisdictions.

112 B Guastaferro, 'Beyond the Exceptionalism of Constitutional Conflicts: The Ordinary Functions of the Identity Clause' (2012) Jean Monnet Working Paper 01/12, 4.

113 German Bundesverfassungsgericht Case 2 BvR 2735/14 *Mr R*. Order of 15 December 2015 http://www.bundesverfassungsgericht.de/SharedDocs/Pressemitteilungen/EN/2016/bvg16-004.html. See also ch 7, s 4.1.2.

114 The same was underlined by the Austrian Constitutional Court, who stated that should a conflict arise, this should not be developed beyond an individual case. National Report: The Constitutional Court of Austria (2014) 9.

115 For instance, Case C-36/02 *Omega* (n 91); Case C-208/09 *Sayn-Wittgenstein* (n 92); Case C-391/09 *Runevič-Vardyn* (n 93).

times on the side of integration.[116] In any event, the outcome will be reached after a careful balancing conducted through applying *both* self-restraint and the strong will to avoid conflict;[117] *and* an EU-friendly interpretation on behalf of national jurisdictions *and/or* the accommodation of national identity claims by the Court of Justice.[118] Individual points of conflict do not bring into question the ability of the auto-correct function to resolve them incrementally, both institutionally and substantively. Over time, the heterarchical setting will inherently work to auto-correct any imbalance and prevent the activation of the doomsday device.

## 4 Analysis of Judicial Vocabulary

The theoretical characteristics of constitutional pluralism—competing claims to ultimate authority in a heterarchical relationship that is sustained by the operation of the auto-correct function—are further strengthened by the formal and informal expressions of all the judicial actors involved when faced with a situation of constitutional conflict. It is important to underline that my argument here is not that the use of certain expressions by courts suffices to demonstrate the main premises of constitutional pluralism. Rather, in this section I aim to offer a broad-brush analysis of judicial vocabulary to serve as prima facie demonstration of the descriptive side of constitutional pluralism. This first indication will be triangulated by an in-depth analysis in the case studies ahead.

However, I do consider it important to look at the expressions used by participants of the EU's constitutional space as interpretative tools in situations of constitutional conflict. It is possible to observe a common reconciliatory vocabulary,

[116] See French Conseil Constitutionnel Case 2007-560 DC *Treaty of Lisbon* Decision of 20 December 2007; German Bundesverfassungsgericht Case *Honeywell* (n 8); Case C-62/14 *Gauweiler* (n 67).

[117] Two further examples highlighting the auto-correct function are: (1) the decision of the Bundesverfassungsgericht in relation to the EAW. In this decision, the German Court was in a position to enter into a discussion on the compatibility of the EAW with the Basic Law. Instead, the Court only focused on interpreting the national law implementing the EAW, avoiding entirely having to entertain the idea of declaring an EU act contrary to the national constitution. German Bundesverfassungsgericht Case 2 BvR 2236/04 *European Arrest Warrant* Decision of 18 July 2005 http://www.bundesverfassungsgericht.de/SharedDocs/Entscheidungen/EN/2005/07/rs20050718_2bvr223604en.html. See also A Hinarejos, '*Bundesverfassungsgericht* (German Constitutional Court), Decision of 18 July 2005 (2 BvR 2236/04) on the German European Arrest Warrant Law' (2006) 43(2) *Common Market Law Review* 583; and (2) Polish Trybunał Konstytucyjny Case SK 45/09 *Brussels Regulation* Judgment of 16 November 2011 http://trybunal.gov.pl/uploads/media/SiM_LI_EN_calosc.pdf. The Polish Trybunał Konstytucyjny provided a broad interpretation of the term 'normative act' and assumed jurisdiction to review secondary acts of EU law against the Constitution. In addition, the tribunal stated that its jurisdiction to do so is only subsidiary to that of the Court of Justice in relation to EU primary law ([2.6]). Nevertheless, it found the provision to be in accordance with the Polish Constitution. I argue that, regardless of expanding its jurisdiction to review secondary EU acts, the Polish Constitutional Tribunal intentionally exhibited self-restraint in order to avoid conflict.

[118] See, in this respect, Opinion of Advocate General Maduro in Joined Cases C-402/05 P and C-415/05 P *Kadi* [2008] EU:C:2008:11 [44]. See also Claes (n 101) 37.

pointing to the existence of a shared understanding of the division of obligations among the participants of the European judicial space, which I argue auto-corrects any imbalance that might arise from a constitutional conflict. In this respect, all Member States are equal and their relationship with the Court of Justice is conducted within the bounds of mutual respect and sincere cooperation.

The argument proceeds as follows: the use of the keywords, the exhibited self-restraint, and the self-imposed obligation to avoid conflict all offer strong proof that a clear (*ex ante*) answer to the question of the final arbiter is indeed unnecessary. Moreover, an insistence upon its resolution might bring about more harm than good, as it may provoke conflicts that are destructive in nature and thus outside of what the auto-correct function can accommodate over time.[119] Subsequently, the analysis of common keywords will be used to depict the functioning of the auto-correct function in preventing constructive constitutional conflict turning into a destructive one. The following figure depicts the keywords and the intensity of their use in the sources under analysis: the horizontal axis represents the number of jurisdictions in which a certain keyword placed on the vertical axis was used.

The keywords under analysis have three common characteristics: (1) they are aimed at conflict prevention, both from the perspective of national constitutional jurisdictions and that of the Court of Justice; (2) they are inherently heterarchical, as none of them contains elements of either superiority or subordination; and (3) their implementation shows institutional awareness of the big (multilateral) picture in the everyday work of the courts under analysis, as they are conscious of the need for a balanced relationship.

As is visible from Figure 3.1, the most commonly used set of keywords is 'EU-friendly interpretation'.[120] In particular, the majority of answers were given in national reports on the question of their approach towards the relationship between national constitutions and EU law and how to proceed in a case of a possible divergence between the two. Such an understanding is a direct application of the principle of sincere cooperation among the courts under analysis.[121] The use of the

[119] See ch 4, s 3.

[120] Italian Corte Costituzionale Case 170/1984 *Granital* Decision of 8 June 1984 [7-3]; Voßkuhle (n 66) 188; German Bundesverfassungsgericht Case *Honeywell* (n 8) [100], [111]; German Bundesverfassungsgericht Case *Lisbon Treaty* (n 11) [221]; Polish Trybunał Konstytucyjny Case *Treaty of Lisbon* (n 11) [3.1]; General Report, Conference of European Constitutional Courts (2014) 2–4; National Report: The Supreme Court of Cyprus (2014) 3; National Report: The Constitutional Court of the Czech Republic (2014) 4; National Report: The Federal Constitutional Court of the Republic of Germany (2014) 2; National Report: The Constitutional Court of Hungary (2014) 3; National Report: The Constitutional Court of the Republic of Latvia (2014) 8; National Report: The Constitutional Court of the Republic of Lithuania (n 8) 15, 26; National Report: The Portuguese Constitutional Court (2014) 23.

[121] The German Bundesverfassungsgericht stated in *Honeywell* (n 8) [100], as regards its principle of openness towards EU law:

> 'When exercising this competence to effect a review, the principle of openness of the Basic Law towards Europe is to be complied with as a correlate of the principle of sincere cooperation' (Article 4.3 TEU) and to be made fruitful.

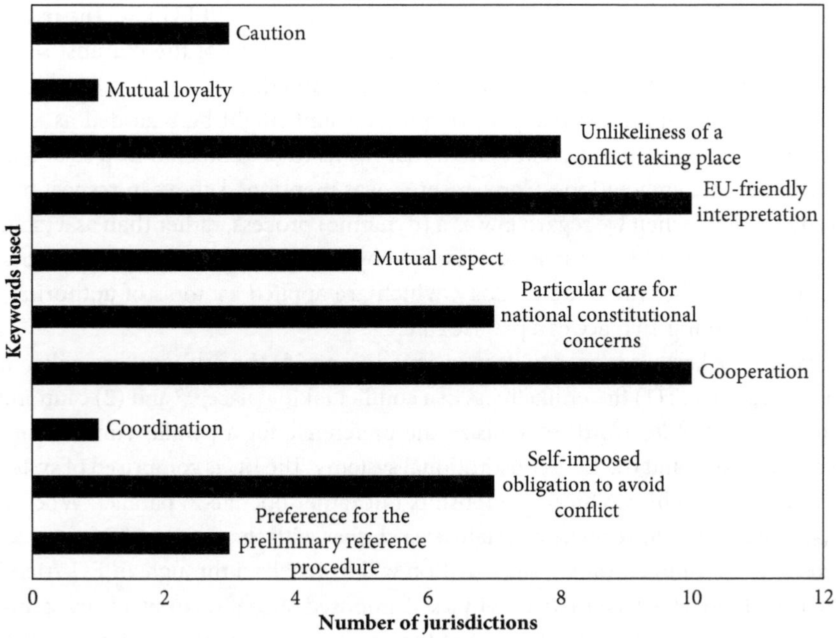


**Figure 3.1** Use of keywords

term was so widespread among national reports that it was also underlined as one of the most common practices in the General Report of the 2014 Conference of European Constitutional Courts.[122] While the use of this term in national reports has little legal value per se, I argue that it reflects a shared attitude that is, in practice, resulting in a coherent application of EU law at the national level.

The second most common set of keywords is the 'self-imposed obligation to avoid conflict'.[123] The term was widely used among European constitutional courts when asked about possible divergences in interpretation between national constitutional law and the exigencies of EU law. In addition, Advocate General Wathelet[124] agreed on the existence of self-restraint that drives the behaviour of the courts involved, in order to prevent a conflict from taking place when a particular

[122] General Report, Conference of European Constitutional Courts (n 120) 2–4.

[123] Polish Trybunał Konstytucyjny Case SK 45/09 *Brussels Regulation* (n 117) [2.6]; Czech Ústavní Soud Case *Lisbon Treaty II* (n 11) [112]; General Report, Conference of European Constitutional Courts (n 120) 2; National Report: The Constitutional Court of the Czech Republic (n 120) 4; National Report: The Supreme Court of Denmark (2014) 12; National Report: German Federal Constitutional Court (n 120) 3; National Report: The Constitutional Court of Hungary (n 120) 2–3; National Report: The Constitutional Tribunal of the Republic of Poland (2014) 2; National Report: The Constitutional Court of Romania (2014) 12. See also, extrajudicially, Lecture of Advocate General M Wathelet: 'Constitutional Courts and the CJEU: Is There a Dialogue? History and Prospects' given at the EU Law discussion group at the Law Faculty, University of Oxford, 23 October 2015; Huber (n 83) 89.

[124] Wathelet (n 123).

case calls into question both national constitutional law and EU law. The use and application of this keyword is central to the preservation of the pluralist setting without any claims to overall superiority or subordination.

From an anti-pluralist perspective, self-restraint might be regarded as an inherent weakness of the current system that needs to be remedied by a clear set of jurisdictional demarcations. Conversely, as was mentioned above in respect of incrementalism, when we regard law as a (dynamic) process, rather than as a (static) rule, the *lacunae* of the system are resolved by interpreting the norms in their societal context, by way of an analogy, which are applied as 'tools of authoritative decision-making' in place of a precise rule.[125]

Two more keywords need to be mentioned alongside the 'self-imposed obligation to avoid conflict': (1) the unlikeliness of a conflict taking place;[126] and (2) caution.[127] All three sets of keywords emphasize the preference for a parallel functioning of Member States' and the EU's constitutional systems. The EU is comprised of systems that are not in a hierarchical relationship, but rather operate in parallel. When the EU's competence to regulate a certain area clashes with the national competence to protect constitutional values, the situation will be resolved through an EU-friendly interpretation, which is also driven by a self-imposed obligation to avoid any conflict, whenever possible. Even in the eyes of the constitutional courts of Member States, such situations are extremely unlikely to take place, but when they do, they should be approached with caution, keeping in mind the ultimate aim of avoiding conflict.

The next group of keywords relevant for the pluralist explanation of judicial interactions in the area of constitutional interpretation are: (1) cooperation;[128] (2) coordination;[129] (3) mutual respect;[130] and (4) mutual loyalty.[131] While the previous group of keywords entailed a more passive attitude of avoiding conflict, in

[125] Higgins (n 101) 10.

[126] National Report: The Constitutional Court of Belgium (2014) 31; Czech Ústavní Soud Case *Lisbon Treaty I* (n 8) [5]; Danish Højesteret Case *Carlsen* (n 8) [9.6]; Italian Corte costituzionale Case *Granital* (n 120) [7–9]; Polish Trybunał Konstytucyjny Case *Brussels Regulation* (n 117) [2.7]; Spanish Tribunal Constitucional Case *Constitutional Treaty* (n 9) [II-4]; Spanish Tribunal Constitucional Case *Melloni* (n 86) [II-3]; National Report: German Federal Constitutional Court (n 120) 3; United Kingdom Supreme Court Case *Pham* (n 8) [91].

[127] Polish Trybunał Konstytucyjny Case *Brussels Regulation* (n 117) [2.5], [2.8]; National Report: The Constitutional Court of Romania (n 123) 12; United Kingdom Supreme Court Case *Pham* (n 8) [91].

[128] German Bundesverfassungsgericht Case *Maastricht Treaty* (n 9) [B.II.b], [B.II.c.5]; Czech Ústavní Soud Case *Sugar Quotas III* (n 9) [VI.A.]; Polish Trybunał Konstytucyjny Case *Brussels Regulation* (n 117) [2.6]; General Report: Conference of European Constitutional Courts (n 120) 12; National Report: The Portuguese Constitutional Court (n 120) 23; National Report: The Constitutional Court of Romania (n 123) 12–13; National Report: The Constitutional Court of the Slovak Republic (2014) 12; National Report: The Constitutional Court of the Republic of Slovenia (2014) 18; United Kingdom Supreme Court Case *HS2* [2014] UKSC 3 [202]; United Kingdom Supreme Court Case *Pham* (n 8) [91].

[129] Italian Corte costituzionale Case *Granital* (n 120) [7–4].

[130] National Report: The Constitutional Court of the Czech Republic (n 120) 11; Polish Trybunał Konstytucyjny Case *Brussels Regulation* (n 117) [2.5]; National Report: The Constitutional Court of Romania (n 123) 58; UK Supreme Court Case *Pham* (n 8) [91]; Portuguese Constitutional Tribunal Decision 711/2020 of 9 December 2020 [12]. See http://www.tribunalconstitucional.pt/tc/acordaos/20200711.html.

[131] National Report: The Constitutional Tribunal of the Republic of Poland (n 123) 2.

the scenario where a conflict does arise, this group of keywords takes a further step forward and engages constitutional jurisdictions in a more active conduct. Not only are the constitutional jurisdictions avoiding conflicting situations, they are also fostering cooperation and coordination in their work. Equally, all interviewees at the Court of Justice confirmed they are participating in judicial networks throughout Europe and benefit greatly from bilateral meetings and visits with national judges at all levels. Read together, this group of keywords shows that all the courts under analysis are implementing the principle of sincere cooperation in practice.

The final group of keywords focuses more on reflecting the attitudes of those making decisions at the Court of Justice—judges and advocates general. In particular, in addition to the tendency of national courts with constitutional jurisdiction to project an EU-friendly jurisprudence, members of the Court of Justice also adhere to the principle of sincere cooperation as well as the obligation to respect the national identities of Member States. Two sets of keywords have been analysed to this end: (1) particular care is taken where national constitutional concerns are involved;[132] and (2) there is a preference for the use of the preliminary reference procedure.[133] When asked about possible clashes in interpretation with national constitutional jurisdictions, six judges/advocates general have confirmed that in their work on a specific case, particular care is taken if a national constitutional concern is involved. In addition, three interviewees expressed their preference for any possible conflict to take place in the realm of the preliminary reference procedure. The importance of such an attitude should not be underestimated: the trust that national constitutional courts have in the Court of Justice complying with the obligation to respect national particularities is not unfounded.

In addition to the use of keywords, the extent of cross-referencing among constitutional jurisdictions throughout the EU is also of relevance, as it represents yet another sign of awareness of constitutional adjudicators of the multilateral momentum of judicial interactions, both institutionally and substantively. The practice of cross-referencing is common among a broad range of constitutional courts in the EU,[134] and the practice has become more widespread in the recent

[132] Interviewee 1; Interviewee 2; Interviewee 3; Interviewee 4; Interviewee 5; Interviewee 6.

[133] Interviewee 1; Interviewee 2, Interviewee 4; National Report: The Supreme Court of Denmark (n 123) 12; National Report: The Portuguese Constitutional Court (n 120) 23; Polish Trybunał Konstytucyjny Case *Brussels Regulation* (n 117) [2.6].

[134] National Report: The Constitutional Court of Austria (n 114) 11; National Report: The Constitutional Court of Croatia (2014) 24; National Report: The Supreme Court of Cyprus (n 120) 5; National Report—The Constitutional Court of the Czech Republic (n 120) 20; National Report: German Federal Constitutional Court (n 120) 17; National Report: The Constitutional Court of Hungary (n 120) 2; National Report—The Supreme Court of Ireland (2014) 5; National Report: The Constitutional Court of the Republic of Latvia (n 120) 8; National Report: The Constitutional Court of the Republic of Lithuania (n 8) 30; National Report: The Constitutional Court of the Republic of Malta (2014) 4; National Report: The Constitutional Tribunal of the Republic of Poland (n 123) 15; National Report: The Portuguese Constitutional Court (n 120) 38; National Report: The Constitutional Court of Romania (n 123) 61–62; National Report: The Constitutional Court of the Slovak Republic (n 128) 9;

years.[135] For example, national judgments concerning the Court of Justice's annulment of the Data Retention Directive showed extensive cross-referencing, increasing the coherent approach to the subject matter that was in that moment not subject to EU legislation.[136] This trend is significant as it further confirms the argument that constitutional courts throughout the EU are aware of the need for a coordinated approach to judicial interactions in the EU.

Cross-referencing is of course not without its shortcomings: the courts that do make use of it may be seen as cherry-picking only those judgments that support their argument.[137] Claes and Reestman analysed the cross-referencing done by the German Bundesverfassungsgericht in its first preliminary reference to the Court of Justice, where case law of nine other Member States was cited in support of its interpretation of constitutional identity.[138] They found that the case law cited is only partially supportive of the view of the German court, while more recent jurisprudence of the cited courts has been omitted. Nevertheless, even such cross-referencing is welcome and contributes to the general awareness of all the courts involved that they are equal counterparts, who are jointly and multilaterally contributing to the development of EU constitutional law broadly understood.[139]

The practice of cross-referencing contains substantive and institutional elements of a pluralist heterarchical judicial setting. Substantively, constitutional jurisdictions in the EU are using each other's jurisprudence to add a comparative element to their reasoning as well as to support their arguments. The use of foreign jurisprudence both enriches the reasoning of the court in question, but also adds to a broader momentum of mutual acknowledgement and the idea of a shared legal culture and standards. As underlined in the General Report of the Conference of European Constitutional Courts, the use of European constitutional jurisprudence contributes to the creation of a 'European standard' of converging jurisprudence in Europe.[140] In that respect, it can be concluded that this type of judicial interactions

National Report: The Constitutional Court of the Republic of Slovenia (n 128) 26; National Report: The Constitutional Tribunal of Spain (2014) 26; United Kingdom Supreme Court Case *Pham* (n 8) [91].

135 General Report: Conference of European Constitutional Courts (n 120) 8.

136 For example, Polish Trybunał Konstytucyjny Case K 23/11 *Data Retention* Judgment of 30 July 2014 paras [3.4]–[3.10] https://trybunal.gov.pl/en/hearings/judgments/art/8821-okreslenie-katalogu-zbieranych-informacji-o-jednostce-za-pomoca-srodkow-technicznych-w-dzialani; Czech Ústavní Soud Case Pl. ÚS 45/17 *Data Retention III* Judgment of 14 May 2019 [75]. See https://www.usoud.cz/fileadmin/user_upload/ustavni_soud_www/Decisions/pdf/Pl-45-17_1_en.pdf.

137 For an analysis of advantages and shortcomings of the use of comparative constitutional law as a method of judicial interpretation, including the problem of cherry-picking see A-B Kaiser, '"It Isn't True that England Is the Moon": Comparative Constitutional Law as a Means of Constitutional Interpretation by the Courts?' (2017) 18(2) *German Law Journal* 294.

138 M Claes and J-H Reestman, 'The Protection of National Constitutional Identity and the Limits of European Integration at the Occasion of the *Gauweiler* Case' (2015) 16(4) *German Law Journal* 917, 941 ff.

139 See also Weatherill (n 60) 245.

140 General Report: Conference of European Constitutional Courts (n 120) 9.

(in the broadest sense) represents a conversation and a discussion on substantive matters of European constitutional law.

Institutionally, cross-referencing acknowledges the multilateral, heterarchical setting among Europe's highest courts.[141] When one constitutional jurisdiction cites another to support its claims, it means in essence that they are regarding each other as peers, equal counterparts.[142] The same logic is applicable in respect of the Court of Justice. Consequently, one should reject Fabbrini's claims concerning the narrow bilateral relationship among courts that would arise as a consequence in case of any exceptions to the principle of primacy of EU law.[143] Conversely, introducing an exception with a common limit for all Member States *contributes* to the equality of Member States. The relationship is characterized by the same mutual respect and self-restraint as between the Court of Justice and national constitutional jurisdictions.[144]

The use of the keywords under analysis, when expressed in the context of possible clashes in constitutional interpretation, resounds immensely. Fundamentally, each set of keywords reflects both an attitude of mutual trust and the principle of sincere cooperation. While at times it is the Court of Justice that will take care of national concerns and particularities,[145] at other times it will be national constitutional courts that will be cautious in the interpretation of matters that involve EU law[146]—all with the same awareness of the importance of EU's pluralist nature and the balance it brings to these judicial interactions, both bilaterally and multilaterally. We can thus see that the descriptive features of constitutional pluralism exist in practice when looking at the behaviour and vocabulary used by relevant courts. I now turn to answering the question of the desirability and normative underpinnings of the EU's system of constitutional pluralism.

[141] See also Czech Ústavní Soud Case *Lisbon Treaty I* (n 8) [105].

[142] The very framework of the Conference of European Constitutional Courts demonstrates how cooperation among judges and courts contributes to what Jacobs famously called the cross-fertilization of legal systems. See generally F G Jacobs, 'Judicial Dialogue and the Cross-fertilization of Legal Systems: The European Court of Justice' (2003) 38 *Texas International Law Journal* 547.

[143] Fabbrini (n 64) 1014–16.

[144] Cooperative programmes, conferences, and networking events of these judicial networks play a role in the coordination of judicial activity and the unification of practices at the national level. One of their main advantages is precisely the level playing field character, where no judicial instance is in a hierarchical position to another. See also Claes and de Visser (n 59) 101.

[145] See in particular on this matter Lord Neuberger and Lord Mance in United Kingdom Supreme Court Case *HS2* (n 128) [201].

[146] Hence heterarchy's ability of different actors to be ranked in a number of ways at different points in time.

# 4

# Constitutional Pluralism as a Normative Theory

The operation of judicial interactions, namely the existence of competing claims to ultimate authority without a predetermined hierarchical order, makes constitutional conflict an unavoidable occurrence in the EU's constitutional space. Given that it rests on the premise of regarding law as a dynamic, incrementally developing creature,[1] constitutional conflict is no exceptional event and represents an important element of the system's functioning. In managing these conflicts, the system has an in-built auto-correct function, which ensures that points of conflict are accommodated through mutual respect and sincere cooperation of all actors involved. Thus, constitutional pluralism is not a theory merely for times of equanimity, but also, crucially, in times of constitutional conflict. However, this does not mean that every point of conflict necessarily means progress for the pluralist system as a whole: it is possible to distinguish constructive from destructive conflict. Contesting the very basic values underpinning the system agreed upon and shared by all Member States results in destructive conflict. However, the 'regular' type of conflict is one that is constructive and has been guiding the development of EU law. It takes place within the 'pluralist', which tells us how far reasonable disagreement concerning the interpretation of the 'constitutional' can go.

The aim of this chapter is thus to introduce and explore the normative core of constitutional pluralism and the way in which it should guide the two types of constitutional conflict. As I will show, convergent standards on EU and national levels of the 'constitutional' will still allow for 'pluralism', both substantively and institutionally. Moreover, strengthening the normative core of constitutional pluralism will result both in decreasing the ability of rogue states[2] to abuse it, and in increasing the capacity of the EU's constitutional system to address such abuses. I will first present the content of the normative core, which defines the shared constitutional essentials of the European Union and all its Member States. I will then distinguish between constructive and destructive conflict, pointing to the benefits of the former and the limits of judicial interactions to solve the latter through the operation of the auto-correct function.

[1] R Higgins, *Problems and Process: International Law and How We Use It* (Clarendon Press 1995) 10.

[2] The term is borrowed from L Pech and K L Scheppele, 'Illiberalism Within: Rule of Law Backsliding in the EU' (2017) 19 *Cambridge Yearbook of European Legal Studies* 3.

*The Jurisprudence of Constitutional Conflict in the European Union*. Ana Bobić, Oxford University Press. © Ana Bobić 2022.
DOI: 10.1093/oso/9780192847034.003.0004

## 1 The Normative Core of Constitutional Pluralism

The normative core of constitutional pluralism consists of the content found in the EU's constitutional sphere that cannot be done away with for the system to function. In other words, the 'constitutional' determines the basis that cannot be questioned by different sites of ultimate authority. The normative core represents the floor below which we can no longer speak of reasonable disagreement, but a destructive denial of one or more of the basic values underpinning the system. It is important to note that, while the formal source of inspiration in defining the normative core is found in formal sources of EU law, this does not mean that the source of national constitutional authority is derived therefrom. Rather, it is the other way around: national constitutional authority created the EU legal order, but not, however, without causing a permanent change on its own part.[3] The EU constitutional sphere is based on an understanding of EU and national constitutional law as permanently enmeshed.[4] In line with these points, the plurality of values agreed upon and shared by all Member States[5] and listed in Article 2 TEU represent the normative core of constitutional pluralism.[6] It is useful to cite the provision in full:

> The Union is founded on the values of respect for human dignity, freedom, democracy, equality, the rule of law and respect for human rights, including the rights of persons belonging to minorities. These values are common to the Member States in a society in which pluralism, non-discrimination, tolerance, justice, solidarity and equality between women and men prevail.

These values operate as the normative core of constitutional pluralism without resulting in an ultimately monist solution. The provision lists values that are common to all Member States and represent the basis for EU membership, in the same way as a geographical link to the European continent, satisfying certain economic

[3] See also M P Maduro, 'Three Claims of Constitutional Pluralism' in M Avbelj and J Komárek (eds), *Constitutional Pluralism in the European Union and Beyond* (Hart Publishing 2012) 76.

[4] A von Bogdandy, 'Principles of a Systemic Deficiencies Doctrine: How to Protect Checks and Balances in the Member States' (2020) 57 *Common Market Law Review* 705, 710; M Claes, *The National Courts' Mandate in the European Constitution* (Hart Publishing 2006) 6. Furthermore, the difficulty with which the United Kingdom Supreme Court attempted to divide EU from national law in order to decide on the government's prerogative to act in the international sphere is further proof of the enmeshment of national and EU law. See United Kingdom Supreme Court Case *Miller* [2017] UKSC 5; and a critical appraisal by M Elliott, 'The Supreme Court's Judgment in *Miller*: In Search of a Constitutional Principle' (2017) 76(2) *Cambridge Law Journal* 257. For a critique of the Bundesverfassungsgericht for its lack of regard for such an enmeshment see C Möllers, 'German Federal Constitutional Court: Constitutional *Ultra Vires* Review of European Acts Only Under Exceptional Circumstances; Decision of 6 July 2010, 2 BvR 2661/06, *Honeywell*' (2011) 7(1) *European Constitutional Law Review* 161, 164.

[5] See eg Case C-284/16 *Achmea* [2018] EU:C:2018:158 [34]; Case C-621/18 *Wightman* [2018] EU:C:2018:999 [62]–[63].

[6] See also S Weatherill, *Law and Values in the European Union* (OUP 2016) 250.

criteria, etc. The shared nature of these values by both levels of constitutional authority thus represents their 'constitutional profile'.[7]

In its essence, the normative core of constitutional pluralism promotes a firmly cosmopolitan, rather than a nationalist, perspective.[8] There is no normative reason why equality of Member States should take precedence over equality of EU citizens, and there is most certainly no basis for the treaties to be interpreted in this way. The Court of Justice's so-called '*Simmenthal* mandate' requires each national court to apply EU law to cases within their jurisdiction and protect the rights that it accords to citizens in their entirety.[9] Keeping the EU as a polity within the conservative confines of the principle of conferral and limited to a 'compound of states' in fact results in more power for the states and diminishes the direct empowerment of their citizens to take ownership of the integration project. This tendency is aided by Member States' governments but also those constitutional courts who employ the retrograde rhetoric of public international law.[10] So, precisely to overcome the 'Member States are the Masters of the Treaties' logic that might allow for a deterioration of the rule of law by abusing the national identity clause, equality of Member States should be read together with equality of EU citizens.

Sovereign equality of states means that once states sign up to a legal obligation in the international sphere, they are all equally bound to abide by it.[11] With the increase in the ability of international (and arguably, supranational) organizations to assume responsibility for carrying out the common interest of its members, it is becoming likelier that those members will decrease their insistence on their 'sovereign status and, correlatively, to equality'.[12] Indeed, placing the individual as the 'fundamental moral unit of concern'[13] demands a move away from the formalistic view of equality of Member States and places further emphasis on individual enforcement of EU law rights in order to ensure a coherent application of Union law across all Member States. The cosmopolitan literature emphasizes the drawbacks that equality of states inflicts upon the equality of individuals:[14]

> [p]olitical equality among states is of value *only* so far as it contributes to justice as goal or as process. Political equality among states is not valuable for its own sake,

[7] A von Bogdandy and M Ioannidis, 'Systemic Deficiency in the Rule of Law: What It Is, What Has Been Done, What Can Be Done' (2014) 51 *Common Market Law Review* 59.
[8] See also von Bogdandy (n 4) 713, 728.
[9] Claes (n 4) 108.
[10] I Pernice, 'Multilevel Constitutionalism and the Crisis of Democracy in Europe' (2015) 11(3) *European Constitutional Law Review* 541, 543.
[11] S R Ratner, *The Thin Justice of International Law* (OUP 2015) 194.
[12] L S Rossi, 'The Principle of Equality among Member States of the European Union' in L S Rossi and F Casolari (eds), *The Principle of Equality in EU Law* (Springer 2017) 10.
[13] A E Eckert, 'Peoples and Persons: Moral Standing, Power, and the Equality of States' (2006) 50 *International Studies Quarterly* 841, 864.
[14] D Chandler, 'New Rights for Old: Cosmopolitan Citizenship and the Critique of State Sovereignty' (2003) 51 *Political Studies* 332, 343.

> and certainly cannot be regarded as a necessary condition in its own right for system legitimacy.[15]

Thus, the principle of equality of Member States is merely an indicator of membership, whereas the normative aim of European integration should be one of partnership.[16] It is therefore regrettable that the Court of Justice employed this logic in its press release following the *Weiss II* judgment of the Bundesverfassungsgericht, where it restated the jurisprudence concerning the preliminary reference procedure, concluding that is 'the only way of ensuring the equality of Member States in the Union they created'.[17] Yet, the preliminary reference procedure has for decades claimed success in allowing individuals to enforce their EU law rights against their governments.[18] This should remain the priority, as Article 9 TEU reminds us that '[in] all its activities, the Union shall observe the principle of the equality of its citizens'. Prioritizing equality of Member States over equality of citizens thus may result in grave long-term consequences on some of the building blocks of EU law and the well-established benefits of judicial cooperation.

Having identified the normative core of the EU's constitutional set-up with reference to Article 2 TEU as its codifying provision, thus the 'constitutional', we are now faced with the question of how the 'pluralist' is ensured. Or, conversely, what outcomes are to be considered below the floor of the 'constitutional' where we no longer speak of reasonable disagreement in interpretation but of destructive constitutional conflict? The following two sections will address each of these situations in turn.

## 2 Constructive Constitutional Conflict

The aim of this section is to better understand the contrasting demands stemming from primacy of EU law on the one hand and from the supremacy of national constitutions on the other. Namely, as I will aim to show, both are far less absolute than the courts interpreting them would have us believe. Rather, both levels of constitutionality are in a permanent relation of mutual influence, developing and changing incrementally through their interactions. In that sense, the famous statement that

15 A Buchanan, *Justice, Legitimacy, and Self-Determination: Moral Foundations for International Law* (OUP 2004) 321.

16 Rossi (n 12) 39.

17 See https://curia.europa.eu/jcms/upload/docs/application/pdf/2020-05/cp200058en.pdf.

18 S Rodin, 'Back to Square One: The Past, the Present and the Future of the *Simmenthal* Mandate' in J M Beneyto and I Pernice (eds), *Europe's Constitutional Challenges in the Light of the Recent Case Law of National Constitutional Courts: Lisbon and Beyond* (Nomos 2011) 298. On the trend of increase of private vis-à-vis Commission enforcement of EU law see A Hofmann, 'Is the Commission Levelling the Playing Field? Rights Enforcement in the European Union' (2018) 40(6) *Journal of European Integration* 737.

Member States are the 'Masters of the Treaties' is no longer accurate: rather, the Treaties have lost a clear master as is the case in the international law sphere. The Court of Justice has famously taken to expanding the self-referential system of the Treaties.[19] While Member States would in principle be at full liberty to negotiate a treaty reform doing away with the cornerstone principles of EU law introduced by the Court of Justice, such a development is almost impossible to imagine. The same goes for national constitutions: the entrenchment of EU integration clauses therein[20] significantly restricts the extent to which EU law can be rejected by way of constitutional review.

The normative core of constitutional pluralism does not lead to homogenization of national constitutions and their content, but rather serves as a codification of their shared values and reduces the incommensurability of constitutional concepts in substance.[21] In other words, the operation of constitutional pluralism is conducive to constructive constitutional conflict. For example, Member States and the EU may not be in perfect agreement as to the precise extent of the rule of law, or how it influences judicial independence in one or another constitutional and institutional context,[22] but can be in agreement on what falls *outside* its borders. In that sense, constructive constitutional conflict forms part of the regular operation of the EU's constitutional set-up and is accommodated by the heterarchical operation of the auto-correct function in the sphere of judicial interactions.[23]

In this process, Maduro stresses the importance of the discursive element between different sites of constitutional authority, who jointly and coherently strive to create the shared European legal space.[24] Recalling his work on principles of contrapunctual law, constitutional pluralism's normative core includes those values and principles that 'make it possible for the processes of justification of national and European decisions to be based on different arguments while their actual application leads to compatible decisions'.[25] This process of remaining above the floor of essential values shared in the EU can be reconciled with a diverse range

[19] Lenaerts concludes that the Court of Justice has 'a constitutional mandate in a self-referential and, in that sense, autonomous legal order'. K Lenaerts, 'The Court's Outer and Inner Selves: Exploring the External and Internal Legitimacy of the Court of Justice' in M Adams and others (eds), *Judging Europe's judges: The Legitimacy of the Case Law of the European Court of Justice* (Hart Publishing 2015) 15.

[20] M Claes, 'Constitutionalizing Europe at Its Source: The 'European Clauses' in the National Constitutions: Evolution and Typology' (2005) 24(1) *Yearbook of European Law* 81.

[21] T Christiansen and C Reh, *Constitutionalizing the European Union* (Macmillan International 2009) 27. See also K Lenaerts and A Wójcik, 'Judges Should Be Fully Insulated from Any Sort of Pressure' *Verfassungsblog* (30 January 2020) https://verfassungsblog.de/judges-should-be-fully-insulated-from-any-sort-of-pressure/.

[22] A von Bogdandy, 'Ways to Frame the European Rule of Law: *Rechtsgemeinschaft*, Trust, Revolution, and Kantian Peace' (2018) 14 *European Constitutional Law Review* 675, 694.

[23] Constructive conflict may be equated with what von Bogdandy terms 'normal violations of law' that do not 'question the foundations of the legal order'. von Bogdandy (n 4) 718.

[24] M P Maduro, 'Contrapunctual Law: Europe's Constitutional Pluralism in Action' in N Walker (ed), *Sovereignty in Transition* (Hart Publishing 2003) 513–14, 518.

[25] ibid 524.

of interpretations in different Member States.[26] As Lenaerts and Gutiérrez-Fons explain:

> [General] principles leave some room for constitutional values that differ from one Member State to another. [ ... ] In this view, the ECJ cannot reply on general principles of EU law, particularly fundamental rights, as an unstoppable centripetal force that would ensure uniformity while destroying constitutional diversity.[27]

In the same vein, Cloots lists a number of interpretative guidelines to both national courts with constitutional jurisdiction and the Court of Justice, in order not only to contain conflict, but also to resolve it in a manner that will be respectful of the values, and ultimately constitutional orders, in balance.[28] Besselink and Ejisbouts explain that the judge faced with situations of constitutional conflict should not address it by 'mere reference to the autonomy or the supremacy of his own legal order, nor by reference to legal hierarchy. He shall do so by reference to fundamental substantive norms valid in the wider circumscription.'[29]

Furthermore, in order to understand how constructive conflict is managed, let us take a look at how the 'pluralism' of 'constitutional' works, where we can distinguish between *institutional* and *substantive* pluralism.[30] Institutional balancing is closely linked to the use of self-restraint, and is the first step to be taken once a national constitutional limit is invoked in a particular case.[31] If the specific case is before the Court of Justice, the use of institutional balancing will mean rendering a decision on which court is to take the final decision. Such an approach is well-known in the case law of the Court and, as Tridimas explains, the Court of Justice employs it regularly in what he calls 'guidance' and 'deference' cases.[32] In particular, the Court of Justice either gives guidance to the national court that is then finally to decide (guidance cases), or it leaves it entirely up to the national court to decide (deference cases). In deciding whether to rule on a certain issue itself, or leave it to the national court, the Court of Justice will be driven by taking into account the sensitivity of the case, which will condition the extent of self-restraint

[26] See also von Bogdandy (n 4) 714.

[27] K Lenaerts and J A Gutiérrez-Fons 'The Constitutional Allocation of Powers and General Principles of EU Law' (2010) 47(6) *Common Market Law Review* 1629, 1662–63.

[28] E Cloots, 'Germs of Pluralist Adjudication: *Advocaten Voor De Wereld* and Other References from the Belgian Constitutional Court' (2010) 47(3) *Common Market Law Review* 645, 668.

[29] W T Ejisbouts and L Besselink, '"The Law of Laws": Overcoming Pluralism' (2008) 4(3) *European Constitutional Law Review* 395, 397.

[30] See also Maduro (n 3) 80.

[31] See also A Bobić 'A Dynamic Analysis of Judicial Behaviour: The Auto-Correct Function of Constitutional Pluralism' in M Derlén and J Lindholm (eds), *The Court of Justice of the European Union. Multidisciplinary Perspectives* (Hart Publishing 2017).

[32] T Tridimas, 'Constitutional Review of Member State Action: The Virtues and Vices of an Incomplete Jurisdiction' (2011) 9(3–4) *ICON* 737, 739.

to be applied.[33] By contrast, when a case takes place before a national constitutional court, regardless of whether the court submitted a preliminary reference or not, national instances will be wary of a possible constitutional conflict. In addition, any situation of a constitutional conflict is to be approached with great self-restraint and in a manner open to European integration.[34]

The institutional balancing – i.e. the determination of which instance will ultimately decide the case, as explained in the preceding paragraph – is followed by the substantive balancing of values in opposition in the particular case.[35] Surely, the result of the institutional balancing will serve as a strong indicator as to the extent of the substantive balancing that a particular court is to exhibit. In essence, when the Court of Justice defers to the national court on the ultimate decision, this undoubtedly means an endorsement for that court to protect the national value in question.

The pluralist nature of constitutional identity more specifically stems from its intrinsically heterarchical nature, as it does not impose an overarching European value over specific national values. In that respect, constitutional identity is in itself a contributing element to the pluralistic nature of EU constitutionalism, endorsing an equal position of a variety of national specificity claims. Such a view outweighs the argument of Advocate General Cruz Villalón in *Gauweiler*[36] in favour of a converging European identity in a *Solange*-like trend.[37] There are two reasons to support this claim. First, the application of the Advocate General's view would create a hierarchical relationship between identity claims on the EU and national level, thus increasing the possibility of constitutional conflict. A clear statement of hierarchy does not appear as something that national constitutional adjudicators would welcome, as their jurisprudence revolves around the reconciliation between the primacy of EU law and the supremacy of national constitutions in their own territory.[38] Second, from an institutional point of view, respecting national particularities contributes to the mutual respect and cooperation between constitutional

[33] See also P M Huber, 'The Federal Constitutional Court and European Integration' (2015) 21(1) *European Public Law* 83, 107, who emphasizes how the principle of cooperation among courts in the European judicial space needs to work in both directions.

[34] See eg German Bundesverfassungsgericht Case 2 BvR 2735/14 *Mr R.* Order of 15 December 2015 key considerations [1.b] http://www.bundesverfassungsgericht.de/SharedDocs/Pressemitteilungen/EN/2016/bvg16-004.html.

[35] For a detailed analysis on how the balancing exercise is to be carried out in order to achieve the rule of law see Lenaerts and Gutiérrez-Fons (n 27) 1649–53.

[36] Opinion of Advocate General Cruz Villalón in Case C-62/14 *Gauweiler* [2015] EU:C:2015:7 [61].

[37] Lord Mance in fact used the argument of the Advocate General against him. In *Pham* he stated: 'This recognises, perhaps, that Europe has not yet reached a situation where it is axiomatic that there is constitutional identity between the Union and its Members.' United Kingdom Supreme Court Case *Pham* [2015] UKSC 19 [79].

[38] To use the wording of the Spanish and Polish Constitutional Tribunals. See Spanish Tribunal Constitucional Case DTC 1/2004 *Constitutional Treaty* Declaration of 13 December 2004 ground 4; Polish Trybunał Konstytucyjny Case K 18/04 *Accession Treaty* Judgment of 11 May 2005 [12] http://trybunal.gov.pl/fileadmin/content/omowienia/K_18_04_GB.pdf.

adjudicators and the Court of Justice, which would be jeopardized if a converging European identity were to replace the current understanding of the identity clause.

In what follows, I will briefly reflect upon a number of cases decided on the EU and national level in order to demonstrate the constructive nature of those constitutional conflicts. More specifically, I aim to show that individual instances of constitutional conflict form part of constructive conflict and are not attacks on the existence of the entire EU legal order (destructive conflicts). The aim of this exercise is not to provide an in-depth analysis of each of the cases, but in analogy to the analysis of judicial vocabulary above, to offer a broad brush, prima facie demonstration of the operation of constructive conflict, and underline how it remains within the confines of constitutional pluralism's normative core.

## 2.1 *Juízes Portugueses*

In the context of the Euro crisis and financial assistance to debt-ridden Member States, the Court of Justice decided that a Memorandum of Understanding grounded in the European Financial Stabilisation Mechanism is justiciable in *Juízes Portugueses*.[39] This unlikely champion of legal accountability in economic governance owes its importance to the current salience of judicial independence in the EU.[40] Namely, the association of judges in Portugal challenged the austerity measure temporarily reducing their salaries, arguing it interfered with their independence guaranteed by Articles 2 and 19 TEU. The Court of Justice, arguably in need of establishing a legal precedent for its jurisdiction concerning the rule of law challenges taking place in Poland and Hungary,[41] found that Article 19(1) TEU[42] was engaged and the preliminary reference was admissible. Importantly, the Court of Justice declared judicial independence the cornerstone of the rule of law, expanding its application to all Member State action, regardless of the applicability of EU law in a specific case.[43]

From the perspective of a national court, this may be seen as intrusion into the division of competences between the EU and the national level. Certainly, the

[39] Case 64/16 *Juizes Portugueses* [2018] EU:C:2018:117 [19]–[26].

[40] M Bonelli and M Claes, 'Judicial Serendipity: How Portuguese Judges Came to the Rescue of the Polish Judiciary ECJ 27 February 2018, Case C-64/16 *Juízes Portugueses*' (2018) 14 *European Constitutional Law Review* 622.

[41] ibid 623.

[42] 'Member States shall provide remedies sufficient to ensure effective legal protection in the fields covered by Union law.'

[43] Case C-64/16 *Juízes Portugueses* (n 39) [21], where the Court of Justice states that: 'In the present case, the order for reference contains sufficient information to enable the Court to understand the reasons why the referring court seeks an interpretation of the second subparagraph of Article 19(1) TEU and Article 47 of the Charter for the needs of the main proceedings.' No such reasons are given beyond stating that the reduction in salaries of judges were the result of austerity measures attached to financial assistance (granted outside of EU law proper).

Court of Justice expanded its jurisdiction to hear cases concerning the rule of law and judicial independence. Upon closer inspection of possible interpretations of Article 2 TEU, there is nothing problematic in placing rule of law and judicial independence obligations on all Member States at all times:[44] precisely because this is the common constitutional core all levels of constitutional authority share. It forms part of the 'constitutional' in constitutional pluralism. And while it can be interpreted in a number of different ways - for example concerning length and renewability of judicial mandates, or powers of courts in the national judicial structure - the core of judicial independence remains (or should remain) untouched.

## 2.2 *FX*

The Romanian High Court of Cassation and Justice submitted a reference concerning the position of the Constitutional Court in relation to corruption cases, and this reference is currently pending before the Court of Justice. The subject matter of the reference is not of much relevance here, but rather, the direct question concerning the principle of primacy and the position of national constitutional courts. In its third question, the Romanian court asks:

> Is the primacy of EU law to be interpreted as permitting a national court to disapply a decision of the constitutional court which has been handed down in a case concerning a constitutional dispute and is binding under national law?[45]

Were present times not as precarious for the rule of law in the EU as they are, the Court of Justice could easily answer this question by referring to its previous Grand Chamber decision in *Križan*:

> The national rule which obliges the Najvyšší súd Slovenskej republiky [Slovakian Supreme Court] to follow the legal position of the Ústavný súd Slovenskej republiky [Slovakian Constitutional Court] cannot therefore prevent the referring court from submitting a request for a preliminary ruling to the Court of Justice at any point in the proceedings which it judges appropriate, and to set aside, if necessary, the assessments made by the Ústavný súd Slovenskej republiky which might prove to be contrary to European Union law.[46]

[44] See on this point ch 5, s 7.
[45] Case C-859/19 *Criminal proceedings against FX, CS and ND* (reference from the High Court of Cassation and Justice, Romania).
[46] Case C-416/10 *Križan* [2013] EU:C:2013:8 [71].

Therefore, we already know the answer to the question the Romanian court asked: primacy of EU law in its EU-exclusive reading demands that all national courts set aside all contradicting jurisprudence, even that of a constitutional court. Yet, given that the question refers directly to the principle of primacy, no doubt will the Court of Justice again conjure a Grand Chamber and use it as an opportunity to elaborate in plenty of detail the meaning of the principle. Taking into account the rule of law backsliding in Poland and Hungary, dealt with also in a number of cases already closed and pending, it is expected that the Court of Justice will follow its approach in *Juízes Portugueses*, where the consequences of this decision will largely be felt in future cases. However, the Court of Justice here needs to be wary of the limits of the normative core of constitutional pluralism, and carefully balance the basic principles of the EU's constitutional sphere with the need to police destructive conflict in other Member States. So while the answer to the question posed will be in the affirmative, it remains to be seen what methods of interpretation the Court of Justice will use to reinforce or perhaps extend the meaning of the principle of primacy.

## 2.3 *Grossmania*

The Court of Justice is further being asked about the temporal limits of the principle of primacy, this time by the Hungarian Administrative and Labour Court:

> Must Article 267 of the Treaty on the Functioning of the European Union be interpreted as meaning that, where the Court of Justice of the European Union, in a decision given in preliminary ruling proceedings, has declared a legislative provision of a Member State to be incompatible with EU law, that legislative provision cannot be applied in subsequent national administrative or judicial proceedings either, notwithstanding that the facts of the subsequent proceedings are not entirely identical to those of the previous preliminary ruling proceedings?[47]

Read together with the preliminary reference from Romania above, the Court of Justice is again in a position to instill further permanent changes to the operation of the principle of primacy. If answered in the affirmative, this may in fact result not in a disapplication of the relevant national provision in the case at hand, but in an invalidation of such a norm for the future. It is less obvious, however, whether the Court of Justice would go as far as turning the obligation of disapplication into one of invalidation for national courts, which would demand a serious reconsideration of the role and scope of the principle of primacy.

[47] Case C-177/20 *Grossmania Kft v Vas Region Administrative Department* (reference from the Győr Administrative and Labour Court, Hungary).

## 3 Destructive Constitutional Conflict

Constitutional conflicts occurring between the EU and national levels of constitutional authority are predominantly of a constructive nature, as described in the previous section. However, the pluralist system is not immune to bugs, which can be characterized as situations in which values contained in Article 2 TEU are put into question in a destructive manner. These conflicts display a bad faith use of constitutional identity that results in disagreements that are no longer reasonable and result in outcomes detracting from the shared values among EU members. In such situations, the auto-correct function of constitutional pluralism is not able incrementally to accommodate the conflict in the sphere of judicial interactions, given that the destructive interpretation detracts from the rule of law and no longer ensures respect of the shared lowest common denominator in Article 2 TEU.

When dealing with destructive constitutional conflict, we are thus no longer operating on a scale of reasonable disagreements that can over time be balanced against each other through the operation of mutual respect and sincere cooperation. While Article 2 TEU allows for a wide array of differing interpretations, there are also types of contestation that cannot be tolerated within its scope.[48] Rule of law is in the process of being dismantled in a number of Member States,[49] primarily through the attacks on the judiciary[50] and an outright disregard for sincere cooperation and mutual respect. Despite a certain conflict fatigue being apparent in the EU constitutional discourse, conflating constructive and destructive conflict disregards the structural properties of the EU's constitutional sphere more generally, and judicial interactions more specifically. This section will thus look further into the nature of destructive constitutional conflict and the limits to the ability of the auto-correct function to resolve it incrementally through judicial interactions.

In *Republikka*, the Court of Justice connected the compliance with Article 2 TEU values to membership of the Union and as a consequence stated that Member States cannot legislate in a manner that reduces its basic protections, and specifically protections of the rule of law.[51] Deteriorations of such a magnitude jeopardize judicial independence and by extension prevent individuals to enforce their rights before national courts, resulting in a situation where not all Member States safeguard the basic shared value of the rule of law.[52] The current rule of law deterioration taking place in Poland is a straightforward example of destructive constitutional conflict, characterized by both the Court of Justice and the Commission

[48] See von Bogdandy (n 4) 734.

[49] For an up-to-date overview of the rule of law cases concerning Poland and Hungary since the *Juizes Portugueses* judgment see L Pech and D Kochenov, 'Respect for the Rule of Law in the Case Law of the European Court of Justice: A Casebook Overview of Key Judgments since the *Portuguese Judges* Case' SIEPS Report (2021).

[50] Pech and Scheppele (n 2) 3.

[51] Case C-896/19 *Republikka* [2021] EU:C:2021:311 [62]–[64].

[52] Case 216/18 PPU *LM* [2018] EU:C:2018:586 [48].

as generalized and systemic deficiencies that go beyond individual instances of breaches of fundamental rights.[53] Destructive constitutional conflict is thus one of such a grave nature that the Member State engaging in it no longer meets the basic EU membership criteria,[54] resulting in a need for a solution on both the legal and the political level.

A useful depiction of how destructive conflict operates can be found in the recent decision of the Disciplinary Chamber of the captured Polish Supreme Court,[55] where a disciplined prosecutor sought the application of the decisions of the Court of Justice concerning judicial independence in the proceedings. Strikingly, the Disciplinary Chamber stated that 'this application did not deserve to be taken into account on substance'.[56] No standard of review has been introduced or presented. The Disciplinary Chamber next had the opportunity to consider the judicial independence of a Supreme Court Chamber of Labour and Social Security that submitted the relevant preliminary reference to the Court of Justice. Here the standard of impartiality is that 'any external observer will easily see the court's lack of neutrality with regards to the interests in the dispute'.[57] Finally, when assessing the validity of the proceedings carried out by said Chamber of Labour and Social Security, including the preliminary reference, the Disciplinary Chamber concluded that 'since the invalidity concerns the entire proceedings, a preliminary ruling of the CJEU which was obtained in such invalid proceedings cannot be valid either'.[58] It is difficult to find standards of review in this judgment, and more difficult still to find any safeguards for sustaining mutual respect and sincere cooperation in the EU judicial space.

Part of academic reactions to *Weiss II* unjustifiably conflate the German decision with examples of Polish decisions, characterizing both as a rule of law issue.[59] Hitherto, there is nothing in the decision of the Bundesverfassungsgericht that questions the judicial independence of the Court of Justice, nor do we have reason to assume that the judges of the Bundesverfassungsgericht were biased or partial. A nuanced understanding of the EU's constitutional space allows for a distinction between these two examples, precisely through the ability of the auto-correct function to accommodate constitutional conflict incrementally. In my view, shielding the Court of Justice from any sort of criticism by national courts would gravely disregard structural properties of judicial cooperation in the EU, which moves forward through constructive conflict. Further, it would also result in a neglect of the

[53] Joined Cases C-404/05 PPU and C-659/15 PPU *Aranyosi and Căldăraru* [2016] EU:C:2016:198 [89], [93], [104]. See more in von Bogdandy (n 4) 718.

[54] See also von Bogdandy (n 4) 710, 733.

[55] See https://ruleoflaw.pl/wp-content/uploads/2020/10/Case-II-DO-52-20.pdf.

[56] ibid 3.

[57] ibid 6.

[58] ibid.

[59] See eg Editorial Comments, 'Not Mastering the Treaties: The German Federal Constitutional Court's PSPP Judgment' (2020) 57 *Common Market Law Review* 965, 966.

constitutional set-up of the EU which does not contain a federal supremacy clause, nor does it subordinate national constitutional orders. Rather, the decision in *Weiss II* should be seen as one where a national court acts as the Court of Justice's counterpart, demanding it to properly exercise competence control as accorded to it by the Treaties, in this case the exercise of monetary policy by the European Central Bank (ECB). There are constructive elements in this finding that can incrementally be resolved through the auto-correct function of constitutional pluralism.

A possible consequence of this litigation is that other national courts incrementally follow the German example[60] and begin imposing their own standards and demands for justification on part of the ECB, leading to a proliferation of diverging national standards and resulting in the creation of an unrealistic burden for the ECB. To prevent this, a coherent improvement in the accountability of the ECB may ultimately call for a more stringent approach by the Court of Justice that would pre-empt the application of national standards of judicial review.[61] However, *solange* this does not take place, national courts demanding more of the ECB in terms of justifying its monetary policy choices with large redistributive effects does not appear to me controversial. In fact, the ECB, despite Article 130 TFEU explicitly prohibiting it from taking instructions from Member States, complied with the request of the Bundesverfassungsgericht[62] to better explain the proportionality of the PSPP. The ECB has, 'in line with the principle of sincere cooperation [ . . . ] decided to accommodate this request'.[63] The Bundesverfassungsgericht subsequently also confirmed that its demands have been met.[64]

Conversely, destructive constitutional conflict is one where judicial accommodation cannot remedy the systemic deficiencies of rule of law in the Member States. Rather, maintaining such conflicts in the realm of judicial interactions and the auto-correct function would legitimize the contestation by the national level and reduce the standards of 'constitutional' for all members of the pluralist system.[65] The prominent example of such a situation is the consistent refusal of the Polish Government to cooperate with the Commission and abide by numerous judgments of the Court of Justice concerning judicial independence.[66] The Court of Justice has, in response, issued an order for an interim measure, requesting Poland to suspend the operation of the above-mentioned Disciplinary Chamber of the

[60] The Commission infringement proceedings against Germany on this matter are arguably sending out a political signal against such a development. See also ch 5, s 6.1.

[61] In the absence of a Treaty review of this matter.

[62] German Bundesverfassungsgericht Cases 2 BvR 859/15, 2 BvR 980/16, 2 BvR 2006/15, 2 BvR 1651/15 *Weiss II* Judgment of 5 May 2020 [235].

[63] See https://www.ecb.europa.eu/pub/pdf/other/ecb.mepletter200629_Simon~ece6ead766.en.pdf.

[64] German Bundesverfassungsgericht Case 2 BvR 1651/15 Order of the Second Senate of 29 April 2021.

[65] See von Bogdandy (n 4) 717.

[66] European Commission Press Release of 31 March 2021 https://ec.europa.eu/commission/presscorner/detail/en/ip_21_1524.

Supreme Court,[67] and ultimately decided that the operation of the Disciplinary Chamber of the Supreme Court contravenes Article 19(1) TEU.[68] In its earlier decision,[69] the Court of Justice found the Disciplinary Chamber to lack judicial independence; however, Poland has continued its operation. The Court of Justice also found that the amendments concerning the appointment procedure to the National Council of the Judiciary are contrary to the rule of law and judicial independence.[70] The decision went so far as to state that the referring court, which has in the meantime been deprived of its jurisdiction to hear the case that was the occasion of the preliminary reference, should continue to assume jurisdiction and, if needed, to apply the provisions of national law that were in force prior to the relevant amendments.[71]

These decisions come in response to the myriad of reforms and actions taken by the Polish Government with the aim of curtailing judicial independence. For example, it is possible for the Minister of Justice personally to delegate a judge to a case.[72] In addition, national judges were warned by the Deputy of the Disciplinary Commissioner of Judges of Common Courts not publicly to question the effectiveness of appointing judges adjudicating in the Chamber of Extraordinary Control and Public Affairs of the Supreme Court.[73] Adding further fuel to the flames, the Polish Prime Minister initiated a requested for constitutional review, asking the Constitutional Tribunal to provide an interpretation concerning the relationship between EU law and the Polish Constitution.[74] More specifically, the Prime Minister is asking whether Articles 1 and 19(1) TEU, read together with Article 4(3) TEU, have any effect on the hierarchical superiority of the Polish Constitution in Poland. Finally, on 14 July 2021, the Polish Constitutional Tribunal ruled that the interim measure issued by the Court of Justice, ordering Poland to suspend the operation of the Disciplinary Chamber of the Supreme Court, is *ultra vires* and that in that respect, Article 4(3) TEU in conjunction with Article 279 TFEU

[67] Case C-791/19 R *Commission v Poland* [2021] EU:C:2020:277.

[68] Case C-791/19 *Commission v Poland* [2021] EU:C:2021:596.

[69] Joined Cases C-585/18, C-624/18 and C-625/18 *AK and Others* [2019] EU:C:2019:982.

[70] Case C-824/18 *AB and Others* [2021] EU:C:2021:153.

[71] ibid [149], [166].

[72] See a line of preliminary references submitted by Polish courts on this point: Case C-748/19 *Prokuratura Rejonowa w Mińsku Mazowieckim v WB* (request from the District Court in Warsaw); Case C-749/19 *Prokuratura Rejonowa Warszawa-Żoliborz w Warszawie v XA and YZ* (request from the District Court in Warsaw); Case C-750/19 *Prokuratura Rejonowa Warszawa—Wola w Warszawie v DT* (request from the District Court in Warsaw); Case C-763/19 *DS v SP, AP, DK, Sz w K* (request from the Court of Appeal in Kraków); Case C-764/19 *C. SA v Administrator in the insolvency of IT in liquidation* (request from the Court of Appeal in Kraków).

[73] Statement of the Deputy of the Disciplinary Commissioner of Judges of Common Courts (6 August 2020) https://www.iustitia.pl/en/activity/informations/3916-statement-of-the-deputy-of-the-disciplinary-commissioner-of-judges-of-common-courts.

[74] Application K 3/21 of 29 March 2021. Unofficial translation available at https://ruleoflaw.pl/wp-content/uploads/2021/05/K_3-21_application.pdf. For further analysis see ch 6, s 2.2.1.

(allowing for the Court of Justice to issue interim measures) are contrary to the Polish Constitution.[75]

All these examples demonstrate that Poland is abusing the concept of constitutional identity and *ultra vires* review through a *contra legem* reading of principles contained in Article 2 TEU. The reaction of the Polish Government to the decision of the Bundesverfassungsgericht in *Wiess II* is a case in point. The Polish Government stated that Polish courts can disapply EU law obligations on the basis of constitutional identity, in the same way as the German Court did.[76] Yet, in the actual decision, the German court found that constitutional identity was *not* breached,[77] but rather, the Court of Justice insufficiently controlled an EU institution in keeping within its mandate (an *ultra vires* finding).[78] It is possible to disagree with the merits of the German decision, but it is *not* possible to claim the findings went beyond a reasonable interpretation of any of the values contained in Article 2 TEU. Conversely, the Polish situation demonstrates a continual interference into judicial independence and an abuse of the pluralist constellation of the EU's constitutional space. The application for constitutional review by the Polish Prime Minister, for example, devoted thirty-five pages analysing German, Italian, Czech, and Danish jurisprudence concerning the conditional primacy of EU law, only to conclude superficially and incorrectly that this results in an outright subordination of EU law in respect of national constitutions.[79]

In addressing these issues, Kelemen and Pech reject constitutional pluralism as a theory able to survive these attacks and in consequence argue that only a full-blown supremacy of EU law[80] can ensure the equality of Member States, recalling Fabbrini's argument on the relationship between equality of Member States and the national identity clause.[81] In other words, they see constitutional identity as the

[75] Polish Trybunał Konstytucyjny Decision P 7/20 of 14 July 2021 https://trybunal.gov.pl/en/hearings/judgments/art/11589-obowiazek-panstwa-czlonkowskiego-ue-polegajacy-na-wykonywaniu-srodkow-tymczasowych-odnoszacych-sie-do-ksztaltu-ustroju-i-funkcjonowania-konstytucyjnych-organow-wladzy-sadowniczej-tego-panstwa.

[76] See https://twitter.com/RULEOFLAWpl/status/1257684311395962880.

[77] German Bundesverfassungsgericht Case *Weiss II* (n 62) [228]. See also the interview with the Bundesverfassungsgericht judge Ulrich Maidowski, explaining how the decision cannot be comparable with the Polish case. See https://dprv.eu/index.php/pl/aktualno%C5%9Bci?fbclid=IwAR3xair3sPdYqoyqlulqWBzw4gHCm3QACvDwmL5NOJBMYL96lLynYM2BsIs.

[78] The difference between identity and *ultra vires* review in the German constitutional jurisprudence is one of consequence: when constitutional identity is breached, it represents an area untouchable by European integration and is without remedy; *ultra vires* review controls *already transferred* competences and how they are used. See Huber (n 33).

[79] Application of the Prime Minister (n 74) 15–50.

[80] In reaction to the decision of the Bundesverfassungsgericht, some academics alongside Kelemen and Pech published the following statement: 'National Courts Cannot Override CJEU Judgments: A Joint Statement in Defense of the EU Legal Order' https://verfassungsblog.de/national-courts-cannot-override-cjeu-judgments/.

[81] R D Kelemen and L Pech, 'The Uses and Abuses of Constitutional Pluralism: Undermining the Rule of Law in the Name of Constitutional Identity in Hungary and Poland' (2019) 21 *Cambridge Yearbook of European Legal Studies* 59, 62. See F Fabbrini, 'After the *OMT* Case: The Supremacy of EU Law as the Guarantee of the Equality of the Member States' (2015) 16(4) *German Law Journal* 1003.

sword threatening the existence of the European Union. Yet, constitutional identity is acting precisely as a shield from authoritarian, anti-democratic tendencies: constitutional identity is a concept necessarily including the rule of law. Pech convincingly and thoroughly shows that the rule of law is indeed a common *constitutional* tradition of both the EU and its Member States.[82] Surely even Fabbrini's reading of Article 4(2) TEU[83] would include the values of Article 2 TEU to be necessarily embedded in national identity of Member States. As was already mentioned above, values contained in Article 2 TEU are entrenched in the accession process to the European Union, and any state aspiring to become a member would, in principle, not be able to follow in the footsteps of Hungary and Poland.[84]

Destructive constitutional conflicts demonstrate the gravity of the disagreement between a Member State and the EU to such an extent that a judicial resolution of the situation is not sufficient in itself to put a halt to the persistent breaches of the rule of law. In this respect, a coherent political and legal action, both top-down (the EU acting vis-à-vis the Member State), and also importantly bottom-up (sourced in the Member State itself, through judicial and civic action), is needed to impose an overhaul to the anti-rule of law developments. Protecting the rule of law can only be successful if both processes are in place: isolated EU action, precisely due to the heterarchical nature of the EU's constitutional space, would result in a hierarchical imposition of EU values over national ones, resulting in reduced legitimacy and increased contestation from the national level. Bottom-up activity, however, has the advantage of creating a contribution to the EU's constitution more broadly conceived, but also promotes its cosmopolitan character. The myriad preliminary references submitted by Polish judges attempting to protect their independence in the face of political intervention is only possible due to the individual enforcement character of EU law that no longer depends on the willingness of political actors to negotiate it and explicitly implement it.

## 4 Conclusion

The geographical space of the European Union is comprised of twenty-seven national and one EU claim to ultimate authority. Such a system is complex and its operation regularly causes headaches, either for the Court of Justice or for national constitutional courts, but most commonly for legal academics trying to make

[82] Emphasis added. L Pech, 'The Rule of Law as a Constitutional Principle of the European Union' (2009) Jean Monnet Working Paper 04/09 https://eclass.uoa.gr/modules/document/file.php/LAW272/rule%20of%20Law.pdf.

[83] Fabbrini (n 81).

[84] For an analysis of the rule of law conditions and compliance during and after the accession process see J B Slapin, 'How European Union Membership Can Undermine the Rule of Law in Emerging Democracies' (2015) 38(3) *West European Politics* 627.

sense of their interactions and the broader ramifications for the character of the EU's constitutional space. In Part I of this book I have shown that the system, despite its non-hierarchical character, does not operate in a haphazard manner, nor are individual constitutional systems in interaction as impervious to the input and demands of other constitutional systems as they may portray themselves to be.

Descriptively, I have presented constitutional pluralism as a system in which different claims to ultimate authority run in parallel, regularly engage in conflict, and are resolved incrementally through the operation of the auto-correct function, sustained by the application of sincere cooperation and mutual respect. The actors in the system are in a relationship of heterarchy, as they continually change their ranking over time. Normatively, constitutional pluralism has a core shared by all participants of the system and is codified in Article 2 TEU, representing the minimum requirements for Union membership. The emergence of constitutional conflict in this constellation is a regular and desirable feature of the system that promotes an interactive development of law and puts in place checks and balances between different sites of constitutional authority. However, when constitutional conflict entails a breach of the basic values in Article 2 TEU and lacks any trace of sincere cooperation and mutual respect, we are speaking of destructive conflict that can only be resolved by both political and legal means.

The preceding chapters have offered a broad-brush presentation and analysis of these characteristics, as well as an empirical demonstration that courts under analysis do indeed behave in a way consistent with the descriptive and normative characteristics of constitutional pluralism. In what comes next, I will provide a comprehensive map of the jurisprudence of constitutional conflict between the Court of Justice and national courts with the power of constitutional review. My aim is to capture the nuances of the relationships under study, providing a comprehensive and comparative account of the actual application of the principle of primacy of EU law and the limits placed on it by national constitutional courts. A detailed and incremental analysis of the full spectrum of the jurisprudence of constitutional conflict will allow us to see beyond individual points of constructive disagreement between the EU and the national level. However, it will also be able to reveal points of conflict that depart from sincere cooperation and mutual respect and thus fall into the category of destructive conflict. To this end, in Part II of this book I will explore jurisprudence in the three areas where constitutional conflict materializes: *ultra vires* review, identity review, and fundamental rights review.

# PART II
# THE JURISPRUDENCE

# 5

# *Ultra Vires* Review

## 1 Introduction

The peculiar nature of the European Union's constitutional set-up, in particular the relatively unclear[1] manner in which competences have been conferred from the Member States to the Union, have made the question of the final arbiter one of the most debated issues in EU constitutional law.[2] The ultimate arbiter in this context is the institution holding the 'interpretative autonomy'[3] concerning the extent of EU competences and the manner of their exercise by Union institutions, which Schilling calls the 'decisive question'.[4] While the Court of Justice established this jurisdiction as early as *Van Gend en Loos*,[5] national constitutional courts have, in their case law, begged to differ.[6] The conflict can be narrowed down to the relationship between the exclusive power of the Court of Justice to interpret (and annul)[7] EU law[8] and the principle of

[1] The lack of clarity has been addressed through a more precise division of competences in the Draft Constitutional Treaty and later transposed to the Lisbon Treaty. On the appraisal of whether this endeavour has been successful (as regards the text of the Constitutional Treaty) see P P Craig, 'Competence: clarity, conferral, containment and consideration' (2004) 29(3) *European Law Review* 323. For a more recent overview see S Weatherill, *Law and Values in the European Union* (OUP 2016) ch 2.

[2] See eg M Kumm, "Who is the final arbiter of constitutionality in Europe? Three conceptions of the relationship between the German Federal Constitutional Court and the European Court of Justice' (1999) 36 *Common Market Law Review* 351; M Kumm, 'The jurisprudence of constitutional conflict: constitutional supremacy in Europe before and after the Constitutional Treaty' (2005) 11(3) *European Law Journal* 262; M Claes, *The National Courts' Mandate in the European Constitution* (Hart Publishing 2006); G Luebbe-Wolff, 'Who Has the Last Word? National and Transnational Courts: Conflict and Cooperation' (2011) 30(1) *Yearbook of European Law* 86; G Beck, 'The Lisbon Judgment of the German Constitutional Court, the Primacy of EU Law and the Problem of *Kompetenz-Kompetenz*: A Conflict between Right and Right in which There Is No *Praetor*' (2011) 17(4) *European Law Journal* 470; J Komárek, 'The Place of Constitutional Courts in the EU' (2013) 9(3) *European Constitutional Law Review* 420.

[3] T Schilling, 'The Autonomy of the Community Legal Order: An Analysis of Possible Foundations' (1996) 37(2) *Harvard International Law Journal* 389. Weiler offers a critique of such an international law prism reading of EU law in J H H Weiler, *The Constitution of Europe. 'Do the New Clothes Have an Emperor?' and Other Essays on European Integration* (CUP 1999) ch 9.

[4] Schilling (n 3) 404. Schilling treats EU law as a public international law entity and thus bases his conclusions on the judicial *Kompetenz-Kompetenz* through a literal reading of the Treaties.

[5] Case 26/62 *Van Gend en Loos* [1963] EU:C:1963:1.

[6] For an analysis of the national case law vocabulary asserting the supremacy of national constitutions and the final say see ch 3, s 1.

[7] Case 314/85 *Foto-Frost* [1987] EU:C:1987:452 [17].

[8] Based on art 19 TEU, art 263 TFEU and art 267 TFEU.

*The Jurisprudence of Constitutional Conflict in the European Union*. Ana Bobić, Oxford University Press. © Ana Bobić 2022.
DOI: 10.1093/oso/9780192847034.003.0005

conferral,[9] which places the Member States as the source of autonomy of EU law. In order to analyse the case law concerning the question of the final say, the remainder of this introduction will address the division of competences between the Union and its Member States and some problems that such a configuration has yielded.

The question of the EU's powers and their limits has been declared a problem in need of a solution in the Declaration on the Future of the Union.[10] This was indeed addressed in the Laeken Declaration,[11] which proposed a makeover in the form of a clear list of Union competences. The Draft Constitutional Treaty[12] followed the same approach, which ultimately made its way into the Lisbon Treaty.[13] Unlike previous Treaties, the Treaty of Lisbon incorporated a list of areas in which the EU has competence, divided into three categories (exclusive, shared, and supporting).[14] In general, this shift represents an improvement in legal certainty and clarity,[15] but it has left the question of how borderline cases are to be resolved without a clear answer.[16] For example, the question on the limits of competence of the European Central Bank (ECB) as regards the scope of monetary policy was tested in the *Gauweiler* and *Weiss* interactions between the Court of Justice and the Bundesverfassungsgericht.[17] Regardless of the actual outcome, both courts remained firm in their respective views that they are the ultimate arbiters on the limits of EU competence.

The criticism against leaving open the question of the final say has been analysed extensively in Chapter 3,[18] but suffice it to mention here that, in order for the pluralist order to be preserved, it is not only desirable, but rather necessary for the question of the final arbiter to remain open. Given the strong positions of both

[9] The German Bundesverfassungsgericht placed the principle of conferral as the 'basic feature of the Community legal order'. German Bundesverfassungsgericht Cases 2 BvR 2134/92 and 2159/92 *Maastricht Treaty* Judgment of 12 October 1993, 94.

[10] Declaration on the Future of the Union attached to the Treaty of Nice [2001] OJ C80/85.

[11] European Council Presidency Conclusions, Laeken (14 and 15 December 2001).

[12] CONV 850/03 Draft Treaty establishing a Constitution for Europe, Brussels (18 July 2003).

[13] TEU, art 5 and TFEU, arts 2–6.

[14] TFEU, arts 3–6.

[15] See eg Czech Ústavní Soud Case Pl. ÚS 19/08 *Lisbon Treaty I* Judgment of 26 November 2008 [133] http://www.usoud.cz/en/decisions/20081126-pl-us-1908-treaty-of-lisbon-i-1/.

[16] Craig (n 1) 327; Mayer (n 2) 10 and F C Mayer, 'The European Constitution and the Courts: Adjudicating European Constitutional Law in a Multilevel System' (2003) Jean Monnet Working Paper 9/03, 69.

[17] The Bundesverfassungsgericht submitted a preliminary reference to the Court of Justice in Case 2 BvR 2728/13 *Gauweiler* Order of 14 January 2014, to determine whether the OMT mechanism is within the competence of the ECB. The response from the Court of Justice came in Case C-62/14 *Gauweiler* [2015] EU:C:2015:400, and was accepted by the German court in Case 2 BvR 2728/13 *Gauweiler* Judgment of 21 June 2016. The second reference from the German court was submitted to concretize the limits to ECB's monetary policy mandate in Cases 2 BvR 859/15, 2 BvR 980/16, 2 BvR 2006/15, 2 BvR 1651/15 *Weiss* Order of 18 July 2017. The Court of Justice confirmed the legality of ECB action in Case C-493/17 *Weiss* [2018] EU:C:2018:1000. However, the German court rejected the reply of the Court of Justice by finding it *ultra vires* in Cases 2 BvR 859/15, 2 BvR 980/16, 2 BvR 2006/15, 2 BvR 1651/15 *Weiss II* Judgment of 5 May 2020. For a further analysis of this interaction see s 6.1 of this chapter.

[18] See s 2 in this chapter.

the Court of Justice and national constitutional adjudicators concerning their ultimate authority, the lack of finality, and heterarchy (the possibility of each of the participants of the European judicial space to be the ultimate arbiter at a certain point in time) is conducive to cooperation and mutual respect between the courts under analysis. It is precisely because winners and losers are not predetermined, and there is a possibility for everyone to prevail at certain times, that all the players remain in the game. That this is a deliberate choice can be seen from the rejection of the Constitutional Treaty, which contained an explicit primacy clause in its Article I-6, which was subsequently excluded from the Lisbon Treaty. Instead, a Declaration on primacy has been added to the Lisbon Treaty:

> The Conference recalls that, in accordance with well settled case law of the Court of Justice of the European Union, the Treaties and the law adopted by the Union on the basis of the Treaties have primacy over the law of Member States, under the conditions laid down by the said case law.[19]

While the role and the authority of the principle of primacy is not diminished by the lack of its express inclusion in the Treaty, it does demonstrate the desire for it to remain on the level of a judicial principle, thus possibly open to differing interpretations in different situations.[20]

In essence, the *ultra vires* conflict reflects the autonomous claims to ultimate authority by the Court of Justice and the parallel replies by national jurisdictions with a constitutional mandate. Accordingly, this chapter aims to determine whether the jurisprudence in this area is supportive of the existence of the auto-correct function of constitutional pluralism as well as its role in constructive and destructive constitutional conflicts. To this end, I will chronologically map the development of *ultra vires* conflicts by first presenting the introduction of the principles of direct effect and primacy of EU law (section 2). This will be followed by the analysis of the explicit assertion on behalf of the Court of Justice to the final say (section 3). I will also present the way in which the Court of Justice has expanded the self-referential system of the Treaties institutionally in respect of judicial independence (section 5) and substantively concerning general principles of EU law (section 5). Section 6 will map the responses to these developments on the national level, by focusing on the claims to *ultra vires* review, the standards of review, and self-imposed safeguards introduced by national constitutional courts. Section 7 will then address recent expansions of the self-referential system of the Treaties in respect of judicial independence and examples of destructive constitutional conflict. The chapter's

[19] Seventeenth Declaration concerning primacy [2008] OJ C115/344.

[20] See G de Búrca, 'Reappraising Subsidiarity's Significance after Amsterdam' (1999) Harvard Jean Monnet Working Paper 7/99 8, where she argues that EU law has more generally evolved through the use of vague and open terms that have deliberately been used to 'mediate between very different understandings and conceptions of the issue under discussion'.. See also Weatherill (n 1) 69.

conclusion will offer some thoughts on the applicability of the theory of constitutional pluralism and its auto-correct function (section 8).

## 2 Introducing Direct Effect and Primacy

In the early days of European integration, the Court of Justice famously stated that the:

> [C]ommunity constitutes a new legal order of international law for the benefit of which the states have limited their sovereign rights, albeit within limited fields, and the subjects of which comprise not only Member States but also their nationals.[21]

In addition to the case law asserting the autonomy, primacy and direct effect of Union law, Article 1 and Article 47 TEU state that the Union is a successor to the European Community and now has legal personality, resulting from the merging of the earlier second and third pillars with the Community. This shift particularly strengthened the position of the Court of Justice as it gained limited jurisdiction in the areas of the Common Foreign and Security Policy[22] and the Area of Freedom, Security and Justice.[23] In what follows, I will analyse the Court's case law in an incremental fashion, starting from the introduction of the principles of direct effect and primacy leading to the autonomy of EU law.

The Court's focus on the autonomy of the EU's legal order comes as a direct response to the understanding of nation states as the exclusive holders of sovereignty.[24] Maduro argues that the Court has taken upon itself the role of ensuring the effectiveness of Union law by underlining its distinctiveness from the public international law realm,[25] whereas Weiler adds that the Court has implied its

[21] Case 26/62 *Van Gend en Loos* (n 5) 12. The same was reiterated by the Court in Case 6/64 *Costa v ENEL* [1964] EU:C:1964:66 593.

[22] According to the Court of Justice: '[a]s regards the provisions of the Treaties that govern the CFSP, the Court of Justice has jurisdiction only to monitor compliance with Article 40 TEU and to review the legality of certain decisions as provided for by the second paragraph of Article 275 TFEU'. Opinion 2/13 [2014] EU:C:2014:2454 [249].

[23] For a more detailed analysis on the legal consequences for the Common Foreign and Security Policy see Opinion 2/13 (n 22) [249]–[257]; D Eisenhut, 'Delimitation of EU-competences under the First and Second Pillar: a view between ECOWAS and the Treaty of Lisbon' (2009) 10 *German Law Journal* 585; as regards the changes concerning the Area of Freedom, Security and Justice see A Hinarejos, 'The Lisbon Treaty Versus Standing Still: A View from the Third Pillar' (2009) 5(1) *European Constitutional Law Review* 99. For a comparison between the two areas see A Engel, 'Delimiting Competences in the EU: CFSP Versus AFSJ Legal Bases' (2015) 21(1) *European Public Law* 47. Finally, for an analysis of the relevant jurisprudence in the former third pillar as regards fundamental rights review see ch 7, s 4.1.

[24] See ch 3, s 1 for a discussion on the legal nature of the EU as a polity and on the resulting claim to ultimate authority by the Court of Justice.

[25] M P Maduro, *We the Court: The European Court of Justice and the European Economic Constitution* (Hart Publishing 1998) 7.

self-perception as a supreme court through the self-referential interpretation of the system of the Treaties.[26] He underlines that the creation of constitutional structural and material doctrines (such as primacy and direct effect) contributed to the creation of EU constitutional law which the Court is legitimized to protect.[27] In support of this view, Lindahl finds that the use of an internal reference point, or the self-referential system of Treaties[28] as Weiler calls it, results in Union law representing an expression of collective self-legislation, meaning the European Union is a sovereign polity within the scope of its objectives.[29]

In order for this new, autonomous and distinct legal order to function properly without attempts at circumvention from the Member States, the Court introduced the principles of direct effect[30] and primacy[31] of EU law. According to Claes, the innovative momentum of introducing the principle of direct effect by the Court of Justice is not in the more general request for direct applicability of a provision with a supranational source, but rather the fact that this appears to be the first time that such a conclusion was reached by a supranational court 'irrespective of domestic preferences as to monism or dualism'.[32] Maduro adds that the Court of Justice, in building its legitimation, did not have to counter claims of democratically legitimate national parliaments, as did national constitutional courts.[33]

In addition to direct effect, the principle of primacy has added another layer to the confidence of the Court of Justice to determine the limits of its own power. Primacy assumes necessary for its existence, but at the same time also legitimizes, the autonomy and independence of the Union legal order.[34] As de Búrca points

[26] Weiler (n 3) 189.

[27] ibid 189–90.

[28] Lenaerts concludes that the Court of Justice has 'a constitutional mandate in a self-referential and, in that sense, autonomous legal order'. K Lenaerts, 'The Court's Outer and Inner Selves: Exploring the External and Internal Legitimacy of the Court of Justice' in M Adams and others (eds), *Judging Europe's Judges: The Legitimacy of the Case Law of the European Court of Justice* (Hart Publishing 2015) 15.

[29] H Lindahl, 'Sovereignty and Representation in the European Union' in N Walker (ed), *Sovereignty in Transition* (Hart Publishing 2003) 107.

[30] ibid. For a useful elaboration see in particular P Pescatore, 'The Doctrine of "Direct Effect": An Infant Disease of Community Law' (2015) 40(2) *European Law Review* 135 (an update from the original article that appeared in (1983) 8 *European Law Review* 155); Claes (n 2) 70–97.

[31] Case 6/64 *Costa v ENEL* (n 21) 594. For an analysis of the role of the principle of primacy in the context of constitutional pluralism see ch 3, s 1.

[32] Claes (n 2) 73. See also H de Waele, 'The Role of the European Court of Justice in the Integration Process: A Contemporary and Normative Assessment' (2010) 6 *Hanse Law Review* 3, 4. A disregard for monism or dualism as legal concepts is advocated by von Bogdandy, who argues they are 'intellectual zombies of another time and should be laid to rest'. See A von Bogdandy, 'Pluralism, Direct Effect, and the Ultimate Say: On the Relationship between International and Domestic Constitutional Law' (2008) 6 *International Journal of Constitutional Law* 397, 400.

[33] Maduro (n 25) 11. In the national setting, this critique is called the counter-majoritarian difficulty, according to which judicial review distorts majoritarian decision-making in democratically elected institutions. See M Tushnet, 'Policy Distortion and Democratic Debilitation: Comparative Illumination of the Countermajoritarian Difficulty' (1995) 94(2) *Michigan Law Review* 245.

[34] Lindahl analysed the Court's circular construction of arguments in *Costa v ENEL* and concluded that: '[in] the same stroke by which supremacy is held to flow from the "special and original nature" of the Treaty, the Treaty acquires a "special and original nature" because the ECJ grants its provisions supremacy over national law'. Lindahl (n 29) 109–10.

out, again taking into account the self-referential nature of the Court's interpretation, primacy of EU law is 'a consequence of the sovereignty of the EC rather than vice versa'.[35]

Discussing the autonomy and independence of the Union's legal order leads us to a more detailed exploration of the consequences for the role and position of the Court of Justice itself. More particularly, although it appears to be widely accepted that Union law is an autonomous and sovereign legal order, does it necessarily follow that the Court of Justice must assume the position of a court akin to a supreme court atop a national judiciary? The autonomy of EU law can in this context be seen as the keystone of the Court's central role in ensuring the uniform interpretation and application of Union law. Interviewees 1, 3, and 5 confirmed this to be the role of the Court, and Interviewee 1 placed a particular emphasis on Article 19(1) TEU as the source of this mandate for the Court of Justice granted by the Member States.[36] The same interviewee concluded that the Court of Justice may be regarded as the EU's court fulfilling the role of a supreme court in the national setting.

Both direct effect and primacy of Union law may lead us to conclude that the Court of Justice is right in claiming the final say concerning the outer limits of EU competence. It can certainly be read as the Court's claim to (a functionally limited) sovereignty in parallel to the claims of constitutional adjudicators. This fact appears rather uncontroversial for Interviewees 1 and 3, and is implied by Interviewee 4.[37] Interviewee 3 stated that the question of *Kompetenz-Kompetenz* has many meanings, and while determining the legislative limits of the EU through Treaty amendments falls to the Member States, the judicial final say is undoubtedly in the hands of the Court of Justice.

During the 1970s and the 1980s, the Court has had the opportunity to further establish itself as the institution designated for and entrusted not only with the uniform interpretation of Union law, but also with determining its validity. In *Internationale Handelsgesellschaft*,[38] the Court was faced with the question of validity of the system of export licences and the deposit attached to them, as a German administrative court considered they are contrary to several fundamental rights protected by the German Basic Law.[39] While the case marked the beginning of a decades-long saga on the status of fundamental rights protection in the European

[35] See de Búrca (n 20) 454. See also Maduro (n 25) 10.

[36] See also the Court's elaboration on the autonomy of EU law and the consequences this has for its position in Opinion 2/13 (n 22) [176], [198]–[199], [246].

[37] Interviewee 4 stated that since the early case law of the Court starting with *Rheinmühlen*, the position of national constitutional and supreme courts in their national judicial structures has irreversibly changed and this is in the view of the Interviewee no longer a controversial issue. See Case 166/73 *Rheinmühlen* [1974] EU:C:1974:3 [4].

[38] Case 11/70 *Internationale Handelsgesellschaft* [1970] EU:C:1970:114.

[39] ibid 1133.

Union,[40] its importance for the focus of the present chapter lies in the Court's re-assertion of its exclusive position to review Union legislation and this solely against the standard of Union law—thus rendering the German constitutional requirements irrelevant for its assessment. On the point of reviewing validity of Union regulations against national constitutional requirements, the Court stated that:

> In fact, the law stemming from the Treaty, an independent source of law, cannot because of its very nature be overridden by rules of national law, however framed, without being deprived of its character as Community law and without the legal basis of the Community itself being called in question.[41]

Simply put, no EU measure's validity could be brought into question due to a contrary national constitutional principle or rule.[42] At this point, the Court faced the possibility of a serious backlash from German courts, as it defied the authority of the German Basic Law during a time when the protection of fundamental rights was beyond the landscape of Union law.[43] Aware nevertheless of the delicate position of primacy of EU law, the Court conceded that:

> However, an examination should be made as to whether or not any analogous guarantee inherent in Community law has been disregarded. In fact, respect for fundamental rights forms an integral part of the general principles of law protected by the Court of Justice. The protection of such rights, whilst inspired by the constitutional traditions common to the Member States, must be ensured within the framework of the structure and objectives of the Community.[44]

The Court broadened the scope of its own self-referential system with general principles which also include the constitutional traditions of Member States, while preserving its own exclusive jurisdiction in this area. It then analysed the regulations in question and found they were appropriate and proportionate, thus not in violation of fundamental rights. This decision of the Court of Justice was ultimately rejected by the German Bundesverfassungsgericht in *Solange I*.[45] Regardless of subsequent developments concerning fundamental rights protection, this judgment marks an

[40] On the relationship between the Court of Justice and national constitutional courts in the area of fundamental rights review see ch 7, and for *Solange* developments more specifically, its s 2.2.

[41] Case 11/70 *Internationale Handelsgesellschaft* (n 38) 1134.

[42] It is the claim of this book that the national identity clause from art 4(2) TEU has changed this unconditional approach initially taken by the Court of Justice. For further analysis see ch 6.

[43] It was not until the mid-1970s that the Court established that fundamental rights are a standard of review of Union action. See Case 4/73 *Nold* [1974] EU:C:1974:51. For a more detailed analysis of this development see ch 7, s 2.2.

[44] Case 11/70 *Internationale Handelsgesellschaft* (n 38) 1134.

[45] German Bundesverfassungsgericht Case 37 BVerfGE 271 *Internationale Handelsgesellschaft (Solange I)* Judgment of 29 May 1974.

important step in limiting national courts' use of national (constitutional) law as a standard of reviewing Union acts.

Doctrines of primacy and direct effect represent the first intrusion of the Court of Justice, and EU law more generally, into the national judicial hierarchy. The relationship of cooperation between the Court of Justice and ordinary national courts is a two-way process, as the latter are now to apply EU law irrespective of possible contrary provisions of their national constitutions.[46] Accordingly, constitutional courts' influence on ordinary national courts was reduced, specifically visible after *Internationale Handelsgesellschaft*. They were still in the position to mandate constitutional interpretation and review, but only to the limit of primacy of EU law. As a result of these relations, the Court of Justice and courts with constitutional jurisdiction are in a relationship of interpretative competition. Initially, thus, the Court of Justice has the advantage.

## 3 An Explicit Assertion to the Final Say by the Court of Justice

More than a decade later, the Court had another opportunity to expand its influence in having the final say, this time in relation to other EU institutions. In *Les Verts*,[47] the Court was faced with an action for annulment of a decision of the Bureau of the European Parliament, which in turn sought, through a broad interpretation of (then) Article 173 of the Treaty, to gain the right to initiate an action for annulment against the Commission and the Council. The Court provided an all-encompassing definition of its role and duties:

> It must first be emphasized in this regard that the European Economic Community is a Community based on the rule of law, inasmuch as neither its Member States nor its institutions can avoid a review of the question whether the measures adopted by them are in conformity with the basic constitutional charter, the Treaty. In particular, in Articles 173 and 184, on the one hand, and in Article 177, on the other, the Treaty established a complete system of legal remedies and procedures designed to permit the Court of Justice to review the legality of measures adopted by the institutions.[48]

[46] The strengthening of ordinary national courts has been subject of extensive scholarship, most prominently addressed by Slaughter and Mattli's empowerment thesis and Alter's inter-court competition thesis. A-M Burley and W Mattli, 'Europe before the Court: A Political Theory of Legal Integration' (1993) 47 *International Organization* 41; and further elaborated in W Mattli and A-M Slaughter, 'Revisiting the European Court of Justice' (1998) 52 *International Organization* 177; K Alter, *Establishing the Supremacy of European Law: The Making of an International Rule of Law in Europe* (OUP 2003).

[47] Case 294/83 *Les Verts* [1986] EU:C:1986:166.

[48] ibid [23].

Regardless of the fact that the provisions cited made no mention of the European Parliament, the Court reviewed the decision in question using a dynamic interpretation of the Treaty, in particular in light of the expanded powers of the European Parliament and the more general spirit and the system of the Treaty.[49]

A year later, in *Foto-Frost*,[50] the Court addressed the relationship between the preliminary reference procedure and its power of judicial review. Drawing upon its conclusions in *Les Verts* about the Treaty's complete system of judicial remedies,[51] the Court found that the preliminary reference procedure, although it does not explicitly determine its exclusive power of declaring an act of the EU invalid, necessarily leads to that conclusion as any other reading of it would be contrary to the coherence of the Treaties.[52]

Read together, *Les Verts* and *Foto-Frost* complete the Union's system of judicial review:[53] privileged applicants[54] are entitled to initiate a direct action before the Court, whereas natural and legal persons are capable of doing so when an act is of a direct and individual concern to them.[55] In addition, the preliminary reference procedure provides another avenue for natural and legal persons as well as national courts questioning the validity of a Union act.[56] Ultimately, it is only through the self-referential system of the Treaties, rooted in the rule of law, that any measure or activity of the Union may be assessed and solely against the standards of EU law. This inherently includes deciding on the outer limits of Union activity in the most general sense of the term.

The Court of Justice did, however, in the same year as *Foto-Frost*, decide that measures of EU law may suffer from defects greater than that of illegality. In *Consorzio Cooperative d'Abruzzo*,[57] the Court differentiated between EU measures that are illegal (to which *Foto-Frost* applies) and those that are non-existent (nullity *ex nunc*) and have accordingly never produced legal effects. In such situations, the

49 ibid [25].

50 Case 314/85 *Foto-Frost* (n 7).

51 ibid [16].

52 ibid [17].

53 See also K Lenaerts, 'The Rule of Law and the Coherence of the Judicial System of the European Union' (2007) 44 *Common Market Law Review* 1625, 1626.

54 According to the current wording of art 263(2) TFEU, these are the Member States, the European Parliament, the Council, and the Commission. TFEU, art 263(3) accords to the Court of Auditors, the European Central Bank, and the Committee of the Regions the right to initiate a direct action for the purpose of protecting their prerogatives.

55 The Treaty of Lisbon omitted the need for individual concern to exist in order to initiate a direct action concerning regulatory acts which do not entail implementing measures (art 263(4) TFEU). This sparked further problems into what exactly regulatory acts entail and the General Court defined them as 'all acts of general application apart from legislative acts' in Case T-18/10 *Inuit Tapiriit Kanatami* [2011] EU:T:2011:419 [56]. On appeal, the Court of Justice confirmed this interpretation in Case C-583/11 P *Inuit Tapiriit Kanatami* [2013] EU:C:2013:625 [61].

56 Case 294/83 *Les Verts* (n 47) [23]; Case 314/85 *Foto-Frost* (n 7) [16]. The special role of the preliminary reference procedure in the system of judicial review of Union acts was confirmed explicitly in eg Case C-50/00 P *UPA* [2002] EU:C:2002:462 [40]; Case C-491/01 *BAT and Imperial Tobacco* [2002] EU:C:2002:741 [39]; Case C-824/18 *AB and Others* [2021] EU:C:2021:153 [90].

57 Case 15/85 *Consorzio Cooperative d'Abruzzo* [1987] EU:C:1987:111.

national court is allowed to declare that the measure in question never produced legal effects in line with the principles of legal certainty and legitimate expectations.[58] The Court of Justice envisaged such an option for measures which 'exhibit particularly serious and manifest effects'.[59] A further elaboration of this exception was given in *Commission v BASF*:

> [Acts] tainted by an irregularity whose gravity is so obvious that it cannot be tolerated by the Community legal order must be treated as having no legal effect, even provisional, that is to say that they must be regarded as legally non-existent. [...]
>
> From the gravity of the consequences attaching to a finding that an act of a Community institution is non-existent it is self-evident that, for reasons of legal certainty, such a finding is reserved for quite extreme situations.[60]

Regardless of the existence of this option, Bast reports that the Court of Justice has not allowed national courts to use it to an extent of any relevance.[61] Such an outcome is unsurprising, as it would otherwise allow national courts to escape their *Foto-Frost* obligation of submitting a preliminary reference when they doubt the validity of an EU act.

But can the Court of Justice ensure that national courts in fact submit preliminary references, in particular when it comes to courts against whose decisions there is no judicial remedy under national law as set out in Article 267(3) TFEU? National courts under analysis in this book are most commonly final instances in the national judicial hierarchy. The Treaties themselves provide no concrete sanction for non-compliance with Article 267(3) TFEU. However, the Court of Justice found in *Köbler* that EU citizens must be able to seek redress in respect of EU law breaches, including when such breaches are done by last instance courts.[62] Yet, infringement proceedings for judicial breaches of EU law, and specifically the failure to refer, have been considered mostly theoretical.[63] In addition, a number

58 ibid [9]–[10].

59 ibid [10].

60 Case C-137/92 P *Commission v BASF* [1994] EU:C:1994:247 [49]–[50]. Confirmed in Case C-245/92 P *Chemie Linz* [1999] EU:C:1999:363 [93]; Case C-475/01 *Commission v Greece* [2004] EU:C:2004:585 [18]–[20].

61 J Bast, 'Don't Act Beyond Your Powers: The Perils and Pitfalls of the German Constitutional Court's *Ultra Vires* Review' (2014) 15(2) *German Law Journal* 167, 171–72. Beyond its use in EU law, Bast suggests another more significant point: the formula used by the Court of Justice seems to have inspired the Bundesverfassungsgericht in defining its own *ultra vires* standard of review in its *Honeywell* decision. See s 6.1 below for the analysis of the German standard.

62 Case C-224/01 *Köbler* [2003] EU:C:2003:513 [36]. See also Case C-173/03 *Traghetti del Mediterraneo* [2006] EU:C:2006:391 [31].

63 M Broberg, 'National Courts of Last Instance Failing to Make a Preliminary Reference: The (Possible) Consequences Flowing Therefrom' (2016) 22(2) *European Public Law* 243, 251.

of Member States' constitutional courts consider the obligation of lower courts to refer as a constitutional requirement of a lawful judge.[64]

This changed in 2018, when the Court for the first time[65] decided that a national court (the French Conseil d'État) breached its obligation under Article 267(3) TFEU for failing to submit a preliminary reference while wrongly applying EU law to the case before it.[66] Advocate General Wathelet specifically addressed the obligation to submit a second preliminary reference should the referring court still have doubts as to the correct interpretation of EU law, finding it is included in Article 267(3) TFEU.[67] However, the Court of Justice entirely omitted this question and treated the situation as one of a total absence of a preliminary reference, concluding it amounts to a breach of Article 267(3) TFEU.[68]

This decision has important consequences for the power relations between the courts under analysis, as it formalizes the obligation[69] of national supreme and constitutional courts to always resort to the preliminary reference procedure when EU law is concerned. This formal obligation disregards the possibility that both levels of judiciary participate in the interpretation of the common content of the EU constitution broadly understood, and reinforces an attempt at instituting a clear hierarchy among the courts involved. Presently, a preliminary reference is pending[70] before the Court of Justice to address explicitly whether there is a need to submit a second reference when a court against whose decisions there is no judicial remedy arguably does not properly apply the interpretation provided by the Court of Justice. An optimistic expectation is, alongside the finding that such an obligation indeed exists,[71] that the Court of Justice will also see this as a signal that references from national courts need to be answered in a clearer way and without a significant reformulation of their questions.[72]

[64] Austria, Czech Republic, Germany, Slovakia, Slovenia. ibid 253.

[65] Opinion of Advocate General Wathelet in Case C-416/17 *Commission v France* [2018] EU:C:2018:626 [87].

[66] Case C-416/17 *Commission v France* [2018] EU:C:2018:811.

[67] Opinion of Advocate General Wathelet in Case C-416/17 *Commission v France* (n 65) [93].

[68] Case C-416/17 *Commission v France* (n 66) [112].

[69] A Turmo, 'A Dialogue of Unequals: The European Court of Justice Reasserts National Courts' Obligations under Article 267(3) TFEU' (2019) 15 *European Constitutional Law Review* 340, 348.

[70] Case C-261/21 *F Hoffmann-La Roche Ltd and Others* (reference from the Italian Consiglio di Stato, the supreme administrative court).

[71] All the case law analysed serves as a strong indication that this will be the reply of the Court of Justice.

[72] On this point see s 6.3 below and in particular n 225.

## 4 Expanding the Self-referential System of the Treaties to External Action

The expansions of the EU's constitutional frame described in the previous section were directed primarily to Member States and their courts. In further developments, the Court has expanded the scope of the EU's constitution in its jurisprudence concerning external action of the EU. In 1991, the Court was asked by the Commission to assess the compatibility of the EEA Agreement with the Treaty provisions on its judicial structure.[73] The Court first explained the difference between the (then) EEC Treaty and the EEA Agreement:

> In contrast, the EEC Treaty, albeit concluded in the form of an international agreement, none the less constitutes the constitutional charter of a Community based on the rule of law. As the Court of Justice has consistently held, the Community treaties established a new legal order for the benefit of which the States have limited their sovereign rights, in ever wider fields, and the subjects of which comprise not only Member States but also their nationals.[74]

The cited paragraph provides interesting insight into how the Court regards the EU as opposed to organizations in the context of public international law. The Court finds primacy and direct effect to have resulted in constitutionalizing the Treaties, based on the rule of law. The Court's move is an HLA Hart-esque one,[75] as it places the rule of law as the ultimate rule of recognition in the EU constitution. This in turn legitimizes the system as a constitutional one and differentiates it from the EEA as an international law one.[76] Ultimately, the Court found that due to the specific nature of the EU as a polity, but also its own powers stemming from the self-referential system of the Treaties, an EEA Court as determined in the EEA Agreement would not be able to achieve legal homogeneity[77] and would undermine the autonomy of Union law.[78]

The Court's rejection did not result in the abandonment of the EEA in itself, as the Member States and the EFTA States subsequently devised a parallel judicial structure (the EFTA Court for EFTA States), whereby the EEA Joint Committee handles disputes between these two pillars.[79] Thus, while it was open to the Member States completely to abandon and amend the system in which the Court

[73] Opinion 1/91 [1991] EU:C:1991:490.
[74] ibid [21].
[75] See H L A Hart, *The Concept of Law* (2nd edn, OUP 1994) 92.
[76] Opinion 1/91 (n 73) [20].
[77] ibid [25]–[29].
[78] ibid [46].
[79] For further background see S Norberg, '20 Years On: Some Reflections on the European Economic Area Judicial Mechanism' in P Cardonnel, A Rosas, and N Wahl (eds), *Constitutionalising the EU Judicial System: Essays in Honour of Pernilla Lindh* (Hart Publishing 2012) 61 ff.

of Justice is powerful enough to reject an international treaty,[80] the opinion of the Court was respected and a different solution was found which respects the Court's Treaty-based, but also self-proclaimed powers.

The constitutional language of the Court of Justice was most recently consolidated in the context of state–investor arbitrations and the possibility of the United Kingdom to withdraw its notification of departure from the EU. Concerning the first, in *Achmea*[81] the Court found that such arbitration is a breach of EU law as it would allow an arbitral tribunal to address matters of EU law.[82] This is problematic precisely because:

> [t]he autonomy of EU law with respect both to the law of the Member States and to international law is justified by the essential characteristics of the EU and its law, relating in particular to the constitutional structure of the EU and the very nature of that law. EU law is characterised by the fact that it stems from an independent source of law, the Treaties, by its primacy over the laws of the Member States, and by the direct effect of a whole series of provisions which are applicable to their nationals and to the Member States themselves. Those characteristics have given rise to a structured network of principles, rules and mutually interdependent legal relations binding the EU and its Member States reciprocally and binding its Member States to each other.[83]

While the Court grounded this statement in 'settled case law', it only by analogy refers to Opinion 2/13 concerning ECHR accession.[84] Placing itself at the centre of ensuring these essential characteristics, the Court underlined that the autonomy of EU law as well as its consistency and uniformity is achieved through the judicial system of cooperation between the EU and national judiciary, specifically through the preliminary reference procedure.[85] When faced with the interpretation of

[80] While this is certainly politically true, legally the Court has, starting with its Opinion concerning the Uruguay round of negotiations, drawn red lines that Member States would not be able to cross when concluding international treaties without 'rise to adverse consequences for all interested parties, including third countries'. See Opinion 3/94 [1995] EU:C:1995:436 [17]; Opinion 1/09 [2011] EU:C:2011:123 [48]; Opinion 2/13 (n 22) [146]. The Court stated in 1971 that 'each time the Community [ … ] adopts provisions laying down common rules [ … ] the Member States no longer have the right [ … ] to undertake obligations with third countries which affect those rules'. Case 22/70 *Commission v Council* [1971] EU:C:1971:32 [17]. In relation to different types of EU competences, the Court held that the: 'duty of genuine cooperation is of general application and does not depend either on whether the Community competence concerned is exclusive or on any right of the Member States to enter into obligations towards non-member countries'. Case C-433/03 *Commission v Germany* [2005] EU:C:2005:462 [64]. For a comprehensive overview of how EU law affects Member States competences in the international sphere see A Arena, 'Exercise of EU Competences and Pre-emption of Member States' Powers in the Internal and the External Sphere: Towards "Grand Unification"?' (2016) 35(1) *Yearbook of European Law* 28, 64–98.

[81] Case C-284/16 *Achmea* [2018] EU:C:2018:158.

[82] ibid [42].

[83] ibid [33].

[84] For the analysis of the Opinion see ch 7, s 3.3.

[85] Case C-284/16 *Achmea* (n 81) [35]–[37]. See also C-362/14 *Schrems* [2015] EU:C:2015:650 [60].

Article 50 TEU and the right of the UK unilaterally to withdraw its notification of departure, the Court referred to *Achmea* to reiterate the autonomy of EU law formula grounded in its special constitutional characteristics.[86]

## 5 Substantive Expansions of the Self-referential System of the Treaties

The expansion of the Court's influence, beyond curbing access to other potential judicial bodies, also took place in relation to the expansion of the general principles of law and their application. In *Mangold*,[87] the Court expanded the application of the general principle of non-discrimination on grounds of age to horizontal situations. The case concerned the application of the Framework Directive,[88] the aim of which was to establish a general anti-discrimination framework, to a contractual relationship between the parties in the procedure prior to the expiry of the Directive's transposition deadline. The Court was thus faced with a national provision which was apparently detrimental for workers of an older age and thus contrary to the Directive, but was not able to apply it before the transposition deadline had expired. The Court instead 'regarded'[89] the prohibition of discrimination on the grounds of age as a general principle of EU law,[90] which must be applied whenever a national rule is within the scope of EU law.[91] The Court stated that the principle of non-discrimination on grounds of age can be found in various international instruments and common constitutional traditions of Member States.[92] In consequence, the general principle of prohibition of discrimination on grounds of age has acquired horizontal effect.[93] However, de Mol rightly points out that

[86] Case C-621/18 *Wightman* [2018] EU:C:2018:999 [45].

[87] Case C-144/04 *Mangold* [2005] EU:C:2005:709.

[88] Council Directive 2000/78/EC of 27 November 2000 establishing a general framework for equal treatment in employment and occupation [2000] OJ L303/16.

[89] Case C-144/04 *Mangold* (n 87) [75]. Mazák and Moser provide a nice comparison to the Court's 'recognition' of this pre-existing general principle, as opposed to its establishment: Michelangelo's alleged explanation of the statue of David was that he was not created from stone, but rather, Michelangelo saw him in it and removed the unnecessary parts of the stone for David to emerge in his full beauty. J Mazák and M K Moser, 'Adjudication by Reference to General Principles of EU Law: A Second Look at the *Mangold* Case Law' in M Adams and others (eds), *Judging Europe's Judges: The Legitimacy of the Case Law of the European Court of Justice* (Hart Publishing 2015) 61.

[90] Case C-144/04 *Mangold* (n 87) [75].

[91] ibid. On the contrary, when a situation is found to be outside the scope of EU law, general principles do not apply. See Case C-427/06 *Bartsch* [2008] EU:C:2008:517 [15]–[16]. It should be noted that the Court does not make any mention of the horizontality of the situation either in *Mangold* or in *Bartsch*.

[92] Case C-144/04 *Mangold* (n 87) [74]. For a direct critique of this point see Opinion of Advocate General Mazák in Case C-411/05 *Palacios de la Villa* [2007] EU:C:2007:106 [88] (indicating only a few Member States had an explicit reference to the principle); Opinion of Advocate General Bot in Case C-555/07 *Kücükdeveci* [2009] EU:C:2009:429 [77].

[93] See on that point Opinion of Advocate General Sharpston in Case C-427/06 *Bartsch* [2008] EU:C:2008:297 [35]. See also M de Mol, '*Kücükdeveci*: *Mangold* Revisited: Horizontal Direct Effect of a General Principle of EU Law' (2010) 6 *European Constitutional Law Review* 293, 302 ff; A Eriksson,

international instruments and national constitutional traditions usually do not accord horizontal effect to the values to which they give expression.[94] Nevertheless, the Court used this reasoning to expand the reach of the general principle of non-discrimination on grounds of age, resulting in an expansion of the self-referential system of primary EU law.

This line of reasoning was further explored in *Kücükdeveci*,[95] where the material difference was the expiry of the transposition period of the Framework Directive and the Charter's entry into force, whose Article 21(1) prohibits discrimination on grounds of age. The reference concerned the provision of the German Civil Code according to which periods of employment before the age of 25 do not count towards the statutory notice period for dismissal. The Court used *Mangold* as a reference that the prohibition of discrimination on grounds of age is a general principle of EU law,[96] which was given specific expression in the Framework Directive. The Court distinguished the situation in *Kücükdeveci* from that of *Bartsch* solely on the basis of the expiry of the implementation deadline,[97] which is central for the Court to place a situation within the scope of Union law:

> On that date, that directive had the effect of bringing within the scope of European Union law the national legislation at issue in the main proceedings, which concerns a matter governed by that directive, in this case the conditions of dismissal.[98]

Subsequently, the Court found that since the Directive's implementation period had passed, which gives a specific expression to the general principle of non-discrimination on the grounds of age, this had the effect of rendering the latter as

'European Court of Justice: Broadening the Scope of European Nondiscrimination Law' (2009) 7(4) *International Journal of Constitutional Law* 731, 736.

[94] de Mol (n 93) 302.

[95] Case C-555/07 *Kücükdeveci* [2010] EU:C:2010:21. Prior to this case, the Court was faced with similar questions concerning the Framework Directive and the status of the non-discrimination on grounds of age, but made no mention of the novelties from *Mangold*. See Case C-411/05 *Palacios de la Villa* [2007] EU:C:2007:604, Case C-427/06 *Bartsch* (n 91), Case C-88/08 *Hütter* [2009] EU:C:2009:381, Case C-388/07 *Age Concern England* [2009] EU:C:2009:128, Case C-229/08 *Wolf* [2010] EU:C:2010:3, and Case C-341/08 *Petersen* [2010] EU:C:2010:4.

[96] Case C-555/07 *Kücükdeveci* (n 95) [21], [50]. Note here how the Court again creates the point of reference (in *Mangold*) and then addresses subsequent cases based on its own self-referential system, as discussed above. Conversely, Advocate General Bot stated that he was of the opinion that the only legal basis for the case is the Directive, because an autonomous position of the general principle of prohibition of discrimination on grounds of age would 'deprive the Directive 2000/78 of all useful effect'. See Opinion of Advocate General Bot in Case C-555/07 *Kücükdeveci* (n 92) [34].

[97] Case C-555/07 *Kücükdeveci* (n 95) [24]. For a critique concerning the inconsistency of this finding with that set out in *Bartsch* see Editorial Comment, 'The Scope of Application of General Principles of Union Law: An Ever Expanding Union?' (2010) 47 *Common Market Law Review* 1589, 1593.

[98] Case C-555/07 *Kücükdeveci* (n 95) [25]. The Court did not explain the difference between *Mangold* and *Bartsch* or why the expiry period was not a decisive factor in *Mangold*.

the basis of review.[99] The Court proceeded with the analysis of the national measure and found it contrary to the principle of non-discrimination on grounds of age.[100] It remained unclear, however, whether the Court is of the view that all general principles of EU law have horizontal direct effect, or whether the case was relevant solely to non-discrimination on the grounds of age.[101] While the Court also established horizontal direct effect of non-discrimination on the grounds of nationality,[102] further cases made it clear that the doctrine in *Mangold* and *Kücükdeveci* applies solely to age discrimination.[103]

The reasoning in *Kücükdeveci* raised more questions than it answered.[104] A particularly pressing one was whether the provisions of the Framework Directive or the principle of non-discrimination on the grounds of age require the national court to disapply, in a horizontal situation, a contrary national provision for which there is no possible interpretation in conformity with EU law. This question was referred to the Court by the Danish Supreme Court (*Højsteret*) in the *Dansk Industri* case.[105] The *Højsteret* also asked whether the general principle of prohibition of discrimination on grounds of age could be balanced against the principles of legitimate expectations and legal certainty.

The Court started answering the question by highlighting that it was faced with a horizontal situation,[106] and reiterated that non-discrimination on grounds of age is a general principle of EU law, as established in *Mangold* and *Kücükdeveci*.[107] The self-referential system established in *Mangold* has been reaffirmed and qualified by the Charter in *Kücükdeveci*, and this qualified form was now used in *Dansk Industri*. Ultimately, the Court further expanded the application of the general principle to horizontal situations, stating that for such a result to occur, it is also necessary for the situation to fall within the scope of the Framework Directive (which the Court found that it did).[108] The Court concluded:

> [t]he general principle prohibiting discrimination on grounds of age, as given concrete expression by Directive 2000/78, must be interpreted as precluding,

[99] ibid [27].
[100] ibid [43].
[101] P P Craig and G de Búrca, *EU Law: Text, Cases and Materials* (6th edn, OUP 2015) 220–21; de Mol (n 93) 302–303; M de Mol, 'The Novel Approach of the CJEU on the Horizontal Direct Effect of the EU Principle of Non-discrimination: (Unbridled) Expansionism of EU Law?' (2011) 18 (1–2) *Maastricht Journal of European and Comparative Law* 109.
[102] Case C-115/08 *ČEZ* [2009] EU:C:2009:660 [139].
[103] Case C-147/08 *Römer* EU:C:2011:286 [61]–[62]; Editorial Comment (n 97) 1596; Mazák and Moser (n 89) 84–85.
[104] Significantly, Interviewee 1 stated that *Kücükdeveci* was a rather controversial decision.
[105] Case C-441/14 *Dansk Industri* [2016] EU:C:2016:278. The Court has already found the Danish provision incompatible with the Directive in Case C-499/08 *Ingeniørforeningen i Danmark* [2010] EU:C:2010:600 where the relationship between the parties was a vertical one.
[106] Case C-441/14 *Dansk Industri* (n 105) [21].
[107] ibid [22].
[108] ibid [24].

including in disputes between private persons, national legislation, such as that at issue in the proceedings before the referring court.[109]

In conclusion, the development of the three cases is a perfect depiction of the dynamic approach that the Court takes in expanding the self-referential system of the Treaties, which results in cementing its position as the ultimate arbiter.[110] From 2005 (*Mangold*) until 2016 (*Dansk Industri*), the landscape of the law on the general principle of non-discrimination on grounds of age has changed considerably and yielded an increase in the scope of influence of the Court. As a result, the general principle of non-discrimination on grounds of age has been granted 'exclusionary effect'.[111]

The expansion of the self-referential system of primary EU law was further strengthened through the expansion of the authority of general principles of EU law in areas of exclusive Member State competence. This entire process started in a case concerning the cross-border provision of health services in *Smits and Peerbooms*,[112] where the Court stated that while Member States are free to regulate their social security systems, they are still bound by Union law.[113] The Court provided no further detail on what this obligation entails and how it affects the regulatory autonomy of Member States. The situation was clarified in cases such as *Watts*[114] and *Stamatelaki*,[115] where the Court explicitly referred to the freedom to provide services as the benchmark against which Member States are not allowed to legislate.

Giving exclusionary effect to written Treaty provisions has long been the approach of the Court;[116] however, this starting position was used to expand the exclusionary effect to non-written general principles.[117] Mr Maruko claimed the right to a widower's pension of his deceased (same-sex) life partner, but was refused on the ground that such an entitlement exists only for spouses and not life partners.[118] This time, the Court was faced with a discriminatory practice in the area of social security, an exclusive competence of Member States. The Court brought the case within the scope of EU law by concluding that the survivor's pension falls within

[109] ibid [27].

[110] The Højsteret rejected the interpretation put forward by the Court as *ultra vires*. For an analysis see s 6.3 of this chapter.

[111] S Rodin, 'Back to Square One: The Past, the Present and the Future of the *Simmenthal* Mandate' in J M Beneyto and I Pernice (eds), *Europe's Constitutional Challenges in the Light of the Recent Case Law of National Constitutional Courts: Lisbon and Beyond* (Nomos 2011) 298, 312.

[112] Case C-157/99 *Smits and Peerbooms* [2001] EU:C:2001:404.

[113] ibid [44]–[46].

[114] Case C-372/04 *Watts* [2006] EU:C:2006:325 [92].

[115] Case C-444/05 *Stamatelaki* [2007] EU:C:2007:231 [23].

[116] See de Mol (n 93) 306.

[117] For a further analysis of the argument that the Court is following an expansive trend see M Cartabia, 'Europe and Rights: Taking Dialogue Seriously' (2009) 5 *European Constitutional Law Review* 5, 11.

[118] Case C-267/06 *Maruko* [2008] EU:C:2008:179 [19]–[22].

the scope of term 'pay' enshrined in Article 141 EC,[119] thus bringing it within the scope of the Framework Directive.[120] The Court continued:

> Admittedly, civil status and the benefits flowing therefrom are matters which fall within the competence of the Member States and Community law does not detract from that competence. However, it must be recalled that in the exercise of that competence the Member States must comply with Community law and, in particular, with the provisions relating to the principle of non-discrimination (see, by analogy, Case C-372/04 Watts [2006] ECR I-4325, paragraph 92, and Case C-444/05 Stamatelaki [2007] ECR I-3185, paragraph 23).[121]

This paragraph is significant in terms of expanding the application of the general principle of non-discrimination as a general obligation for Member States, even when they regulate areas that are within their exclusive competence.[122] The Court cited the cases concerning the cross-border provision of health services where the paragraphs refer to the freedom to provide services as a restriction of Member States regulatory competence. The novelty in *Maruko* is that the Court introduces the principle of non-discrimination, which does not have a written expression in the Treaties, as a limit to Member State regulatory competence.[123] Tobler and Waaldijk do not find this development controversial and list a number of areas where the Court has already mentioned a limit to Member States' regulatory autonomy.[124] They fail, however, to mention the specificity of the benchmark (a non-written general principle) and the novel exclusionary effect of the general principle of non-discrimination.

Furthermore, the Court does not specify grounds of non-discrimination that are capable of limiting Member States' freedom to regulate in areas of their exclusive competence. It also remains unclear whether the principle hinders national regulatory autonomy solely in vertical situations or also produces effects among private parties. The Court has therefore positioned itself as the ultimate arbiter not only in matters of EU law, but also as regards Member States' exclusive competence.

[119] Now art 157 TFEU.

[120] Case C-267/06 *Maruko* (n 118) [56].

[121] ibid [59].

[122] Such an expansion of Union law obligations is often termed as 'competence creep'. In relation to the exclusive Member State competence in particular, Weatherill cites Lenaerts: 'there simply is no nucleus of sovereignty that the Member States can invoke, as such, against Union law'. K Lenaerts, 'Constitutionalism and the Many Faces of Federalism' (1990) 38(2) *American Journal of Comparative Law* 205 in S Weatherill, *Law and Values in the European Union* (OUP 2016) 30. See also S Weatherill, 'Competence Creep and Competence Control' (2004) 23(1) *Yearbook of European Law* 1.

[123] On how different areas of Member States' exclusive competence were hindered by Treaty provisions on free movement see Weatherill (n 1) 45–51.

[124] C Tobler and K Waaldijk, 'Case C-267/06, *Tadao Maruko v. Versorgungsanstalt der deutschen Bühnen*, Judgment of the Grand Chamber of the Court of Justice of 1 April 2008, Not Yet Reported' (2009) 46 *Common Market Law Review* 723, 734.

Despite the expansions of its jurisdiction beyond the letter of the Treaties, the Court of Justice has not been particularly active or rigorous in policing the EU institutions' use of conferred competences. The well-known *Tobacco Advertising I*[125] decision is still a lonely example of an EU act of general application that has been annulled due to an excess in the use of conferred competences.[126] In brief, Germany, after being outvoted in the Council, argued that the EU had no competence to regulate the advertising of tobacco, as it is a measure of public health, where the EU has no harmonizing competence. The Court of Justice analysed the aims of the directive, and found that:

> [A] measure adopted on the basis of Article 100a of the Treaty must genuinely have as its object the improvement of the conditions for the establishment and functioning of the internal market. If a mere finding of disparities between national rules and of the abstract risk of obstacles to the exercise of fundamental freedoms or of distortions of competition liable to result therefrom were sufficient to justify the choice of Article 100a as a legal basis, judicial review of compliance with the proper legal basis might be rendered nugatory.[127]

The Commission therefore cannot use the most convenient legal basis and distort the principle of conferral. In assessing the scope of the Directive, the Court of Justice differentiated between various types of advertising and found that they only in part exceed the regulation of disparities among Member States.[128] The Court of Justice thus annulled the Directive in its entirety. It later became clear that the Court of Justice will not take up a more active role in policing EU legislative action. As Weatherill points out, since the annulment of the Directive, the decision turned into a circular drafting guide for the Commission to satisfy the requirements of conferral,[129] resulting in a high benchmark for finding a violation

[125] Case C-376/98 *Germany v Parliament and Council* [2000] EU:C:2000:544.

[126] In ch 7, s 4.2. I analyse the annulment of the Data Retention Directive due to its breach of fundamental rights. In respect of the same Directive, the Court of Justice previously decided, cross-referring to the decision in *Tobacco Advertising*, that the EU has not exceeded its competence to regulate the internal market given that it addressed disparities between national rules, regardless of the Directive's second aim to fight serious crime. See Case C-301/06 *Ireland v Parliament and Council* [2009] EU:C:2009:68 [63]. On the discussion on the Court's omission to address the relationship between the two objectives of the Directive see O Lynskey, 'The Data Retention Directive Is Incompatible with the Rights to Privacy and Data Protection and Is Invalid in its Entirety: *Digital Rights Ireland*' (2014) 51 *Common Market Law Review* 1789, 1802.

[127] Case C-376/98 *Germany v Parliament and Council* (n 125) [84].

[128] ibid [99]. Usher equates this formula with 'selling arrangements' from *Keck*, which also lack influence upon trade between Member States. J Usher, 'Case C-376/98, Germany v. European Parliament and Council (tobacco advertising). Judgment of the Full Court of 5 October 2000, [2000] ECR I-8419' (2001) 38(6) *Common Market Law Review* 1519, 1525. See Joined Cases C-267/91 and C-268/91 *Keck* [1993] EU:C:1993:905.

[129] S Weatherill, 'The Limits of Legislative Harmonization Ten Years after Tobacco Advertising: How the Court's Case Law Has Become a "Drafting Guide"' (2011) 12(3) *German Law Journal* 827, 828.

thereof.[130] Subsequent cases have confirmed this scepticism[131] and leave considerable doubt as to the Court of Justice's willingness to keep the EU legislative institutions in check.

The Court of Justice thus again has the advantage. Ordinary national courts are bound to apply the general principle of non-discrimination on grounds of age in horizontal situations that are in the scope of EU law (per *Mangold* and *Dansk Industri*). Without referring to a specific ground of discrimination, the general principle of non-discrimination furthermore applies in areas of exclusive Member State competence (per *Maruko*). Consequently, the influence of EU law is expanded in the everyday work of ordinary national courts. Accordingly, the role of constitutional adjudicators has been additionally marginalized, in particular given that general principles predominantly correspond to fundamental rights, where constitutional adjudicators were an undisputed authority. Finally, the leverage of the Court of Justice vis-à-vis constitutional adjudicators is increased, as countervailing constitutional principles are rarely taken into account by the Court of Justice (per *Dansk Industri*). This imbalance was at least part of the reason national courts with constitutional jurisdiction have insisted on maintaining their right to *ultra vires* review, as will be seen in the following section.

## 6 Claims to *Ultra Vires* Review of EU Action

Constitutional pluralism presupposes the existence of parallel claims to ultimate authority in the same geographical space. Accordingly, Member States' courts performing constitutional review have had a variety of reactions to the penetration of the new autonomous legal order into their respective constitutional orders,[132] including that of rejecting the Court of Justice's claim to the final say. The aim of this section is to explore specifically: (1) the different limits that national constitutional adjudicators have placed upon the principle of primacy in relation to the final say; and (2) the possible scenarios they envisage in the event that a constitutional conflict takes place. The analysis will aim to show that, regardless of the controversy surrounding the question of the final say, the auto-correct function of constitutional pluralism serves to mediate any constructive conflict that might arise as a result.

[130] Weatherill (n 1) 38. After the Directive was amended to include the Court's recommendations, Germany failed in its attempt to annul it. Case C-380/03 *Germany v Parliament and Council* [2006] EU:C:2006:772.

[131] Weatherill (n 129) 834–42.

[132] Mancini referred to them as 'some grumblings by the French *Conseil d'État*, the Italian *Corte Costituzionale* and a couple of English law lords'. F Mancini, 'The Making of a Constitution for Europe' (1989) 26(4) *Common Market Law Review* 595, 600.

## 6.1 Germany

The position of the Bundesverfassungsgericht[133] in the German constitutional set-up is in some ways analogous to the constitution-making activities of the Court of Justice.[134] The jurisprudence of the Bundesverfassungsgericht has been central not only to matters of European integration, but for the preponderance of major political issues in Germany.[135] With its progressive interpretations of individual rights, the law-making activities of the Bundesverfassungsgericht moved significantly beyond its original mandate.[136] The dominant position of the Bundesverfassungsgericht among the three branches of government has sparked criticism, mainly associated with the counter-majoritarian difficulty,[137] but according to Huber, this did little to change the practice of the German court.[138]

This exceptionally strong domestic position was translated into the Bundesverfassungsgericht becoming one of the most influential courts in the European Union, widely cited among other constitutional courts in Europe.[139] It therefore comes as little surprise that it was the Bundesverfassungsgericht that first introduced the *ultra vires* review of EU acts, after which other constitutional courts in the EU followed suit. In what follows, I will chronologically present the case law of the Bundesverfassungsgericht establishing its claim to the final say in competence monitoring, ending with the *ultra vires* finding in the *Weiss II* decision from May 2020.

The notion of sovereignty has been central to the German constitutional thought[140] and has been at the forefront of the constitutional challenge to the German ratification of the Maastricht Treaty.[141] The Bundesverfassungsgericht

133 A more thorough analysis of the Bundesverfassungsgericht goes beyond the scope of this chapter. The literature on the topic is vast. For a recent and thorough presentation see M Hailbronner, *Traditions and Transformations: The Rise of German Constitutionalism* (OUP 2015). For a comprehensive analysis of the Bundesverfassungsgericht's case law see D P Kommers and R A Miller, *The Constitutional Jurisprudence of the Federal Republic of Germany* (3rd edn, Duke University Press 2012).

134 A-M Burley and W Mattli, 'Europe before the Court: A Political Theory of Legal Integration' (1993) 47 *International Organization* 41, 42; K Alter, *Establishing the Supremacy of European Law: The Making of an International Rule of Law in Europe* (OUP 2001) 2–3; Lenaerts (n 28) 15.

135 P M Huber, 'The Federal Constitutional Court and European Integration' (2015) 21(1) *European Public Law* 83, 83; D P Kommers, 'The Federal Constitutional Court in the German Political System' (1994) 26(4) *Comparative Political Studies* 470, 470–71.

136 Huber (n 135) 85. See also C Joerges, 'Pereat Iustitia, Fiat Mundus: What Is Left of the European Economic Constitution after the *Gauweiler* Litigation?' (2016) 23(1) *Maastricht Journal of European and Comparative Law* 99, 101.

137 See n 33.

138 Huber (n 135) 85.

139 General Report: Conference of European Constitutional Courts (2014) 9; G Anagnostaras, 'Activation of the *Ultra Vires* Review: The *Slovak Pensions* Judgment of the Czech Constitutional Court' (2013) 14(7) *German Law Journal* 959, 959.

140 For an analysis of its development in the post-war Germany see M Aziz, 'Sovereignty *Über Alles*: (Re)configuring the German Legal Order' in N Walker (ed), *Sovereignty in Transition* (Hart Publishing 2003).

141 German Bundesverfassungsgericht *Maastricht Treaty* (n 9). For a fierce critique of the judgment see J H H Weiler, 'Does Europe Need a Constitution? Demos, Telos and the German Maastricht Decision' (1995) 1(3) *European Law Journal* 219. For a comparison to the Italian 'lack of worry' for

has found itself torn between the exigencies of sovereignty and the requirements stemming from autonomy of EU law, most importantly its principle of primacy. Accordingly, sovereignty has been forcefully reasserted and relied upon by the Bundesverfassungsgericht when it introduced its claim to perform *ultra vires* review of EU primary law.[142] The decision was consequentially characterized as marking the beginning of constitutional pluralism,[143] as the Bundesverfassungsgericht countered the Court of Justice's claim to the final say with its own. In addition, this was the first time that the German court allowed a constitutional complaint against an EU act, directly contradicting the decisions of the Court of Justice in *Les Verts* and *Foto-Frost*.[144] This created a space of co-existing claims to the ultimate authority of competence monitoring.[145]

The litigation concerning the constitutionality of the Maastricht Treaty revolved around two issues:[146] (1) its compatibility with the right to democratically legitimate representation enshrined in Article 38 of the German Basic Law;[147] and (2) its effect on the German statehood.[148] The Bundesverfassungsgericht turned its focus to the democratic legitimation of EU institutions based on the Maastricht Treaty. The starting premise bodes well with an understanding of EU's legitimacy as qualitatively different from that of Member States: 'democratic legitimation for these purposes cannot be produced in the same way as it is within a national order governed uniformly and conclusively by a state constitution'.[149] For the Bundesverfassungsgericht, genuine devotion to the integration project requires the acceptance of the majority principle. Such adherence is further positively and negatively qualified:

national sovereignty when compared to Germany see M Cartabia, 'The Legacy of Sovereignty in Italian Constitutional Debate' in N Walker (ed), *Sovereignty in Transition* (Hart Publishing 2003) 319 ff.

142 Aziz significantly calls the Bundesverfassungsgericht's case law on the ultimate say 'sovereignty jurisprudence'. Aziz (n 140) 293.

143 Most notably in the seminal piece by N MacCormick, 'The Maastricht-Urteil: Sovereignty Now' (1995) 1(3) *European Law Journal* 259.

144 J Kokott, 'Report on Germany' in A-M Slaughter, A Stone Sweet, and J H H Weiler (eds), *The European Court and National Courts, Doctrine and Jurisprudence: Legal Change in its Social Context* (Hart Publishing 1998) 81.

145 However, as will be explained in ch 7, s 2.2, the argument in this book is that multiple claims to ultimate authority in the European judicial space started as early as the *Frontini* and *Solange I* decisions of the Italian Corte Costituzionale and the German Bundesverfassungsgericht, respectively. I am especially grateful to Richard O. Melanzana for a challenging and illuminating conversation concerning the German and Italian jurisprudence in this context.

146 Complaints regarding the protection of fundamental rights were rejected as inadmissible in line with the *Solange II* doctrine. German Bundesverfassungsgericht case *Maastricht Treaty* (n 9) [B.2.b]. See also Kommers and Miller, *The Constitutional Jurisprudence of the Federal Republic of Germany* (n 133) 335.

147 German Bundesverfassungsgericht Case *Maastricht Treaty* (n 9) [A.II.1.a].

148 ibid [A.II.1.b] and [A.II.2.a].

149 ibid.

> In any event the majority principle, in accordance with the requirement of mutual consideration entailed by loyalty to the community, finds its limits in the constitutional principles and basic interests of the member-States.[150]

The Court thus managed to reconcile the requirements of the democratic principle enshrined in the German constitution with its participation in the European project. It further analysed the notion of *demos* and its centrality to the creation of a state, concluding that there is no such thing as a European nation,[151] which might be the basis of creation of a 'United States of Europe, in a way comparable to the United States of America'.[152] Yet, despite its state-centred reasoning,[153] the Bundesverfassungsgericht found that establishing the European Union necessarily entails a transfer of sovereignty from the Member States, for the purposes of jointly exercising it through the European institutions.[154] For the Bundesverfassungsgericht, the foundation for finding the EU institutions' democratic credentials was the derivation of the democratic credentials of Member State institutions participating in the integration project, while the increased powers of the European Parliament were marked as a step forward in improving the democratic deficiencies of the Union.[155]

Weiler rightly points to several inconsistencies in the reasoning of the German court related to the *no demos* thesis and the democratic credentials of the Union. First, *demos* can be many things, and by saying it can only exist on the Member State level, the Court in essence pre-empts the possibility for the Union to develop into a democratic polity on a basis different from that of Member States.[156] Secondly, by then restating how the European Parliament may contribute to the resolution or improvement of the EU's current democratic deficit, it is contradicting its own statement that the existence of a *demos* is central to democratic legitimacy.[157]

Ultimately, the Bundesverfassungsgericht's introduction of *ultra vires* review is the control of the democratic pedigree of Union acts,[158] the limits of which are

150 ibid. As will be seen in ch 6, s 2.1, the limits mentioned here may be seen as the basis for the introduction of the identity review in the *Lisbon* decision of the Bundesverfassungsgericht, where review is carried out against the standard of the unamendable constitutional core.

151 See also E Vranes, 'German Constitutional Foundations of, and limitations to, EU Integration: A Systematic Analysis' (2013) 14(1) *German Law Journal* 75, 91.

152 German Bundesverfassungsgericht Case *Maastricht Treaty* (n 9) [II.a].

153 The Court remained on the thesis that Member States are the 'Masters of the Treaties'. German Bundesverfassungsgericht Case *Maastricht Treaty* (n 9) [II.a]. In addition, the Court stated that the Member States are the ones 'continuously breathing life into the Treaty'. See [II.d.2.1].

154 ibid.

155 ibid [A.II.2.a], [C.I.2.b.1], and [C.I.2.b.2].

156 Weiler (n 141) 222, 230.

157 ibid 235. For an analogous criticism of the *Lisbon* judgment of the Bundesverfassungsgericht see C Calliess, 'The Future of the Eurozone and the Role of the German Federal Constitutional Court' (2012) 31(1) *Yearbook of European Law* 402, 406. For a broader critique of the Bundesverfassungsgericht's reasoning in both judgments see M Everson, 'An Exercise in Legal Honesty: Rewriting the Court of Justice and the Bundesverfassungsgericht' (2015) 21(4) *European Law Journal* 474, 484.

158 Kokott (n 144) 81; Huber (n 135) 98; Kumm (n 2) 264. For a converse opinion according to which democracy control is to be considered a separate head of review see M Claes, 'Luxembourg, Here We

defined by Article 79(3) of the Basic Law.[159] This meant that primacy of EU law only extends to acts within *vires*[160] and it was the Bundesverfassungsgericht who has retained the right to control the division between intra and *ultra vires*.

*Ultra vires* was confirmed as a head of review of EU acts in the decision concerning the constitutionality of the Lisbon Treaty in Germany,[161] alongside which the Bundesverfassungsgericht added constitutional identity as a separate head of review, measured against the standards of the unamendable core of the Basic Law.[162] The *Lisbon* judgment repeated the state-centrist views first set out in *Maastricht*, according to which Member States are the Masters of the Treaties and the imminent source of any legitimation of EU action. The Bundesverfassungsgericht additionally reflected upon how such a finding affects the autonomy of the EU as a supranational legal order:

> In a functional sense, the source of Community authority, and of the European constitution that constitutes it, are the peoples of Europe with democratic constitutions in their states. The "Constitution of Europe", international treaty law or primary law, remains a derived fundamental order. [ … ] autonomy can only be understood - as is usual regarding the law of self-government - as an autonomy to rule which is independent but derived, i.e. is granted by other legal entities.[163]

It would therefore be logically impossible for the EU to be able to decide on the scope of its own competence,[164] as the principle of conferral is a principle of both European and national constitutional law.[165] By way of conclusion of this analysis, the Bundesverfassungsgericht stated that 'it must be possible within the German jurisdiction to assert the responsibility for integration if obvious transgressions of the boundaries occur when the European Union claims competences'.[166] The

Come? Constitutional Courts and the Preliminary Reference Procedure' (2015) 16(6) *German Law Journal* 1331, 1335.

159 German Bundesverfassungsgericht case *Maastricht Treaty* (n 9) [B.1.a[5]–[6]].

160 Kokott (n 144) 81.

161 German Bundesverfassungsgericht Case 2 BVerfG 2/08 *Lisbon Treaty* Judgment of 30 June 2009 [240] http://www.bverfg.de/e/es20090630_2bve000208en.html.

162 For a detailed analysis of identity review in general see ch 6; for a detailed analysis of the identity review in Germany see s 2.1 of that chapter.

163 German Bundesverfassungsgericht Case *Lisbon Treaty* (n 161) [231].

164 ibid [233].

165 ibid [234]. Such an understanding is very much in line with constitutional pluralism, according to which the lines between national and EU law are blurred and their division can only be conceived upon functional, rather than territorial criteria. For a critique of the Bundesverfassungsgericht for its lack of regard for such an enmeshment see C Möllers, 'German Federal Constitutional Court: Constitutional *Ultra Vires* Review of European Acts Only under Exceptional Circumstances; Decision of 6 July 2010, 2 BvR 2661/06, *Honeywell*' (2011) 7(1) *European Constitutional Law Review* 161, 164.

166 German Bundesverfassungsgericht Case *Lisbon Treaty* (n 161) [240].

Bundesverfassungsgericht also revisited the principle of openness to European integration[167] and found the Lisbon Treaty in line with the Basic Law.

A further, more detailed elaboration of the precise standards for review of EU action took place in *Honeywell*,[168] which reached the Bundesverfassungsgericht in the subsequent application of the *Mangold* doctrine.[169] The constitutional complaint of the applicant was based on three assertions:[170] (1) the *Mangold* reasoning is a manifest transgression of the competences allocated to the Court of Justice;[171] (2) the Court of Justice's decision in *Mangold* was an interpretation of national private law, which is outside its powers; and finally (3) the Court of Justice stepped out of bounds in finding the applicability of the Framework Directive prior to the expiry of its implementation period.[172]

The Bundesverfassungsgericht was thus presented with a perfect opportunity to carry out an *ultra vires* review of the Court of Justice's actions. Elaborating first upon the operation of the principle of primacy of EU law as developed by the Court of Justice,[173] the Bundesverfassungsgericht linked the limited extent of primacy to the principle of conferral.[174] Before detailing further the standard of review, an important point was made for the viability of constitutional pluralism: 'The obligation incumbent on the Federal Constitutional Court to pursue substantiated complaints of an *ultra vires* act on the part of the European bodies and institutions is to be coordinated with the task which the Treaties confer on the Court of Justice.'[175] In accordance with constitutional pluralism, the Bundesverfassungsgericht considers the EU judicial space is a cooperative one and any review of EU acts thus needs to be carried out in a manner mindful of such a set-up.[176]

[167] ibid [221]. See also ch 3, s 4 for a more detailed vocabulary analysis of this jurisprudence and how it fits into the structure of constitutional pluralism.

[168] German Bundesverfassungsgericht Case 2 BverfG 2661/06 *Honeywell* Order of 6 July 2010 http://www.bundesverfassungsgericht.de/SharedDocs/Entscheidungen/EN/2010/07/rs20100706_2bvr266106en.html.

[169] ibid [28]–[31]. See also Möllers (n 165) 163.

[170] German Bundesverfassungsgericht Case *Honeywell* (n 168) [40].

[171] Arguments along similar lines were put forward in the *Dansk Industri* case before the Danish Højesteret, also including a reference to the principle of legitimate expectations. See below n 325.

[172] See also Kommers and Miller (n 133) 350.

[173] Note here that the Bundesverfassungsgericht uses the term 'primacy of application' and not 'supremacy', which would otherwise indicate a hierarchical superiority of the entirety of Union law over the entirety of national law. The Bundesverfassungsgericht then goes on to explain primacy as a rule of collision, fully in line with the centrality of heterarchy in constitutional pluralism. German Bundesverfassungsgericht Case *Honeywell* (n 168) [53]; Kokott (n 144) 83. See also to this effect MacCormick (n 143) 264.

[174] German Bundesverfassungsgericht Case *Honeywell* (n 168) [55]. See also n 163.

[175] ibid [56].

[176] The language the Bundesverfassungsgericht uses fits perfectly with the theoretical framework based on the auto-correct function of constitutional pluralism as set out in ch 3: 'If each Member State claimed to be able to decide through their own courts on the validity of legal acts of the Union, the primacy of application could be circumvented in practice, and the uniform application of Union law would be placed at risk. If, however, on the other hand the Member States were to completely forgo *ultra vires* review, disposal of the treaty basis would be transferred to the Union bodies alone, even if their understanding of the law led in the practical outcome to an amendment of a Treaty or to an expansion of competences. [ . . . ] The tensions, which are basically unavoidable according to this construction, are

The *ultra vires* standard of review[177] was set out in significant detail, ultimately resulting in a significant narrowing[178] of the Bundesverfassungsgericht's scope of review. First, prior to any finding, the Court of Justice must have a say through the preliminary reference procedure. Thus, the Bundesverfassungsgericht is putting into effect its obligation of sincere cooperation and mutual respect.[179] Its function is to avoid conflict 'whenever possible'.[180] Secondly, the Bundesverfassungsgericht will police only 'manifest transgressions', a rather high threshold.[181] Thirdly, not only must the transgression be manifest, it also needs to fall into an area which is highly significant[182] in the structure of competence division between the EU and its Member States. Beyond the test itself, there are two further qualifications in *Honeywell* that restrict the applicability of *ultra vires* review: first, only the Bundesverfassungsgericht is allowed to carry out the review; and second, 'the Court of Justice has a right to tolerance of error'.[183]

After having set out the test and its qualifications, the Bundesverfassungsgericht applied it to the *Mangold* judgment of the Court of Justice and found that it does not meet the threshold of a 'manifest transgression' and is consequently intra vires.[184] Justice Landau dissented from the majority, arguing they departed from its *Lisbon* state-oriented language and reasoning,[185] thus leaving the Court of Justice operating without any institution or Member State being able effectively to keep it in check.[186] It is argued that when considered together with fundamental rights and identity review, the Bundesverfassungsgericht's control of the Court of Justice is not as negligible as Justice Landau presents it. Indeed, had it not been for the expansive German jurisprudence adding further layers of review of Union action, it is questionable whether other constitutional courts of Member States would join to also contribute to keeping the Court of Justice in check. The very addition of

to be harmonised cooperatively in accordance with the European integration idea and relaxed through mutual consideration' ibid [57].

177 ibid [60]–[61].

178 Kommers and Miller (n 133) 350.

179 Möllers notes that *Honeywell* adds the obligation to carry out the review in a 'restrained' manner, confirming the importance of self-restraint in the conduct of courts involved in a possible constitutional conflict. Möllers (n 165) 165.

180 Huber (n 135) 89.

181 In his dissent, Justice Landau states that manifest must mean 'each expanding interpretation of the Treaties which is tantamount to a non-permissible autonomous amendment of the Treaty'. German Bundesverfassungsgericht Case *Honeywell* Dissenting Opinion of Justice Landau (n 168) [101].

182 This requirement has subsequently been made part of the Danish *ultra vires* review standard. See n 321 below.

183 German Bundesverfassungsgericht Case *Honeywell* (n 168) [66].

184 ibid [71] (as regards the significant breach of the principle of conferral), [75] (concerning the law-making activities of the Court of Justice being *ultra vires*), and [80] (in relation to the principle of legitimate expectations).

185 German Bundesverfassungsgericht case *Honeywell* Dissenting Opinion of Justice Landau (n 168) [96]–[98].

186 ibid [99]. Möllers sides with Justice Landau's finding that the Bundesverfassungsgericht effectively waived its review powers by setting an unreachable *ultra vires* standard. Möllers (n 165) 167.

different heads of review created a cooperative judicial space in the EU and has forced the Court of Justice to take notice of national constitutional concerns and adjust its case law accordingly. It is precisely the permanent contestation and incremental accommodation (the auto-correct function) that results in a coherent interpretation and application of Union law, but keeping in line with conferral as its defining principle.

The Bundesverfassungsgericht applied the *Honeywell* standard in its review of the European Central Bank's Outright Monetary Transactions (OMT) programme in the *Gauweiler* case. The Bundesverfassungsgericht doubted the compatibility of the OMT mechanism with primary EU law, specifically the extent of powers accorded to the ECB within its monetary policy mandate.[187] In line with the requirements of *Honeywell*, the Bundesverfassungsgericht first submitted a preliminary reference to the Court of Justice.[188] More specifically, for the OMT to be *ultra vires*, it needed to exceed monetary policy and the prohibition of monetary financing, resulting in an encroachment of Member States' economic policy.[189] Framing monetary and economic policy as mutually exclusive disregards the functional nature of EU competences, which necessarily influence each other and may at times partially overlap.[190] After carrying out the analysis of the OMT programme and its effects on monetary and economic policy, in which the Bundesverfassungsgericht preliminarily concluded that it is *ultra vires*, it also offered a Treaty interpretation that would be compliant with the current division of competences.[191] By defining the possible interpretation of the Treaty in relation to the mandate of the ECB, the Bundesverfassungsgericht narrowed the scope of the Court of Justice's answer and according to Kumm, invited it in the game of 'chicken'.[192] Such a move was touted as problematic for both the Court of Justice and the Bundesverfassungsgericht, as it significantly restricted the latter's subsequent manoeuvring space.[193]

Justice Lübbe-Wolff joined the critique of the Bundesverfassungsgericht in her dissent, where she found that the Order for reference is itself a judicial *ultra vires* act, which disregards the constitutional position and role of the Bundesverfassu

[187] The case will also be analysed in ch 6, s 2.1 as regards the identity review aspects of the case. For a wide array of opinions and analyses of the preliminary reference see the *Special Issue: The OMT Decision of the German Federal Constitutional Court* (2014) 15(2) *German Law Journal* 281.

[188] See n 17.

[189] German Bundesverfassungsgericht Order *Gauweiler* (n 17) [36], [39], [63], and [80].

[190] Bast (n 61) 175; M Dawson and A Bobić, 'Quantitative Easing at the Court of Justice: Doing Whatever It Takes to Save the Euro: *Weiss and Others*' (2019) 56(4) *Common Market Law Review* 1005, 1017–18. The political science literature on the theory of neo-functionalism explains European integration mainly through the spill over of conferred competences into new areas which also may impinge upon Member States' exclusive competences. See A Wiener and T Diez (eds), *European Integration Theory* (2nd edn, OUP 2009) 48–49. See also on the spill-over of existing competences into ever wider areas Weatherill (n 1) 29–30.

[191] German Bundesverfassungsgericht Order *Gauweiler* (n 17) [100].

[192] M Kumm, 'Rebel without a Good Cause: Karlsruhe's Misguided Attempt to Draw the CJEU into a Game of "Chicken" and what the CJEU Might Do about It' (2014) 15(2) *German Law Journal* 203, 206.

[193] ibid 203–204.

ngsgericht.[194] She emphasized that the admissibility criteria applied to allow the constitutional complaint were too wide, not least since the case relates to matters of European integration.[195] Finally, Fabbrini[196] and Kelemen[197] both found that the wording of the Bundesverfassungsgericht left no space for the Court of Justice to reach a satisfactory interpretation, concluding that a constitutional conflict is inevitable and with it the fall of constitutional pluralism. Conversely, the possibility or even the emergence of a conflict is not contrary to constitutional pluralism, but is rather its essential element.

Among the options available to the Court of Justice, it chose to preserve the OMT programme. It first analysed the powers of the ECB and concluded that indirect effects of monetary policy on economic policy do not make them equivalent, leading to the conclusion that the ECB was acting within its mandate.[198] The Court of Justice set out the conditions necessary for compliance with the Treaties,[199] albeit these were different from those in the Bundesverfassungsgericht's order for reference.[200] In relation to the relationship between the two courts, the Court of Justice omitted any analysis of the claims to constitutional identity and *ultra vires* review of the Bundesverfassungsgericht, stating only that the decisions provided by way of preliminary reference procedure concerning the interpretation and validity of Union acts are binding on the national court.[201]

The academic community read the reply from the Court of Justice as being firmly on a 'collision course'[202] with the Bundesverfassungsgericht, predicting the final decision in the case to activate the doomsday device.[203] Perhaps due to the time passed between the announcement of the OMT programme by Mario Draghi (which had the effect of calming the market) and the final judgment, it appeared the actual use of the programme might not be necessary and the Bundesverfassungsgericht accepted the Court of Justice's findings.[204] In the substantive part of its judgment, the Bundesverfassungsgericht first set out the

[194] German Bundesverfassungsgericht Order *Gauweiler* Dissenting Opinion of Justice Lübbe-Wolff (n 17) [1], [5]–[10].

[195] ibid [14].

[196] F Fabbrini, 'After the *OMT* Case: The Supremacy of EU Law as the Guarantee of the Equality of the Member States' (2015) 16 (4) *German Law Journal* 1003.

[197] R D Kelemen, 'On the Unsustainability of Constitutional Pluralism: European Supremacy and the Survival of the Eurozone' (2016) 23 *Maastricht Journal of European and Comparative Law* 136.

[198] Case C-62/14 *Gauweiler* (n 17) [52], [56], relying on its findings in Case C-370/12 *Pringle* [2012] EU:C:2012:756.

[199] For a more detailed analysis of each of these conditions see T Tridimas and N Xanthoulis, 'A Legal Analysis of the Gauweiler Case: Between Monetary Policy and Constitutional Conflict' (2016) 23(1) *Maastricht Journal of European and Comparative Law* 17, 23–30.

[200] ibid 30–31.

[201] Case C-62/14 *Gauweiler* (n 17) [16].

[202] Fabbrini (n 196) 1012.

[203] Kelemen (n 197) 138.

[204] German Bundesverfassungsgericht Case 2 BvR 2728/13 *Gauweiler* Judgment of 21 June 2016 [9] http://www.bundesverfassungsgericht.de/SharedDocs/Entscheidungen/EN/2016/06/rs20160621_2bvr272813en.html.

relationship between the principle of primacy and the Basic Law, addressing also the identity and *ultra vires* review it carries out in relation to EU acts. The conclusion is that any such review must be done cautiously, with restraint and in a way open to European integration.[205] This reasoning closely follows the framework of constitutional pluralism, whereby an initial expression of the right to the final say is followed by a reconciliatory vocabulary aimed at a final balancing exercise through which conflicts are managed and resolved in a dynamic manner. This set-up confirms the cooperative relationship[206] between the Bundesverfassungsgericht and the Court of Justice and is summed up in the following paragraph which addresses a situation of diverging interpretations of Union law by the two courts:

> Against this backdrop, it is not the task of the Federal Constitutional Court to replace the interpretation of the Court of Justice with its own when faced with issues of interpretation of Union law that can—even when handled in a methodologically correct manner within the usual bounds of legal debate—yield differing results [ … ]. On the contrary, as long as the Court of Justice applies recognised methodological principles and does not act in a way that is objectively arbitrary, the Federal Constitutional Court must respect judicial development of the law by the Court of Justice even when the Court of Justice adopts a view against which weighty arguments could be made.[207]

Substantively, the Bundesverfassungsgericht accepted the conditions attached to the OMT programme as defined by the Court of Justice,[208] as well as the standard of review of Union acts it exercises.[209] Should the ECB, in a potential use of the OMT mechanism, sideline any of these conditions, such an action would be considered *ultra vires*.[210]

The ECB afterwards introduced a second quantitative easing programme, the public sector purchase programme (PSPP).[211] The Bundesverfassungsgericht was

[205] ibid [121], [154], [156].

[206] ibid [157].

[207] ibid [161].

[208] ibid [174]. The Bundesverfassungsgericht does however mention the arguments it found to be important for the review of the OMT programme, which were not taken into account by the Court of Justice, and the question submitted in the preliminary reference concerning the independence of the ECB that the Court of Justice did not answer ([181]–[189]).

[209] ibid [179]. The Bundesverfassungsgericht mentions specifically that the standard of review is now more explicit in relation to the ECB ([180]).

[210] ibid [193], [205].

[211] ECB Decision 2015/774 of 4 March 2015 on a secondary markets public sector asset purchase programme [2015] OJ L121/20, amended by Decision 2015/2101 of 5 November 2015 amending Decision (EU) 2015/774 on a secondary markets public sector asset purchase programme [2015] OJ L303/106, Decision 2015/2464 of 16 December 2015 amending Decision (EU) 2015/774 on a secondary markets public sector asset purchase programme [2015] OJ L344/1, Decision 2016/702 of 18 April 2016 amending Decision (EU) 2015/774 on a secondary markets public sector asset purchase programme [2016] OJ L121/24, and Decision (EU) 2017/100 of 11 January 2017 amending Decision (EU) 2015/774 on a secondary markets public sector asset purchase programme [2017] OJ L16/51. For a comparison between the characteristics of the OMT and PSPP programmes see A Bobić and M Dawson, 'Making

again presented with a constitutional complaint concerning the limits of ECB's mandate and the decision of the German court in *Weiss II* is at present the last instance of this back and forth. This reference revolved around three issues: whether the ECB had complied with its duty to state reasons in devising the PSPP programme, whether said programme falls within the monetary policy mandate of the ECB, and whether it is contrary to the Treaty prohibition of monetary financing. The principle of proportionality was mentioned by the Bundesverfassungsgericht only in relation to the first two issues. After receiving the response from the Court of Justice, the Bundesverfassungsgericht found that the proportionality test as applied by the Court of Justice deprives it of its ability to protect Member State competence.[212] It declared the judgment of the Court of Justice[213] and the PSPP programme[214] of the ECB *ultra vires*.

Having rejected the findings of the Court of Justice, the Bundesverfassungsgericht then took it upon itself to interpret the scope of the monetary policy mandate of the ECB. The ECB failed to take into account the economic policy effects of the PSPP programme and, importantly, to balance a number of competing interests against each other.[215] In defining the relevant steps of the proportionality test, the Bundesverfassungsgericht stated that the fourth *stricto sensu* step has been omitted by the Court of Justice[216] and there was no review of the sufficiency of information provided by the ECB in balancing the relevant interests at stake.[217] The ECB thus failed in its duty to state reasons concerning the proportionality of the PSPP.[218]

The way that the *ultra vires* test from *Honeywell* was applied in *Weiss II* leaves some space for doubting that the Bundesverfassungsgericht complied with its own obligation of sincere cooperation and a EU-friendly interpretation. For example, when is a competence highly significant in the structure of the division of competences? We know that this does not cover the substance of constitutional identity, which is automatically excluded from European integration.[219] But that provides us with little knowledge as to what highly significant is, leaving the Bundesverfassungsgericht in danger of a *laesio enormis* fallacy[220] concerning the boundaries of the German constitutional obligation to participate in the

Sense of the "Incomprehensible": The PSPP Judgment of the German Federal Constitutional Court' (2020) 57(6) *Common Market Law Review* 1953, 1956–57.

212 German Bundesverfassungsgericht Cases 2 BvR 859/15, 2 BvR 980/16, 2 BvR 2006/15, 2 BvR 1651/15 *Weiss II* (n 17) [123].

213 ibid [116], [163].

214 ibid [117], [178].

215 ibid [133], [138]–[145].

216 Here, the Bundesverfassungsgericht infamously stated that the decision of the Court of Justice is 'simply not comprehensible'. ibid [116].

217 ibid [169], [176].

218 ibid [177].

219 German Bundesverfassungsgericht Case *Lisbon Treaty* (n 161) [240]–[241].

220 K Schneider, 'Gauging "Ultra-Vires": The Good Parts' (2020) 21 *German Law Journal* 968, 976.

integration programme. To demand of the Bundesverfassungsgericht to define this boundary more clearly would be in line with its own jurisprudence on the relationship between German and EU constitutional law, as well as on the cooperation with the Court of Justice.

In response, the European Commission initiated infringement proceedings against Germany for breaching the principle of primacy and not submitting a second preliminary reference to the Court of Justice.[221] Indeed, part of the fierce academic reaction to the *Weiss II* decision argued that the Bundesverfassungsgericht should have submitted a second preliminary reference before an *ultra vires* finding.[222] However, the Treaties themselves do not prescribe such an obligation on the part of the national court.[223] In addition, there were no new legal questions that would warrant a second reference,[224] even more so given that the *Weiss* reference relied heavily on the already existing interpretation by the Court of Justice given in *Gauweiler*.[225] Requiring repeated references from national courts may reduce confidence in the usefulness and procedural economy of the preliminary reference procedure. While there may be merit in the argument that national courts can, through subsequent references, force the Court of Justice to rethink its approach,[226] it remains unclear how long[227] the national court should wait or how many references are necessary for such a change to take place. This does not appear to me a sustainable manner of managing judicial interactions between the Court of Justice and highest national courts tasked with constitutional review.

More important, however, is the requirement of impartiality that the Court of Justice is lacking should the infringement proceedings reach it: the Court of Justice already made it public that it considers the *Weiss II* decision a breach of EU law in the press release following the German decision.[228] Finally, given the

[221] European Commission, June infringements package: key decisions. Brussels (9 June 2021) https://ec.europa.eu/commission/presscorner/detail/en/inf_21_2743.

[222] Editorial Comments, 'Not Mastering the Treaties: The German Federal Constitutional Court's PSPP judgment' (2020) 57 *Common Market Law Review* 965.

[223] See also s 3 above on the infringement proceedings for the failure to refer a second preliminary reference.

[224] In that sense see Broberg (n 63) 255.

[225] Šadl and Wallerman found that the Court of Justice tends to reformulate questions and avoids answering the original one when the referring court presents a forceful argument for a particular interpretation. This suggests that a clearer formulation of the issues at hand by the Bundesverfassungsgericht would result in an even less clear answer from the Court. U Šadl and A Wallerman, '"The Referring Court Asks, in Essence": Is Reformulation of Preliminary Questions by the Court of Justice a Decision Writing Fixture or a Decision-making Approach?' (2019) 25 *European Law Journal* 416, 428.

[226] T Tridimas, 'Knocking on Heaven's Door: Fragmentation, Efficiency and Defiance in the Preliminary Reference Procedure' (2003) 40(1) *Common Market Law Review* 9, 39. On how the Court of Justice indeed succumbed to the repeated references of the Italian courts see M Bonelli, 'The Taricco Saga and the Consolidation of Judicial Dialogue in the European Union' (2018) 25(3) *Maastricht Journal of European and Comparative Law* 357, 363–64. On the identity review aspects of the Italian judicial interaction see ch 6, s 2.2.4.

[227] R Voss, 'The National Perception of the Court of First Instance and the European Court of Justice' (1993) 30(6) *Common Market Law Review* 1119, 1124.

[228] See https://curia.europa.eu/jcms/upload/docs/application/pdf/2020-05/cp200058en.pdf. For a critique of the press release see J Lindeboom, 'Is the Primacy of EU Law Based on the Equality of the

political indecisiveness to pursue destructive rule of law breaches in Poland and Hungary, this action on behalf of the Commission appears misguided, as it focuses on a constructive conflict, maintained within the delicate equilibrium in the long-established jurisprudence of two courts. Moreover, there is little previous practice of the Commission pursuing such decisions. Indeed, the numerous national decisions analysed in this book have not seldom departed from what the Court of Justice required, however, without the Commission initiating infringement proceedings. According to the main argument of constitutional pluralism, constructive conflict has value for advancing the development of the EU's constitution broadly understood and should remain within the judicial, rather than political sphere. Political solutions are needed once the auto-correct function of constitutional pluralism is not able to accommodate conflicts by way of reasonable disagreements in the interpretation of the values in Article 2 TEU, as will be argued below in respect of destructive conflicts.[229]

As the subsequent sections will show, the *Honeywell* standard of *ultra vires* review has been the source of inspiration for other courts performing constitutional review, most notably the Czech and Danish courts, who have applied them in their respective jurisprudence and found two judgments of the Court of Justice to be *ultra vires*. In addition, Lithuania, Poland, and Hungary have put forward similar constraints on the application of the principle of primacy, grounded in the authority of their constitutions as the source of authority of EU law.[230]

## 6.2 The Czech Republic

The Ústavní Soud was established in the aftermath of the dissolution of Czechoslovakia in 1993, but its design was to a great extent inspired by its federal precursor, established in 1992 as the strong guardian of the constitution following the fall of communism.[231] Post-communist constitutional courts generally took up an active role in the process of democratic transition and the EU accession process.[232] The Czech Republic's accession to the EU was preceded by a constitutional amendment, which introduced a monist approach to incorporating international

Member States? A Comment on the CJEU's Press Release Following the PSPP Judgment' (2020) 21(8) *German Law Journal* 1649.

[229] See s 7 of this chapter.

[230] National Report: The Constitutional Court of the Republic of Lithuania (2014) 5, 28; Polish Trybunał Konstytucyjny Case P 37/05 Order of 19 December 2006 [7]; Hungarian Magyarország Alkotmánybírósága Case 143/2010 *Treaty of Lisbon* Judgment of 12 July 2010 (press release) http://hunconcourt.hu/letoltesek/en_0143_2010.pdf; Hungarian Magyarország Alkotmánybírósága Judgment No 22/2016 *Refugee Allocation Scheme* of 5 December 2016 [54] https://hunconcourt.hu/uploads/sites/3/2017/11/en_22_2016-1.pdf.

[231] M de Visser, *Constitutional Review in Europe: A Comparative Analysis* (Hart Publishing 2014) 70.

[232] F Biagi, *European Constitutional Courts and Transitions to Democracy* (CUP 2020).

law into its legal order and accorded the jurisdiction to the Constitutional Court to review international treaties prior to their ratification.[233]

The *Sugar Quotas III* judgment was the first occasion for the Ústavní Soud to set out its approach to EU law.[234] The Court was asked to assess the constitutionality of Government regulations implementing the allocation of sugar quotas in the internal market. Accordingly, the court had the task of answering 'the question of degree to which it is even authorised to adjudge the constitutional conformity of such legal norms as are tied up with Community law'.[235] The analysis in the judgment is extremely useful as it sets out the main findings concerning the consequences of primacy[236] and direct effect for the Constitutional Court's referential framework, how this affects the question of the final say, its relationship to the Court of Justice, and its role in the preliminary reference procedure.

The Ústavní Soud started its analysis in line with constitutional pluralism. It first stated that the Court of Justice has exclusive jurisdiction to assess the validity of Union law, after which it proceeded to analyse the challenges to this power by constitutional courts of other Member States, such as Germany, Italy, Denmark and Ireland,[237] demonstrating the parallel existence of claims to the final say. The Ústavní Soud stated that none of these circumstances can be overlooked in determining its own approach to the doctrines of primacy and direct effect, concluding that these issues represent the 'constitutional exegesis for the entire [Union] and that these issues have certain implications not just in the legal sphere, but also the political'.[238] The Czech court kept in mind not only the interpretation put forward by the Court of Justice, but also the bigger picture painted by other constitutional courts in the EU, where primacy and direct effect are not absolute and unlimited, but rather operate in a collaborative EU judicial space.[239]

The Court proceeded with the assessment of the relationship between Member State discretion and the exigencies of EU law, taking into account the principle of sincere cooperation as well as the principle of subsidiarity. The two principles should in the view of the Ústavní Soud result in the Union applying restraint when

[233] National Report: The Constitutional Court of the Czech Republic (2014) 2.

[234] Czech Ústavní Soud Case Pl. ÚS 50/04 *Sugar Quotas III* Judgment of 8 March 2006 http://www.usoud.cz/en/decisions/20060308-pl-us-5004-sugar-quotas-iii-1/.

[235] ibid [VI.A].

[236] Ústavní Soud calls it 'applicational precedence', presumably guided by an attempt to avoid mentioning the supremacy of one legal order over another. The same was done by the Spanish Constitutional Tribunal when it distinguished between primacy and supremacy. Spanish Tribunal Constitucional Case DTC 1/2004 *Constitutional Treaty* Declaration of 13 December 2004 [II-4]. For the same development in the German constitutional jurisprudence see n 173.

[237] Czech Ústavní Soud Case *Sugar Quotas III* (n 234) [VI.A].

[238] ibid.

[239] The Constitutional Court should also be commended for the amount of cross-referencing to other constitutional courts concerning national constitutional limits to primacy of EU law, but also concerning the participation of constitutional courts in the preliminary reference procedure. See Czech Ústavní Soud Case *Sugar Quotas III* (n 234) [VI.A], [VI.A-1]. It goes to show that the Czech court views the EU judicial space as one shared among the Court of Justice and guardians of national constitutions.

exercising its competences and leaving space for Member States to implement their EU obligations.[240] Conversely, when Member States act to meet their EU obligations, their discretion is curbed by the objectives of the EU norm in question and general principles of EU law.[241] By way of conclusion as to the position of EU law in relation to constitutional review, the Constitutional Court stated that:

> Although the Constitutional Court's referential framework has remained, even after 1 May 2004, the norms of the Czech Republic's constitutional order, the Constitutional Court cannot entirely overlook the impact of [Union] law on the formation, application, and interpretation of national law, all the more so in a field of law where the creation, operation, and aim of its provisions is immediately bound up with [Union] law. In other words, in this field the Constitutional Court interprets constitutional law taking into account the principles arising from [Union] law.[242]

The Court provided a thorough analysis of the case law of the Court of Justice concerning sugar quotas and its own case law on the matter. Subsequently, it proceeded in the reconciliatory fashion introduced in Chapter 3 and sought to establish whether there were any inconsistencies between the two lines of jurisprudence that would require a change in its case law.[243] It concluded that it required amendments as the case law of the Court of Justice prohibits implementation measures for directly applicable EU law such as regulations and found the Government regulation to be *ultra vires*.[244]

Finally, the Constitutional Court emphasized that the transfer of powers to the EU level is conditional upon the Czech Republic remaining a democratic, rule of law-based state. It accordingly reserved for itself the power of the final say should the EU institutions carry out their delegated powers in a manner that is 'regressive' to that condition.[245] Crucially, the Constitutional Court found this conditionality essential for the dynamic development of the operation of EU law in national law.

Regardless of this reservation, the Ústavní Soud took a reconciliatory approach to possible inconsistencies in its judgment concerning the constitutionality of the European Arrest Warrant. Similar to the approach taken by the Polish

[240] Czech Ústavní Soud Case *Sugar Quotas III* (n 234) [VI.A].

[241] ibid [VI.A-1].

[242] ibid.

[243] ibid [VI.A-3].

[244] ibid. For a comparison of the German and Czech language concerning the state-rooted conceptions of sovereignty see J Priban, 'The Semantics of Constitutional Sovereignty in Post-sovereign "New" Europe: A Case Study of the Czech Constitutional Court's Jurisprudence' (2015) 13(1) *International Journal of Constitutional Law* 180, 182–83.

[245] Czech Ústavní Soud Case *Sugar Quotas III* (n 234) [VI.B]. See also National Report: The Constitutional Court of the Czech Republic (n 233) 3–4.

Constitutional Tribunal in the area of identity review,[246] the Constitutional Court stated that:

> If the Constitution [ ... ] can be interpreted in several manners, only certain of which lead to the attainment of an obligation which the Czech Republic undertook in connection with its membership in the EU, then an interpretation must be selected with supports the carrying out of that obligation, and not an interpretation which precludes [it].[247]

The judgments in *Sugar Quotas III* and *European Arrest Warrant* represented the general approach of the Ústavní Soud towards EU law,[248] at least until a constitutional complaint was lodged against the ratification of the Lisbon Treaty. The Constitutional Court assumed jurisdiction to review the Treaty amendment,[249] stating that this is the first time it will be undertaking a review of an international treaty,[250] thus expanding its powers of review as regards treaty amendments of EU law. However, more importantly, it reiterated the conditionality of the transfer of powers to the EU as well as its power to review EU law should it deform the essential elements of a democratic law-based state.[251] It thus concluded by underlining its own right to a final say in matters of both identity review and *ultra vires* review:

> The Constitutional Court of the Czech Republic will (may) also—although in view of the foregoing principles—function as an ultima ratio and may review whether any act of Union bodies exceeded the powers that the Czech Republic transferred to the European Union under Art. 10a of the Constitution. However, the Constitutional Court assumes that such a situation can occur only in quite exceptional cases; these could be, in particular, abandoning the identity of values and, as already cited, exceeding the scope of conferred competences.[252]

The Constitutional Court proceeded with its analysis of the final say. It cited the Bundesverfassungsgericht's *Maastricht* decision in parts where it reserved for itself the right to the final say,[253] stating that the decision should be read as a warning without any need to be used in practice.[254] The Ústavní Soud cited the Polish

[246] Polish Trybunał Konstytucyjny Case K 18/04 *Accession Treaty* Judgment of 11 May 2005 [14] http://trybunal.gov.pl/fileadmin/content/omowienia/K_18_04_GB.pdf. See ch 6, s 2.2.1 for a more detailed analysis of the identity review aspects of the case.

[247] Czech Ústavní Soud Case Pl. ÚS 66/04 *European Arrest Warrant* Judgment of 3 May 2006 [61] http://www.usoud.cz/en/decisions/20060503-pl-us-6604-european-arrest-warrant-1/.

[248] National Report: The Constitutional Court of the Czech Republic (n 233) 4.

[249] Limited, however, by the scope of the petition request. Czech Ústavní Soud Case *Lisbon Treaty I* (n 15) [77].

[250] ibid abstract.

[251] ibid [120].

[252] ibid [120].

[253] ibid [118].

[254] ibid [139].

Constitutional Tribunal on the same issue, stating, however, that its position is comparable only to a certain extent, since the Czech court does not regard the question of the final say as being one of purely domestic constitutional law.[255] Finally, the Ústavní Soud addressed the role of the Court of Justice in policing the boundaries of EU action, but also the new position for national parliaments in respect of the principle of subsidiarity. The Constitutional Court concluded this analysis in the spirit of cooperation and mutual respect: '[r]eview of observing the limits of the conferral of competences is thus the joint role of all participating bodies, both at the European level and at the domestic level'.[256] The behaviour of the Czech court thus falls squarely into the framework of constitutional pluralism.

The remainder of the Czech court's analysis places emphasis on self-restraint and Euro-friendly interpretation as necessary interpretative tools in review of the treaties, where the Czech Constitution will only take precedence if there is a clear and insurmountable conflict.[257] The Constitutional Court further compared its standard of review in this case to that in *Sugar Quotas III*, where secondary EU law enjoyed a presumption of constitutionality and was only reviewed against individual provisions of the Czech Constitution. Conversely, the Ústavní Soud concluded it necessary to review a revision of primary EU law against the entire Czech constitutional order.[258] The Ústavní Soud was subsequently faced with a second challenge for review of the Lisbon Treaty, where it rejected the petitions and restated its main findings from *Lisbon Treaty I*.[259]

The relationship between the Court of Justice and the Ústavní Soud took a rather unexpected turn after these EU-friendly interpretations. The *Slovak Pensions* case[260] concerned a specific issue of entitlements to pensions rights after the break-up of Czechoslovakia. The original agreement[261] between the Czech Republic and Slovakia provided rules on the allocation to a particular social security system based on the seat of the former employer.[262] This commonly resulted

[255] ibid. See Priban (n 244) 189–92.

[256] Czech Ústavní Soud Case *Lisbon Treaty I* (n 15) [140].

[257] ibid [85], [94].

[258] Expanding for itself the referential scope of review. Czech Ústavní Soud Case *Lisbon Treaty I* (n 15) [94]. It also repeated that, should a conflict arise, it might also be necessary to change the Czech Constitution. The Ústavní Soud thus fell in the company of those Member States' constitutional courts who have in their jurisprudence addressed possible ways of reconciliation should a constitutional conflict arise between the EU and the national level.

[259] Czech Ústavní Soud Case Pl. ÚS 29/09 *Lisbon Treaty II* Judgment of 3 November 2009 http://www.usoud.cz/en/decisions/20091103-pl-us-2909-treaty-of-lisbon-ii/. See also J Komárek and Editors, 'The Czech Constitutional Court's Second Decision on the Lisbon Treaty of 3 November 2009' (2009) 5(3) *European Constitutional Law Review* 345.

[260] Czech Ústavní Soud Case Pl. ÚS 5/12 *Slovak Pensions* Judgment of 31 December 2012 http://www.usoud.cz/en/decisions/?tx_ttnews%5Btt_news%5D=37&cHash=911a315c9c22ea1989d19a3a848724e2.

[261] Treaty between the Czech Republic and the Slovak Republic on Social Security (29 October 1992).

[262] For a more detailed analysis of the case see M Bobek, '*Landtová, Holubec*, and the Problem of an Uncooperative Court: Implications for the Preliminary Ruling Procedure' (2014) 10 *European Constitutional Law Review* 54; Anagnostaras (n 139); J Komárek, 'Czech Constitutional Court Playing with Matches: The Czech Constitutional Court Declares a Judgment of the Court of Justice of the

in a considerably lower amount of pension for those Czech nationals who were working for companies whose seat was located in Slovakia.[263] In order to allow these workers to receive the same amount of pension as workers whose entire employment was carried out in the Czech Republic, the Constitutional Court decided that Czech nationals residing in the Czech Republic were entitled to a pension supplement for periods they worked in the territory of Slovakia.[264] The Constitutional Court justified the introduction of the supplement through the constitutional right to material security in old age, guaranteed by the Czech Charter of Fundamental Rights and Freedoms.

Although the original agreement between the Czech Republic and Slovakia was compliant with EU law, the case law of the Constitutional Court was problematic as it awarded a pension supplement based on nationality and residence in the Czech Republic, constituting nationality-based discrimination prohibited by EU law. Accordingly, the Czech Supreme Administrative Court was faced with a number of cases in which it had to juggle the requirements of the Czech–Slovak Agreement and EU law on the one hand and the authoritative jurisprudence of the Constitutional Court on the other. With the aim of resolving this conundrum, the Supreme Administrative Court submitted a preliminary reference to the Court of Justice, asking it to decide on the compliance of the pension supplement with EU law.[265] The Court of Justice found that while a pension supplement as such is not contrary to Regulation 1408/71,[266] the fact that it is awarded solely based on Czech nationality and residence in the Czech Republic constituted prohibited direct and indirect discrimination.[267]

While the outcome established by the Court of Justice seems straightforward, Interviewee 4 stated that the Court has made its fair share of mistakes. Specifically, the Ústavní Soud sought to intervene in the preliminary reference procedure and submitted an *amicus curiae* brief of sorts to present its view of the situation to the Court of Justice.[268] Since the Rules of Procedure of the Court envisage no such

EU *Ultra Vires*; Judgment of 31 January 2012, Pl. ÚS 5/12, *Slovak Pensions XVII*' (2012) 8 *European Constitutional Law Review* 323.

[263] Bobek (n 262) 57.

[264] Czech Ústavní Soud Case II. ÚS 405/02 *Pension Insurance* Judgment of 3 June 2003 http://www.usoud.cz/fileadmin/user_upload/ustavni_soud_www/Decisions/pdf/2-405-02.pdf. As Bobek reports, between this decision and the decision in *Slovak Pensions*, there were 17 cases in total where the Constitutional Court confirmed its original decision granting the right to a pension supplement. Bobek (n 262) 59.

[265] Case C-399/09 *Landtová* [2011] EU:C:2011:415.

[266] ibid [40].

[267] ibid [49].

[268] See also Bobek (n 262) 80. The Ústavní Soud subsequently addressed this point, concluding that the Court of Justice regularly uses *amicus curiae* briefs (it remains unclear how the Ústavní Soud reached this conclusion) and that the 'the ECJ's statement that the Constitutional Court was a "third party" in the case at hand cannot be seen otherwise than as abandoning the principle audiatur et altera pars'. Czech Ústavní Soud Case *Slovak Pensions* (n 260) [VII].

correspondence, the Court of Justice returned the letter. Interviewee 4 stated that this could have been handled better—for example, there could have been an effort on behalf of the Court to explain to the Ústavní Soud that it cannot receive such letters. Moreover, the same interviewee considered that the Court of Justice took too long to realize and take into account the constitutional implications of the case, thus confirming that in the EU pluralist judicial space, the Court of Justice is obliged to take note of national constitutional specificities. The members of the Court of Justice confirmed in their interviews this is the regular practice upon receiving a preliminary reference.[269]

The *Landtová* decision resulted in a conflict between the Supreme Administrative Court and the Constitutional Court and ultimately led to the *Slovak Pensions* decision.[270] The constitutional complaint submitted to the Ústavní Soud was factually analogous to *Landtová*, granting it the opportunity to respond to the findings of the Court of Justice. The Constitutional Court started its substantive review by reiterating its case law on the relationship between national and EU law analysed above, where it compared its position to that of the German Bundesverfassungsgericht as set out in the *Solange* and *Maastricht* judgments.[271]

The Constitutional Court further stated that the Court of Justice failed to take into account the specificities of the dissolution of Czechoslovakia, which cannot simply be translated into the language of the uniform social security system in the European Union.[272] Keeping these findings in mind, the Court proceeded:

> [We] cannot do otherwise than state, in connection with the effects of ECJ judgment of 22 June 2011, C-399/09 on analogous cases, that in that case there were excesses on the part of a European Union body, that a situation occurred in which an act by a European body exceeded the powers that the Czech Republic transferred to the European Union under Art. 10a of the Constitution; this exceeded the scope of the transferred powers, and was *ultra vires*.[273]

The decision to disapply the judgment of the Court of Justice due to its alleged transgression of conferred powers, while being within the theoretical possibilities after the *Lisbon Treaty I* judgment, seems antagonistic when read together with other options available to the Constitutional Court in case of a conflict with EU law.

However, this judgment cannot be assessed solely based on the relationship between the Court of Justice and the Constitutional Court: a complete reading needs to include the relationship and clashes that took place between the Supreme

[269] Interviewee 1; Interviewee 2; Interviewee 3; Interviewee 4; Interviewee 5; Interviewee 6. See ch 3, s 4 for a more detailed analysis.

[270] Bobek (n 262) 62.

[271] Czech Ústavní Soud Case *Slovak Pensions* (n 260) [VII].

[272] ibid.

[273] ibid.

Administrative Court and the Constitutional Court, as reported in detail by Bobek.[274] The Constitutional Court also pointed out that the Czech Government failed properly to inform the Court of Justice of the legal situation revolving around the Czech and Slovak pensions.[275] In addition, the marginality of the case has been underlined by AG Wathelet,[276] Fabbrini,[277] and Interviewee 4.[278] Finally, the 2014 National Report for the Conference of European Constitutional Courts prepared by the Czech court itself does not mention this judgment among those relevant for the relationship between EU law and national constitutional law, but only mentions it as an example of a divergence in jurisprudence, stating that the Court of Justice 'overlooked'[279] the facts of the case. Significantly, the Czech court never applied the judgment again, but rather complied with the initial interpretation put forward by the Court of Justice,[280] which may be considered an implicit admission of its overly zealous behaviour.

In conclusion, the Czech jurisprudence may be seen as crossing the line of a constructive dialogue between the Court of Justice and national constitutional adjudicators. However, the *Slovak Pensions* decision should be read in context: the *ultra vires* review conducted by the Ústavní Soud was misdirected, as the original conflict was in fact one with the Supreme Administrative Court. As Komárek puts it, the *ultra vires* declaration of a Court of Justice decision was collateral damage.[281] In that respect, the defiance of the Ústavní Soud has little to do with a constructive critique of the Court of Justice's jurisprudence[282] and more to do with its perceived loss of influence due to the preliminary reference procedure.[283] If read in an incremental fashion, the extent of the conflict is considerably reduced. Conversely, it can be concluded that the position taken by the Ústavní Soud in the *Lisbon Treaty I* judgment is the leading authority on the approach to be taken in a situation of another constitutional conflict, which is led by a preference for an EU-friendly interpretation.[284]

[274] Bobek (n 262).

[275] Czech Ústavní Soud Case *Slovak Pensions* (n 260) [VII].

[276] Lecture of Advocate General M Wathelet: 'Constitutional Courts and the CJEU: Is There a Dialogue? History and Prospects' given at the EU Law discussion group at the Law Faculty, University of Oxford (23 October 2015).

[277] F Fabbrini, 'The European Court of Justice, the European Central Bank and the Supremacy of European Law: Introduction' (2016) 23 *Maastricht Journal of European and Comparative Law* 1, 2.

[278] Who stated that the case should not be taken into account as a representation of anything, as is it vitiated by numerous mistakes on behalf of both the Czech Constitutional Court and the Court of Justice.

[279] National Report: The Constitutional Court of the Czech Republic (n 233) 18.

[280] Bobek (n 262) 66, 71.

[281] Komárek (n 262) 323.

[282] As I argue is the case with the *ultra vires* declaration by the Danish Supreme Court below.

[283] Komárek (n 262) 332.

[284] See National Report: The Constitutional Court of the Czech Republic (n 233) 6, 15–16, 32.

## 6.3 Denmark

Denmark, a majoritarian democracy, has a decentralized system of constitutional review, where all courts can review legislation with the Supreme Court (Højesteret) at the top of the hierarchy. Regardless of this broad power, Nordic courts have more generally applied self-restraint in favour of the supreme parliament.[285] This tradition was characterized by the former president of the Højesteret Mr Pontoppidan as a long-standing tradition of utmost judicial self-restraint towards the *Folketing* (the Danish Parliament).[286]

Such a constitutional division of labour results in a different relationship between the legislature and the judiciary than that found in Germany and the Czech Republic. In addition, such a structure makes it less likely for the Supreme Court to find itself in conflict with other national courts, as may well be the case in countries with a specialized constitutional court.[287] Finally, it is important to note that while all courts in Denmark can theoretically strike down primary legislation, it is only the Supreme Court that has done it for the first and only time in 1999.[288]

The well-established principle of self-restraint on the national level resulted in an equally passive position of Danish courts as regards constitutional review of statutes, in particular in the area of fundamental rights.[289] In the same 1996 statement, Mr Pontoppidan indicated that the time may have come for the Danish courts more actively to police the constitutionality of statutes.[290] According to Rytter and Wind, it was the appearance and expansion of supranational adjudication that created a pressure for national courts to abandon blindly applying self-restraint vis-à-vis acts of Parliament.[291] It is thus the aim of this section to address the relationship that the Danish court has since developed with the Court of Justice and to determine whether the Danish principle of judicial self-restraint towards the legislator extended also towards the Court of Justice.

The story began when the Højesteret was faced with a challenge to the constitutionality of the Maastricht Treaty. The first indication that the case would mark a shift in the jurisprudence was allowing the appeal—the Danish court is only trying cases of a precedential nature, narrowing admissibility to only some cases (as opposed to the more lenient doctrine of only some cases being refused).[292] As

285 J E Rytter and M Wind, 'In Need Of Juristocracy? The Silence of Denmark in the Development of European Legal Norms' (2011) 9(2) *International Journal of Constitutional Law* 470, 471.

286 In an interview given in 1996, two years ahead of the *Maastricht* decision of the Danish Højesteret. H Rasmussen, 'Denmark's Maastricht Ratification Case: Some Serious Questions about Constitutionality' (1998) 21(1) *Journal of European Integration* 1, 5.

287 H Kelsen, 'Judicial Review of Legislation: A Comparative Study of the Austrian and the American Constitution' (1942) 4 *The Journal of Politics* 183.

288 National Report: The Supreme Court of Denmark (2011) 2.

289 Rasmussen (n 286) 6.

290 ibid.

291 Rytter and Wind (n 285) 471.

292 P H Lindblom, 'The Role of Supreme Courts in Scandinavia' (2000) 39 *Scandinavian Studies in Law* 325, 329.

Rasmussen reports, allowing the case to be heard represented a radical shift in the century-old tradition of Danish courts not to question the constitutionality of parliamentary statutes via class action.[293] The Højesteret justified the reversal by emphasizing the 'radical significance' of the transfer of powers by the Maastricht Treaty for the Danish population.[294]

The principal question of the dispute was whether the Danish Constitution allowed for the transfer of powers to the EU as defined in the Maastricht Treaty. Once the case reached the Højesteret, the appellants made two main assertions. First, the conditions of s 20(1) of the Danish Constitution[295] for the transfer of sovereignty, which was the basis for accepting the Maastricht Treaty, have not been met. The appellants referred to the broad scope of the then Article 235 EC[296] as well as the 'law-making activities of the Court of Justice'.[297] Secondly, the appellants claimed that the transfer of sovereignty under the Maastricht Treaty was contrary to the premise of a democratic form of government.[298]

The length of the Supreme Court's decision[299] may be read as the first sign of a new approach taken by the Højesteret, whose decisions are usually extremely short.[300] The Danish court then proceeded with the analysis of s 20 of the Danish Constitution, finding that it was first necessary to read it broadly, since it was introduced in 1953 and envisaged to regulate Danish membership in international organizations more generally.[301] However, any reading of this provision cannot be so broad as to assume that the international organization in question may specify the limits to its powers.[302]

Having concluded that the transfer of powers to the EU under the principle of conferral is in essence in line with s 20(1) of the Danish Constitution, the Court

293 Rasmussen (n 286) 8, 15.

294 ibid 8.

295 Section 20 of the Danish Constitution reads as follows:

(1) Powers vested in the authorities of the realm under this Constitutional Act may, to an extent specified by statute, be delegated to international authorities set up by mutual agreement with other states for the promotion of international rules of law and co-operation.

(2) For the enactment of a bill dealing with the above, a majority of five-sixths of the members of the Folketing shall be required. If this majority is not obtained, whereas the majority required for the passing of ordinary bills is obtained, and if the Government maintains it, the bill shall be submitted to the electorate for approval or rejection in accordance with the rules for referenda laid down in section 42.

296 Today's art 352 TFEU. See T Konstantinides, 'Drawing the Line between Circumvention and Gap-filling: An Exploration of the Conceptual Limits of the Treaty's Flexibility Clause' (2012) 31(1) *Yearbook of European Law* 227.

297 Danish Højesteret Case I 361/1997 *Carlsen* Judgment of 6 April 1998, 857.

298 ibid.

299 Harck and Olsen report that this was the longest judgment in the history of Højesteret's case law. S Harck and H P Olsen, 'Decision Concerning the Maastricht Treaty: 1998 Ugeskrift for Retsvaesen, H 800' (1999) 93(1) *The American Journal of International Law* 209, 211.

300 Rasmussen (n 286) 28.

301 Danish Højesteret Case *Carlsen* (n 297) 857.

302 ibid 858. See also by analogy German Bundesverfassungsgericht Case *Maastricht Treaty* (n 9) [C.I.3].

proceeded with a more detailed analysis of Article 235 EC, which the appellants flagged as specifically breaching a precise transfer of powers as required by s 20(1). The Højesteret referred to Opinion 2/94 of the Court of Justice, where it provided for a narrow reading of Article 235[303] to establish that its scope was in line with s 20 of the Constitution. In addition, it referred to the Article's unanimity requirement, which ensured that the Member State may even subsequently control the extent of the exercise of transferred powers.[304]

The Højesteret then turned to the appellants' argument concerning the law-making powers of the Court of Justice, addressing its powers of interpretation and review of EU action. It is here that the Supreme Court established its power of *ultra vires* review:

> [The] Supreme Court finds that it follows from the demand for specification in section 20(1) of the Constitution, held against the Danish court's access to test the constitutionality of acts, that the courts of law cannot be deprived of their right to try questions as to whether an E.C. act of law exceeds the limits for the surrender of sovereignty made by the Act of Accession. Therefore, Danish courts must rule that an E.C. act is inapplicable in Denmark if the extraordinary situation should arise that with the required certainty it can be established that an E.C. act which has been upheld by the European Court of Justice is based on an application of the Treaty which lies beyond the surrender of sovereignty according to the Act of Accession. Similar interpretations apply with regard to Community law rules and legal principles which are based on the practice of the European Court of Justice.[305]

The Supreme Court thus established its right to the final say on the constitutionality of primary and secondary EU law and the judgments of the Court of Justice. It went on to dismiss the remaining arguments of the appellants and found the Maastricht Treaty to be in line with the Danish Constitution.

The Supreme Court's *ultra vires* standard does not come without a safeguard. In particular, and similar to the German Bundesverfassungsgericht's finding in its own *Maastricht* decision, the Supreme Court stated that any finding of unconstitutionality by the Danish courts can only be established after the Court of Justice has had the opportunity to assess its compatibility with primary law. This approach follows a clear pluralist line of reasoning: the Danish Constitution is found to be central and supreme in Denmark and it is the Supreme Court who is entrusted with its interpretation, albeit with a strong self-restraint applied in favour of the national parliament. Subsequently, in a reconciliatory fashion, the Supreme Court

303 Opinion 2/94 [1996] EU:C:1996:140 [29]–[30].
304 Danish Højesteret Case *Carlsen* (n 297) 860.
305 ibid 861–62.

considers the Court of Justice the ultimate interpreter of EU primary law and will only assume the position of the ultimate arbiter in an 'extraordinary situation'.[306]

In addition to the awareness of the extraordinary conditions that would need to be met in order for the Højesteret to declare an EU act *ultra vires*, Danish courts more generally follow the 'rule of interpretation'—an obligation to interpret Danish law in line with Denmark's obligations under international (including EU) law 'to the fullest extent possible'.[307] This method is outlined by the Supreme Court as the guiding principle for avoidance of divergences with decisions of international courts, including the Court of Justice.[308] This obligation may be considered a more general expression of the obligation of an EU-friendly interpretation found in the jurisprudence of a number of Member States. As was discussed in Chapter 3, 'EU-friendly interpretation' is the most widespread common keyword in national constitutional jurisprudence guiding relationships in the European judicial space.

The Supreme Court has demonstrated, using a cautious vocabulary, that it forms part of the pluralist European judicial space. Its vocabulary is in line with that used by other constitutional courts under analysis. Thus, the Supreme Court established its position as the final arbiter as regards the application of EU law in Denmark, but found the Maastricht Treaty in line with it. Such a concession is in line with the pluralist auto-correct function, as it balances out opposing claims by the Court of Justice and national constitutional adjudicators.

With the aim of determining the existence of a balanced relationship of mutually assured trust between the Danish Supreme Court and the Court of Justice through a dynamic lens, I will address the case law of the Danish Supreme Court leading up to and including its *ultra vires* finding concerning a judgment of the Court of Justice. In so doing, the next benchmark is the Danish ratification of the Lisbon Treaty, the constitutionality of which was questioned before the Højesteret.[309]

The basis for the appellants' action revolved around the proper interpretation of s 20 of the Danish Constitution, and its requirement for a five-sixths majority in the Parliament when parts of sovereignty are transferred to a supranational organization.[310] The Government's position was that the Lisbon Treaty did not entail a new transfer of sovereignty to the European Union and thus s 20 and its majority requirement did not apply. Conversely, the Government claimed that s 19, regulating the powers of the Government in international affairs, applied.[311] The appellants' case rested on the claim that the changes in the decision-making procedures (in particular the expansion of qualified majority voting in the Council)

306 ibid 861.

307 National Report: The Supreme Court of Denmark (2014) 2.

308 ibid 12.

309 Danish Højesteret Case 199/2012 *Hausgaard* Judgment of 20 February 2013 http://www.hoejesteret.dk/hoejesteret/nyheder/ovrigenyheder/Documents/199-12engelsk.pdf.

310 See n 295.

311 H P Olsen, 'The Danish Supreme Court's Decision on the Constitutionality of Denmark's Ratification of the Lisbon Treaty' (2013) 50 *Common Market Law Review* 1489, 1489.

and the administration of delegated powers were fundamental enough to warrant the application of s 20 of the Danish Constitution to the ratification of the Lisbon Treaty.[312]

The Supreme Court's decision continued the trend of the *Maastricht* decision as regards its length and verbosity. What is specifically telling is its explicit reference to methods of interpretation: starting from reference to the wording of the provision, but also including the interpretation of the legislative history and the general purpose of s 20 of the Danish Constitution.[313] The Højesteret concluded that a transfer of new powers or a reform of the international organization that would result in its new identity are of such a fundamental importance to warrant the use of s 20.[314] However, even if the powers have been delegated without any further specification as to the structure and design of such an organization, the use of s 20 would not be warranted, so long as the delegated powers are defined precisely.[315]

Having carried out the analysis of the substantive changes brought about by the Lisbon Treaty, the Supreme Court concluded that they do not amount to changes 'so fundamental in nature that the EU has in effect assumed a new identity'.[316] The declaration on the principle of primacy,[317] the legal status of the Charter of Fundamental Rights, and the new wording of Article 352 TFEU[318] were all labelled by the appellants as extending the Union's powers. The Supreme Court did not accept these arguments, given the reservations included in each of the mentioned provisions.[319] The Højesteret concluded:

> If an act or a judicial decision which has a specific and real impact on Danish citizens etc. raises doubts as to whether it is based on an application of the Treaties which lies beyond the surrender of sovereignty according to the Accession Act, as amended, this may be made subject to a judicial review, as stated in paragraph 9.6 of the Maastricht judgment. The same applies if EU acts are adopted—or if the Court of Justice delivers judgments—based on such application of the Treaties with reference to the Charter of Fundamental Rights.[320]

[312] Danish Højesteret Case *Hausgaard* (n 309) 5.

[313] ibid 7.

[314] ibid 8.

[315] ibid.

[316] ibid 10. Olsen adds that this 'identity principle' is an added criterion for the application of s 20 of the Danish Constitution and was deliberately left vague to leave the Court with some manoeuvring space in future reviews. Olsen (n 311) 1495–96. For the same tendency in the context of EU law see n 20.

[317] See n 19.

[318] The former art 235 EC was also subject of review in the Supreme Court's *Maastricht* judgment. See n 304.

[319] The Supreme Court stated that it can still perform an *ultra vires* review of the Court of Justice's case law on primacy (according to its decision in *Maastricht*); TEU, art 6(1) expressly prevents the Charter from extending the Union's competences; and the unanimity requirement attached to the flexibility clause from art 352 TFEU prevents its broad application. Danish Højesteret Case *Hausgaard* (n 309) 12–15.

[320] Danish Højesteret Case *Hausgaard* (n 309) 15.

This conclusion fits the pluralist framework: the Supreme Court reserved for itself the right to perform *ultra vires* review of Union action (and specifically the Court of Justice's action). Further, in a reconciliatory fashion of mutually assured trust, the Court found the text of the Lisbon Treaty and the related case law of the Court of Justice to fall within the boundaries of what the Danish Constitution allows. The reluctance and self-restraint of the Danish court may seem as all bark and no bite, but when regarded from the perspective of the role and position of Danish courts in their constitutional set-up, it becomes clear that the Supreme Court did bare its teeth. Olsen also adds that the very language of the Danish court is more stringent than that of its German counterpart introducing the right to *ultra vires* review of 'structurally significant' transgressions of delegated competences.[321] Nevertheless, it is argued that the Danish court's language relies on the 'extraordinary' character of any such transgression, which ultimately results in a high threshold to meet.

The Court of Justice's case law on the scope of general principle of non-discrimination on grounds of age and the Framework Directive[322] triggered a series of interactions with the Supreme Court.[323] As mentioned above, the Danish law regulating retirement discriminated between workers' right to severance package based on their age. The expansion of the general principle non-discrimination on grounds of age to horizontal situations as decided in *Kücükedeveci* was almost automatically applied to the situation referred by the Danish court. In its longest judgment to date, the Højesteret rejected the obligation to interpret the Danish Law on salaried employees *contra legem* in order to afford horizontal effect to the general principle of non-discrimination on grounds of age. The Danish Law on Salaried Employees had, in the course of the procedure been amended, but not in time for it to be applicable to the case at hand.[324]

The Supreme Court provided an extensive interpretation of the limits to the competences that Denmark conferred upon the EU. It interpreted the Danish Act of Accession to the EU, all the ratifying acts of Treaty amendments, and to what extent that includes the law-making activities carried out by the Court of Justice through its jurisprudence. Essentially, the Danish court rejected the expanded self-referential system of the Treaties as created by the Court of Justice; more precisely, its jurisprudence on the direct effect of general principles of EU law.[325] Article 6(3) TEU was used as the central provision to determine the extent to which general principles of Union law are applicable in Denmark and the

[321] Olsen (n 311) 1502.

[322] See s 5 above.

[323] See n 105.

[324] M R Madsen, H P Olsen, and U Šadl, 'Competing Supremacies and Clashing Institutional Rationalities: The Danish Supreme Court's Decision in the *Ajos* Case and the National Limits of Judicial Cooperation' (2017) 23(1–2) *European Law Journal* 140, 146.

[325] Danish Højesteret Case 15/2014 *Dansk Industri* Judgment of 6 December 2016 45–46 https://europeanlawblog.eu/wp-content/uploads/2020/05/Judgment-15-2014-Danish-Constitutional-Court-DI-Final-Judgment.pdf.

Højesteret found no basis in that provision for the Court of Justice's findings in *Mangold* and *Kücükdeveci*.[326]

The Supreme Court's analysis is far from logically flawless. It accepts direct effect and primacy, but solely in relation to Treaty provisions and not general principles of EU law. In her dissent, Judge Scharling pointed out that both the *Maastricht* and the *Lisbon* decisions of the Supreme Court did not set such a high 'specificity' requirement of s 20 of the Constitution so as not to be able to include the case law of the Court of Justice using interpretative methods beyond the literal one.[327]

The second inconsistency is the conclusion that the Danish legislature was aware in 1972, when the Law on Accession came into force, of the doctrines of direct effect and primacy.[328] Conversely, even though *Mangold* was analogously decided before the Lisbon Treaty Ratification Act, this was not enough to include it in its scope, solely because the *travaux préparatoires* of the Ratification Act did not mention it.[329]

While the logic of the Supreme Court may be thin and the Danish Law on Salaried Employees is now amended, the substantive criticism directed at the Court of Justice for expanding the self-referential system of the Treaties through the horizontal application of general principles remains and is constructive.[330] The Supreme Court thus decided to dismiss the appeal and not allow the application of the general principle in a horizontal situation. Consequentially, the Supreme Court decision leads to the conclusion that the judgments of the Court of Justice in *Mangold* and *Kücükdeveci* were *ultra vires* of what the Danish Law on Accession allows. The Supreme Court also applied the more classical Nordic principle of self-restraint[331] and decided it would be acting outside its constitutional powers if it allowed the application of a principle (arguably) not covered by the transfer of powers from Denmark to the EU.[332]

The reaction of the academic community to the decision did not pick up the existing critique directed to the Court of Justice in relation to its *Mangold*-initiated jurisprudence, but rather turned on the Supreme Court for stepping out of bounds. The decision was called an act of 'defiance of clear guidelines from the Court of Justice'[333] and 'controversial',[334] which 'took the European legal community by

[326] ibid 45.

[327] ibid Dissenting Opinion of Judge Scharling 49.

[328] ibid 45–46. Similar criticism was voiced in the Dissenting Opinion of Judge Scharling 49–50.

[329] ibid 47.

[330] See also Möllers (n 165) 163–64.

[331] See n 285.

[332] Danish Højesteret Case *Dansk Industri* (n 325) 48.

[333] M R Madsen, H P Olsen, and U Šadl, 'Legal Disintegration? The Ruling of the Danish Supreme Court in AJOS' *Verfassungsblog* (30 January 2017) http://verfassungsblog.de/legal-disintegration-the-ruling-of-the-danish-supreme-court-in-ajos/.

[334] S Klinge, 'Dialogue or Disobedience between the European Court of Justice and the Danish Constitutional Court? The Danish Supreme Court Challenges the Mangold-principle' *EU Law Analysis Blog* (13 December 2016) http://eulawanalysis.blogspot.nl/2016/12/dialogue-or-disobedience-between.html.

surprise'.[335] I do not share the shock of those commentaries. While the Supreme Court could have justified its decision through a more coherent and less formalistic argument, rooted almost exclusively in the textual interpretation of the Law on Accession and the Treaties, substantively its decision complements the criticisms already made to the Court of Justice.

In the description of the background of the case, the Supreme Court mentioned opinions of several Advocates General concerning the same criticism. First, the Supreme Court cited the analysis of Advocate General Trstenjak[336] concerning the implications of *Kücükdeveci* for the principle of legal certainty and in particular her questioning of the remaining scope of the Framework Directive beyond the general principle of anti-discrimination.[337] The Supreme Court also cited Advocate General Kokott, who called the outcome in *Mangold* and *Kücükdeveci* a 'makeshift arrangement'[338] for resolving discrimination situations between individuals.[339] Finally, in support for its formalistic reading of the application of general principles of EU law, the Supreme Court cited Advocate General Bot[340] in *Kücükdeveci*, where he criticized the Court of Justice's overestimation of how common is the constitutional protection of antidiscrimination on grounds of age across EU Member States.[341] Rather, he recommended a more formalistic reading of the principle, based on the prohibition of discrimination in the then Article 13 TEC and Article 21(1) of the Charter.[342] These concerns have been present since the *Mangold* judgment,[343] and, accordingly, reactions to the Danish Supreme Court's decision seem to me blown out of proportions.

First, the Supreme Court was in doubt as to the counter-balance that the principles of legal certainty and legitimate expectations provide to the horizontal application of the principle of prohibition of discrimination. The same concerns were endorsed by different Advocates General in the development of the Court of Justice's jurisprudence as set out above, which should have signalled to the Court of Justice to reconsider the importance of the two principles and their scope of application. The Court of Justice dismissed the importance of these countervailing principles, without affording enough weight to national constitutional concerns,

335 Madsen, Olsen, and Šadl (n 324) 1.

336 Opinion of Advocate General Trstenjak in Case C-282/10 *Dominguez* [2011] EU:C:2011:559.

337 Danish Højesteret Case *Dansk Industri* (n 325) 4.

338 Opinion of Advocate General Kokott in Case C-499/08 *Ingeniørforeningen i Danmark* [2010] EU:C:2010:248 [22].

339 Danish Højesteret Case *Dansk Industri* (n 325) 40.

340 ibid 38.

341 Opinion of Advocate General Bot in Case C-555/07 *Kücükdeveci* (n 92) [77].

342 ibid. In addition to the three Advocate Generals mentioned in the Danish judgment, it is also worth revisiting the Opinion of Advocate General Mazák in Case C-411/05 *Palacios de la Villa* (n 92) [133]–[139]. He criticizes *Mangold* on the basis of legal certainty and jeopardizing the Treaty structure on the division of competences between the EU and its Member States, but also between different Union institutions.

343 Mazák and Moser called the *Mangold/Kücükdeveci* case law as having an 'evading, transgressing flavour'. Mazák and Moser (n 89) 85.

contrary to the general approach affirmed by all the interviewees at the Court of Justice.

Secondly, the rejection of the Court of Justice's decision in *Dansk Industri* likely serves an even more important purpose—that of keeping the Court of Justice in check[344] and reminding it that, in the pluralist setting in which they all operate, constitutional adjudicators are to be considered peers. Unlike the most recent literature critical of constitutional pluralism, which sources the demise of the theory in individual cases of disobedience by national constitutional courts,[345] precisely the opposite is true. On the one hand, if all the national courts performing constitutional review always remained supportive of all the Court of Justice's decisions, this would result in a hierarchical supremacy of EU law over national constitutions. EU institutions and the Member States, on the other hand, have little to no recourse to keep the Court of Justice in check, namely because any significant control would require a Treaty change. It is therefore essential for the healthy functioning of the pluralist constellation for all the courts involved constructively to contest the Court of Justice.[346]

The Danish court has undergone significant shifts in its behaviour since Denmark joined the EU. Its starting position was one of 'ultimate judicial self-restraint' towards the parliament,[347] but it subsequently evolved into a court ready to review acts of parliament by allowing the *Maastricht* appeal. A further change can be witnessed in the Supreme Court's willingness to review EU acts and the jurisprudence of the Court of Justice (in its *Maastricht* decision) and to do so using an expanded set of interpretative methods. Finally, in the *Dansk Industri* decision, and what might be a result of a changed composition of the Supreme Court,[348] self-restraint towards the national parliament appears to have reassumed its previous prominence. However, this return to judicial self-restraint can also be read as a pretext for the Supreme Court to challenge the demands of EU law and the Court of Justice's jurisprudence, while designating the political arena as the proper forum for the resolution of constitutional conflict.

[344] Justice Huber of the Bundesverfassungsgericht has, in his extrajudicial writing, critiqued the Court of Justice's lack of interest for a fiercer policing of the principles of conferral and subsidiarity. He argued that national courts performing *ultra vires* review will incentivize the Court of Justice not to 'overstretch' the competences of the EU. Huber (n 135) 106.

[345] See eg D Sarmiento, 'The *OMT* Case and the Demise of the Pluralist Movement' *Despite Our Difference Blog* (21 September 2015) https://despiteourdifferencesblog.wordpress.com/2015/09/21/the-omt-case-and-the-demise-of-the-pluralist-movement/.

[346] In the same vein, Huber argues for a constructive policing of the boundaries of EU action by national constitutional courts, which ultimately contribute to the 'balance between the unitarian and diversity-oriented dimensions of European law'. Huber (n 135) 106.

[347] See n 286.

[348] Madsen, Olsen, and Šadl (n 324) 13. They note, however, that the changes on the bench cannot lead to a conclusion that the new judges have a normatively different view on the position of the Supreme Court in the new era of increased supranational adjudication.

## 7 Rule of Law and Judicial Independence

Most recently, the principle of primacy has been further elaborated upon by the Court of Justice in the context of rule of law breaches in some Member States. As will be seen from the analysis, these latter expansions are addressing destructive contestation from the national level, but will have long lasting effects in the management of constructive conflict in the future.

The centrality of the judicial in the EU's constitutional set-up is closely connected to its strong cosmopolitan character, where Member States are no longer sole central decision-makers in the EU. Rather, individuals are provided with access to effective judicial protection and thus themselves become agents of enforcement of EU law. The Court of Justice has in the early days of European integration established the so-called '*Simmenthal* mandate', according to which each national court must apply EU law to cases within their jurisdiction and protect the rights that it accords to citizens in their entirety.[349] Keeping the EU as a polity within the conservative confines of the principle of conferral and limited to a 'compound of states' in fact results in more power for the states and diminishes the direct empowerment of their citizens to take ownership of the integration project. The preliminary reference procedure has for decades claimed success in allowing individuals to enforce their EU law rights against their governments.[350]

That the Polish government would invest significant efforts into reducing judicial independence is thus not surprising in a context where national courts play such a prominent role in the enforcement of EU law and the shared basic values from Article 2 TEU. In response to these developments,[351] the Court of Justice has incrementally expanded the scope of application of Article 19(1) TEU and differentiated it from the right to an effective remedy under Article 47 of the Charter in the 'far-reaching'[352] decision in *Juízes Portugueses*.[353] Namely, for the latter provision to apply, the condition of 'implementation of EU law' from Article 51(1) of the Charter must be met.[354] Conversely, the former right to effective legal protection in Article 19(1) TEU only refers to 'fields covered by EU law' and is thus of a broader scope.[355] This distinction has become crucial in order for judicial independence to acquire a central position in the normative core of the EU's constitution. Using

[349] Claes (n 2) 108.
[350] Rodin (n 111) 298.
[351] M Bonelli and M Claes, 'Judicial Serendipity: How Portuguese Judges Came to the Rescue of the Polish Judiciary ECJ 27 February 2018, Case C-64/16 *Juízes Portugueses*' (2018) 14 *European Constitutional Law Review* 622.
[352] Opinion of Advocate General Bobek in Joined Cases C-748/19 to C-754/19 *Prokuratura Rejonowa* [2021] EU:C:2021:403 [132].
[353] Case C-64/16 *Juízes Portugueses* [2018] EU:C:2018:117.
[354] Although this concept itself is already subject to wide interpretation under *Fransson*. For the analysis of the expansive interpretation of the scope of the Charter see ch 7, s 3.2.
[355] Case C-64/16 *Juízes Portugueses* (n 353) [29].

*Juízes Portugueses* as groundwork for this finding, the Court of Justice has in subsequent cases that deal with Poland in specific, clarified that:

> Under the second subparagraph of Article 19(1) TEU, every Member State must thus in particular ensure that the bodies which, as 'courts or tribunals' within the meaning of EU law, come within its judicial system in the fields covered by EU law and which, therefore, are *liable* to rule, in that capacity, on the application or interpretation of EU law, meet the requirements of effective judicial protection. (emphasis added)[356]

According to this expansion, the only relevant criterion for the requirement of judicial independence to apply is that the national court in question may in theory apply EU law. As Advocate General Bobek clarified, there is nothing controversial in the requirement that the case before a national court need not specifically deal with matters of EU law.[357] However, this decreases the likelihood of destructive conflicts in the EU's judicial space, ensuring that no Member State outright denies the operation of the shared normative core contained in Article 2 TEU.[358] In that respect, Advocate General Bobek called Article 19(1) TEU:

> [a]n extraordinary remedy for extraordinary situations. Its purpose is not to catch all possible issues arising with regard to the national judiciary, but only those of a certain gravity and/or of a systemic nature, to which the internal legal system is unlikely to offer an adequate remedy.[359]

The judicial independence expansions of the Court developed in two further directions. First, the Court addressed a situation in which the national court has been deprived, by legislative or executive intervention, of the possibility to apply Article 267 TFEU and Article 4(3) TEU. Here, the Court for the first time explicitly advised the national court to disapply the new procedural rules and continue assuming jurisdiction under the rules previously in force.[360] The national court in this case would not be able to abide by the obligation to interpret national law in an EU-friendly manner.[361] Rather, it offers an absolute reading of primacy of

[356] Case C-619/18 *Commission v Poland (Independence of the Supreme Court)* [2019] EU:C:2019:531 [55]; Case C-192/18 *Commission v Poland (Independence of Ordinary Courts)* [2019] EU:C:2019:924 [103]; Joined Cases C-585/18, C-624/18 and C-625/18 *AK and Others* [2019] EU:C:2019:982 [83]; Case C-824/18 *AB and Others* (n 56) [112].

[357] 'It is absurd to claim that a national rule on judicial organisation would be unproblematic in purely domestic cases while potentially being an issue each time a provision or principle of EU law becomes applicable.' Opinion of Advocate General Bobek in Joined Cases C-748/19 to C-754/19 *Prokuratura Rejonowa* (n 352) [136].

[358] ibid [144].

[359] ibid [147].

[360] Case C-824/18 *AB and Others* (n 56) [149].

[361] Polish Trybunał Konstytucyjny K 32/09 *Treaty of Lisbon* Judgment of 24 November 2010 [3.1] http://trybunal.gov.pl/fileadmin/content/omowienia/K_32_09_EN.pdf.

EU law in the face of destructive conflict, where the basic tenets of the rule of law are not respected in the Member State. Secondly, the Court of Justice has also addressed compliance with Article 2 TEU as the continuation of respect for EU membership criteria in the accession process. As a consequence of this connection, in *Republikka*, it stated that Member States cannot legislate in a manner that reduces its basic protections and specifically protections of the rule of law.[362]

In contesting these expansions of the Court of Justice, Poland is not the only Member State whose constitutional court engages in destructive conflict. When Romania joined the EU in 2007, issues pertaining to judicial reforms and corruption remained in need of addressing. Given its more general loss of leverage in ensuring compliance post-accession,[363] the EU was hard pressed to ensure the continuation of its influence. For this purpose, the Commission set up the Cooperation and Verification Mechanism (CVM)[364] established by Commission Decision 2006/928/EC.[365] The CVM operates as a monitoring tool, albeit sanction-free. The Commission issues regular progress reports including recommendations. The CVM also sets out rule of law benchmarks to be regularly reported on by Romania.[366]

With the parliamentary elections in 2016 bringing about a change in government, Romania has witnessed a consistent attack on its judiciary, climaxing in 2018 with the introduction of disciplinary proceedings for magistrates and their personal responsibility for judicial errors, without objections from the Constitutional Court.[367] In such a climate, Commission recommendations under the CVM focused on remedying these issues, but the Constitutional Court found that they have no legal value as they do not form part of EU law, given that this question was not, as of yet, interpreted by the Court of Justice. In this situation, similarly to Poland, the Constitutional Court becomes part of the problem as it endorses the legislative changes reducing judicial independence. In such a constellation, the Constitutional Court no longer participates in constructive constitutional conflict but forms part of the systemic, destructive nature of contesting the values in Article 2 TEU, namely the rule of law.

362 Case C-896/19 *Republikka* [2021] EU:C:2021:311 [62]–[64].

363 C Lacatus and U Sedelmeier, 'Does Monitoring without Enforcement Make a Difference? The European Union and Anti-corruption Policies in Bulgaria and Romania after Accession' (2020) 27(8) *Journal of European Public Policy* 1236, 1237.

364 Information on the Cooperation and Verification Mechanism for Bulgaria and Romania is available at https://ec.europa.eu/info/policies/justice-and-fundamental-rights/upholding-rule-law/rule-law/assistance-bulgaria-and-romania-under-cvm/cooperation-and-verification-mechanism-bulgaria-and-romania_en.

365 Commission Decision of 13 December 2006 establishing a mechanism for cooperation and verification of progress in Romania to address specific benchmarks in the areas of judicial reform and the fight against corruption [2006] OJ L354/56.

366 R Carp, 'The Struggle for the Rule of Law in Romania as an EU Member State: The Role of the Cooperation and Verification Mechanism' (2014) 10(1) *Utrecht Law Review* 1, 6.

367 E S Tănăsescu, 'The Independence of Justice as Proxy for the Rule of Law in the EU Case Study: Romania' (2021) 3(1) *Nuovi Autoritarismi e Democrazie: Diritto, Istituzioni e Società* 103, 114.

In response, six ordinary Romanian courts submitted preliminary references to the Court of Justice seeking the interpretation of the CVM and the resulting recommendations.[368] This is again analogous to the Polish situation where ordinary courts have took up the task of defending their position in the face of rule of law breaches and are using the EU's normative frame for this purpose. Building on its case law concerning judicial independence, the Court of Justice found that the Decision establishing the CVM and the resulting recommendations form part of EU law and have direct effect.[369] The Court specifically addressed this in the context of shared values in Article 2 TEU, which represent the conditions for accession as well as for continued membership in the EU.[370]

The Constitutional Court addressed this decision only several weeks later,[371] finding that primacy of EU law applies only to ordinary legislation and not to the constitution.[372] The following statement of the Constitutional Court adds a level of both confusion and incoherence with even such a weak treatment of primacy: 'a national court does not have the power to examine the conformity of a provision of national law, found to be constitutional in the light of Article 148 of the Constitution, with the provisions of EU law'.[373] In other words, every time the Constitutional Court sanctions an ordinary national law as constitutional, it acquires constitutional status and primacy of EU law does not apply to it.[374] Such a reduction in the operation of EU law in the Romanian legal order grants virtually free reign to the government under whose control the Constitutional Court currently operates. Any and all legislation that undermines the rule of law simply needs to be confirmed as constitutional and is no longer subject to Article 2 TEU nor Article 19(1) TEU control by the Court of Justice, in direct contradiction of the judicial independence findings of the Court of Justice in *Juízes Portugueses*[375] and most recently in *AB and Others*.[376]

Destructive constitutional conflicts that lie at the source of these expansions by the Court of Justice demonstrate the gravity of the disagreement between a Member State and the EU. The conflict of such a degree also shows the limits of the auto-correct function of constitutional pluralism, where a judicial resolution of the situation is not sufficient in itself to put a halt to the persistent breaches of the rule of law. In this respect, a coherent political and legal action, both top-down (the EU

[368] Joined Cases C-83/19, C-127/19, C-195/19, C-291/19, C-355/19 and C-397/19 *Asociația 'Forumul Judecătorilor din România'* [2021] EU:C:2021:393.

[369] ibid [178], [249].

[370] ibid [160], [162].

[371] Romanian Curtea Constituțională Decision No 390 of 8 June 2021 https://www.ccr.ro/wp-content/uploads/2021/07/Decizie_390_2021_EN.pdf.

[372] ibid [76].

[373] ibid.

[374] See also B Selejan-Gutan, 'A Tale of Primacy Part II: The Romanian Constitutional Court on a Slippery Slope' *Verfassungsblog* (18 June 2021) https://verfassungsblog.de/a-tale-of-primacy-part-ii/.

[375] Case C-64/16 *Juízes Portugueses* (n 353).

[376] Case C-824/18 *AB and Others* (n 56).

acting vis-à-vis the Member State), but also importantly, bottom-up (sourced in the Member State itself) is needed to impose an overhaul to the anti-rule of law developments. Protecting the rule of law can only be successful if both processes are in place: due to the heterarchical nature of the EU's constitutional space, isolated EU action would result in a hierarchical imposition of EU values over national ones, resulting in reduced legitimacy and increased contestation from the national level. Bottom-up activity, however, has the advantage of creating a contribution to the EU's constitution more broadly conceived, but also promotes its cosmopolitan character. The myriad preliminary references submitted by Polish and Romanian judges attempting to protect their independence in the face of political intervention is only possible due to the individual enforcement character of EU law that no longer depends on the willingness of Member States to negotiate it and explicitly implement it.

## 8 Conclusion

The question of the final arbiter in the European Union appears to be unsettled to everyone except the courts under analysis. The Court of Justice has, for its part, consistently held that it has the final say for all matters EU law, and it has for this purpose created its own self-referential framework. Drawing upon Germany's model of *ultra vires* review, courts with constitutional jurisdiction in the Czech Republic and Denmark have both found judgments of the Court of Justice *ultra vires*. Parallel claims to the final say by the courts under analysis are therefore beyond obvious.

The analysed jurisprudence offers a perfect occasion to test the applicability and usefulness of the auto-correct function of constitutional pluralism in the event of a constitutional conflict. As advocated by Huber,[377] the role of national constitutional courts should be to constructively keep the Court of Justice in check and control its jurisprudence. On the one hand, the Danish case demonstrates precisely this point—none of the criticism by the Advocates General or academic commentary propelled the Court of Justice to rethink the role of general principles and their applicability between private parties. Furthermore, the German decision in *Weiss II* can be seen as an attempt to control the European Central Bank more stringently in the exercise of its mandate. These decisions also fall squarely into Walker's framework of conflict resolution, in which conflict should be resolved through mutual negotiation, learning, open dialogue and cross-examination.[378]

The Czech decision, on the other hand, demonstrates that we should look beyond individual points of conflict and regard the jurisprudence of constitutional

[377] Huber (n 135) 106.
[378] N Walker, 'The Idea of Constitutional Pluralism' (2002) 65(3) *Modern Law Review* 317, 358–59.

conflict incrementally, equally presupposed by constitutional pluralism. A single decision did not lead to an overall deterioration in the relationship between the Court of Justice and the Ústavní Soud: the 2014 National Report for the Conference of European Constitutional Courts prepared by the Ústavní Soud itself does not mention this judgment among those relevant for the relationship between EU law and national constitutional law.[379] *Weiss II* is again instructive in this regard, as the German court twice submitted a preliminary reference concerning the accountability of the ECB, asking the Court of Justice to apply its own standard of review from *Gauweiler*. A pronunciation of a judgment as *ultra vires* is but one link in the long incremental chain of interactions between these two courts.[380]

It was also visible that not all instances of contestation of EU law follow a constructive pattern of reasonable disagreement within the scope of Article 2 TEU. Courts in Poland and Romania are rejecting rulings of the Court of Justice concerning the basic principles shared by all Member States, most importantly the rule of law. As was stated in the analysis, such conflicts remove the constitutional courts in those Member States from the scope of constructive conflict. In contrast, ordinary national courts take centre stage in protecting their own position by submitting preliminary references to the Court. It is also crucial to note here that in respect of constitutional courts, the auto-correct function of constitutional pluralism cannot accommodate destructive conflicts, as they are no longer applying the necessary self-restrain and mutual respect.[381] Destructive conflicts can only be resolved through cumulative legal and political actors at the national and EU level.

In the area of competence monitoring, as the analysis has shown, there is no single final arbiter. There are advantages for all the actors in the European judicial space to engage in competence monitoring. On the one hand, it is essential for the Court of Justice to be the final interpreter of Union law to ensure its uniform application throughout the Member States. On the other hand, it would be contrary to the principle of conferral for the Court of Justice to decide on the limits of its own competence, since the source of its mandate—the Treaties—was created by the Member States. In this context, constitutional pluralism appears to best capture these tensions, where constitutional adjudicators compete with the Court of Justice and through it engage in a constructive dialogue on the development of EU and national constitutional law. Such dialogue takes place not in a single case, but in an incremental fashion, where tensions and conflicts are settled through progressive interpretations on both the EU and the national level.

[379] See n 279.

[380] Which, as was explained above in s 6.3, may be broken with the infringement proceedings initiated by the Commission.

[381] See ch 3, s 4 for the analysis of the recurring judicial vocabulary behind the operation of the auto-correct function. Crucially, Member States currently engaging in destructive conflict were earlier also using the same vocabulary in their interpretations of the relationship between constitutional and EU law.

# 6
# Identity Review

## 1 Introduction

The long-celebrated EU motto 'united in diversity' strikes at the heart of the inherent tension between two main drivers behind Member State action: the inclination towards integration, while preserving national particularities and interests. The 'national identity' clause in Article 4(2) TEU, introduced first in the Maastricht Treaty in 1992, lies at the intersection between these two directions. Reliance on the clause before the Court of Justice has been confined mainly to its use as a justification of Member State failure to respect EU law obligations. A more important role of the national identity clause for the Member States may be seen in its potential to become a substantive expression of national constitutional concerns,[1] minimizing future constitutional and institutional conflicts.[2]

In the wider constitutional dialogue of the EU, the terms 'national' and 'constitutional' identity have been used as synonyms.[3] However, in its first preliminary reference to the Court of Justice, the Bundesverfassungsgericht stated that the terms were not interchangeable, and more importantly, that the protection of constitutional identity of a Member State falls within the exclusive jurisdiction of national constitutional courts.[4] Constitutional identity is thus a concept developed by national constitutional courts in the process of identity review as one of the heads of review in the area of constitutional conflict. Constitutional adjudicators have referred to constitutional identity with the aim of determining constitutional limits

[1] For an analysis of the introduction of national constitutional concepts in the Constitutional Treaty see J Ziller, 'National Constitutional Concepts in the New Constitution for Europe' (2005) 1(2) *European Constitutional Law Review* 247.

[2] One should bear in mind that the application of art 4(2) TEU is not restricted solely to address the conflicts between existing EU law and national law, but also has a role in the legislative procedure itself. However, its use in the legislative procedure lies outside the scope of the book, insofar as it does not involve courts as relevant actors.

[3] Opinion of Advocate General Maduro in Case C-53/04 *Marrosu* [2006] EU:C:2006:569 [40]. See also L F M Besselink, 'National and Constitutional Identity before and after Lisbon' (2010) 6(3) *Utrecht Law Review* 36, 37; S Rodin, 'National Identity and Market Freedoms after the Treaty of Lisbon' (2011) 7 *Croatian Yearbook of European Law and Policy* 11; A von Bogdandy and S Schill, 'Overcoming Absolute Primacy: Respect for National Identity under the Lisbon Treaty' (2011) 48 *Common Market Law Review* 1417, 1435; G van der Schyff, 'The Constitutional Relationship between the European Union and its Member States: The Role of National Identity in Article 4(2) TEU' (2012) 37(5) *European Law Review* 563, 568.

[4] German Bundesverfassungsgericht Case 2 BvR 2728/13 *Gauweiler* Order of 14 January 2014 [29] https://www.bundesverfassungsgericht.de/SharedDocs/Entscheidungen/EN/2014/01/rs20140114_2bvr272813en.html.

*The Jurisprudence of Constitutional Conflict in the European Union*. Ana Bobić, Oxford University Press. © Ana Bobić 2022.
DOI: 10.1093/oso/9780192847034.003.0006

to the primacy of Union law, thus reasserting their own position in judicial power relations in the EU.[5]

These two different interpretations of the national identity clause portray the nature of the constitutional conflict in the EU. After looking in more detail at the case law of national constitutional adjudicators and the Court of Justice on identity review, several conclusions will be drawn as to the substantive use of identity review. It will become visible that the question of who is the final arbiter on matters of national and/or constitutional identity will not yield a single winner, but, beneficially for the more general development of EU's judicial architecture, it will render the question immaterial.[6]

Section 2 will offer an analysis of the national constitutional jurisprudence and its approach to constitutional identity. In so doing, I will present the wide range of national approaches to safeguarding constitutional identity: the German unconditional take on constitutional identity as a limit to the principle of primacy of EU law; the Polish shift from constructive to destructive use of constitutional identity; and finally other Member States that envisage some identity-based limits to primacy, while at the same time offering a range of reconciliatory options should a conflict arise. The case law of the Court of Justice will be explored in section 3, by looking at the different ways in which Article 4(2) TEU has featured in its decisions on free movement. Section 4 will conclude with suggesting a pluralist interpretation of the national identity clause that would accommodate both national constitutional concerns and the requirements of the principle of primacy of EU law.

## 2 Constitutional Identity

Jurisprudence of national constitutional adjudicators has influenced, if not even shaped, fundamental constitutional concepts of EU law. It is argued that the identity review jurisprudence on the national level can be placed on a spectrum between an unconditional limit to the principle of primacy (for example the German Bundesverfassungsgericht) on one end, the middle where constitutional identity is operating as a conditional limit to the principle, and examples on the other end where trust is placed in the Court of Justice to safeguard national constitutional values through the application of Article 4(2) TEU (the Spanish Tribunal

[5] I will refer to 'identity review' throughout the chapter so as to encompass review carried out on the basis of both the national identity clause and constitutional identity as conceived by constitutional adjudicators. When the difference between national and constitutional identity is relevant, this will be flagged in the analysis.

[6] In this respect, Halberstam claims that the lack of a determined final authority is in fact an 'essential characteristic' of the system. D Halberstam, 'Constitutional Heterarchy: The Centrality of Conflict in the European Union and the United States' in J L Dunoff and J P Trachtman (eds), *Ruling the World? Constitutionalism, International Law, and Global Governance* (CUP 2009) 331.

Constitucional).[7] In between is a range of jurisprudence introducing identity-based constitutional limits and concessions to the principle of primacy, aimed at avoiding or managing constitutional conflict in a constructive manner. On this spectrum, all courts strive to envisage parameters of conflict management with the Court of Justice with the aim of preserving the atmosphere of mutual respect and self-restraint.

Identity-based conflicts are not always constructive. In the past decade, with the rise of populist and authoritarian tendencies in a number of Member States, constitutional identity developed into an effective tool for justifying intrusions into judicial independence and democratic institutions more generally.[8] These conflicts display a bad faith use of constitutional identity that results in disagreements that are no longer reasonable and result in outcomes detracting from the shared values among EU members. In such situations, the auto-correct function of constitutional pluralism is not able to incrementally accommodate the conflict in the sphere of judicial interactions, given that the destructive interpretation detracts from the rule of law and no longer ensures respect of the shared lowest common denominator in Article 2 TEU.

In addressing identity review constitutional conflicts this section will explore in particular: (1) the different limits that national constitutional adjudicators placed on the principle of primacy in relation to the protection of national/constitutional identity; and (2) the possible scenarios that they envisage in the event a constitutional conflict takes place. In addition, I will also present destructive identity conflicts that have recently emerged in Poland and other Member States, underlining the limitations they pose for legal enforcement of primacy of EU law more generally, and the operation of the auto-correct function more specifically.

## 2.1 Constitutional Identity as an Unconditional Limit to the Primacy of EU Law

In this section I will be focusing on the German jurisprudence concerning identity review, in particular in the light of the Bundesverfassungsgericht's recent interpretation of the Basic Law, underscoring the difference between national and constitutional identity.[9] However, in order to draw a complete picture of the German

[7] Spieker makes a distinction between soft-conflict and hard-conflict identity reviews to illustrate the absolute and relative consequences such review has in limiting the operation of the principle of primacy. L D Spieker, 'Framing and Managing Constitutional Identity Conflicts: How to Stabilize the Modus Vivendi Between the Court of Justice and National Constitutional Courts' (2020) 57(2) *Common Market Law Review* 361, 373.

[8] For an overview of the literature addressing these developments see J Scholtes, 'Abusing Constitutional Identity' (2021) 22 *German Law Journal* 534, 545.

[9] German Bundesverfassungsgericht Order *Gauweiler* (n 4) [29].

court's understanding of constitutional identity and how it affects the primacy of EU law, I will start with initial cases where identity was flagged as a limit to EU law.

The first mention of constitutional identity can be found in *Solange I*.[10] Here, the Bundesverfassungsgericht, apart from introducing the preferable standard for the review of fundamental rights protection at the Union level, explained the limits to integration referring to the core of the German Basic Law as a basis for its identity.[11] While the judgment in *Solange I* concerned a regulation, the scope of EU's competence at that time did not extend to the protection of fundamental rights, resulting in the leverage unquestionably on the side of the Bundesverfassungsgericht and its constitutional role to protect fundamental rights guaranteed by the Basic Law.[12]

Several decades later, a number of constitutional complaints against the ratification of the Lisbon Treaty proved to be an excellent opportunity for the Bundesverfassungsgericht to present its complete vision of identity review, added as a third head of review of EU acts, alongside *ultra vires* and fundamental rights review.[13] While the complaints were admitted based on an allegation that the right to vote under Article 38(1) of the Basic Law would be infringed, the Bundesverfassungsgericht engaged in a full review of the Treaty Amendment pending ratification. The identity review introduced in the judgment is defined in rather vague terms:

> [i]t must be possible within the German jurisdiction to assert the responsibility for integration if obvious transgressions of the boundaries occur when the European Union claims competences [ ... ] and to preserve the inviolable core content of the Basic Law's constitutional identity by means of a identity review.[14]

The Bundesverfassungsgericht went on to give examples of 'core areas' that are not subject to integration, including criminal law (both substantive and procedural), the monopoly on the use of force by the police and by the military, fundamental fiscal decisions on public revenue and expenditure, the social state, the school and education system, as well as the relationship with religious communities.[15]

[10] German Bundesverfassungsgericht Case 37 BVerfGE 271 *Internationale Handelsgesellschaft (Solange I)* Judgment of 29 May 1974 [279].

[11] See also German Bundesverfassungsgericht Case 2 BvR 197/83 *Re the Application of Wünsche Handelsgesellschaft (Solange II)* Judgment of 22 October 1986 [375]-[376].

[12] See in that respect the Dissenting Opinion of Justice Gerhardt in German Bundesverfassungsgericht Order *Gauweiler* (n 4) [3].

[13] German Bundesverfassungsgericht Case 2 BVerfG 2/08 *Lisbon Treaty* Judgment of 30 June 2009 [240]–[241] http://www.bverfg.de/e/es20090630_2bve000208en.html.

[14] ibid [240].

[15] ibid [252]–[260]. The Bundesverfassungsgericht added the budgetary autonomy of the German Parliament to the list of areas pertaining to the untouchable constitutional core in Case 2 BVerfG 987/10 *Aids for Greece and EFSF* Judgment of 7 September 2011 [126] http://www.bundesverfassungsgericht.de/SharedDocs/Entscheidungen/EN/2011/09/rs20110907_2bvr098710en.html. See also P M Huber, 'The Federal Constitutional Court and European Integration' (2015) 21(1) *European Public Law* 83, 92.

The decision does not entail definitions or examples of what an 'obvious transgression' might entail. However, it underlined that undertaking identity review needs to go hand in hand with the principle of sincere cooperation from Article 4(3) TEU and should furthermore be performed taking into account the Basic Law's openness towards EU law.[16] Wendel is pessimistic about the actual use of the principle of friendliness towards EU law when conducting identity review; he views it as a trick through which the Bundesverfassungsgericht will place further limits on the applicability of EU law in Germany.[17] Pernice offers a more optimistic reading of the reference to the principle of friendliness towards European law, interpreting the seemingly contradictory statement as a turn to a 'non-hierarchical or pluralist' understanding of the relationship between European and national constitutional law.[18]

I argue that the wording of the Bundesverfassungsgericht should be read in support of a pluralist understanding of the European constitutional space. In particular, the Bundesverfassungsgericht referred to the *Kadi* judgment of the Court of Justice[19] as an example of a situation in which the EU's identity claim overrides its legal obligations in the international sphere.[20] In so doing, the Bundesverfassungsgericht addressed the 'contexts of political order which are not structured according to a strict hierarchy',[21] and subsequently applied the analogy to a hypothetical situation of a conflict between the German constitutional identity and the requirements of EU law.[22]

The German court stated that the right to perform an identity review is 'rooted in constitutional law'[23] and exists because 'the guarantee of national constitutional

[16] German Bundesverfassungsgericht Case 2 BVerfG 2/08 *Lisbon Treaty* (n 13) [240]. See also E Vranes, 'German constitutional foundations of, and limitations to, EU integration: a systematic analysis' (2013) 14(1) *German Law Journal* 75, 92.

[17] M Wendel, 'Lisbon before the courts: a comparative perspective' (2011) 7 *European Constitutional Law Review* 96, 134. In general, it seems that the literature dealing with the judgment is mainly pessimistic as regards the use of the principle of openness to European law. See D Halberstam and C Möllers, 'The German Constitutional Court Says "Ja zu Deutschland!"' (2009) 10(8) *German Law Journal* 1241; D Thym, 'From Ultra-vires-control to Constitutional Identity Review: The Lisbon Judgment of the German Constitutional Court' in J M Beneyto and I Pernice (eds), *Europe's Constitutional Challenges in the Light of the Recent Case Law of National Constitutional Courts: Lisbon and Beyond* (Nomos 2011); S Theil, 'What Red Lines, If Any, Do the Lisbon Judgments of European Constitutional Courts Draw for Future EU Integration?' (2014) 15(4) *German Law Journal* 599.

[18] I Pernice, 'Motor or Brake for European Policies? Germany's New Role in the EU after the Lisbon-Judgment of Its Federal Constitutional Court' in J M Beneyto and I Pernice (eds), *Europe's Constitutional Challenges in the Light of the Recent Case Law of National Constitutional Courts: Lisbon and Beyond* (Nomos 2011) 355, 385. See also D Thym, 'In the Name of the Sovereign Statehood: A Critical Introduction to the Lisbon Judgment of the German Constitutional Court' (2009) 46 *Common Market Law Review* 1795, 1805.

[19] Joined Cases C-402/05 P and C-415/05 P *Kadi and Al Barakaat International Foundation* [2008] EU:C:2008:461.

[20] German Bundesverfassungsgericht Case *Lisbon Treaty* (n 13) [340].

[21] ibid.

[22] Nicolaïdis argues that the Bundesverfassungsgericht in fact praises the heterarchical setting. See K Nicolaïdis, 'Germany as Europe: How the Constitutional Court Unwittingly Embraced EU Demoicracy. A Comment on Franz Mayer' (2011) 9(3-4) *International Journal of Constitutional Law* 786, 791.

[23] German Bundesverfassungsgericht Case *Lisbon Treaty* (n 13) [240].

identity under constitutional and under Union law go hand in hand in the European legal area'.[24] This point treats national and constitutional identity as synonyms[25] and therefore represents a reading of Article 4(2) TEU similar to that employed by the Court of Justice and the majority of the academic community.[26] In addition, Thym notes that the use of the expression 'hand in hand' for describing the relationship between national and constitutional identity might also serve as a subscription to the pluralist understanding of the EU constitutional framework.[27]

Somewhat surprising in comparison to the reasoning of its judgment concerning the Lisbon Treaty, the Bundesverfassungsgericht set out a more detailed account of identity review in its first preliminary reference to the Court of Justice.[28] The case concerned the announced Outright Monetary Transactions mechanism, which is not a binding piece of EU law, but merely a press release issued by the Governing Council of the European Central Bank (ECB).[29] However, the legal nature of the document was not disputed by the Bundesverfassungsgericht or by the Court of Justice, although some of the intervening Member States and EU institutions in the procedure raised issues of admissibility.[30] The Court of Justice stated that the reference concerns the interpretation of Treaty provisions regulating the competences of the ECB and was therefore admissible.[31]

As regards identity review, the Bundesverfassungsgericht in its reference divided constitutional values in two categories: those underpinning national 'fundamental structures, political and constitutional' as set out in Article 4(2) TEU and the core constitutional values that represent the national constitutional identity, therefore being beyond the reach of EU law. The main difference between the two is that the latter are not subject to the principle of primacy of EU law and the Bundesverfassungsgericht has exclusive jurisdiction as to their interpretation.[32] Furthermore, the German court stated that values representing constitutional identity cannot be subject to any kind of balancing exercise and must be unconditionally protected by the Bundesverfassungsgericht.[33]

24 ibid Headnote 4 and [240].

25 Thym (n 17) 41; Halberstam and Möllers (n 17) 1247.

26 See in particular n 3 and Thym (n 18) 1811.

27 Thym (n 18) 1811.

28 German Bundesverfassungsgericht Order *Gauweiler* (n 4). For an analysis of the *ultra vires* reasoning of the Bundesverfassungsgericht in the reference see ch 5, s 6.1.

29 'Technical features of Outright Monetary Transactions' Governing Council of the European Central Bank 6 September 2012 http://www.ecb.europa.eu/press/pr/date/2012/html/pr120906_1.en.html.

30 Admissibility was challenged, in one way or another, by the Dutch, Finnish, French, Greek, Irish, Italian, Portuguese, and Spanish Government, as well as by the European Commission, the ECB, and the European Parliament. Case C-62/14 *Gauweiler* [2015] EU:C:2015:7 [18]–[23]. For a more detailed analysis of the admissibility point of the judgment see S Simon, 'Direct Cooperation Has Begun: Some Remarks on the Judgment of the ECJ on the OMT Decision of the ECB in Response to the German Federal Constitutional Court's First Request for a Preliminary Ruling' (2015) 16(4) *German Law Journal* 1025, 1027 ff.

31 Case C-62/14 *Gauweiler* (n 30) [30].

32 German Bundesverfassungsgericht Order *Gauweiler* (n 4) [29].

33 ibid.

The distinction between constitutional and national identity seems at odds with the reasoning employed in the *Lisbon Treaty* decision of the Bundesverfassungsgericht. In particular, the German court has abandoned its view that the two notions go 'hand in hand'[34] and put forward an interpretation which sets out a *domaine réservé* for the constitutional court. The Court of Justice, in its reply to the preliminary reference, refrained from entering into any discussion on this point and focused solely on the substantive questions concerning the ECB's mandate in relation to the OMT mechanism. I argue that the Court of Justice was prudent not to enter a discussion on this matter, but rather deferred to the Bundes verfassungsgericht.[35] In turn, the Bundesverfassungsgericht also acted in a manner of mutual respect and self-restraint, by not disputing the interpretation on the validity of the OMT mechanism as given by the Court of Justice.[36] It has, in a clear pluralist fashion, done so after underlining its vision of identity review as a limit to European integration.[37]

In December 2015, the Bundesverfassungsgericht decided not to refer a preliminary reference to the Court of Justice in a case where an EAW was to be applied to an American citizen, who was to be extradited to Italy where he was sentenced *in absentia*.[38] The Düsseldorf Higher Regional Court allowed such an extradition, but the American citizen submitted a constitutional complaint to the Bundesverfassungsgericht claiming he was sentenced *in absentia* and would not have a chance of a new evidentiary hearing in Italy, as required by Article 5(1) of the EAW Framework Decision.[39]

The Bundesverfassungsgericht quashed the decision of the Higher Regional Court, but the Order is of interest as it gives further information on the Bundesverfassungsgericht's view of identity review. First, the Bundesverfassungsgericht found that, although the requirements of its *Bananas Market Regulation* decision for fundamental rights review had not been met,[40] it would carry out an identity review. Specifically, the right to a fair trial

[34] German Bundesverfassungsgericht Case *Lisbon Treaty* (n 13) Headnote 4 and [240].

[35] See on this point M Claes and J-H Reestman, 'The Protection of National Constitutional Identity and the Limits of European Integration at the Occasion of the Gauweiler Case' (2015) 16(4) *German Law Journal* 917, 970.

[36] German Bundesverfassungsgericht Case 2 BvR 2728/13 *Gauweiler* Judgment of 21 June 2016 http://www.bundesverfassungsgericht.de/SharedDocs/Entscheidungen/EN/2016/06/rs20160621_2bvr272813en.html.

[37] ibid [120]–[121]. See also the analysis of the Portuguese identity review standard in s 2.2.5. below.

[38] German Bundesverfassungsgericht Case 2 BvR 2735/14 *Mr R* Order of 15 December 2015 http://www.bundesverfassungsgericht.de/SharedDocs/Pressemitteilungen/EN/2016/bvg16-004.html.

[39] Council Framework Decision 2002/584/JHA of 13 June 2002 on the European arrest warrant and the surrender procedures between Member States [2002] OJ L190/1. Council Framework Decision 2009/299/JHA of 26 February 2009 amending Framework Decisions 2002/584/JHA, 2005/214/JHA, 2006/783/JHA, 2008/909/JHA and 2008/947/JHA, thereby enhancing the procedural rights of persons and fostering the application of the principle of mutual recognition to decisions rendered in the absence of the person concerned at the trial [2009] OJ L81/24. For the analysis on the fundamental rights protection developments concerning the EAW see ch 7, ss 4.1.1. and 4.1.2.

[40] See ch 7, s 4.1.1.2 for the analysis of the decision.

was considered inextricably linked to human dignity, which forms part of the unamendable core of the Basic Law.[41]

Second, the Bundesverfassungsgericht reiterated the view introduced in *Gauweiler* that the constitutional identity of Germany is a matter for it alone to interpret and protect, and is not subject to European integration or open to European interpretation.[42] However, it continued by reiterating its stance from the *Lisbon Treaty* decision that such an understanding of constitutional identity is inherent to the national identity clause from Article 4(2) TEU and is in line with the principle of sincere cooperation from Article 4(3) TEU.[43] Nevertheless, the Bundesverfassungsgericht, taking into account the principle of openness to European integration, reserved solely for itself any possibility of declaring a provision of EU law inapplicable in Germany, underlining the extremely exceptional nature of such a scenario.[44] Yet, 'this does not entail a substantial risk for the uniform application of Union law, as the powers of review reserved for the Federal Constitutional Court have to be exercised with restraint and in a manner open to European integration'.[45]

Although such reasoning might come across as contrary to the principle of primacy, it in fact fits the pluralist heterarchical scheme. The role of the national identity clause is precisely to underline differences between Member States and their constitutional values. However, national courts are not able to use this exception to circumvent the principle of primacy and the most extreme remedy is reserved for the constitutional court,[46] under strict conditions.

Finally, in the decision concerning the Public Sector Purchase Programme (PSPP) of the ECB,[47] the Bundesverfassungsgericht found that the ECB acted in excess of its monetary policy powers. However, the decision is of relevance here as it includes identity based arguments used in a way that detracts from the balancing between constitutional and EU law demands and is possibly absolute, unilateral, and thus destructive. The Bundesverfassungsgericht's initial worry in *Gauweiler* concerned the possibility that quantitative easing may involve unforeseeable risks for national budgets beyond those directly approved by the Bundestag. It ultimately accepted the assurances of the Court of Justice that the OMT programme

41 German Bundesverfassungsgericht Order *Mr R* (n 38) [34].

42 ibid Key considerations [1]. The case law of the United Kingdom Supreme Court might be interpreted as similar to the position of Germany. In a United Kingdom Supreme Court case, Lord Mance stated that should an unlikely situation of a constitutional conflict arise between the national and the EU constitutional order, it should be for the Supreme Court itself to decide on consistency of national constitutional requirements. He then went on to underline that such a situation would be unlikely and should be treated with mutual respect and caution. United Kingdom Supreme Court Case *Pham* [2015] UKSC 19 [90]–[91].

43 German Bundesverfassungsgericht Order *Mr R* (n 38) Key considerations [1].

44 ibid.

45 ibid Key considerations [1.b].

46 See also the practice of the Italian Constitutional Court below in s 2.2.4.

47 For the *ultra vires* analysis of the decision see ch 5, s 6.1.

entails safeguards preventing such an outcome.[48] The same concern was raised in relation to the PSPP, where the Court of Justice dismissed the question about risk-sharing as hypothetical.[49] The Bundesverfassungsgericht took this to mean that the Treaties prohibit risk-sharing as such and added that this would also be contrary to Germany's constitutional identity protected by Articles 23(1) and 79(3) of the Basic Law.[50] In that sense, identity review is a weapon of a strength incomparable to that of *ultra vires* review: while the latter allows for the situation to be remedied by an action of the Bundestag, the former is embedded in an unamendable characteristic of the Basic Law and does not allow for any departures.[51]

The good news is that the Bundesverfassungsgericht seems to use identity review in a self-restrained manner and abiding by its well-established self-imposed obligation of an EU-friendly interpretation.[52] In other words, although statements of an uncompromising protection of constitutional identity now feature more prominently in the text of the judgments, in effect quantitative easing programmes of the ECB are nevertheless accepted when it comes to their compliance with the prohibition of monetary financing. And this is so, although each new programme departs further from the original conditions of compliance set out by the Court of Justice in *Gauweiler*.[53] We can therefore speak of a (perhaps not very sophisticated) constructive attempt of the German court to underline the magnitude of the issue under review in order to demand a higher standard of review of ECB's activities in the monetary field. The German court has used identity review to demonstrate the importance of budgetary autonomy in the Basic Law. As a result, we have witnessed the ECB complying with its request to publish its proportionality analysis and rejected an application for an order of execution relating to the PSPP judgment.[54]

At present, the EU's 'Next Generation EU' pandemic programme that forms part of the EU's Own Resources Decision[55] is being challenged before the Bundesverfassungsgericht by the founder of the Alternative für Deutschland

[48] Case C-62/14 *Gauweiler* (n 30) [123]–[126] accepted by the Bundesverfassungsgericht in *Gauweiler* (Judgment) (n 36) [218]–[219].

[49] Case C-493/17 *Weiss* [2018] EU:C:2018:1000 [165]–[166].

[50] German Bundesverfassungsgericht Cases 2 BvR 859/15, 2 BvR 980/16, 2 BvR 2006/15, 2 BvR 1651/15 *Weiss II* Judgment of 5 May 2020 [227]–[228].

[51] German Bundesverfassungsgericht in *Gauweiler* (Judgment) [29].

[52] In addition, this approach may also be seen as confirming interpretative pluralism: 'In offering a constitutional interpretation which reasonably accommodates but also constrains European institutions [ . . . ] constitutional courts go into novel terrain, and if they manage to stick to some of their constitutional values they almost inevitably do so at the cost of others.' G Davies, 'Interpretative Pluralism and the Constitutionalisation of the EU Legal Order' in M Dawson and M Jachtenfuchs (eds), *Autonomy without Collapse in a Better European Union* (OUP forthcoming 2022).

[53] A Bobić and M Dawson, 'Making sense of the "incomprehensible": The PSPP judgment of the German Federal Constitutional Court' (2020) 57(6) *Common Market Law Review* 1953, 1956–1957.

[54] German Bundesverfassungsgericht Case 2 BvR 1651/15 Order of 29 April 2021 https://www.bundesverfassungsgericht.de/SharedDocs/Entscheidungen/DE/2021/03/rs20210326_2bvr054721.html.

[55] Council Decision (EU, Euratom) 2020/2053 of 14 December 2020 on the system of own resources of the European Union and repealing Decision 2014/335/EU [2020] OJ L424/1.

(AfD) precisely on the basis of constitutional identity.[56] On 26 March 2021, the Bundesverfassungsgericht issued an unreasoned decision[57] to the Federal President to hold off signing the bill until it decides whether to grant the applicants interim relief.[58] The central argument of the applicants revolves around the possibility that Germany becomes liable for the entire amount of the pandemic fund, effectively introducing risk-sharing into EU law. Afterwards, the Bundesverfassungsgericht rejected the interim relief request, allowing the Own Resources Decision to be ratified by Germany.[59] It nevertheless continued the proceedings on merits that might subsequently find that the Decision is either *ultra vires* or breaches Germany's constitutional identity. In such a scenario, the Order itself envisages a preliminary reference to be submitted to the Court of Justice on the interpretation of the risk-sharing elements of the Own Resources Decision.[60]

The final decisions analysed in this section conclude the identity review of the Bundesverfassungsgericht. The German court continued on its path of conducting identity review and distinguishing it from the scope of Article 4(2) TEU by excluding any possible integration to take place as regards constitutional identity. Yet, it remains bound to sincere cooperation by the self-imposed obligation to submit a preliminary reference should doubts arise as to the intrusion of an EU act into an area of constitutional identity. In the Own Resources Decision in specific, the Bundesverfassungsgericht acknowledged that, although it is possible that constitutional identity is engaged, the consequences of stopping the ratification of the Decision are too great to trigger it before a full review is undertaken.[61]

## 2.2 Constitutional Identity as a Conditional Limit to the Principle of Primacy

The rigour of identity review across Member States follows the normal distribution curve, where the majority of constitutional adjudicators declared some kind of identity-based constitutional limit to the principle of primacy, while allowing

[56] More information on the initiative is available at https://buendnis-buergerwille.de/verfassungsbeschwerde/.

[57] German Bundesverfassungsgericht Case 2 BvR 547/21 Decision of the Second Senate of 26 March 2021 https://www.bundesverfassungsgericht.de/SharedDocs/Entscheidungen/DE/2021/03/rs20210326_2bvr054721.html.

[58] For a brief analysis of the procedural intricacies of the decision see R Repasi, 'Karlsruhe, Again: The Interim-interim Relief of the German Constitutional Court Regarding Next Generation EU' (EU Law Live 29 March 2021) https://eulawlive.com/analysis-karlsruhe-again-the-interim-interim-relief-of-the-german-constitutional-court-regarding-next-generation-eu-by-rene-repasi/.

[59] German Bundesverfassungsgericht Case 2 BvR 547/21 Order of the Second Senate of 15 April 2021 https://www.bundesverfassungsgericht.de/SharedDocs/Entscheidungen/DE/2021/04/rs20210415_2bvr054721.html.

[60] ibid [110].

[61] ibid [106].

for a possibility of a constitutional amendment as one of the reconciliatory options should a situation of conflict arise. Poland, France, Spain, Italy, and Portugal will be analysed in further detail to demonstrate the way identity review operates in such a setting. The analysis will underline the pluralist elements in the reasoning of these institutions, demonstrating further the viability of constitutional pluralism. I will also reflect upon destructive ways in which constitutional identity has been used to reject the primacy of EU law and the limits of the auto-correct function of constitutional pluralism to remedy such developments.

### 2.2.1 Poland

The analysis of the Polish jurisprudence in this section will be done in two stages. Until 2015, the Polish Trybunał Konstytucyjny was an independent institution of unmatched credibility and legitimacy in the Polish public sphere,[62] in many respects being a success story of the Polish democratic transition.[63] Established in 1982 after the Solidarity movement, the Tribunal was retained after the fall of the communist regime with an expanded set of powers, although subject to subsequent parliamentary override until the new Constitution of 1997.[64] This period will thus be analysed through the lens of constructive constitutional conflict. However, in the course of 2015 and 2016, the Law and Justice Party (PiS) that won parliamentary majority in 2015 radically transformed the Constitutional Tribunal.[65] After a period of resistance to legislative interventions into its appointment procedures, the Tribunal ultimately succumbed to governmental capture and is currently operating as a non-independent institution, rubber-stamping any and all legislative changes.[66] This second period is thus marked by the destructive nature of the constitutional conflict the Tribunal is entering into with the Court of Justice. The consequences of these interventions were already mentioned in respect of destructive constitutional conflict in Chapter 4[67] and in the context of the responses to these changes by the Court of Justice in Chapter 5.[68] The analysis here will focus on the effects this has had on the abuse of constitutional identity by the Constitutional Tribunal for the purposes of rejecting the primacy of EU law.

Until 2015, the Polish Trybunał Konstytucyjny was singled out as being the closest to the German position of preserving constitutional identity,[69] but as will

[62] L Garlicki, 'The Experience of the Polish Constitutional Court' in W Sadurski (ed), *Constitutional Justice, East and West: Democratic Legitimacy and Constitutional Courts in Post-Communist Europe in a Comparative Perspective* (Kluwer Law International 2002).

[63] M F Brzezinski and L Garlicki, 'Judicial Review in Post-Communist Poland: The Emergence of a Rechtsstaat?' (1995) 31 *Stanford Journal of International Law* 13.

[64] M de Visser, *Constitutional Review in Europe: A Comparative Analysis* (Hart Publishing 2014) 72.

[65] L Garlicki, 'Constitutional Court and Politics: The Polish Crisis' in C Landfried (ed), *Judicial Power. How Constitutional Courts Affect Political Transformations* (CUP 2019) 145 ff.

[66] ibid 155.

[67] s 3.

[68] s 7.

[69] See in particular Claes and Reestman (n 35) 956.

become evident, its jurisprudence in fact provided ample space for concessions and compromises. There are three cases in particular that will be used to depict the limits that the Tribunal placed on the principle of primacy of EU law, but also to sketch out the various options it leaves in the event of a constitutional conflict taking place.[70] They concern first, the review of the Polish Accession Treaty that has already been ratified; second, the Lisbon Treaty, again after the ratification has been deposited; and, finally, the Brussels Regulation,[71] where the tribunal assumed jurisdiction to review it in relation to the Polish Constitution. In all three situations, the tribunal acted in direct opposition to the *Foto-Frost* jurisprudence,[72] which ultimately shaped its decisions.

In 2004, the Constitutional Tribunal was faced with a review of the Polish Accession Treaty[73] with the Constitution. While the judgment itself is not relevant specifically for identity review, it is nevertheless necessary to touch upon some of its reasoning on the relationship between EU and Polish constitutional law. In the judgment, the Tribunal offered an extensive account of its prerogative to interpret the Constitution as well as the supremacy of the Constitution in the territory of Poland. Article 91(3) of the Polish Constitution states: 'If an agreement, ratified by the Republic of Poland, establishing an international organisation so provides, the laws established by it shall be applied directly and have precedence in the event of a conflict of laws.' The Tribunal hence faced the well-known omnipotence paradox:[74] if the Polish Constitution is supreme, can it allow an external legal order to take precedence? For the Trybunał Konstytucyjny the answer was no and it emphasized that the Constitution is the 'supreme law of the Republic of Poland'.[75] Regardless of its seemingly firm stance, subsequent reasoning in the judgment follows the pluralist logic:

> The concept and model of European law created a new situation, wherein, within each Member State, autonomous legal orders co-exist and are simultaneously operative. Their interaction may not be completely described by the traditional concepts of monism and dualism regarding the relationship between domestic law and international law. The existence of the relative autonomy of both, national

[70] For a more detailed analysis of the difference between these three cases and the German position, in particular as they were cited by the Bundesverfassungsgericht in support of its claims on constitutional identity in its *Gauweiler* reference see Claes and Reestman (n 35) 957–59.

[71] Council Regulation 44/2001/EC of 22 December 2000 on jurisdiction and the recognition and enforcement of judgments in civil and commercial matters [2001] OJ L12/1.

[72] Case 314/85 *Foto-Frost* [1987] EU:C:1987:452 [15].

[73] Polish Trybunał Konstytucyjny Case K 18/04 *Accession Treaty* Judgment of 11 May 2005 http://trybunal.gov.pl/fileadmin/content/omowienia/K_18_04_GB.pdf.

[74] Most usually expressed through: 'Can God, if omnipotent, create an immovable stone?' https://en.wikipedia.org/wiki/Omnipotence_paradox.

[75] Polish Trybunał Konstytucyjny Case K 18/04 *Accession Treaty* (n 73) [8], [11].

and Community, legal orders in no way signifies an absence of interaction between them. [ ... ][76]

In addressing the possibility of an 'irreconcilable inconsistency'[77] between an EU law and a constitutional norm, the Tribunal listed three possible outcomes, the first being an amendment of the Constitution, the second the amendment of the Union norm in question, and finally, if none of the previous is possible, Poland's withdrawal from the EU.[78] The Tribunal, however, emphasized that in any event, an EU-friendly interpretation of the Constitution should be employed.[79] Unlike the German view of the unamendable character of the core of Germany's constitutional identity, the Constitutional Tribunal seemed open, at least in theory, to make concessions in order to avoid or reconcile possible future conflicts.

The second judgment relevant for the analysis of identity review in Poland was handed down on the occasion of the ratification of the Lisbon Treaty.[80] The Tribunal stated that a ratified treaty benefits a presumption of constitutionality. Rebutting this presumption would require a situation to occur without a possible reconciling interpretation of the Constitution nor of the treaty, keeping in mind the consequences that such a judgment might have for the sovereignty of the state and its constitutional identity.[81] In consequence, it seems that an interpretation that might go against Polish constitutional identity would not be acceptable for the Tribunal.

Differing again from the German approach to the relationship between constitutional identity and the national identity clause, the Trybunał Konstytucyjny considered the two equivalents.[82] The Tribunal goes on to emphasize the underlying logic of the national identity clause and the way it functions: 'The idea of confirming one's national identity in solidarity with other nations, and not against

[76] Polish Trybunał Konstytucyjny Case K 18/04 *Accession Treaty* (n 73) [12]. For an opposite reading see W Sadurski, '"Solange, Chapter 3": Constitutional Courts in Central Europe: Democracy: European Union' (2008) 14(1) *ELJ* 1, 19. I argue that the inability to retort to monism and dualism to explain the status of the EU demonstrates that the Polish Trybunał Konstytucyjny cannot place the EU in the category of a classical international organization. At [6], the Tribunal does discuss the lack of the term 'supranational organisation' in the Polish Constitution and the Accession Treaty, the latter itself being an act of public international law. Nevertheless, subsequent reasoning of the tribunal suggests it is aware that defining the EU is no simple task resolvable by resorting to public international law terminology and categories.

[77] Polish Trybunał Konstytucyjny Case K 18/04 *Accession Treaty* (n 73) [13].

[78] ibid. I argue the tribunal lists these options in order of preference, regardless of the use of the conjunction 'or' between them, as it calls the third option (leaving the EU altogether) as the ultimate one.

[79] ibid [14]. It should be added that in the same passage, the Trybunał Konstytucyjny placed fundamental rights as the limit to the principle of Euro-friendly interpretation. For the analysis of this limit see ch 7, s 4.1.1.1.

[80] Polish Trybunał Konstytucyjny Case K 32/09 *Treaty of Lisbon* Judgment of 24 November 2010 http://trybunal.gov.pl/fileadmin/content/omowienia/K_32_09_EN.pdf.

[81] ibid [1.1.2].

[82] 'An equivalent of the concept of constitutional identity in the primary EU law is the concept of national identity.' ibid [2.1].

them, constitutes the main axiological basis of the European Union, in the light of the Treaty of Lisbon.'[83]

This understanding confirms the pluralist interpretation of the identity clause as set out in this book. In other words, if the national identity clause is used as a general exception for national particularities (constitutional identities) of all Member States, which are subject to the same limits determined by the Court of Justice, it only reinforces and strengthens the heterarchical relationship between national and EU law. It also confirms that the Tribunal does not only make conclusions regarding the bilateral relationship between the Polish Constitution and EU law, but is aware of the multilateral consequences that must not be overlooked in order for the system to function.

The judgment of the Trybunał Konstytucyjny concerning the Brussels Regulation is significant as it assumed jurisdiction to review secondary EU law against the Constitution.[84] The tribunal emphasized, however, that such review must be performed with great caution and restraint, taking into account the principle of sincere cooperation.[85] More importantly, the Tribunal used this opportunity to further explain two points: (1) the relationship between national and constitutional identity and (2) the way in which potential constitutional conflict is to be resolved.

The Tribunal addressed constitutional identity as the essential component of national identity in Article 4(2) TEU.[86] Read in conjunction with the *Lisbon Treaty* judgment, it is possible to infer the Tribunal's more general stance concerning the relationship between national and constitutional identity: the Tribunal regarded the national identity clause in Article 4(2) TEU as a general clause allowing for protection of national particularities. It then went on to state that the Polish equivalent of such a concept is constitutional identity.[87] If we are to apply the Polish reasoning universally, this would mean that Article 4(2) TEU is the EU concept for each identity-based limit to integration and the principle of primacy put forward by the national level. Such an approach endorses a multilateral understanding of the protection of national identity, as it creates a common denominator on the Union level under which national particularities can be placed.

The Trybunał Konstytucyjny is, however, well aware that the protection of constitutional identity might give rise to constitutional conflict. It therefore engaged in a detailed analysis of possible reconciliatory methods that would need to be employed so as to avoid the conflict actually taking place, elaborating further on what

[83] ibid.

[84] Polish Trybunał Konstytucyjny Case SK 45/09 *Brussels Regulation* Judgment of 16 November 2011 [2.2] http://trybunal.gov.pl/uploads/media/SiM_LI_EN_calosc.pdf.

[85] ibid [2.5].

[86] ibid.

[87] Polish Trybunał Konstytucyjny Case K 32/09 *Treaty of Lisbon* (n 80) [2.1]; Case SK 45/09 *Brussels Regulation* (n 84) [2.5].

has been introduced in its *Accession Treaty* judgment.[88] The Tribunal advanced the idea of a cooperative relationship, based on mutual loyalty, which should result in a mutually acceptable interpretation of EU law and national constitutional law. Therefore, considerable efforts should be put in place to provide for an interpretation that is EU-friendly (by the Tribunal), but also respective towards national particularities (by the Court of Justice). It can therefore be concluded that the Polish tribunal endorsed a pluralist, heterarchical understanding of the relationship between EU and national constitutional law, which should be based on mutual respect and self-restraint in order to avoid conflict. Only subsequently, when all efforts fail to provide for a mutually satisfactory interpretation, the *ultima ratio* decision that might take place would declare the secondary act of EU law contrary to the Constitution and therefore inapplicable in Poland. The Polish tribunal was aware of the fact that such a ruling would be contrary to obligations undertaken when signing the Treaties and stated that this might result in proceedings being brought by the European Commission against Poland before the Court of Justice.[89] This scenario regrettably materialized itself beyond the extent that anyone at this point in time could probably have imagined it.

In this period, thus, the Polish view of constitutional identity and the prospect of a constitutional conflict taking place fit the pluralist understanding of the relationship between a number of constitutional orders in the EU, but also the judicial interactions between constitutional adjudicators. While there are some limits placed on European integration in the form of constitutional identity, the Polish tribunal was well aware of the grave consequences that would arise should such a protection be applied without caution and observance of mutual respect and self-restraint. I argue that the Trybunał Konstytucyjny found all acts under review to be in accordance with the Constitution precisely due to these reservations. Things then took quite an unfortunate turn for the Constitutional Tribunal.

Throughout 2015 and 2016, PiS, the new political majority in the country, worked tirelessly[90] on establishing decisive political influence over the Constitutional Tribunal.[91] The Tribunal in response declared the legislative interventions into its composition and procedure unconstitutional.[92] Although the new parliamentary majority ultimately imposed only the legislative changes that the Tribunal found constitutional, fewer and fewer cases of political relevance were reaching it.[93] In addition, as the mandates of the judges appointed by the old political majority

[88] Polish Trybunał Konstytucyjny Case K 18/04 *Accession Treaty* (n 73) [13].

[89] Polish Trybunał Konstytucyjny Case SK 45/09 *Brussels Regulation* (n 84) [2.7].

[90] T Tadeusz Koncewicz, 'Of Institutions, Democracy, Constitutional Self-defence and the Rule of Law: The Judgments of the Polish Constitutional Tribunal in Cases K 34/15, K 35/15 and Beyond' (2016) 53(6) *Common Market Law Review* 1753, 1768.

[91] For a detailed presentation of the legislative and political interventions into the operation of the Tribunal see Garlicki (n 65).

[92] For a detailed analysis of the two most relevant decisions see Tadeusz Koncewicz (n 90).

[93] Garlicki (n 65) 155.

were expiring, PiS ultimately managed to secure the majority of supportive judges (perhaps obedient is the more fitting term).[94] Over time, the Tribunal no longer found issues with PiS-initiated reforms, including that of the Supreme Court, the National Council of the Judiciary and the Ministry of Justice, expanding the latter's control over ordinary courts.[95]

In the context of these reforms, the Prime Minister has requested[96] the Constitutional Tribunal to assess the constitutionality of the interpretations by the Court of Justice of Article 2 TEU, Article 4(3) TEU, and Article 19(1) TEU from its recent case law.[97] The application of the Prime Minister grounds the arguments in constitutional pluralism and presents the jurisprudence of a number of Member States[98] analysed throughout this book. The practice of *ultra vires* review, fundamental rights review, and identity review carried out in other Member States is used in the application as reason to support the claim of the Prime Minister that EU law should not have primacy over the Polish Constitutional Order.

This reasoning is flawed and extremely superficial, given that it does not acknowledge the significant safeguards in the application of the three heads of review of EU law by national constitutional courts, nor does it account for the exceptional nature of such practice.[99] It also omits from the analysis conclusions by national courts that do not deny the operation of the principle of primacy of EU law. Finally, all national decisions cited in the application in fact confirm the autonomy and authority of EU law, something that the application itself seeks to disregard.

The decision of the Constitutional Tribunal on the Prime Minister's application is still pending, but the Constitutional Tribunal gave us a sneak peek preview of what awaits us once the decision does come out. The Disciplinary Chamber of the Supreme Court asked the Tribunal to assess the compatibility of the Court of Justice's interim measures issued in infringement proceedings. The Court of Justice has requested Poland to suspend the operation of the abovementioned Disciplinary Chamber of the Supreme Court,[100] and ultimately decided that the operation of the Disciplinary Chamber of the Supreme Court contravenes Article 19(1) TEU.[101] On 14 July 2021, the Polish Constitutional Tribunal ruled (in merely two paragraphs)

[94] ibid 153–54.

[95] ibid 156; A Śledzińska-Simon and M Ziółkowski, 'Constitutional Identity in Poland: Is the Emperor Putting On the Old Clothes of Sovereignty?' in C Calliess and G van der Schyff (eds), *Constitutional Identity in a Europe of Multilevel Constitutionalism* (CUP 2019) 265.

[96] Application K 3/21 of 29 March 2021. Unofficial translation available at https://ruleoflaw.pl/wp-content/uploads/2021/05/K_3-21_application.pdf.

[97] For the presentation of this case law see ch 5, s 7.

[98] Germany, Italy, Czech Republic, and Denmark.

[99] For example, the Czech decision in *Slovak Pensions* analysed in ch 5, s 6.2. is taken at face value as the representative example of the Czech position to the relationship between EU and Czech constitutional law. Such a view omits the subsequent developments and the ultimate irrelevance that the Czech Constitutional Court itself accords to that judgment.

[100] Case C-791/19 R *Commission v Poland* [2021] EU:C:2020:277.

[101] Case C-791/19 *Commission v Poland* [2021] EU:C:2021:596.

that the interim measure is *ultra vires* and that in that respect, Article 4(3) TEU in conjunction with Article 279 TFEU (allowing for the Court of Justice to issue interim measures) are contrary to the Polish Constitution.[102]

It is difficult to analyse these developments through the framework of constitutional pluralism, given that the Trybunał Konstytucyjny no longer applies the principles of sincere cooperation and mutual respect towards the Court of Justice. Even outside the relationship between EU and national constitutional law, the Tribunal is endorsing the deterioration of conditions of judicial independence in the country, thus contributing to the country's departure from the basic membership conditions in Article 2 TEU.[103] It must be said that identity review, when applied as the ultimate limit of what the national constitution allows in the context of EU integration, represents the strongest weapon among the three heads of review analysed in this book. It demands utmost self-restraint on behalf of national constitutional courts and strict limits as to its application.

The ease with which some of the constitutional courts have introduced this limit, in particular in the context of constitutional capture,[104] gives rise to concerns as to the constructive use of such review.[105] A comparable example might be found in Hungary, where the Constitutional Court introduced constitutional identity review, but its standard of review was presented in an entirely open-ended fashion:

> The Constitutional Court of Hungary interprets the concept of constitutional identity as Hungary's self-identity and it unfolds the content of this concept from case to case, on the basis of the whole Fundamental Law and certain provisions thereof, in accordance with the National Avowal and the achievements of our historical constitution [...].[106]

A dynamic reading of constitutional identity here allows the Constitutional Court to stretch or squeeze its scope in any possible way needed. In order to legitimize such practice, both Polish and Hungarian examples refer to Article 4(2) TEU as endorsing such an application of constitutional identity.[107] Constitutional identity

[102] Polish Trybunał Konstytucyjny Decision P 7/20 of 14 July 2021 https://trybunal.gov.pl/en/hearings/judgments/art/11589-obowiazek-panstwa-czlonkowskiego-ue-polegajacy-na-wykonywaniu-srodkow-tymczasowych-odnoszacych-sie-do-ksztaltu-ustroju-i-funkcjonowania-konstytucyjnych-organow-wladzy-sadowniczej-tego-panstwa.

[103] To that effect see Case C-896/19 *Republikka* [2021] EU:C:2021:311 and the discussion in ch 5, s 7.

[104] P Castillo-Ortiz, 'The Illiberal Abuse of Constitutional Courts in Europe' (2019) 15 *European Constitutional Law Review* 48.

[105] Another example is the decision of the Romanian Constitutional Court concerning the applicability of the Cooperation and Verification Mechanism in Romania. Romanian Curtea Constituţională Decision No 390 of 8 June 2021 https://www.ccr.ro/wp-content/uploads/2021/07/Decizie_390_2021_EN.pdf. See ch 5, s 7 for the analysis of the decision and its *ultra vires* aspects.

[106] Hungarian Magyarország Alkotmánybírósága Judgment No 22/2016 *Refugee Allocation Scheme* of 5 December 2016 [64] https://hunconcourt.hu/uploads/sites/3/2017/11/en_22_2016-1.pdf.

[107] The Chancellery of the Prime Minister, 'White Paper on the Reform of the Polish Judiciary' (7 March 2018) 82 https://www.statewatch.org/media/documents/news/2018/mar/pl-judici

as a concept, given its specificity in the national context, has shown to be a particularly useful tool for illiberal governments and their captured constitutional courts to detract from the rule of law as well as from the obligations under EU law. However, as was shown in Chapter 3, a pluralist approach in placing limits to the principle of primacy requires a number of safeguards. For example, the use of constitutional identity should be an extremely unlikely possibility, only to take place after all reconciliatory methods (such as EU-friendly interpretation, mutual respect, and a self-imposed obligation to avoid conflict) have been put to use. It must be said that the Polish Constitutional Tribunal does not demonstrate a cooperative approach as it does not use the preliminary reference procedure beforehand either, depriving the Court of Justice from making a contribution to the discussion on the matter.

Destructive conflicts thus require political as well as legal action beyond judicial accommodation. The Constitutional Tribunal no longer operates as an independent institution that in good faith participates in the European judicial space. Normatively, it has sunk below the common shared values in Article 2 TEU, as it does not adhere to the rule of law in upholding the constitution. By extension, this is then also strongly reflected in Poland's relationship with the EU. Poland is therefore an example of a Member State whose constitutional court has shifted from a constructive to a destructive use of identity review.

### 2.2.2 France

The French Conseil Constitutionnel also set out its view of constitutional identity and the role it plays in the relationship between EU and national constitutional law. As will be shown below, the French position seems to be close to the pre-capture Polish jurisprudence presented above, whereas there are significant differences between the German and the French court in their understanding of constitutional identity and the extent of judicial review to be applied in this regard.

The Conseil Constitutionnel was called to assess the conformity of the Constitutional Treaty with the French Constitution.[108] Prior to the French and Dutch referenda which ultimately decided the destiny of the Constitutional Treaty, the Conseil Constitutionnel decided on the constitutionality of the new Treaty. The Council, aware of the intricacies of EU judicial relations and the broader complexity of the EU constitutional context, concluded, among other things, that the new proposed primacy clause set out in Article I-6 would not extend the existing

ary-reform-chanceller-white-paper-3-18.pdf; Hungarian Magyarország Alkotmánybírósága *Refugee Allocation Scheme* (n 106) [62].

[108] For a detailed analysis of the decision see G Carcassonne, 'Case note: *Conseil Constitutionnel* on the European Constitutional Treaty: Decision of 19 November 2004, 2004–505 DC' (2005) 1(2) *European Constitutional Law Review* 293.

scope of the principle, in particular referring to the new identity clause contained in the proposed Article I-5 that functions as a safeguard in this context.[109]

In 2006, the Conseil Constitutionnel further explained its vision of identity review.[110] In its decision on the validity of a national law literally transposing a directive,[111] the Conseil Constitutionnel was faced with an assessment of whether a directive complies with the French Constitution. It is important to note that this case is placed in the context of review of secondary EU acts, against the background of the exclusive jurisdiction of the Court of Justice to interpret and possibly annul them. This situation in my view conditioned the extent of self-restraint that was applied by the Conseil Constitutionnel.

In deciding the case, the Conseil Constitutionnel replaced its previous reasoning, which held that the implementing act of a directive can only be reviewed against an expressly conflicting provision of the Constitution.[112] Instead, constitutional identity was placed as a benchmark against which the constitutionality of an act implementing a directive can be reviewed.[113] Nevertheless, the Council did not leave this statement as final and unconditional—in the same paragraph it allowed for the possibility of a constitutional amendment that would remedy such a situation.[114] The Conseil Constitutionnel certainly did not go as far as the Trybunał Konstytucyjny to assume jurisdiction to review secondary acts of EU law, but it did reserve for itself the power to do so should the act in question go against French constitutional identity. Again, similarly to the Trybunał Konstytucyjny, a provision of the Constitution denoting French constitutional identity seems to be the one for which no other interpretation is possible, which in turn means that an EU-friendly interpretation is the first step in approaching a constitutional conflict. Only subsequently does the Conseil Constitutionnel mention the option of amending the Constitution.

Apart from the Conseil Constitutionnel, the Conseil d'État (Supreme Administrative Court) has also expressed its understanding of constitutional identity on the occasion of the preliminary reference concerning data retention and

[109] French Conseil Constitutionnel Case 2004-505 DC *Constitutional Treaty* Decision of 19 November 2004 [12]. The wording of the decision seems to reflect its reasoning from five months earlier, when it was faced with a review of a national law which almost literally transposed an EU directive. The Conseil Constitutionnel stated that the transposition of a directive into the national legal order is a constitutional obligation, and it would be possible to disregard this obligation only in the event of an express provision of the Constitution to the contrary. See Conseil Constitutionnel Case 2004-496 DC Decision of 10 June 2004 [7]. Such a wording of the Council was seen as declaring a limit to the primacy of EU law based on the new national identity clause and as a basis of the subsequent pronunciation of the Council on the notion of constitutional identity. Further on this point see also J-H Reestman, 'The Franco-German constitutional divide' (2009) 5(3) *European Constitutional Law Review* 374.

[110] Unlike the Bundesverfassungsgericht, the Conseil Constitutionnel never expressly uses this term.

[111] French Conseil Constitutionnel Case 2006-540 DC *Information Society* Decision of 27 July 2006.

[112] French Conseil Constitutionnel Case 2004-505 DC (n 109).

[113] French Conseil Constitutionnel Case 2006-540 DC *Information Society* (n 111) [19].

[114] See also Reestman (n 109) 388.

national security, in *Quadrature du Net*.[115] The preliminary reference decision by the Court of Justice dealt with the relationship between national security threats addressed by data retention and fundamental rights protection. The Court of Justice found that national security is an important enough concern of a Member State to justify indiscriminate retention of data.[116] The Conseil d'État applied this exception to find the French law only partially invalid, insofar as it does not provide for regular review of the existing threat to national security, and legislation allowing for indiscriminate retention for purposes other than national security.[117]

After refusing to conduct *ultra vires* as proposed by the government, the Conseil d'État focused on constitutional identity. Preventing breaches of public order, tracking down the perpetrators of criminal offences and combating terrorism are of a constitutional value safeguarding the fundamental interest of the nation.[118] While these interests can to a certain extent be subsumed under Article 6 of the Charter and subsequently justified by its Article 52 through the principle of proportionality, the French court found that the specific French security interests of the nation do not find equivalent protection in EU law.[119] It was thus for the French constitutional order to safeguard them and preserve most of the data retention legislation in force.

This decision can to a certain extent be compared to the below analysed decision of the Italian Corte Costituzionale in *Taricco II*.[120] The interpretation of EU law provided by the Court of Justice is accepted but also expanded to reinforce the national interests at stake. At this point in time, judicial power relations thus favour the national court who has the last (procedural) word and provided their own understanding of the relationship between the requirements of primacy and fundamental constitutional interests. This outcome remains within the limits of constructive constitutional conflict, as it allows for further developments of the law, should either the national judiciary be confronted with further legislation or the Court of Justice with additional questions of interpretation in the sphere of the right to private and family life and data protection.

### 2.2.3 Spain

On the far end of the spectrum of identity review we find the Spanish Tribunal Constitucional. Its position is characterized by the trust it places in the Court of Justice in protecting its national identity through Article 4(2) TEU and the correspondingly high level of judicial restraint it exercises. The following section

[115] French Conseil d'État Decision No 393099 *Quadrature du Net* of 21 April 2021 https://www.conseil-etat.fr/fr/arianeweb/CE/decision/2021-04-21/393099.

[116] Joined Cases C-511/18, C-512/18 and C-520/18 *Quadrature du Net* [2020] EU:C:2020:791 [72]. For the analysis of the fundamental rights aspects of the case see ch 7, s 4.2.3.

[117] French Conseil d'État *Quadrature du Net* (n 115) [35], [46].

[118] ibid [9].

[119] ibid [10].

[120] s 2.2.4.

will analyse the Declaration of the Tribunal Constitucional on the Constitutional Treaty,[121] as well as its judgment in *Melloni* after receiving the answer from the Court of Justice on its first preliminary reference.[122]

In its declaration on the constitutionality of the Constitutional Treaty, the Tribunal Constitucional offered some insight into its view on the Treaty structure and how it safeguards national constitutional concerns. While the declaration concerned a treaty that never entered into force, the reasoning of the Tribunal Constitucional is valid, insofar as it relates to the provisions that are still contained in the Treaty of Lisbon, in particular the national identity clause. The Tribunal Constitucional, in its assessment of the Constitutional Treaty, first described how the Spanish Constitution is the source of the transfer of competences from Spain to the EU, and subsequently, for the penetration of EU law into national law.[123] The Tribunal Constitucional went on to accept the need for a supranational institution to oversee the application of the Treaties (the Court of Justice) and provide its interpretation.[124] In its view, the Treaty ensures the protection of the basic constitutional values and principles and is based on the protection of identity of its Member States, which should be preserved regardless of the extent of the transfer of competences to the Union.[125] In the eyes of the Tribunal Constitucional, therefore, the Treaty framework is set up so as to include the protection of national constitutional particularities:

> In other words, the limits referred to by the reservations of said constitutional justifications now appear proclaimed unmistakably by the Treaty under examination, which has adapted its provisions to the requirements of the constitutions of the member states.[126]

Such an interpretation is placing a considerable amount of trust in the Court of Justice and its interpretation of the Treaties, whose role is to ensure at all times that the obligation to respect national identities of Member States is complied with.[127]

[121] Spanish Tribunal Constitucional Case DTC 1/2004 *Constitutional Treaty* Declaration of 13 December 2004.

[122] Spanish Tribunal Constitucional Case 26/2014 *Melloni* Judgment of 13 February 2014. For the answer of the Court of Justice see Case C-399/11 *Melloni* [2013] EU:C:2013:107.

[123] Spanish Tribunal Constitucional Case DTC 1/2004 *Constitutional Treaty* (n 121) ground 2 states in particular: 'Metaphorically, it could be said that Art. 93 CE [Spanish Constitution] operates as a door through which the Constitution itself allows the entry of other legislations into our constitutional system through the transfer of the exercise of competence.'

[124] ibid.

[125] ibid ground 3. The tribunal stated that the identity of Member States and their fundamental constitutional structures should not become unrecognizable in the process of transfer of competences to the EU. It can therefore be inferred that the basic constitutional features of Member States that form their national identity represent the limit to the reach of Union law.

[126] ibid. On this point see also the Opinion of Advocate General Cruz Villalón in Case C-62/14 *Gauweiler* [2015] EU:C:2015:7 [59]–[61].

[127] See also Claes and Reestman (n 35) 961.

The Tribunal Constitucional also presented its understanding of primacy of Union law and its heterarchical character: EU law does not enjoy an absolute hierarchical supremacy over national law, but is rather relevant only in situations of conflict between national and EU law.[128] Such an understanding of primacy is crucial for the sound functioning of the pluralist setting.

Ten years later, in the *Melloni* judgment, the Tribunal once again addressed the relationship between national and EU constitutional law, and in particular the limits to the transfer of competences to the EU and the preservation of basic constitutional structures through the national identity clause. In this case, the Tribunal Constitucional first asked the Court of Justice for an interpretation of the EAW Framework Decision; specifically, whether it allows for the protection as set out in the Spanish Constitution, which gives a right to a constitutional complaint to those that have been convicted *in absentia* in a criminal procedure. This is a higher level of protection than that of the Charter and the EAW.[129] The Court of Justice stated that the EAW and the Charter provide for a satisfactory level of protection of fundamental rights and should therefore be applied instead of the rules set out in the Spanish Constitution.[130]

The Tribunal Constitucional was faced with a clear constitutional conflict, where the standard of protection provided by the Spanish Constitution was higher than that provided by the EAW and the Charter. Based on its declaration on the Constitutional Treaty, the Tribunal had to change its case law in order to accommodate the answer of the Court of Justice.[131] Such a move may be the ultimate expression of the trust the Tribunal Constitucional is placing in the Court of Justice in the protection of constitutional identity, as was stated in its declaration on the Constitutional Treaty. This approach places the Tribunal Constitucional on the far end of the spectrum regarding national jurisprudence on identity review—a position that it does not seem to share with many other Member States. The Tribunal Constitucional nevertheless also put forward a claim of jurisdiction in the unlikely case where constitutional conflict would jeopardize the sovereignty of the Spanish people.[132]

In conclusion, the Spanish position considers the national identity clause and the system of the Treaties as accommodating national constitutional traditions and structures. It therefore reserves for itself the power to protect these values only in the unlikely event where the basic characteristics of Spain as a sovereign state

[128] Spanish Tribunal Constitucional Case DTC 1/2004 *Constitutional Treaty* (n 121) ground 4. On this distinction see ch 3, s 2.

[129] For the analysis of the fundamental rights aspects of the decision see ch 7, s 4.1.2. For a more detailed analysis of the preliminary reference see N de Boer 'Addressing rights divergences under the Charter: Melloni' (2013) 50(4) *Common Market Law Review* 1083.

[130] Case C-399/11 *Melloni* (n 122) [55]–[61].

[131] Spanish Tribunal Constitucional Case 26/2014 *Melloni* (n 122) grounds 3–4.

[132] Spanish Tribunal Constitucional Case DTC 1/2004 *Constitutional Treaty* (n 121) ground 4; Case 26/2014 *Melloni* (n 122) ground 3.

become unrecognizable. Until such a situation takes place, it trusts the Court of Justice to do so.

### 2.2.4 Italy

The Italian Corte Costituzionale has for the longest time considered itself not to be a court or a tribunal within the meaning of Article 267 TFEU[133] and thus refrained from submitting preliminary references to the Court of Justice. Furthermore, the Italian court was the first one to introduce limits to the primacy of EU law by introducing the *controlimiti* doctrine. According to the doctrine, the fundamental principles of the Italian constitutional order and the inalienable rights of man stand as a limit to EU action.[134] Over time, this position has changed[135] and the Italian court began submitting preliminary references and was praised in legal scholarship as an EU-friendly constitutional court.[136] It is against this background that we arrive at the first expression of a possible identity review by the Italian court.

In 2015, the Court of Justice decided on a preliminary reference submitted by an ordinary Italian court concerning limitation periods in the prosecution of tax and financial offences.[137] In essence, the new Italian law on limitation periods significantly shortened them, leading to *de facto* impunity in the event where proceedings were interrupted.[138] The Court of Justice significantly reformulated the question from the national court and focused its analysis on the financial interests of the Union under Article 325 TFEU through the support of its decision in *Fransson*.[139] In consequence, it concluded that Member States are obliged to institute effective and dissuasive penalties for financial fraud and that criminal penalties are essential for achieving this aim.[140]

While granting the referring court the discretion to verify whether the limitation periods interfere with the effectiveness and dissuasiveness of the penalty,[141] it added that they most likely do.[142] As a consequence:

[133] Italian Corte Costituzionale Decision 13/1960 of 16 March 1960; Decision 536/1995 of 15 December 1995.

[134] Italian Corte Costituzionale Case 183/73 *Frontini* Decision of 27 December 1973 [21]. For a detailed analysis of the *controlimiti* doctrine see ch 7, s 2.2.

[135] For example, by stating in Case 232/1989 Decision of 21 April 1989 that the application of the doctrine is highly unlikely. Reported in F Fabbrini and O Pollicino, 'Constitutional Identity in Italy. Institutional Disagreements at a Time of Political Change' in Callies and van der Schyff (n 95) 214.

[136] S Sciarra and G Nicastro, 'A New Conversation: Preliminary References from the Italian Constitutional Court' (2016) 23 *Maastricht Journal of European and Comparative Law* 195.

[137] Case C-105/14 *Taricco* [2015] EU:C:2015:555.

[138] M Bonelli, 'The Taricco Saga and the Consolidation of Judicial Dialogue in the European Union' (2018) 25(3) *Maastricht Journal of European and Comparative Law* 357, 359.

[139] On the Charter-related aspects of that decision see ch 7, s 3.2.

[140] Case C-105/14 *Taricco* (n 137) [39].

[141] ibid [44].

[142] ibid [47].

> [t]hat court would have to ensure that EU law is given full effect, if need be by disapplying those provisions and thereby neutralising the consequence referred to in paragraph 46 above, without having to request or await the prior repeal of those articles by way of legislation or any other constitutional procedure.[143]

In short, the referring court is to disapply the amendment with due regard to fundamental rights, such as the principle of legality and proportionality of criminal offences and penalties from Article 49 of the Charter.[144] The Court concluded that not shortening the limitation period does not interfere with the rights of the accused as these pertain to procedural and not substantive criminal law, thus not subject to the prohibition of non-retroactivity. This finding in particular was in direct conflict with the case law of the Corte Costituzionale concerning Article 25 of the Italian Constitution and is the cause of what transpired next.[145]

Some ordinary courts began complying with the decision of the Court of Justice, in opposition to the case law of the Corte Costituzionale, while others found the judgment contrary to the constitutional core concerning the principle of legality in criminal matters.[146] Two such proceedings resulted in a reference to the Constitutional Court for an assessment of the relationship between the Constitution and the primacy of EU law, suggesting an application of the *controlimiti* doctrine.[147] The Order submitting the preliminary reference to the Court of Justice by the Italian court constitutes the first description of the Italian review based on the constitutional identity.

In an excellent constructive move, the Italian court stated that the principle of legality is in any event a common constitutional tradition of the Member States and should thus be understood as a general principle of EU law that the Court of Justice should protect.[148] The Italian court then reflected upon the findings of the Court of Justice in *Taricco* concerning the limitation periods pertaining the procedural criminal law and the need for the national judge to make the assessment of compliance of national law with Article 325 TFEU. It proceeded:

143 ibid [49].

144 ibid [53]–[54].

145 Bonelli (n 138) 361.

146 G Piccirilli, 'The "Taricco Saga": The Italian Constitutional Court Continues Its European Journey' (2018) 14 *European Constitutional Law Review* 814, 819.

147 ibid.

148 Italian Corte Costituzionale Order 24/2017 23 November 2016 [5]. A similar point was made by the Austrian Constitutional Court in its preliminary reference concerning the Data Retention Directive. The Austrian court proposed that the common constitutional traditions of Member States in the area of the right to private and family life should serve as a source of inspiration for the Court of Justice to interpret the Charter under its art 52(4). See Austrian Verfassungsgerichtshof Decision in Cases G 47/12-11, G 59/12-10, G 62,70,71/12-11 of 28 November 2012 [5.2]. For a more detailed analysis of this point see ch 7, s 4.2.2.

> It is the view of this Court, whose confirmation is sought from the Court of Justice, that these statements are intended to state that the rule laid down in Article 325 TFEU is applicable only if it is compatible with the constitutional identity of the Member State, and that it is for the competent authorities of that State to undertake such an assessment.[149]

The Italian court went on to underline that should it be concluded that *Taricco* goes against Italian constitutional identity, such an outcome would still be in line with the principle of sincere cooperation and proportionality. This is so given that an understanding of limitation periods as pertaining to substantive criminal law is outside the material scope of Article 325 TFEU as interpreted by the Court of Justice and would not undermine the uniform application of EU law.[150]

The Court of Justice started its reply with an equally constructive preliminary remark that we might read as an implicit acknowledgement that it did not abide entirely by its obligation to take note of national constitutional specificities:[151]

> [...] the Court, when answering questions referred for a preliminary ruling, must take account, under the division of jurisdiction between the EU judicature and the national courts and tribunals, of the factual and legislative context of the questions as described in the order for reference.
>
> It is therefore for the Court, in the light of the questions raised by the referring court with regard to that principle, which were not drawn to its attention in the case in which the *Taricco* judgment was given, to clarify the interpretation of Article 325(1) and (2) TFEU in that judgment.[152]

The Court of Justice did not make reference to national or constitutional identity,[153] but rather focused on the prohibition of retroactivity being a common constitutional tradition of Member States.[154] In short, it addressed the concerns of the Italian court by focusing its analysis on Article 49 of the Charter and the principle of legality.[155]

The Corte Costituzionale, while acknowledging the shift in the interpretation from *Taricco* to *MAS and MB*, concluded that because rules of criminal law must be precisely determined, Article 325 TFEU lacks the required certainty,[156]

[149] Italian Corte Costituzionale Order 24/2017 (n 148) [7]. My own translation.

[150] ibid [8].

[151] Although it is also possible to read these statements as shifting the blame to the referring court in *Taricco*. However, I will maintain a more optimistic interpretation whereby the Court of Justice is capable of accepting constructive criticism and improve its previous decisions.

[152] Case C-42/17 *MAS and MB* [2017] EU:C:2017:936 [24], [28].

[153] The same approach was taken in *Gauweiler*. See s 3.

[154] Case C-42/17 *MAS and MB* (n 152) [53].

[155] C Rauchegger, 'National Constitutional Rights and the Primacy of EU Law: MAS' (2018) 55(5) *Common Market Law Review* 1521.

[156] Italian Corte Costituzionale Decision 115/2018 of 10 April 2018 [11] https://www.cortecostituzionale.it/documenti/download/doc/recent_judgments/S_2018_115_EN.pdf.

thereby effectively concluding it does not have direct effect.[157] It also disregarded the finding of the Court of Justice that the *Taricco* rule can only be applied non-retroactively, instead finding that it cannot be applied at all as it is contrary to the Italian Constitution.[158] More importantly, the Italian court reserved the right to conduct the assessment of the constitutionality of measures under the *Taricco* rule exclusively for itself 'since it alone is entitled to ascertain whether EU law contrasts with the supreme principles of the constitutional system'.[159] From the perspective of judicial power relations, this is arguably a move intended not for the Court of Justice. Rather, it is a signal for national courts to submit mandatory constitutionality references to the Corte Costituzionale instead of submitting preliminary references to the Court of Justice.[160]

Judicial interactions on this occasion are, in contrast to the *Gauweiler* and *Weiss II* decisions of the Bundesverfassungsgericht, praised in academic commentary as the right way to go about the situation of constitutional conflict.[161] From a pluralist perspective, the Italian court's approach is of particular interest. First, it is praiseworthy that even a constitutional identity review is preceded by submitting a preliminary reference to the Court of Justice and can be conducted only by the Constitutional Court, thus envisaging safeguards before embarking upon the highly exceptional route of identity review.[162] Second, in line with the incremental operation of the auto-correct function, the Constitutional Court is right to conclude that a single point of conflict does not undermine the overall sincere cooperation among the two constitutional orders (and by extension, between courts claiming the final say). Rather, it substantively promotes a higher level of protection of fundamental rights that the Court of Justice is also incrementally increasing through such contestation, thus strengthening the normative core of constitutional pluralism. The Italian court is not the lonely example of recently introducing the language of constitutional identity. Next up is Portugal.

### 2.2.5 Portugal

In Portugal, the tradition of judicial review and disapplication of legislation long predates the establishment of the Constitutional Tribunal. Centralized constitutional review was introduced as early as 1933, through the then Overseas Council,

[157] C Amalfitano and O Pollicino, 'Two Courts, Two Languages? The Taricco Saga Ends on a Worrying Note' *Verfassungsblog* (5 June 2018) https://verfassungsblog.de/two-courts-two-languages-the-taricco-saga-ends-on-a-worrying-note/.

[158] Italian Corte Costituzionale Decision 115/2018 (n 156) [10].

[159] ibid [8].

[160] Amalfitano and Pollicino (n 157).

[161] For example in Editorial Comments, 'Not Mastering the Treaties: The German Federal Constitutional Court's PSPP Judgment' (2020) 57 *Common Market Law Review* 965.

[162] In the same way that only the Bundesverfassungsgericht is entitled to conduct a review of EU law and is obliged to submit a preliminary reference to the Court of Justice before undertaking such review. See ch 5, s 6.1.

overseeing legislative reforms in Portuguese colonies.[163] Today's Constitutional Tribunal was established by constitutional amendment in 1982 and began its operation in its current set-up in 1983.[164] The system of constitutional review in Portugal operates as a hybrid between centralized and decentralized models: all courts in Portugal can perform constitutional review, whereas the Constitutional Tribunal operates as a centralized appeal instance of such review.[165] In addition, decisions of the Constitutional Tribunal on appeal are binding *inter partes*, whereas only actions initiated by privileged applicants result in *erga omnes* effects.[166]

In respect of EU law, the Portuguese court attracted some attention during the Euro crisis, when it found the budget based on new austerity measures imposed by the Troika unconstitutional.[167] Furthermore, the Tribunal found solidarity among the Portuguese people and different regions of the country to be a justification for limitations of regional autonomy that were interfered with due to austerity measures.[168] More recently, the Constitutional Tribunal introduced its own identity-based limits to the primacy of EU law.[169] Subsequently, it also for the first time submitted a preliminary reference to the Court of Justice.[170]

What amounts to Portuguese constitutional identity? The Portuguese court defined it as the democratic state based on the rule of law, exemplified by constitutional provisions concerning Portuguese territory or its character as a unitary state.[171] Only exceptionally, when constitutional commitments are at stake, will the Constitutional Tribunal as the inalienable guardian of the Constitution exercise its review. The Tribunal found this to be safeguarded by Article 4(2) TEU,[172] which places it in close proximity to the Spanish Tribunal Constitucional's understanding of the relationship between constitutional identity and Article 4(2) TEU.[173] The Portuguese court considered these to be situations where the Court of Justice cannot ensure equivalent control,[174] which resembles the pluralist understanding

[163] M L Amaral and R A Pereira, 'The Portuguese Constitutional Court' in A von Bogdandy, P Huber, and C Grabenwater (eds), *The Max Planck Handbooks in European Public Law: Volume III: Constitutional Adjudication: Institutions* (OUP 2020) 682.

[164] ibid 683.

[165] ibid 689.

[166] According to G Almeida Ribeiro, 'Judicial Review of Legislation in Portugal: A Brief Genealogy' in F Biagi, J O Frosini, and J Mazzone (eds), *Constitutional History: Comparative Perspectives* (Brill 2020) 4, this legal solution is arcane and departs from traditional set-ups of constitutional review in Europe.

[167] M Canotilho, T Violante, and R Lanceiro, 'Austerity Measures under Judicial Scrutiny: The Portuguese Constitutional Case-law' (2015) 11 *European Constitutional Law Review* 155; R De Brito Gião Hanek and D Gallo, 'Constitutional Change through Euro Crisis Law: Report of Portugal' (2015) Annex I 10 https://eurocrisislaw.eui.eu/wp-content/uploads/sites/44/2019/05/Portugal.pdf.

[168] De Brito Gião Hanek and Gallo (n 167) 6, 38, 57.

[169] Portuguese Constitutional Tribunal Case 422/2020 Decision of 15 July 2020.

[170] Portuguese Constitutional Tribunal Case 711/2020 Decision of 9 December 2020.

[171] Portuguese Constitutional Tribunal Case 422/2020 (n 169) [2.6.2.2.], [2.6.4.1.].

[172] ibid [2.6.4.1.]

[173] As well as the earlier understanding of the Bundesverfassungsgericht, when it stated in its *Lisbon Treaty* decision that the two concepts 'go hand in hand'. See s 2.1 above, and specifically n 24.

[174] R Tavares Lanceiro, '"The Portuguese Constitutional Court Judgment 422/2020: A 'Solange' Moment?"' *EU Law Live* (24 July 2020) https://eulawlive.com/op-ed-the-portuguese-constitutio

of primacy of EU law that accords precedence to EU law solely in functionally accorded areas of authority.[175] This reasoning also corresponds to the reasoning of the French Conseil d'État that EU law will not be reviewed against constitutional identity lest it does not provide equivalent protection as the national constitution.[176]

The Tribunal also engaged in an extensive comparative analysis of limits to primacy imposed by other constitutional courts, such as Germany and Italy, as well as the relevant jurisprudence of the Court of Justice.[177] From a pluralist perspective, such an analysis falls squarely into the logic of a cooperative judicial space in the EU, where the jurisprudence of other constitutional courts is instructive for maintaining a coherent approach to limits to primacy of EU law. In the end, the Tribunal refused to conduct identity review in this particular case. This resembles strongly the practice of the Court of Justice, where novel doctrines are introduced but not applied in the case at hand, serving rather as the foundation to be applied in future cases.[178]

In addition to the analysed Member States, other constitutional adjudicators in the EU[179] have also introduced identity-based constitutional limits to the principle of primacy of EU law, offering at the same time possible reconciliatory methods when a constitutional conflict takes place.

## 3 Article 4(2) TEU (the National Identity Clause)

Before the Lisbon Treaty entered into force, the national identity clause was outside the jurisdiction of the Court of Justice,[180] resulting in a limited discussion of the clause in the Court's jurisprudence.[181] The Lisbon Treaty eliminated this exclusion;

nal-court-judgment-422-2020-a-solange-moment-by-rui-tavares-lanceiro/#:~:text=Primacy%20and%20the%20Portuguese%20Constitution&text=This%20provision%20expressly%20allows%20the,basis%20for%20primacy%20in%20Portugal.

[175] See ch 3, s 2.

[176] See s 2.2.2 above.

[177] Portuguese Constitutional Tribunal Case 422/2020 (n 169) [2.3.3.2], [2.5.1].

[178] See eg Joined Cases C-8/15 P to C-10/15 P *Ledra* [2016] EU:C:2016:701 and Joined Cases C-105/15 P to C-109/15 P *Mallis* [2016] EU:C:2016:702 in the context of admissibility of direct actions against Memoranda of Understanding concluded within the framework of the Troika.

[179] Czech Ústavní Soud Case Pl. ÚS 29/09 *Lisbon Treaty II* Judgment of 3 November 2009 [150] http://www.usoud.cz/en/decisions/20091103-pl-us-2909-treaty-of-lisbon-ii-1/; Czech Ústavní Soud Case Pl. ÚS 45/17 Decision of 14 May 2019 [54] https://www.usoud.cz/fileadmin/user_upload/ustavni_soud_www/Decisions/pdf/Pl-45-17_1_en.pdf; Latvian Satversmes Tiesa Case 2008-35-01 *Treaty of Lisbon* Judgment of 7 April 2009 [16.3] http://www.satv.tiesa.gov.lv/wp-content/uploads/2008/09/2008-35-01_Spriedums_ENG.pdf; Belgian Cour Constitutionnelle Case 62/2016 *Stability Pact* Judgment of 28 April 2016, summary http://www.const-court.be/cgi/judgments_popup.php?lang=en&ArrestID=4097. See also Huber (n 15) 92.

[180] The exclusion was expressed in the pre-Lisbon art 46 TEU.

[181] The Court has so far addressed national identity in Case 379/87 *Groener* [1989] EU:C:1989:599 [18]; Case C-473/93 *Commission v Luxembourg* [1996] EU:C:1996:263 [32], [35]–[36]; Case C-36/02 *Omega* [2004] EU:C:2004:614 [32]; Case C-208/09 *Sayn-Wittgenstein* [2010] EU:C:2010:806 [92]; Case C-391/09 *Runevič-Vardyn* [2011] EU:C:2011:291 [86]; Case C-393/10 *O'Brien* [2012] EU:C:2012:110

however, the use of the clause is still at a level that can hardly allow us to reach any serious conclusions as to its scope, meaning and use.[182] The small number of cases where the national identity clause has been invoked by national authorities predominantly concern internal market law.

The Court of Justice has also not, in interpreting Article 4(2) TEU, declared national identity an autonomous concept of EU law. In situations where a certain concept in EU law requires interpretation, and no reference is made to national law, the Court of Justice grants it an autonomous interpretation to be identical and uniformly applied in all Member States.[183] Advocate General Maduro argued that national identity is a legal concept shared between the EU and the national level, given that its content is to be defined by the national level (this will predominantly be constitutional courts),[184] while the Court of Justice controls the compliance with fundamental rights and the objectives of EU law.[185] Article 4(2) TEU indeed makes reference to national constitutional structures and it would be counter-intuitive to define it as an autonomous concept of EU law and give its content identical meaning in all Member States.[186] Rather, it is inherent in the purpose of this provision that it accounts for diverse constitutional structures across Member States. Importantly, this also means that the provision concerns structural constitutional solutions on the national level, rather than substantive values.[187]

Despite the lack of litigation, scholars have offered predictions as to the role and use of the national identity clause. Leczykiewicz determines three uses of the national identity clause: (1) a justification for a national measure breaching internal

[49]; Case C-202/11 *Las* [2013] EU:C:2013:239 [26]; Case C-127/12 *Commission v Spain* [2014] EU:C:2014:2130 [61]; Case C-151/12 *Commission v Spain* [2013] EU:C:2013:690 [37]; Joined Cases C-58/13 and C-59/13 *Torresi* [2014] EU:C:2014:2088 [55]; Case C-156/13 *Digibet* [2014] EU:C:2014:1756 [34]; Case C-438/14 *Bogendorff von Wolffersdorff* [2016] EU:C:2016:401 [73]; Case C-51/15 *Remondis* [2016] EU:C:2016:985 [40]–[41]; Case C-673/16 *Coman* [2018] EU:C:2018:385 [43]–[44]. Moreover, in only a few cases has the principle been elaborated upon in more detail, whereas the majority of the cases involved the Court's rejection of national authorities' invocation of the national identity clause.

[182] This trend is also confirmed in the recent judgment of the Court of Justice in Case C-62/14 *Gauweiler* (n 30), where the Court omitted to address the claims of the Bundesverfassungsgericht concerning the difference between national identity as enshrined in art 4(2) TEU and constitutional identity.

[183] See eg Case C-516/19 *NMI Technologietransfer GmbH v EuroNorm GmbH* [2020] EU:C:2020:754 [45]. For a broader analysis concerning autonomous concepts of EU law see L Mancano, 'Judicial Harmonisation through Autonomous Concepts of European Union Law: The Example of the European Arrest Warrant Framework Decision' (2018) 43(1) *European Law Review* 69.

[184] He stated that: 'Those authorities are best placed to define the constitutional identity of the Member States which the European Union has undertaken to respect.' Opinion of Advocate General Maduro in *Marrosu* (n 3) [40].

[185] ibid.

[186] In that sense see also van der Schyff, 'Member States of the European Union, Constitutions, and Identity' in C Calliess and G van der Schyff (eds), *Constitutional Identity in a Europe of Multilevel Constitutionalism* (CUP 2019) 328.

[187] B de Witte, 'The Lisbon Treaty and National Constitutions: More or Less Europeanisation?' in C Closa (ed), *The Lisbon Treaty and National Constitutions: Europeanisation and Democratic Implications* (Oslo Centre for European Studies 2009) 34.

market rules; (2) a means to invoke the validity of an EU act; and (3) a codification of the case law of national constitutional courts.[188] Guastaferro calls for a horizontal application of the national identity clause, in order to interpret the existing EU law principles in a manner more favourable towards the regulatory autonomy as well as constitutional and cultural diversity of Member States.[189] Perhaps on a more fundamental basis, there is a prevalent view in the literature that the national identity clause will have its greatest significance in the field of constitutional conflict.[190] Hence, the clause confirms the relevance of national constitutional concerns, but also, institutionally, of national constitutional adjudicators, with the aim of minimizing the potential of conflicts taking place in the future.

Advocates General have had an important role in positioning the national identity clause in the wider architecture of EU law by underlining the Union's obligation to respect national identities of Member States. The first substantial contribution aimed at providing an analysis of this Union's duty was made by Advocate General Maduro. In *Marrosu*,[191] he took the position that national authorities, and in particular national constitutional courts, are best placed to define the content of national identity, while the Court of Justice has the role of determining how far Member States can go in derogating from EU law obligations on the basis of national identity.[192] In *Michaniki*, he highlighted the role of the national identity clause as a legitimate aim for derogating from free movement rules.[193] He also shed further light on the relationship between national and constitutional identity, finding the two concepts to be inherently overlapping due to the reference to fundamental constitutional structures in Article 4(2) TEU.[194]

In *Gauweiler*, Advocate General Cruz Villalón had the opportunity to analyse the claim of the Bundesverfassungsgericht on the different scopes of constitutional as opposed to national identity.[195] He shares Advocate General Maduro's understanding of the overlapping scope of constitutional and national identity,[196] and

[188] D Leczykiewicz, 'The 'National Identity Clause' in the EU Treaty: A Blow to Supremacy of Union Law?' *UK Constitutional Law Association Blog* (12 June 2012) http://ukconstitutionallaw.org/2012/06/21/dorota-leczykiewicz-the-national-identity-clause-in-the-eu-treaty-a-blow-to-supremacy-of-union-law/.

[189] B Guastaferro, 'Beyond the Exceptionalism of Constitutional Conflicts: The Ordinary Functions of the Identity Clause' (2012) Jean Monnet Working Paper 01/12 69.

[190] See von Bogdandy and Schill (n 3) 1452; Wendel (n 17) 137; Besselink (n 3) 45; and Leczykiewicz (n 188). Conversely, Guastaferro calls for an 'ordinary use' of the national identity clause; see Guastaferro (n 189) 5.

[191] Opinion of Advocate General Maduro in Case C-53/04 *Marrosu* (n 3) [40].

[192] ibid. See also Opinion of Advocate General Maduro in Case C-213/07 *Michaniki* [2008] EU:C:2008:544 [33].

[193] Opinion of Advocate General Maduro in Case C-213/07 *Michaniki* (n 192) [32].

[194] ibid [31].

[195] Opinion of Advocate General Cruz Villalón in Case C-62/14 *Gauweiler* (n 126). For a more detailed comparison of the Advocate General's Opinion and the judgment of the Court of Justice see D Sarmiento, 'The Luxembourg "Double Look": The Advocate General's Opinion and the Judgment in the *Gauweiler* Case' (2016) 23(1) *Maastricht Journal of European and Comparative Law* 40.

[196] He notes, rather dramatically: '[i]t seems to me an all but impossible task to preserve this Union, as we know it today, if it is to be made subject to an absolute reservation, ill-defined and virtually at the

warns of the dangers that a different understanding of Article 4(2) TEU could have for the principle of primacy—rendering Union law subordinate to twenty-seven different legal systems.[197] It thus seems that the views of Advocates General on the role and scope of the national identity clause broadly correspond to the mainstream academic understanding of the clause.

A remark should be added here on the Court's judgment in *Gauweiler*,[198] as it had the opportunity to address the claim of the Bundesverfassungsgericht on the difference in the scope of national identity as formulated in Article 4(2) TEU and constitutional identity. Perhaps disappointingly for some,[199] the Court made no reference to national identity at all. Although this was raised by the Italian Government in the course of the procedure and referred to by the Advocate General in his Opinion, and while due reference was inserted in the preliminary points of the judgment,[200] the substantive part of the judgment made no assessment or assertion to respond to or address this claim of the Bundesverfassungsgericht.

The lack of attention paid to this issue might be explained as a reflection of the great importance this case holds more generally for the determination of the powers pertaining to the ECB, and it only seems reasonable for the Court to address as few controversial points as possible in order to avoid unnecessary constitutional conflicts. The short-term importance of the survival of mechanisms apt to address the Euro crisis overtook the thrust of the judgment. The Court made a trade-off between these two claims, in order to preserve the OMT mechanism in the short run and to maintain the relationship of mutual respect with the Bundesverfassungsgericht. In particular, although the Bundesverfassungsgericht referred its first preliminary reference to the Court only in *Gauweiler*, the dialogue that these two courts have had in the development of European integration has been constructive and highly relevant for the advancement of the European project. A brief look at the past case law of both courts concerning fundamental rights, treaty amendments, and the division of competences between the Union and the Member States shows a well-thought-out, balanced approach without rushed and controversial decisions.

In the same vein, the wording of the Court in the judgment does not put forward any statement that would pose a direct threat to the Bundesverfassungsgericht

discretion of each of the Member States, which takes the form of a category described as "constitutional identity"'. Opinion of Advocate General Cruz Villalón in Case C-62/14 *Gauweiler* (n 126) [59].

[197] ibid [60].

[198] Case C-62/14 *Gauweiler* (n 30).

[199] 'Whether the ECJ should enforce the EU Treaty's identity clause against other Union institutions is, in my view, one of the primary issues raised by the *Gauweiler* case and a question of paramount importance.' E Cloots, 'Cruz Villalón's "Gauweiler" Opinion: Lost in Platitudes' *Verfassungsblog* (15 January 2015) http://www.verfassungsblog.de/en/cruz-villalons-gauweiler-opinion-lost-platitudes/#.Va16HF9Viko.

[200] Case C-62/14 *Gauweiler* (n 30) [17].

as regards its interpretation of constitutional identity.[201] The Court rightly recognized that, regardless of the importance of the participation of the Bundesverfassungsgericht in the preliminary reference procedure, this is not and should not be the focus of the case. Moreover, precisely because the central point of the case is the scope of the ECB's mandate, there was no need to enter a potentially problematic discussion on the relationship between constitutional and national identity. Such an omission of the Court of Justice demonstrates the functioning of the pluralist relationship among constitutional courts of Member States and the Court of Justice, which includes self-restraint not only on the national, but also on the EU level. It therefore best depicts the inherent heterarchy that is at the heart of the relations among the participants of the EU judicial space.

The case law analysis ahead will be divided into three main areas: (1) cases connected to the public policy justification; (2) cases where the national identity clause was invoked in relation to the national language; and (3) cases where the national identity clause was used to argue an EU act is invalid.

## 3.1 National Identity as an Expression of Public Policy

The case law prior to the entry into force of the Lisbon Treaty reveals the tendency of Member States to put forward their national constitutional concerns as justification for hindering free movement. While the Court was willing to engage in the assessment of those claims in its interpretation of the limits of and acceptable derogations from free movement rules, it has done so mainly through the public policy exception. Initially, this was due to the lack of an explicit provision in the Treaty aimed at the protection of national particularities and, subsequently, due to the lack of jurisdiction of the Court of Justice to interpret the national identity clause once it was inserted in the Maastricht Treaty.

There is hardly any scholarly inquiry into the protection of national identity in EU law that does not refer to the Court's judgment in *Omega*,[202] where the Court stated that the special protection of human dignity in the German Basic Law is a justified restriction of the free provision of services. Although the judgment makes no explicit reference to national identity, its relevance for research into national

[201] The Opinion of Advocate General Cruz Villalón is more direct in this respect. The specific legal nature of an Advocate General opinion served as a perfect platform for the Advocate General Cruz Villalón to put forward a statement concerning the overlapping scope of constitutional and national identity, as well as to put forward the idea of a converging European identity, a statement that is still difficult to imagine coming from the Court in such a direct form. See Opinion of Advocate General Cruz Villalón in Case C-62/14 *Gauweiler* (n 126) [59]–[61]. I owe great thanks to Richard O. Melanzana for the interesting discussions concerning the role and position of the Advocate General.

[202] Case C-36/02 *Omega* (n 181). The Court in the case does not refer to the term national identity as such, but rather focuses on the public policy exception through which the German constitutional concern is framed.

identity in the context of EU law results from the Court's treatment of a *national* constitutional concern from which a restriction of a fundamental freedom ensued. *Omega* concerned the ban by the city of Bonn, Germany of laser games that simulated killing.[203] The basis for the ban was the violation of human dignity, a value of particular importance in the German Basic Law. The Court applied the four-step proportionality test, a well-established practice regarding national measures restricting free movement.[204] The Court found that the German ban did restrict the freedom to provide services and went on to assess the aim that Germany was seeking to protect by the ban. Human dignity was recognized by the Court not only as a value of specific importance in Germany, but also as a part of general principles of Union law.[205]

The Court first addressed the post-Lisbon version of the national identity clause in *Sayn-Wittgenstein*, a case concerning Austria's ban on using references to nobility in personal names as part of a wider abolition of nobility and a constitutional enforcement of the principle of equality.[206] The applicant in the case was an Austrian national, who was later adopted by a German national and acquired his last name that entailed a nobility reference. Although several identity documents were issued to her in Austria under the new last name, the administrative authorities in Austria informed her that her documents would be changed so as to exclude the reference to nobility. She appealed this decision, claiming that the mandatory change of her last name was contrary to the right to free movement and the freedom to provide services in the EU, as it would interfere with her business of luxury real estate, carried out predominantly in Germany, but also in other Member States.

The Court confirmed the existence of a restriction on her right of free movement enshrined in Article 21 TFEU.[207] It then turned to the question of justification, which was, according to Austria, the constitutional status of the abolition of nobility (as a more particular expression of the general principle of equal treatment) forming part of the country's national identity.[208] The Court, faced with the need to accommodate the invocation of Article 4(2) TEU into its existing free movement case law, stated that the national identity claim should be 'interpreted

[203] The prohibition of the laser game was issued by the Bonn police authority, and was therefore applicable solely on that territory. There was no argument raised in the proceedings concerning the geographical scope of the ban, but it is interesting to note that there was no obligation in the wording of the national identity clause for the Union to respect local and regional self-government until the Treaty of Lisbon. Most recently, the Court underlined the importance of regional and local self-government, and subsequently, that the division of competences between different levels of governance cannot be called into question by Union law. See Case C-156/13 *Digibet* (n 181) [34]; Case C-51/15 *Remondis* (n 181) [40].

[204] Opinion of Advocate General Maduro in Case C-434/04 *Leppik* [2006] EU:C:2006:462 [23]–[31].

[205] Case C-36/02 *Omega* (n 181) [34].

[206] Case C-208/09 *Sayn-Wittgenstein* (n 181).

[207] ibid [71], [80].

[208] ibid [82].

as reliance on public policy'.[209] It proceeded, by referring to its *Omega* reasoning, to find that the concept of public policy may vary across Member States and they are thus allowed a certain margin of appreciation.[210] The subsequent examination of the justification followed the proportionality test. The Court of Justice found that the national measure *was* proportionate to the 'fundamental constitutional objective pursued'.[211]

There is a difference between *Omega* and *Sayn-Wittgenstein* that has thus far been overlooked in scholarly writings. The Court in *Omega* addressed the value of human dignity as a German specificity, but added that the protection of human dignity is a general principle that Union law is striving to protect.[212] The Court concluded that the specific position of the protection of human dignity in Germany was *immaterial*, as it coincided with the general principle of protection of human dignity, determined as a European value of high regard.[213] The wording of *Sayn-Wittgenstein* does not appear to follow the same logic, as the Court includes a reference to the specificity of the abolition of nobility in the context of Austrian constitutional history.[214] While the abolition of nobility in Austria is, according to the Court, an expression of the principle of equality, which is also a general principle of EU law, it is precisely the Austrian *national* context that justifies the national provision. The importance of this difference becomes clear when placed in the broader context of EU primary law: on the one hand, *Omega* was a pre-Lisbon case, when the Court had no jurisdiction to interpret the national identity clause and recourse to general principles of EU law was a safe harbour. *Sayn-Wittgenstein*, on the other hand, was a case where the Court was free to interpret and apply Article 4(2) TEU and give some insight as to its future scope and application, regardless of the fact that the value invoked was confined to a single Member State.

There are also similarities in the Court's reasoning in *Omega* and *Sayn-Wittgenstein* that paint a broader picture on the use of Article 4(2) TEU in the area of free movement. First, the Court seems to take a unified approach in relation to Member State reliance on national identity, categorizing it as an expression of public policy.[215] Second, Member States invoking national identity as a legitimate aim benefit from a wider margin of discretion,[216] in particular as the Court stressed

[209] ibid [84].

[210] ibid [87].

[211] ibid [93].

[212] Case C-36/02 *Omega* (n 181) [34]. The Opinion of Advocate General Stix-Hackl is even more telling in this regard, as she spends a great part of her opinion in determining the status of fundamental rights in the EU ([46]–[73]), human dignity as a legal concept ([74]–[81]), and its position in Community law ([82]–[91]). Opinion of Advocate General Stix-Hackl in Case C-36/02 *Omega* [2004] EU:C:2004:162. See also C Dupré, 'Human Dignity in Europe: A Foundational Constitutional Principle' (2013) 19(2) *European Public Law* 319.

[213] Case C-36/02 *Omega* (n 181) [34]. The status of human dignity in the EU is now highlighted in art 2 TEU.

[214] Case C-208/09 *Sayn-Wittgenstein* (n 181) [82]–[83].

[215] Case C-36/02 *Omega* (n 181) [28]; Case C-208/09 *Sayn-Wittgenstein* (n 181) [84].

[216] Guastaferro advocates for such a reading of the case law as well. Guastaferro (n 189) 43.

that the values protected need not be uniform across Member States.[217] Finally, the Court clearly determined the division of tasks in the process of justification of a national measure, explaining that it is for the national authorities to spell out the content of the national value, whereas the Court is to set the limit to the application of such a value through the proportionality test. In both cases, the Court did not leave it to the national court to assess the proportionality of the measure in question, but undertook the evaluation itself.[218]

This approach of the Court to national identity in *Omega* and *Sayn-Wittgenstein* mirrors a method that the Court employs in cases concerning the public policy justification.[219] The following statement by the Court sums up its approach to the use of and limits to the public policy exception:

> The Court has always emphasised that while Member States essentially retain the freedom to determine the requirements of public policy and public security in accordance with their national needs, which can vary from one Member State to another and from one era to another, the fact still remains that, in the European Union context and particularly as justification for a derogation from the fundamental principle of free movement of persons, those requirements must be interpreted strictly, so that their scope cannot be determined unilaterally by each Member State without any control by the institutions of the European Union.[220]

The Court's division of tasks in the application of the public policy exception is extremely useful in this regard: there is scope for the discretion of national authorities in determining the public policy requirements, which can also express national particularities. Once the national value is voiced as a justification, it is for the Court to perform the control in accordance with the principle of proportionality. While it would be misplaced to regard the national identity clause as merely an adjacent claim when Member States invoke the public policy exception, it would be equally wrong to ignore the Court's recurring application of the public policy

[217] Case C-36/02 *Omega* (n 181) [31]; Case C-208/09 *Sayn-Wittgenstein* (n 181) [87]. However see analysis of Case C-673/16 *Coman* (n 181) in respect of same-sex marriage recognition below.

[218] Case C-36/02 *Omega* (n 181) [39]; Case C-208/09 *Sayn-Wittgenstein* (n 181) [93]. Both cases therefore meet the standard of what Tridimas calls 'outcome cases'. According to his categorization, '[t]he ECJ may give an answer so specific that it leaves the referring court no margin for manoeuvre and provides it with a ready-made solution to the dispute (outcome cases); it may, alternatively, provide the referring court with guidelines as to how to resolve the dispute (guidance cases); finally, it may answer the question in such general terms that, in effect, it defers to the national judiciary on the point in issue (deference cases)'.

See T Tridimas, 'Constitutional Review of Member State Action: The Virtues and Vices of an Incomplete Jurisdiction' (2011) 9(3–4) *International Journal of Constitutional Law*, 737, 739. This will, however, change in Case C-438/14 *Bogendorff von Wolffersdorff* (n 181) as we will see below.

[219] See in this respect K Lenaerts, 'EU Values and Constitutional Pluralism: The EU System of Fundamental Rights Protection' (2014) 34 *Polish Yearbook of International Law* 135, 156.

[220] Case C-434/10 *Aladzhov* [2011] EU:C:2011:750 [34]. See also Case C-33/07 *Jipa* [2008] EU:C:2008:396 [23]; and Case C-420/07 *Apostolides* [2009] EU:C:2009:271 [57].

jurisprudence to national identity cases. For the purposes of uniform application of Union law, thus, the Court interprets Article 4(2) TEU in the context of previously established principles in the area of free movement.

Matching the application of Article 4(2) TEU to the public policy exception to free movement does, however, grant the Court of Justice a significant influence on political choices across Member States. To explore this situation, I will contrast two further decisions of the Court dealing with national identity as an expression of public policy: *Bogendorff von Wolffersdorff*[221] and *Coman*.[222] In both cases, the Court of Justice repeated its previous position on the strict interpretation of the exception. For the Court, this means that there needs to be a 'genuine and sufficiently serious threat to a fundamental interest of society'.[223] The way that this exception was applied to the two cases was nevertheless rather different, which may pertain to the exceptions sought by Germany and Romania, respectively.

In *Bogendorff von Wolffersdorff*, a dual German and British citizen has sought Germany to recognize the change of his name carried out in the UK. Similarly to the situation in *Sayn-Wittgenstein*, this name change was refused as it included a title of nobility, which is also prohibited in German law, albeit not by a constitutional provision such as is the case in Austria. Unlike in *Sayn-Wittgenstein*, however, in *Bogendorff von Wolffersdorff* the name change was done freely rather than as a result of a personal status change (adoption in *Sayn-Wittgenstein*). The German referring court thus asked whether the refusal to recognize this change can be justified by reasons of public policy, protecting the principle of equality through the abolition of nobility titles.

The Court of Justice found that the German principle of equality before the law, expressed also in the prohibition of nobility titles, does fall in the scope of public policy.[224] The Court continued:

> The fact remains, however, that the specific circumstances which may justify recourse to the concept of public policy may vary from one Member State to another and from one era to another. In that regard, it is therefore necessary to accord the competent national authorities a certain discretion within the limits laid down in the Treaty.[225]

In line with this discretion, the Court of Justice affirmed that Member States may protect different fundamental rights or legitimate interests, recalling the obligation of the EU to protect national identities.[226] Unlike in *Sayn-Wittgenstein*, where the

[221] Case C-438/14 *Bogendorff von Wolffersdorff* (n 181).
[222] Case C-673/16 *Coman* (n 181).
[223] Case C-438/14 *Bogendorff von Wolffersdorff* (n 181) [67]; Case C-673/16 *Coman* (n 181) [44].
[224] Case C-438/14 *Bogendorff von Wolffersdorff* (n 181) [65].
[225] ibid [68].
[226] ibid [72].

Court itself analysed the proportionality of the measure, here the proportionality is left to the assessment of the referring court, with minor instructions as to what should be taken into account in this exercise.[227]

However, the Court does not always remain on the margins when it comes to national public policy preferences. The Romanian Constitutional Court submitted a reference to the Court of Justice concerning the right to family reunification of same-sex spouses in *Coman*. The couple had lawfully been married in Belgium, but Romanian law, not recognizing same-sex marriage, refused to grant Mr Coman's spouse the right of residence based on family reunification. The Court, after finding this to be a breach of Article 21(1) TFEU[228] granting EU citizens the right to move and reside freely across all EU Member States, analysed possible justifications of that restriction.[229]

Here is where the difference in approach took shape. The Court stated that national identity entails political and constitutional choices of Member States and repeated that any such public policy exception must be interpreted restrictively. It did not, however, repeat the finding that national authorities are granted certain discretion as regards their public policy choices that may vary across Member States and across time.[230] Rather, it concluded that national identity is not breached as the Member State is not obliged to institute the institution of same-sex marriage, but merely to recognize it when lawfully concluded in another Member State.[231] There is only one reference made to the countervailing obligation of Member States to protect fundamental rights when restricting free movement, but this point has not been explored in much depth. With a simple reference to the ECtHR case law concerning the right to private and family life, the Court found that a restriction of this right trumps the autonomy granted to the Member States under the national identity clause.[232] The Court here decided the outcome entirely without leaving any leeway to the referring court.[233]

We may thus conclude that the respect for national identity used under the public policy heading stands in an uneasy relationship with free movement and fundamental rights. In *Bogendorff von Wolffersdorff* the Court of Justice found that the German protection of equality is also a general principle under EU law.[234] This

[227] ibid [75], [78]. It appears from these paragraphs that the reason why the discretion is given to the referring court lies in the lack of a strict prohibition of maintaining titles of nobility (as is the case in Austria), thus leaving some leeway to the German court to assess the proportionality of the prohibition in this particular case. This increased deference may be placed in Tridimas' middle category (guidance cases) explained above. See Tridimas (n 217).

[228] Case C-673/16 *Coman* (n 181) [40].

[229] ibid [41].

[230] See n 225.

[231] Case C-673/16 *Coman* (n 181) [45]–[46].

[232] ibid [47]–[50]. On this point see also M van den Brink, 'Is the Reasoning in "Coman" as Good as the Result?' *Verfassungsblog* (10 June 2018) https://verfassungsblog.de/is-the-reasoning-in-coman-as-good-as-the-result/.

[233] What Tridimas calls outcome cases. See Tridimas (n 217).

[234] Case C-438/14 *Bogendorff von Wolffersdorff* (n 181) [70].

might lead us to conclude that the Court is more willing to accept, despite saying Member States need not have the same public policy preferences, restrictions to free movement when they are justified by interests which also coincide with those protected by the EU. Without prejudice to the overall positive development that *Coman* has in championing rights of same-sex couples, we may find the reasoning of the Court to be more outcome-oriented than in other public policy cases analysed above.

The Romanian Constitutional Court accepted the decision of the Court of Justice[235] and granted the right to family reunification to same-sex spouses legally married in another Member State. The Romanian court did not go further than this requirement, but focused exclusively on the findings of the Court of Justice in the area of free movement. The role of national identity in free movement may ultimately become a spill over avenue for the Court of Justice to engage in further harmonizing activities as regards fundamental rights protection. However, it remains to be seen whether national constitutional courts will be as willing to accept choices contrary to their constitutional preferences.[236]

## 3.2 Language as an Expression of National Identity

Another use of Article 4(2) TEU is connected to one of the most vivid expressions of a nation's identity—its language.[237] While the content of national identity throughout Member States is anything but clear and determined,[238] language appears to be the value broadly appreciated across the European Union as a determination of identity. Furthermore, the competence for language policies lies almost exclusively with the Member States;[239] the EU has only a supporting competence in promoting linguistic diversity,[240] and EU secondary legislation might sporadically touch upon the different national language arrangements.[241]

While the competence of Member States in language policy is so far undisputed, the respect for linguistic diversity inevitably obstructs the smooth functioning of

[235] Romanian Curtea Constituţională Decision no. 534 of 18 July 2018 [40]–[41] https://www.ccr.ro/wp-content/uploads/2020/11/Decizia-534_EN.pdf.

[236] van den Brink uses the example of the French constitutional protection of *laïcité* and how it may well clash with the fundamental right to religious expression. van den Brink (n 232).

[237] See in particular E Cloots, *National Identity in EU Law* (OUP 2015) 288.

[238] ibid 139.

[239] B de Witte, 'Internal Market Law and National Language Policies' in K Purnhagen and P Rott (eds), *Varieties of European Economic Law and Regulation:* Liber Amicorum *for Hans Micklitz* (Springer 2014) 421.

[240] TFEU, art 165.

[241] de Witte mentions Directive 2010/64/EU of the European Parliament and of the Council of 20 October 2010 on the right to interpretation and translation in criminal proceedings [2010] OJ L280/1, which sets out rules for the use of languages, rather than harmonizing national language policies. de Witte (n 239) 420.

the internal market, creating additional costs to market operators across the EU.[242] The inherent heterogeneity of national language policies and the homogeneity required by the liberalization of economic activity represent the crux of the problem with which the internal market is faced. It thus comes as little surprise that the first case to refer to the concept of national identity concerned a reference to the promotion of a (minority) national language.[243]

Ms Groener, a Dutch national, applied for a teaching position at the College of Marketing and Design in Dublin, only to be rejected based on the Irish law which requires all permanent teaching staff to speak Gaelic, regardless of the actual use of the language in their work. The Court stated that the promotion of Gaelic was an expression of national identity worthy of protection, subject to the principle of proportionality.[244] Hence, the promotion of a national language, as an expression of national identity, may serve as a derogation from the free movement rules, so long as it is proportionate. The same rationale was used by the Court when Luxembourg attempted to use the national identity argument in a case where it reserved teaching posts to Luxembourgish nationals, claiming they were best placed to safeguard the Luxembourgish language.[245] The Court found the nationality requirement disproportionate to the aim pursued, stating that the same could be achieved through language requirements.[246]

Ever since the Lisbon Treaty underlined the importance of linguistic diversity in Article 3(3) TEU[247] and Article 22 of the Charter,[248] the Court has consistently referred to it when interpreting national identity claims concerning the protection of an official language, emphasizing even further the obligation of the Union to respect such an aim in the face of market integration. The first such case, *Runevič-Vardyn*, concerned a Lithuanian provision determining that documents indicating civil status must be in accordance with the rules governing the spelling of the official national language. Based on such legislation, a Lithuanian national of Polish origin was unable to obtain her birth and marriage certificate to include the original Polish spelling of her last name. As she lived in Belgium with her husband, a Polish national, her appeal was based on a breach of the free movement provisions. The Court upheld the importance of the national rules governing the official

242 In that respect see I Urrutia, 'Approach of the European Court of Justice on Accommodation of the European Language Diversity in the Internal Market: Overcoming Language Barriers or Fostering Linguistic Diversity?' (2012) 18(2) *Columbia Journal of European Law* 243, 245.

243 Case C-379/87 *Groener* (n 181).

244 ibid [18]–[19].

245 Case C-473/93 *Commission v Luxembourg* (n 181).

246 ibid [35]. The Court reiterated its position when dismissing a recent (post-Lisbon) Luxembourgish attempt to confine the notary function to Luxembourgish nationals only. See Case C-51/08 *Commission v Luxembourg* [2011] EU:C:2011:336 [124].

247 The fourth subparagraph of art 3(3) TEU reads: [The Union] shall respect its rich cultural and linguistic diversity, and shall ensure that Europe's cultural heritage is safeguarded and enhanced.

248 Article 22 of the Charter states: 'The Union shall respect cultural, religious and linguistic diversity.'

language, in particular in the light of Articles 3(3) and 4(2) TEU, and Article 22 of the Charter.[249]

Consistently, the Court puts the protection of the official language, formulated as a national identity claim, to the proportionality test. In that respect, it seems that the Court is, as in the case law involving the public policy exception, making use of the same division of tasks between the national and EU levels: it is for the national authorities to define the national language policy, while it is for the Court to interpret the limits up to which such a derogation can be used. Again, the principle of proportionality has proved to be a useful and well-known tool to delineate the outer limits of the applicability of Article 4(2) TEU.

### 3.3 Invoking the Invalidity of an EU Act Based on Article 4(2) TEU

The duty of the Union to respect national identities, as previously mentioned, is not limited to judicial review by the Court of Justice, but exists also in the legislative process on the EU level. It is therefore possible for a Member State to call into question the validity of an EU measure based on the EU's breach of the obligation to respect the Member State's national identity. The first such doubt was voiced by the Italian *Consiglio Nazionale Forense* (National Bar Council), in respect of the conformity of Article 3 of the Directive 98/5/EC[250] with Article 4(2) TEU.[251] In particular, the National Bar Council considered that the possibility for Italian nationals to register in Italy with a professional legal qualification obtained in another Member State was contrary to the constitutional provision according to which the profession of a lawyer is reserved to those having successfully passed the Italian State examination.[252]

The answer of the Court contained a brief introductory reference to Article 4(2) TEU,[253] while dismissing the concerns of the National Bar Council, given that the Directive did not open access to the Italian professional title and concluding that this in no way breaches the constitutional provisions concerning the Italian profession of a lawyer.[254] The brevity of the case unfortunately does not allow us to draw any relevant conclusions regarding the level of scrutiny that the Court will apply to

[249] Case C-391/09 *Runevič-Vardyn* (n 181) [86]. The same reasoning was reiterated by the Court in the context of free movement of workers. See Case C-202/11 *Las* (n 181).

[250] Directive 98/5/EC of the European Parliament and of the Council of 16 February 1998 to facilitate practice of the profession of lawyer on a permanent basis in a Member State other than that in which the qualification was obtained [1998] OJ L77/36.

[251] Joined Cases C-58/13 and C-59/13 *Torresi* (n 181).

[252] ibid [14].

[253] ibid [54].

[254] ibid [58]. See also G di Federico, 'Joined Cases 58 and 59/13, C-58/13 and C-59/13 *Angelo Alberto Torresi and Pierfrancesco Torresi v. Consiglio dell'Ordine degli Avvocati di Macerata*, Judgment of the Court (Grand Chamber) of 17 July 2014' (2015) 21(3) *European Public Law* 481.

EU measures that are potentially contrary to the obligation to respect the national identities of Member States. Nevertheless, it points to the fact that Article 4(2) TEU will be used in order to challenge the validity of EU acts, which might result in placing a greater burden on the political process at the EU level.

## 4 Conclusion

In the preceding sections, I have analysed the case law of national constitutional courts performing identity review and the interpretation of the national identity clause by the Court of Justice. The aim of this section is to propose a coherent interpretation of identity review grounded in the framework of constitutional pluralism and draw some conclusions concerning the question of the ultimate arbiter.

The EU and national case law provides us with broadly two different views of identity review. According to the first interpretation, there are essentially two sets of constitutional values: those underpinning national 'fundamental structures, political and constitutional' as set out in Article 4(2) TEU; and the core constitutional values that represent the national constitutional identity and, in the view of constitutional adjudicators, lie beyond the reach of the primacy of EU law. The second line of interpretation (by the Court of Justice and some constitutional courts) offers a more homogeneous understanding of Article 4(2) TEU, according to which the concept of fundamental political and constitutional structures encompasses core constitutional values of Member States.

The first line of interpretation singles out national constitutional provisions that have a higher degree of constitutional entrenchment, such as provisions on the basic principles of state organization, sovereignty, the principle of democracy, and human dignity.[255] In substantive terms, such a reading of the identity clause in relation to national constitutions creates an area of constitutional interpretation that runs counter to the principle of primacy of EU law. Interviewee 5 stated that the scope of the national identity clause is broader in its content and encompasses constitutional identity. The same Interviewee stated that when it comes to constitutional identity as interpreted by the Bundesverfassungsgericht, there should be some areas of national constitutions that remain in the exclusive realm of constitutional adjudicators. Such a view opposes the Court's case law whereby Member States are bound by general principles of EU law even when exercising their exclusive competences.[256] From an institutional point of view, it represents an area of primacy for constitutional adjudicators, where their interpretative jurisdiction remains intact. However, as was shown in the preceding analysis, constitutional courts that have introduced some form of identity review have themselves also

255 von Bogdandy and Schill (n 3) 1432.
256 See ch 5, s 5 on this point.

imposed limits to such review, grounded in the principles of EU-friendly interpretation and self-restraint.[257]

It is difficult to imagine the Court of Justice subscribing to an understanding of Article 4(2) TEU, which would undermine its decades-long jurisprudence on the primacy of Union law over all sources of national law, including national constitutions, that are possibly in conflict with provisions of EU law. At the same time, the Court of Justice has not been very active in interpreting the scope of the national identity clause. Advocates General have been more elaborate in proposing a comprehensive interpretation of the notion, which has only exceptionally found its way into the judgments of the Court. In the view of Interviewee 6, since the national identity clause is contained in the Treaties, it is only natural that the Court of Justice treats it as an autonomous concept of EU law.[258]

The Court of Justice has not undertaken an exploratory mission to determine the scope of the newly-worded national identity clause, but has remained in the area of well-established concepts and principles. It is my argument that the Court was applying a contextual interpretation of the relevant value identified as 'national identity' in accordance with the already established principles in other areas of EU law in order to ensure its coherence with existing jurisprudence. For example, when invoked in the area of free movement, the clause has been interpreted as a public policy justification of national restrictive measures.[259] The case law where the clause was invoked on the basis of protection of a national language confirms this hypothesis: in *Runevič-Vardyn*, the Court stated that the protection of national language forms part of the national identity of a Member State and is as such considered a legitimate aim for restricting free movement protected by Article 21 TFEU.[260] Once defined as a legitimate aim, it is subject to the same test that is consistently used in the context of restrictions on free movement.[261] In effect, the Court of Justice introduced a common denominator for all national identity claims: the principle of proportionality.[262]

Such an approach endorses the principle of uniform interpretation and contributes to the consistency of the Court's case law. Furthermore, the use of well-known

[257] The limits can, as was shown, be placed on a spectrum from a seemingly uncompromising identity review (Germany), to a position whereby the Court of Justice is trusted to be the one protecting the national identity on the EU level (Spain).

[258] However, the Court of Justice has not been explicit about this.

[259] The Court's reasoning in Case C-208/09 *Sayn-Wittgenstein* (n 181) is particularly useful in this regard: the Court first analysed the status of the value invoked by the Austrian authorities ([74], [83]), after which it introduced its connection to the already existing public policy justification ([84]). Finally, it stated that 'the concept of public policy as justification for a derogation from a fundamental freedom must be interpreted strictly, so that its scope cannot be determined unilaterally by each Member State without any control by the European Union institutions' ([86]).

[260] Case C-391/09 *Runevič-Vardyn* (n 181) [87].

[261] ibid [88] ff.

[262] The academic literature in the field mainly seems to agree on this point. In opposition to the usefulness of the principle of proportionality in the balancing exercise before the Court of Justice see Cloots (n 237) 196 ff. See also Lenaerts (n 218) 156.

and developed principles is also beneficial for national authorities, as they are aware of the benchmark by which their measures will have to abide, as well as the standard of scrutiny to which they will be subject in potential subsequent litigation. However, the Court has not developed a clear pattern of the actual application of the proportionality test—in certain cases, the Court itself found the national measure proportionate or disproportionate,[263] while in others it left it to the national court to take into account the circumstances of the case and finally decide on proportionality.[264]

Cloots argues that the proportionality test is not an adequate method of adjudication and should be replaced by a more rule-like method of adjudication by the Court,[265] which would leave the Court with less space for balancing based on values and would result in more certainty for all the parties concerned. While there is some merit in calls for more legal certainty, it was precisely the wide latitude of the Court in applying the proportionality test that has provided clearer regulation of the internal market in the absence of a political consensus in the remainder of the Union institutions.

Despite the *prima facie* contradictions between European and national case law, when analysed through the lens of constitutional pluralism, this jurisprudence is nevertheless coherent: the underlying assumption of such an interpretation is that all the courts involved are aware of the need to preserve a peaceful relationship in the European judicial space, without a clear or prior declaration of superiority or subordination. The exercise of self-restraint is therefore key in situations of potential constitutional conflict.

The proposed pluralist interpretation of identity review is twofold: (1) the national identity clause is to serve as an exception to accommodate national particularities in the application of EU law on the national level, while the role of the Court of Justice is to apply a uniform method in determining the limits to this exception through the application of the principle of proportionality;[266] (2) the proportionality analysis will highlight issues of jurisdictional and constitutional conflict, both between the EU and national level, but potentially also conflicts within the Member State. The balancing of these issues will determine the extent of self-restraint to be applied in a particular case. In addition, Interviewee 6 underlined that the Court of Justice will, in taking into account national identity concerns, undertake a balancing exercise in reaching its final judgment. The same Interviewee also stated that the Court of Justice should carry out this balancing carefully, taking into

[263] Case C-36/02 *Omega* (n 181) [39]; Case C-208/09 *Sayn-Wittgenstein* (n 181) [93].

[264] Case C-391/09 *Runevič-Vardyn* (n 181) [91]; Case C-438/14 *Bogendorff von Wolffersdorff* (n 181) [75].

[265] Cloots (n 237) 196 ff.

[266] Case C-420/07 *Apostolides* (n 219) [57]. See also Besselink (n 3) 46; Wendel (n 17) 134–35; K Lenaerts, 'La Vie après l'Avis: Exploring the Principle of Mutual (Yet Not Blind) Trust' (2017) 54(3) *Common Market Law Review* 805, 822.

account the historical underpinnings of a particular national value, as was done in the case of *Sayn-Wittgenstein*. Such a division of interpretative tasks between national and EU judiciaries is inherently pluralist.

From an institutional point of view, respecting national particularities contributes to the mutual respect and cooperation between constitutional adjudicators and the Court of Justice, which would be jeopardized if a converging European identity were to replace the current understanding of the identity clause. If we were to accept the view of Advocate General Cruz Villalón in *Gauweiler*[267] that we are witnessing an emergence of a European identity in a converging trend, the purpose of Article 4(2) TEU would be significantly weakened, particularly having in mind Article 2 TEU which serves to underline the shared and common values among EU Member States. Finally, respect for national specificities, subject to the principle of proportionality, reinforces the role of the Court of Justice in ensuring the uniform application of Union law through providing a common method of determining the limit(s) to Article 4(2) TEU and ultimately contributes to equality among Member States.

Fabbrini has argued that the principle of primacy must be applied without exceptions to all Member States, so as to preserve the multilateral, rather than a bilateral, framework of the Union constitutional order.[268] In contrast, I argue that the use of Article 4(2) TEU as an exception to the primacy of EU law would not reduce the EU's constitutional order to bilateral relations between individual Member States and the EU. It would create a Union-wide the procedure for determining the limits to Article 4(2) TEU and Member States would be able to invoke each other's case law and practice in order to reinforce the national identity clause.[269] Understood in this way, a proper implementation of the national identity clause and identity review can in fact contribute to a further connection between national constitutional jurisdictions throughout the EU.

Furthermore, through incrementalism, the development of the case law in this area will create a common approach to the substantive issues connected to the national identity clause,[270] as it can be expected that recourse to Article 4(2) TEU will become more frequent over time. Interviewee 1 stated that one of the functions of the Court of Justice as a supreme court of the EU of sorts (based on the mandate in Article 19(1) TEU), is to accommodate national constitutional provisions in a

[267] Opinion of Advocate General Cruz Villalón in Case C-62/14 *Gauweiler* [2015] EU:C:2015:7 [61].

[268] F Fabbrini, 'After the *OMT* Case: The Supremacy of EU Law as the Guarantee of the Equality of the Member States' (2015) 16(4) *German Law Journal* 1003, 1005.

[269] As was the practice of, for example, the Portuguese Constitutional Tribunal. See s 2.2.5.

[270] A common approach to substantive issues does not mean a convergence of values towards a European identity, as proposed by Advocate General Cruz Villalón. Instead, it means that the sheer volume of cases that will arise over time will establish a unified jurisprudence of the Court of Justice and create expectations on behalf of national authorities as regards the extent to which a particular national value can be protected. It was possible to witness such an approach in the Italian understanding of the principle of legality in criminal proceedings in the *Taricco* interactions. See s 2.2.4 above.

substantive sense, so as to give them a coherent meaning throughout the European Union. However, for sensitive issues (for example abortion, but as we have seen, not same-sex marriage) answers are limited to the single case and do not draw on wider implications that this could have on all member states.[271]

In essence, the national identity clause should be interpreted so as to follow the main characteristics of a pluralist constitutional order. First, the national identity clause, due to its broad wording, is constituted to encompass a wide range of values and its particular national expressions are translated into notions such as constitutional identity.[272] While they cannot be used as synonyms in terms of content, they are functionally equivalent.[273] It is also crucial to emphasize that constitutional identity values cannot depart from the shared normative core in Article 2 TEU. This ensures that constitutional conflicts remain constructive, rather than descend into judicially irreparable destructive conflicts.

Second, the aim of the system is conflict prevention and management, both from the perspective of constitutional adjudicators and that of the Court of Justice, who aim to avoid constitutional conflict and find it highly unlikely. In addition, remedies for resolving possible conflict have also been put in place, without clear hierarchical solutions. Destructive uses of constitutional identity depart from this practice: constitutional courts that have used constitutional identity to reject primacy of EU law have, for example, not made use of the preliminary reference procedure or referred to an EU-friendly interpretation or any other reconciliatory method.

Third, the protection of national identity through Article 4(2) TEU is necessarily multilateral in its nature. Its implementation shows an institutional awareness of the big picture in the everyday work of the courts under analysis, as they are conscious of the need for a balanced relationship among all constitutional jurisdictions in the EU.[274] Destructive conflicts have regrettably demonstrated a superficial engagement with practices in other Member States in order to rubber-stamp their own departure from the principle of primacy and rule of law standards. Apart from cross-referencing, judicial formal and informal networks have been a great

[271] In support of this view see also D Thym, 'Separation Versus Fusion—or: How to Accommodate National Autonomy and the Charter? Diverging Visions of the German Constitutional Court and the European Court of Justice' (2013) 9(3) *European Constitutional Law Review* 391, 419; K Lenaerts and J A Gutiérrez-Fons, 'The Constitutional Allocation of Powers and General Principles of EU Law' (2010) 47(6) *Common Market Law Review* 1629, 1663 (discussing 'value diversity' that the Court of Justice appreciates and strives to protect).

[272] According to von Bogdandy and others, the role of art 4(2) TEU is to protect constitutional pluralism. A von Bogdandy and others, 'Reverse Solange: Protecting the Essence of Fundamental Rights against EU Member States' (2012) 49(2) *Common Market Law Review* 489, 491.

[273] To use the wording of the Polish Trybunał Konstytucyjny (n 82).

[274] Perhaps the best example of this is the vast number of cross-references among constitutional jurisdictions in the EU in their jurisprudence on national identity. See eg United Kingdom Supreme Court Case *Pham* (n 42); German Bundesverfassungsgericht Order *Gauweiler* (n 4); Polish Trybunał Konstytucyjny Case K 18/04 *Accession Treaty* (n 73).

resource to ensure that cross-references and cross-Member State engagement is meaningful and constructive. In that respect, the national identity clause, despite its particularistic character, can contribute to a connection between constitutional courts of different Member States.

Finally, as a consequence, in order for the clause to work for everyone, and not against anyone, it is the role of the Court of Justice to set common limits through the application of a careful balancing exercise.[275] This means that sometimes national particularities will prevail, while at other times it will be the primacy of Union law. This ultimately renders the question of the final arbiter immaterial, as the system is one of a clear-cut heterarchy: one where there are no predetermined winners and losers, but rather, all courts maintain the ability to have a final say at a certain point in time.

[275] See in that sense J H H Weiler, *The Constitution of Europe; 'Do the New Clothes Have an Emperor?' and Other Essays on European Integration* (CUP 1999) 122.

# 7

# Fundamental Rights Review

## 1 Introduction

The story of fundamental rights protection in the European Union has been analysed in the literature from top to toe, substantively and institutionally.[1] In this chapter I aim to add the analysis of the role this story has played in constitutional conflict. The Court of Justice, in its expansion of the self-referential system of the Treaties, could not avoid this question, as the creation of the single market necessarily touched upon the national protection of fundamental rights.[2] In managing this interaction, the Court of Justice *de facto* elevated free movement rules to the status of a fundamental right.[3] Unsurprisingly, thus, the (standard of) fundamental rights protection was the first area of constitutional conflict between national courts performing constitutional review and the Court of Justice.[4]

Given that—in a pre-EU world—national courts performing constitutional review were the foremost protectors of fundamental rights,[5] it was entirely expected that the Court of Justice's jurisdictional claim in fundamental rights protection led to a constitutional clash. Fundamental rights have been central in defining the EU as a constitutional order in its own right.[6] So, while the initial goals of European integration were purely economic,[7] the Court of Justice

[1] The literature is too vast to be cited here. Important contributions include P Alston and J H H Weiler, 'An "Ever Closer Union" in Need of a Human Rights Policy' (1998) 9 *European Journal of International Law* 658; P Alston (ed), *The EU and Human Rights* (OUP 1999); A Torres Pérez, *Conflicts of Rights in the European Union: A Theory of Supranational Adjudication* (OUP 2009); F Fabbrini, *Fundamental Rights in Europe. Challenges and Transformations in Comparative Perspective* (OUP 2014); M Bobek and J Adams-Prassl (eds), *The EU Charter of Fundamental Rights in the Member States* (Hart Publishing 2020).

[2] A classic example is Case C-112/00 *Schmidberger* [2003] EU:C:2003:333, where the Austrian constitutionally protected right to protest was restricting the free movement of goods.

[3] M P Maduro, *We, the Court: The European Court of Justice and the European Economic Constitution* (Hart Publishing 1998) 168.

[4] The structure of the book's analytical chapters in Part II are, however, not ordered in a chronological fashion, but rather in order of relevance of the jurisprudence of constitutional conflict.

[5] Some of them were established after the Second World War primarily with the purpose of safeguarding fundamental rights against the majority of the day. See Fabbrini (n 1) 17; M de Visser, *Constitutional Review in Europe. A Comparative Analysis* (Hart Publishing 2014) 410.

[6] See further Maduro (n 3) 8. For an analysis of the development by which fundamental rights are being placed at the centre of the integration project see A von Bogdandy, 'The European Union as a Human Rights Organization? Human Rights at the Core of the European Union' (2000) 37(6) *Common Market Law Review* 1307.

[7] See von Bogdandy (n 6) 1308. See also G de Búrca, 'The Road Not Taken: The European Union as a Global Human Rights Actor' (2011) 105 *American Journal of International Law* 649.

*The Jurisprudence of Constitutional Conflict in the European Union.* Ana Bobić, Oxford University Press. © Ana Bobić 2022.
DOI: 10.1093/oso/9780192847034.003.0007

built[8] a constitutional structure protecting fundamental rights through the spillover of existing competences.

Fundamental rights protection is one of the areas where the federalist argument bites strongest: the multilevel system of fundamental rights protection (national, supranational, international)[9] provides an almost perfect laboratory for exploring the possibilities of the normative side of EU federalism.[10] This is even more so given the prominence of what is in the literature termed as the 'federal question':[11] are the Member States subject to the fundamental rights control by the Court of Justice? However, while the multi-layered architecture of fundamental rights protection may lead us to imagine it in vertical and hierarchical terms, the relationship between national courts performing constitutional review and the Court of Justice is inherently heterarchical.[12] For that reason, the monism intrinsic to federal systems cannot adequately capture the European judicial space where each of the courts under analysis can at times have the final say as regards fundamental rights review.

For the purposes of defining the subject of analysis, I will follow Torres Pérez's definition of the term 'fundamental rights': all rights which are recognized as fundamental by the legal orders under analysis will be regarded as such.[13] In instances when both the EU and national level of adjudication are dealing with the same fundamental right, I will address possible differences in the scope or standard of protection. Equally, as Fabbrini posits, the constitutional dynamics of fundamental rights protection in Europe[14] apply to all fundamental rights, regardless of whether they are civil, political, social, or a new generation right.[15] This chapter will likewise

[8] Although, as will be seen in the case law analysis, the Court of Justice viewed this development not as a creation, but rather as giving expression to fundamental rights as the essential value of the integration project. See J H H Weiler, *The Constitution of Europe: 'Do the New Clothes Have an Emperor?' and Other Essays on European Integration* (CUP 1999) 102. The wording used by Lenaerts and Gutiérrez-Fons follows this logic, as they conclude that one of the functions of the Charter of fundamental rights is its operation 'as a source for the *discovery* of general principles of EU law' (emphasis added). K Lenaerts and J A Gutiérrez-Fons, 'The Constitutional Allocation of Powers and General Principles of EU Law' (2010) 47(6) *Common Market Law Review* 1629, 1656. For the commentary on the same approach of the Court in the context of general principle of non-discrimination on grounds of age see J Mazák and M K Moser, 'Adjudication by Reference to General Principles of EU Law: A Second Look at the *Mangold* Case Law' in M Adams and others (eds), *Judging Europe's Judges: The Legitimacy of the Case Law of the European Court of Justice* (Hart Publishing 2015) 61.

[9] Fabbrini (n 1) 4; Torres Pérez (n 1) 3.

[10] Fabbrini sides explicitly with the federalist argument. Fabbrini (n 1) 3. See also D Kochenov (ed), *EU Citizenship and Federalism: The Role of Rights* (CUP 2017).

[11] P Eeckhout, 'The EU Charter of Fundamental Rights and the Federal Question' (2002) 39(5) *Common Market Law Review* 945.

[12] Again explicitly, Fabbrini rejects pluralism as unable to 'offer a comprehensive and persuasive account of the complex implications produced by the interaction between the multiple human rights standards in Europe'. Fabbrini (n 1) 4. Conversely, Torres Pérez compares the US and EU contexts of fundamental rights protection, concluding that a federal approach is not an appropriate solution for the EU. Torres Pérez (n 1) ch 4.

[13] Torres Pérez (n 1) 9.

[14] And by deduction, then, in the EU.

[15] Fabbrini (n 1) 48–49.

prove the descriptive and normative prescriptions of constitutional pluralism in relation to all fundamental rights irrespective of their generation.[16]

The aim of this chapter is not to retell the history of the development of protection of fundamental rights in the EU,[17] but rather to address two points connected to the jurisprudence of constitutional conflict in this area: the different limits that constitutional adjudicators have placed on the principle of primacy in the area of fundamental rights protection and the possible scenarios they envisage in the event of a constitutional conflict. The argument running through both these themes is that constitutional pluralism can both explain and guide the relations among the courts under analysis in the area of fundamental rights protection. As will also be visible from the analysis, the area of fundamental rights protection has not yielded destructive constitutional conflict, as all the courts are striving towards a substantive level of protection that remains within the reasonable disagreement in interpreting the values in Article 2 TEU.

The remainder of this chapter is divided into five sections. I will first analyse the initial judicial interactions that led to the development of fundamental rights protection at the EU level (section 2). In section 3, I will address the case law of the Court of Justice in the area of fundamental rights review, in particular in relation to the expansion of its scope and the Charter of Fundamental Rights.[18] Section 4 will again look at the joint jurisprudence of the EU and the national level in relation to the application of fundamental rights review in the Area of Freedom, Security and Justice (AFSJ) and the field of data retention. The last section (5) will offer conclusions concerning the role and position of fundamental rights review in the system of constitutional pluralism and in respect of the question of the final arbiter.

## 2 The Common Perspective: The Beginning of Constitutional Conflict

The principle of primacy of EU law, as developed by the Court of Justice,[19] was first challenged in the context of fundamental rights protection. The principles behind the protection of fundamental rights, according to Bobek, transcend 'a nation state, ancestry, or ethnicity'[20] and have 'universal meaning'.[21] They may therefore be expected to serve as a unifying factor in the development of EU constitutional law. However, as Weiler analyses in detail, this view is over simplified.[22] The very

[16] For a brief description of the different generations of rights see ibid 48 and the literature cited.

[17] Although this will at certain points be inevitable, as it is inextricably linked to the jurisprudence of constitutional conflict.

[18] Charter of Fundamental Rights of the European Union [2012] OJ C326/391.

[19] See ch 5, s 2.

[20] M Bobek, *Comparative Reasoning in European Supreme Courts* (OUP 2013) 61.

[21] ibid.

[22] Weiler (n 8) 102.

definition of fundamental rights and differing standards of protection throughout the European Union created further tensions and differentiation in the European judicial space. Weiler points out that these differences 'reflect fundamental societal choices and form an important part in the different identities of polities and societies'.[23]

The protection of fundamental rights can subsequently also lead to institutional frictions, given the overlapping jurisdictions of national courts performing constitutional review and the Court of Justice. In the course of European integration, constitutional conflict in fundamental rights review developed from a predominantly institutional one (as national courts performing constitutional review have been faced with an expansion of the Court of Justice's jurisdiction in this area), towards a more substantive conflict (related to the appropriate standard of fundamental rights protection).[24] This section will divide its analysis in three periods to reflect this shift: (1) the period before fundamental rights entered the scope of EU law (until 1970); (2) the period of institutional conflict over the jurisdiction to perform fundamental rights review (1970 to 1984); (3) the period of accommodation of parallel jurisdictional claims (after 1984).

## 2.1 The Period until 1969

The position of constitutional courts with respect to fundamental rights protection was at this point in time undisputed.[25] The power relations among the courts under analysis are balanced as both the Court of Justice and national constitutional courts have their respective spheres of authority, resulting from a lack of overlap in jurisdiction to perform the fundamental rights review. The constitutional court is atop the national judicial hierarchy[26] and their constitutional role in fundamental rights protection was not affected by the principle of primacy of EU law. The constitutional court remains an undisputed final authority over ordinary national courts in the area of fundamental rights. The Court of Justice's authority is confined to areas

[23] ibid.

[24] A Bobić, 'Developments in the EU-German Judicial Love Story: The Right to Be Forgotten II' (2020) 21(S1) *German Law Journal* 31.

[25] In this period, these were the constitutional courts of Italy and Germany. Weiler (n 8) 108. See also F Mancini, 'The Making of a Constitution for Europe' (1989) 26(4) *Common Market Law Review* 595, 611.

[26] Save for the authority of the European Court of Human Rights, which was created specifically for the purpose of protecting fundamental rights, and the High Contracting Parties have accepted its jurisdiction. In addition, the ECHR functions as the minimum standard and states are allowed to confer protection higher than that required by the European Court of Human Rights, something that will not be the case in relation to the EU Charter of Fundamental Rights. In relation to the former see also Weiler (n 8) 105. For the analysis of the jurisprudence of constitutional conflict in relation to the Charter see s 3.2 of this chapter.

of existing EU competences, where it has developed a relationship of cooperation through the preliminary reference procedure.

An example which reflects this power balance well is the German *EEC Regulations Constitutionality* decision.[27] The Bundesverfassungsgericht was to decide on a constitutional complaint against two regulations which allegedly breached fundamental rights protected by the Basic Law. The decision was praised by the academic community as EU-friendly for a rejection of the jurisdiction to review the constitutionality of regulations, due to the autonomous status of the EU's legal order.[28] Nevertheless, the Bundesverfassungsgericht reserved for itself the power to review EU law should it breach fundamental rights enshrined in the Basic Law.

## 2.2 The Start of the Conflict (the Period between 1969 and 1984)

The judicial power relations started shifting towards the end of the 1960s, as the requirements of EU law began to coincide with fundamental rights protection in the Member States. The competition between the participants of the European judicial space resulted in a protective approach of the Court of Justice as regards its autonomy, by offering its own contribution to the fundamental rights protection landscape.[29] According to Mancini, it was the 'brutal blow'[30] of the above *EEC Regulations Constitutionality* decision that provoked the Court of Justice to address fundamental rights protection. Interviewee 1 stated that, although at this time there was no political consensus on the matter, introducing fundamental rights review at the EU level was a 'necessity'. Whether this was a defensive or offensive move,[31] collision was inevitable[32] and fundamental rights slowly but surely entered

[27] German Bundesverfassungsgericht Case 22 BVerfGE 293 *EEC Regulations Constitutionality* Decision of 18 October 1967.

[28] M Claes, *The National Courts' Mandate in the European Constitution* (Hart Publishing 2006) 597–98.

[29] F Schimmelfennig, 'Competition and Community: Constitutional Courts, Rhetorical Action, and the Institutionalisation of Human Rights in the European Union' (2006) 13(8) *Journal of European Public Policy* 1247, 1248. See also H Kaila, 'The Scope of Application of the Charter of Fundamental Rights of the European Union in the Member States' in P Cardonell, A Rosas, and N Wahl (eds), *Constitutionalising the EU Judicial System: Essays in Honour of Pernilla Lindh* (Hart Publishing 2012) 292; J Coppel and A O'Neill, 'The European Court of Justice: Taking Rights Seriously?' (1992) 12(2) *Legal Studies* 227, 229. For a critique of the latter see J H H Weiler and N J S Lockhart, '"Taking Rights Seriously" Seriously: The European Court and Its Fundamental Rights Jurisprudence—Part I' (1995) 32(1) *Common Market Law Review* 51.

[30] Mancini (n 25) 609–10.

[31] Weiler reports that during the 1960s, it was a political and legal imperative to complete the constitutional charter of the Community with the protection of fundamental rights. Weiler (n 8) 108. See also B-O Bryde, 'The ECJ's Fundamental Rights Jurisprudence: A Milestone in Transnational Constitutionalism' in M P Maduro and L Azoulai (eds), *The Past and Future of EU Law: The Classics of EU Law Revisited on the 50th Anniversary of the Rome Treaty* (Hart Publishing 2010) 122.

[32] Mancini (n 25) 611. See also F G Jacobs, 'Human Rights in the European Union: The Role of the Court of Justice' (2001) 26(4) *European Law Review* 331, 332.

the scope of the Union legal order. Equally, judicial power relations started changing, as the jurisdiction of national courts under analysis and the Court of Justice started to overlap as regards fundamental rights protection.

The story begins with the well-known *Stauder* decision.[33] Mr Stauder claimed that the Commission's welfare scheme of issuing coupons for a subsidized butter price that included his name breached his fundamental right to human dignity. National fundamental rights were, it was long decided, not the acceptable standard of review of EU action.[34] The Court of Justice could not allow national standards to play a role in review and interpretation of EU law, given that its own function is to achieve and maintain the uniformity and effectiveness of EU law. Nevertheless, the Court of Justice found a fairly easy way out of the situation, and deciding that since only the German version of the Commission's decision indicated the name as an identifier on the subsidies coupon, German authorities were allowed to employ other methods of identification.[35] More importantly,[36] the Court stated that '[i]nterpreted in this way, the provision at issue contains nothing capable of prejudicing the fundamental human rights enshrined in the general principles of Community law and protected by the Court'.[37] The Court employed the same technique as regards the expansion of general principles of EU law,[38] by solely *giving expression* to a pre-existing state of affairs.

A year later, the Court of Justice expanded the scope of fundamental rights protection. In *Internationale Handelsgesellschaft*,[39] the Administrative Court of Frankfurt-am-Main was in doubt as to the compatibility of a regulation concerning export licences with principles of freedom of action and disposition, economic liberty, and proportionality.[40] Again repeating that national law cannot be the standard of review of EU acts, the Court of Justice provided an autonomous definition of its fundamental rights catalogue:

> In fact, respect for fundamental rights forms an integral part of the general principles of law protected by the Court of Justice. The protection of such rights, whilst inspired by the constitutional traditions common to the Member States, must be ensured within the framework of the structure and objectives of the Community.[41]

[33] Case 29/69 *Stauder* [1969] EU:C:1969:57. For an analysis see N Fennelly, 'Pillar Talk: Fundamental Rights Protection in the European Union' (2008) 8(1) *Judicial Studies Institute Journal* 95, 98.

[34] Case 1/58 *Stork* [1959] EU:C:1959:4 [4(a)].

[35] Case 29/69 *Stauder* (n 33) [2].

[36] More importantly is used here as a reference to the consequence, since the Court of Justice only mentions fundamental rights at the end of the judgment, 'in passing', to borrow the phrasing from Coppel and O'Neill (n 29) 228.

[37] Case 29/69 *Stauder* (n 33) [7].

[38] See ch 5, s 5.

[39] Case 11/70 *Internationale Handelsgesellschaft* [1970] EU:C:1970:114.

[40] See ch 5, s 2 for the analysis of the case in relation to the principle of primacy.

[41] Case 11/70 *Internationale Handelsgesellschaft* (n 39) [4].

General principles of law, thus, *materially* comprised of common constitutional traditions of Member States. While a single national standard was a threat to the primacy, uniformity and effectiveness of EU law,[42] it was impossible to ignore national constitutional standards of protection of fundamental rights altogether. In the structure of constitutional pluralism, national and EU law are inherently intertwined, thereby ensuring that cross-fertilization is a two-way process between national and EU constitutional orders.[43]

After the case returned to the Administrative Court, which was not satisfied with the finding of the Court of Justice as regards the status of fundamental rights protection,[44] it referred the case to the Bundesverfassungsgericht, resulting in the famous *Solange I* decision.[45] The decision requires an analysis from the perspective of constitutional pluralism, regardless of the fact the theory has developed and is mostly connected to the much later *Maastricht* judgment of the Bundesverfassungsgericht. The Bundesverfassungsgericht first addressed the nature of the EU's legal system: 'Community law is neither a component part of the national legal system nor international law, but forms an independent system of law flowing from an autonomous legal source.'[46] Avoiding thus to define the nature of the EU's legal order, the Bundesverfassungsgericht nevertheless acknowledged it is, in MacCormick's terms,[47] an institutional normative order, and continued: '[i]t follows from this that, in principle, the two legal spheres stand independent of and side by side one another in their validity'.[48] This may in fact be the first expression of the existence of multiple co-existing claims to ultimate authority, the first premise of constitutional pluralism.

The Bundesverfassungsgericht went further to address the situation of a possible conflict in the spirit of constitutional pluralism:

> This does not lead to any difficulties as long as the two systems of law do not come into conflict with one another in their substance. There therefore grows forth from the special relationship which has arisen between the Community and its members by the establishment of the Community first and foremost the duty for

[42] 'According to the evaluation of the Verwaltungsgericht, the system of deposits is contrary to certain structural principles of national constitutional law which must be protected within the framework of Community law, with the result that the primacy of supranational law must yield before the principles of the German Basic Law.' Case 11/70 *Internationale Handelsgesellschaft* (n 39) [2].

[43] To use the phrasing of Thym, these orders are 'separate, but not separable'. D Thym, 'Separation Versus Fusion—or: How to Accommodate National Autonomy and the Charter? Diverging Visions of the German Constitutional Court and the European Court of Justice' (2013) 9(3) *European Constitutional Law Review* 39, 41.

[44] Claes (n 28) 599.

[45] German Bundesverfassungsgericht Case 37 BVerfGE 271 *Internationale Handelsgesellschaft (Solange I)* Judgment of 29 May 1974.

[46] ibid [19].

[47] N MacCormick, *Questioning Sovereignty: Law, State and Nation in the European Commonwealth* (OUP 1999), 102–103. See also ch 3, s 1.

[48] German Bundesverfassungsgericht Case *Solange I* (n 45) [20].

> the competent organs, in particular for the two courts charged with reviewing law—the European Court of Justice and the Bundesverfassungsgericht—to concern themselves in their decisions with the concordance of the two systems of law.[49]

The incremental functioning of the auto-correct mechanism of constitutional pluralism is visible from the joint obligation on behalf of the two courts to accommodate each other's claims to ultimate authority in their respective areas of jurisdiction. The Bundesverfassungsgericht continued by stating that even an exceptional disapplication of a Community or a German obligation would not bring into question the validity of claims of those two legal orders.[50] The obligation of mutual respect should thus drive the two courts in their decision-making, as the emergence of any possible conflict does not lead to a violation of the Treaty nor of the Basic Law.[51] In addition, a possibility of an exceptional 'victory' of one legal order over the other and vice versa is in line with the definition of heterarchy,[52] a system in which there is no single permanent winner, but one where participants can be positioned differently in relation to one another at different times.

The remainder of the judgment is widely known: the Bundesverfassungsgericht stated that the Community at that time did not have a catalogue of protecting fundamental rights[53] and the conflict should be resolved as follows:

> Provisionally, therefore, in the hypothetical case of a conflict between Community law and a part of national constitutional law or, more precisely, of the guarantees of fundamental rights in the Constitution, there arises the question of which system of law takes precedence, that is, ousts the other. In this conflict of norms, the guarantee of fundamental rights in the Constitution prevails as long as the competent organs of the Community have not removed the conflict of norms in accordance with the Treaty mechanism.[54]

Six months earlier, the Italian Corte Constituzionale had put forward criticism concerning the protection of fundamental rights along very similar lines. In its *Frontini* decision,[55] it introduced the *controlimiti* doctrine.[56] It first addressed the

[49] ibid [20].
[50] ibid [21].
[51] ibid.
[52] See ch 3, s 2.
[53] Although it did not rule out the possibility that this might change. German Bundesverfassungsgericht Case *Solange I* (n 45) [23].
[54] ibid [24].
[55] Italian Corte Costituzionale Case 183/73 *Frontini* Decision of 27 December 1973.
[56] Cartabia reports this was already implicitly announced already in 1965, but was given explicit expression in *Frontini*. M Cartabia, 'The Italian Constitutional Court and the Relationship Between the Italian Legal System and the European Union' in A-M Slaughter, A Stone Sweet, and J H H Weiler (eds), *European Court and National Courts: Doctrine and Jurisprudence—Legal Change in its Social Context*

nature of the EU's legal order: 'Community norms, which cannot be characterised as a source of international law, nor of foreign law, nor of internal law of the individual States';[57] as well as the relationship of such a legal order with those of its Member States: 'its laws and the internal law of the individual member-States can be described as autonomous and distinct legal systems, albeit co-ordinated in accordance with the division of power laid down and guaranteed by the Treaty'.[58]

Thus, the vision of the Corte Costituzionale as regards the EU's legal order and its relationship to national law also closely follows the structure of constitutional pluralism—the co-existence of multiple *autonomous* legal orders claiming authority in overlying areas of regulation. The overlap of functions is all the more evident in *Frontini*, as the applicants were seeking review of the Community's powers to regulate customs duties, which overlap with the constitutionally guaranteed state monopoly (*riserva di legge*) to regulate personal and financial obligations of individuals.[59] The Corte Costituzionale then proceeded with its claim to the ultimate say as regards fundamental rights:

> It is hardly necessary to add that by Article 11 of the Constitution limitations of sovereignty are allowed solely for the purpose of the ends indicated therein, and it should therefore be excluded that such limitations of sovereignty, concretely set out in the Rome Treaty, signed by countries whose systems are based on the principle of the rule of law and guarantee the essential liberties of citizens, can nevertheless give the organs of the EEC an unacceptable power to violate the fundamental principles of our constitutional order or the inalienable rights of man.[60]

The language of the Corte Costituzionale certainly stems from a dualist approach to external sources of law.[61] However, the Corte Costituzionale talks about the specific nature of the EU's legal order, not pertaining to the sphere of either public international or national law. Rather, taking into account primacy and direct effect,[62] the vocabulary of dualism becomes obsolete as it lacks an ultimate monist solution (a *Grundnorm*, or a rule of recognition, which is traditionally found in the national constitution). The Corte Costituzionale talks about coordination of the two legal orders, rather than a single ultimate solution, which can only exceptionally be the disapplication of the principle of primacy. Again, much like the analysis in *Solange I*, such a solution corresponds to the definition of heterarchy following

(Hart Publishing 1998) 138; Italian Corte Costituzionale Case 98/1965 *Società Acciaierie San Michele* Decision of 27 December 1965.

[57] Italian Corte Costituzionale Case *Frontini* (n 55) [12].
[58] ibid.
[59] ibid [6].
[60] ibid [21].
[61] Cartabia (n 56) 133–34.
[62] Italian Corte Costituzionale Case *Frontini* (n 55) [12].

the parallel operation of multiple claims to ultimate authority within the same space, descriptively thus aligning with constitutional pluralism.

The two courts' decisions display important similarities. For the Bundesverfassungsgericht, the status of European integration did not satisfy the German standard of protection of fundamental rights and it rejected the primacy of EU law 'provisionally, therefore, in the hypothetical case of conflict'[63] in the area of fundamental rights. The standpoint of the Corte Costituzionale was that of a conditional primacy, subject to the counter-limits of the constitutional core and fundamental rights. Judicial power relations have therefore shifted from the original position of balance to one favouring constitutional courts. The relationship between ordinary national courts and the Court of Justice remained virtually the same as before, save for the situation in which the ordinary national court would be obliged to follow the constitutional court should it find that an EU measure violates the constitutional standard of fundamental rights protection. The position of the constitutional court is accordingly strengthened in relation to ordinary national courts, as it is the undisputed final authority over ordinary national courts in the area of fundamental rights protection, given that the EU does not (yet) have an appropriate catalogue of fundamental rights. The constitutional court accordingly took up the review of EU legislation against the constitutional standard of fundamental rights protection.

The German and Italian constitutional courts thus had the upper hand. The next development brings us back to Luxembourg. The case of *Nold* was,[64] according to some commentators,[65] a response to the 'conditional primacy' jurisprudence of the Italian and German constitutional courts.[66] It involved an action for annulment of a Commission decision concerning the retail of coal in the Ruhr area of Germany, based on, among others, a claim that the decision breaches the fundamental right of a free pursuit of business, enshrined in the German Basic Law, but also in constitutions of other Member States and the European Convention on Human Rights (ECHR). In its judgment, the Court of Justice set out a comprehensive catalogue of fundamental rights in the EU:

> As the Court has already stated, fundamental rights form an integral part of the general principles of law, the observance of which it ensures. In safeguarding

[63] German Bundesverfassungsgericht Case *Solange I* (n 45) [24].

[64] Case 4/73 *Nold* [1974] EU:C:1974:51. It should be noted that the judgment in *Nold* was handed down two weeks before *Solange I*, but its findings were not taken into account by the Bundesverfassungsgericht.

[65] J Kühling, 'Fundamental Rights' in A von Bogdandy and J Bast (eds), *Principles of European Constitutional Law* (Hart Publishing 2006) 501; Schimmelfennig (n 29); both cited in Fabbrini (n 1) 9; de Visser (n 5) 410.

[66] While the decision in *Solange I* was handed down two weeks after *Nold*, the commentators refer more generally to the German jurisprudence initiated by the mentioned *EEC Regulations Constitutionality* decision (n 27) of the Bundesverfassungsgericht, as well as the Italian *controlimiti* jurisprudence.

> these rights, the Court is bound to draw inspiration from constitutional traditions common to the Member States, and it cannot therefore uphold measures which are incompatible with fundamental rights recognized and protected by the Constitutions of those States. Similarly, international treaties for the protection of human rights on which the Member States have collaborated or of which they are signatories, can supply guidelines which should be followed within the framework of Community law.[67]

This was the first time that the Court of Justice, in describing the content of general principles of law, referred to an international source of law, seeking to establish 'external coherence for its human rights protection and thereby enhance its legitimacy'.[68] By including international treaties in the scope of fundamental rights protection, the Court of Justice was able to encompass the ECHR. As explained by Henckaerts, the ECHR was of use to the Court of Justice as all the Member States were signatories. This way, the Court of Justice did not have to engage in a comparative constitutional law study in devising a fundamental rights protection catalogue, having the ECHR at its disposal to serve as the common denominator.[69]

### 2.3 The Incremental Accommodation of Conflict

Both the Bundesverfassungsgericht and the Corte Costituzionale watered down their approach in subsequent case law. The language of the Italian decision in *Granital*[70] is in line with the incremental nature of constitutional pluralism, as the Corte Costituzionale stated that its own jurisprudence concerning the relationship between EU and Italian constitutional law had undergone an evolution:[71] EU regulations have primacy over national law and the latter must be interpreted as much as possible in light of the former.[72] The Corte Costituzionale then further elaborated upon the primacy of EU law and retained for itself the right to invalidate a conflicting national provision which was enacted after the EU act in question. In a situation of conflict, it reiterated its position from *Frontini*—it is the ultimate arbiter as regards the basic principles of the Italian state and fundamental rights—only this time with an additional use of reconciliatory vocabulary, emphasizing that a conflict is an 'unlikely possibility'.[73] In sum, the Italian court will perform a

[67] Case 4/73 *Nold* (n 64) [13].

[68] Schimmelfennig (n 29) 1254.

[69] J-M Henckaerts, 'The Protection of Human Rights in the European Union: Overview and Bibliography' (1994) 22 *International Journal of Legal Information* 228, 232.

[70] Italian Corte Costituzionale Case 170/1984 *Granital* Decision of 8 June 1984.

[71] G Gaja, 'Constitutional Court (Italy), Decision No 170 of 8 June 1984, S.p.a. Granital v. Amministrazione delle Finanze dello Stato' (1984) 21(4) *Common Market Law Review* 756, 758.

[72] ibid.

[73] ibid 764. Note here the resemblance to the *Solange I* vocabulary of the Bundesverfassungsgericht, when it talks about a 'hypothetical case of a conflict'. See n 54.

fundamental rights review only if the exceptional situation takes place whereby a constitutionally protected fundamental right is breached due to adhering to an EU law obligation.[74]

The German *Solange II* decision[75] resembles the Italian approach more than its own from *Solange I* and more generally follows the framework of constitutional pluralism. First, the Bundesverfassungsgericht called the Court of Justice 'a sovereign organ of judicature' that has 'judicial monopoly' as regards the interpretation and validity of EU law,[76] acknowledging multiple claims to ultimate authority in overlapping areas of jurisdiction. The Bundesverfassungsgericht proceeded:

> That partly functional incorporation of the European Court into the jurisdictions of member-States expresses the fact that the legal orders of member-States and that of the Community are not abruptly juxtaposed in a state of mutual insulation but are in numerous ways related to each other, interconnected and open to reciprocal effects.[77]

This understanding of the relationship between EU and national law, and accordingly their respective judiciaries, points to a greater degree of cooperation than a relationship that is subject to a hierarchical monist structure. In the same incremental fashion as the Corte Costituzionale, its German counterpart changed its view as regards fundamental rights review, addressing at length how the Court of Justice changed its approach to fundamental rights. It then concluded:

> In view of those developments it must be held that, so long as the European Communities, and in particular in the case law of the European Court, generally ensure an effective protection of fundamental rights as against the sovereign powers of the Communities which is to be regarded as substantially similar to the protection of fundamental rights required unconditionally by the Constitution, and in so far as they generally safeguard the essential content of fundamental rights, the Federal Constitutional Court will no longer exercise its jurisdiction to decide on the applicability of secondary Community legislation cited as the legal basis for any acts of German courts or authorities within the sovereign jurisdiction of the Federal Republic of Germany, and it will no longer review such legislation by the standard of the fundamental rights contained in the Constitution.[78]

[74] This approach was further refined in 1989, where the Corte Costituzionale stated that it will test individual provisions of EU law against fundamental rights. Italian Corte Costituzionale Case 232/1989 *Fragd* Decision of 21 April 1989.

[75] German Bundesverfassungsgericht Case 2 BvR 197/83 *Re the Application of Wünsche Handelsgesellschaft (Solange II)* Judgment of 22 October 1986.

[76] ibid [4], [6].

[77] ibid [7].

[78] ibid [48].

At this point, the position of the Bundesverfassungsgericht is very similar to that of the Corte Costituzionale, in that they will both perform fundamental rights review only if the Court of Justice fails to adhere to the standards of their national constitutions and the ECHR. The Italian and German constitutional courts have thus instituted a rebuttable presumption that EU law generally complies with the constitutional level of fundamental rights protection. The judicial power relations are now back in balance. This balance is, however, sourced in a different legal structure, as the spheres of jurisdiction of the Court of Justice and constitutional courts now overlap. Nevertheless, the relationship between their opposing claims to fundamental rights review is heterarchical, given that the jurisprudence on both levels leaves open the possibility of such review under specific circumstances.[79]

The relationship of cooperation of ordinary national courts with the Court of Justice will only be put in question if the presumption is rebutted. The constitutional court remains the undisputed final authority for ordinary national courts in fundamental rights review of national law. Finally, the constitutional court will exhibit self-restraint in matters of EU law, according to the presumption established by *Solange II* and *Granital*, whereas the Court of Justice will safeguard the standard of fundamental rights protection in line with the standard of national constitutions.

*Solange II* thus marks the end of the initial period of an institutional constitutional conflict in the European Union, settling the question of whether the Court of Justice has jurisdiction in the area of fundamental rights. The conflict opened the door for a substance-oriented discussion between the participants of the European judicial space, in relation to the proper standard of fundamental rights protection. In this respect, national constitutional courts acted as a check to the Court of Justice in the cooperative, heterarchical setting of the European judicial space.[80] The next development is marked by an expansion of the Court of Justice's jurisdiction in fundamental rights review (by instituting review of national measures and the enactment of the Charter).

## 3 Further Expansions of Fundamental Rights Review by the Court of Justice

Having established a catalogue of fundamental rights protection for matters of EU law, ultimately expanding the self-referential system of the Treaties,[81] the Court of

[79] For the Court of Justice, this is a situation when an EU law obligation allegedly breaches fundamental rights. For constitutional courts, this is the situation when the standard of fundamental rights protection on the EU level sinks below the constitutional level of protection.

[80] See also in that sense P M Huber, 'The Federal Constitutional Court and European Integration' (2015) 21(1) *European Public Law* 83, 106.

[81] The protection of fundamental rights first entered the text of the Treaties in the Preamble to the Single European Act (1987) and in art F of the Maastricht Treaty (1992).

Justice proceeded by attempting to establish itself as the constitutional court of the European Union.[82] For this purpose, it extended its jurisdiction of fundamental rights review, and this section will look more closely at three such expansions: (1) the review of national measures; (2) the scope of the Charter of Fundamental Rights; and (3) external actors.

## 3.1 National Measures

The Court of Justice has, by defining the fundamental rights catalogue in *Nold*, surpassed the initial constitutional conflict with the German and Italian constitutional courts. As a further development, the Court of Justice expanded its fundamental rights review by subjecting national measures to its scrutiny.

Advocate General Jacobs proposed the review of national measures directly in *Wachauf*,[83] relying upon the analogous obligation of Union institutions. As Weiler explains, given that Member States are implementing EU law on a daily basis, it would be arbitrary to review only the Union's institutions' compliance with fundamental rights.[84] Thus, according to Advocate General Jacobs, when Member States act 'in pursuance of powers granted under Community law' it is 'self-evident' they must act in compliance with fundamental rights.[85] The Court of Justice followed suit, equally deriving Member States' obligations from that of the Union legislator:

> [It] must be observed that Community rules which [would be equal to the German rules in question] would be incompatible with the requirements of the protection of fundamental rights in the Community legal order. Since those requirements are also binding on the Member States when they implement Community rules, the Member States must, as far as possible, apply those rules in accordance with those requirements.[86]

The power of review is thus expanded from its original focus on EU law measures and will be carried out when Member States are acting in their capacity of implementing EU law (labelled as the 'agency situation' in the literature).[87]

[82] J J Barceló III, 'ECJ Review of Member State Measures for Compliance with Fundamental Rights' (2009) Cornell Law School Legal Studies Research Paper No 10-001 [4] http://scholarship.law.cornell.edu/cgi/viewcontent.cgi?article=1096&context=clsops_papers; S Weatherill, *Law and Values in the European Union* (OUP 2016) 152. For an argument on the existence of supranational constitutional courts see F Fabbrini and M P Maduro, 'Supranational Constitutional Courts' (2017) iCourts Working Paper Series 98/2017 https://papers.ssrn.com/sol3/papers.cfm?abstract_id=2990277.

[83] Opinion of Advocate General Jacobs in Case 5/88 *Wachauf* [1989] EU:C:1989:179 [22].

[84] Weiler (n 8) 120–21.

[85] Opinion of Advocate General Jacobs in Case 5/88 *Wachauf* (n 83) [22].

[86] Case 5/88 *Wachauf* [1989] EU:C:1989:321 [19].

[87] Weiler (n 8) 120; Kaila (n 29) 296.

In addition, the Court of Justice introduced fundamental rights review of national measures which derogate from EU law in *ERT*.[88] The Court of Justice linked the adherence to fundamental rights to public policy derogations in Treaty Articles concerning free movement: 'the national rules in question can fall under the exceptions provided for by [ . . . ] Articles 56 and 66 only if they are compatible with the fundamental rights the observance of which is ensured by the Court.'[89] It is generally accepted that this is an expansion of the Court's jurisdiction,[90] but Weiler is right to note that the extent of the derogation is still a matter within the scope of EU law and thus within the jurisdiction of the Court.[91] A reservation in relation to the *ERT* reasoning on the scope of EU law may be found in *Annibaldi*,[92] where the Italian authorities denied the right to Mr Annibaldi to grow an orchard in the park he owns due to its cultural heritage status and environmental concerns. He claimed his right to property is infringed and attempted to prove the relevant national legislation falls in the scope of Union law. The Court of Justice did not establish a connection between the national law and the EU's common agricultural policy:

> [Even] if the Regional Law be capable [sic] of affecting indirectly the operation of a common organization of the agricultural markets, it is not in dispute that, the park having been created to protect and enhance the value of the environment and the cultural heritage of the area concerned, the Regional Law pursues objectives other than those covered by the common agricultural policy, or that the Law itself is general in character.[93]

*Annibaldi* thus offered some reassurance that the Court of Justice will carry out a more detailed analysis of the connection between the national measure and EU law. Lenaerts stated that the *ERT* expansion sources its importance in providing reassurance to national (constitutional) courts that the basic values of their constitutions are adhered to.[94] In order to test whether this is indeed the case, let us take a look at the post-*Wachauf* and *ERT* judicial power relations.

[88] Case C-260/89 *ERT* [1991] EU:C:1991:254.

[89] ibid [43]. The Court of Justice confirmed in later cases that this relates to implementing all sources of EU law. See Case C-309/96 *Annibaldi* [1997] EU:C:1997:631 [14]–[21]; Case C-384/05 *Piek* [2007] EU:C:2007:21 [34]. The Court of Justice confirmed explicitly that this also entails situations where the Member States have a wide discretion in the implementation obligation. Case C-292/97 *Karlsson* [2000] EU:C:2000:202 [35]. For the analogous tendency in the operation of the national identity clause as a public policy derogation see ch 6, s 3.1.

[90] Jacobs (n 32) 335–36; Fabbrini (n 1) 210. This point will also be of relevance in relation to the scope of the Charter of Fundamental Rights in s 3.2 below.

[91] Weiler (n 8) 122. See also K Lenaerts, 'The Court of Justice of the European Union and the Protection of Fundamental Rights' (2011) 31 *Polish Yearbook of International Law* 79, 88–90.

[92] Case C-309/96 *Annibaldi* (n 89).

[93] ibid [22].

[94] Lenaerts (n 91) 89.

Lenaerts may have overestimated the benefits that constitutional courts would yield after *Wachauf* and *ERT*. The leverage at this point in time is on the side of the Court of Justice. First, it has the advantage in relation to constitutional courts thanks to the presumption of compliance with constitutional protection of fundamental rights, according to *Solange II* and *Granital*. Second, it now also has the advantage of reviewing national measures implementing or derogating from EU law that may have not been questioned for their constitutionality on the national level. This results in a more influential relationship towards ordinary national courts, as they will be bound by the fundamental rights review of national measures carried out by the Court of Justice.

Constitutional courts remain firmly influential towards their ordinary national courts solely in situations of constitutional review of measures that fall outside the scope of EU law, which results in an additional decrease of their authority in the national judicial hierarchy. Yet, the existence of the rebuttable presumption from *Solange II* and *Granital* retained some power for the constitutional courts towards the Court of Justice. Finally, the power of the Court of Justice to review national measures has increased the overlap of its jurisdiction with that of national courts performing constitutional review. Constitutional pluralism presupposes such an overlap, whereas in line with the definition of heterarchy, at this particular point in time, it was the Court of Justice that had the upper hand. Having established the catalogue of fundamental rights (in accordance with *Nold*) and the scope of fundamental rights review of both EU and national measures in the scope of EU law (in accordance with *Internationale Handelsgesellschaft*, *Wachauf*, and *ERT*),[95] the Court of Justice holds most influence at this point in time.

## 3.2 The Scope of the Charter of Fundamental Rights

The Charter of Fundamental Rights marks the next step in the development of fundamental rights review on the EU level. The Charter was initially envisaged as a non-binding EU bill of rights, proposed during the German presidency in 1999.[96] The Cologne Conclusions of the Council affirmed that the role of the Charter is to, first and foremost, improve the visibility of the EU as a fundamental rights actor to its citizens, and second, to codify the *existing* jurisprudence of the Court of Justice in fundamental rights protection.[97] Consequently, the Charter was not

[95] To Lenaerts and Gutiérrez-Fons, this is inherent in the mandate of the Court of Justice, enshrined in today's art 19(1) TEU, to ensure that in the interpretation and application of the Treaties the law is observed. Lenaerts and Gutiérrez-Fons (n 8) 1650.

[96] G de Búrca, 'The Drafting of the European Union Charter of Fundamental Rights' (2001) 26(2) *European Law Review* 126, 130.

[97] ibid 130–31. On the extent to which the final text of the Charter introduces innovations see C Ladenburger, 'Protection of Fundamental Rights Post-Lisbon: The Interaction between the Charter of Fundamental Rights, the European Convention of Human Rights and National Constitutions' FIDE Institutional Report (2012) 2 http://www.fide2012.eu/index.php?doc_id=88.

intended to introduce any novelties in fundamental rights protection in the EU. It was proclaimed as a non-binding legal document by the European Parliament, the Council, and the Commission in Nice in 2000. Its legal status remained non-binding until it was attached to the Lisbon Treaty and gained the status of primary EU law.[98] Prior to the entry into force of the Lisbon Treaty, the Charter was used as inspiration for the establishment of general principles.[99] The scope is set out in Article 51(1) of the Charter:

> The provisions of this Charter are addressed to the institutions, bodies, offices and agencies of the Union with due regard for the principle of subsidiarity and to the Member States only when they are implementing Union law. They shall therefore respect the rights, observe the principles and promote the application thereof in accordance with their respective powers and respecting the limits of the powers of the Union as conferred on it in the Treaties.

The Explanations relating to the Charter[100] refer to *Wachauf* and *ERT* as the relevant case law in determining the proper reading of Article 51(1) of the Charter. As the following analysis will demonstrate, the Court of Justice has, again incrementally, expanded the outer limits of Article 51(1) through an expansive interpretation of what it means to 'implement Union law'.

According to Lenaerts, this expression covers 'all situations where Member States fulfil their obligations under the Treaties as well as under secondary EU law, [ ... ] i.e. [ ... ] whenever Member States fulfil an obligation imposed by EU law'.[101] This definition lacks precision and is susceptible to being stretched and narrowed according to the needs of a particular case. In *Scattolon*,[102] Advocate General Bot argued for a wide reading of Article 51(1) of the Charter, arguing that it does not

[98] For an analysis of the Court's treatment of the Charter from 2000 until 2009 when the Charter became binding see Eeckhout (n 11); S Iglesias Sánchez, 'The Court and the Charter: The Impact of the Entry into Force of the Lisbon Treaty on the ECJ's Approach to Fundamental Rights' (2012) 49(5) *Common Market Law Review* 1565. It should be added that Poland and the United Kingdom added a Protocol to the Charter, exempting them from the judicial expansion of the rights and principles set out in the Charter and in particular its Title IV (concerning workers' protection, social and environmental protection). See Protocol on the application of the Charter on Fundamental Rights of the European Union to Poland and to the United Kingdom [2007] OJ C306/156. In 2011, the Court of Justice found that the Protocol does not exempt the two countries from their obligations under the Charter. Joined Cases C-411/10 and C-493/10 *NS* [2011] EU:C:2011:865 [120]. For a detailed analysis see V Belling, 'Supranational Fundamental Rights or Primacy of Sovereignty? Legal Effects of the So-called Opt-out from the EU Charter of Fundamental Rights' (2012) 18(2) *European Law Journal* 251 (concluding the Protocol will not lead to substantively lower fundamental rights protection in the United Kingdom and Poland).

[99] Case C-540/03 *Parliament v Council* [2006] EU:C:2006:429 [38]. See also Ladenburger (n 97) 2.

[100] Explanations relating to the Charter of fundamental rights [2007] OJ C303/17.

[101] Lenaerts (n 91) 83.

[102] Opinion of Advocate General Bot in Case C-108/10 *Scattolon* [2011] EU:C:2011:211 [119]–[120]. Advocate General Bot also cited *Annibaldi* as an example of a situation without sufficient connection to EU law, in which the Charter did not apply. *Annibaldi* is also cited in the Explanations relating to the Charter concerning art 51 of the Charter. Case C-309/96 *Annibaldi* (n 89).

seem to be the intention of the drafters of the Charter that general principles of EU law and the Charter have a different scope of application.[103] He cited *Kücükdeveci* in support of such a wide reading and concluded that (in relation to directives) the Charter should apply to 'all situations in which national legislation concerns or affects a matter governed by a directive the period for the transposition of which has expired'.[104]

In contrast, former Advocate General Jacobs and Lord Goldsmith both advocated for a narrower reading of Article 51(1) of the Charter, arguing it should be confined solely to the 'agency situation'.[105] Situations not covered by *Wachauf* should remain outside the scope of the Court of Justice's powers of review and their compliance with fundamental rights should be ensured in accordance with the national constitution and the ECHR.[106] The analysis of the case law below will illustrate the difference these various views make in practice.

In *Kücükdeveci*,[107] the Court of Justice found that for the general principles and the Charter to apply, it suffices that the national measure in question falls within the scope of the Directive.[108] The Court mentions no further conditions, nor does it differentiate between implementation and derogation. A further progressive interpretation of Article 51(1) of the Charter was given in *Estov*,[109] where the Court of Justice rejected a preliminary reference as inadmissible for the following reason:

> Given that the order for reference does not contain any specific information to show that the decision of the Ministerski savet na Republika Bulgaria of 16 December 2009 would constitute a measure implementing European Union law or would be *connected in any other way* with that law, the jurisdiction of the Court to rule on the present reference for a preliminary ruling is not established.[110]

The Court of Justice employed a very wide reading of Article 51(1) of the Charter, as it refers, aside from implementation, to any other connection with EU law.[111] The 'any other connection' formula has a strong *Dassonville*-ian taste to it,[112] as it is capable of being stretched even beyond the derogation situation envisaged in

[103] Lenaerts (n 91) 82.
[104] Opinion of Advocate General Bot in Case C-108/10 *Scattolon* (n 102) [119].
[105] Lord Goldsmith, 'A Charter of Rights, Freedoms and Principles' (2001) 38(5) *Common Market Law Review* 1205, 1206; Jacobs (n 32) 336.
[106] Jacobs (n 32) 336.
[107] Case C-555/07 *Kücükdeveci* [2010] EU:C:2010:21. For the analysis of the case in the context of the horizontal effect of the general principle of non-discrimination on grounds of age see ch 5, s 5.
[108] ibid [23]–[26].
[109] Order C-339/10 *Estov* [2010] EU:C:2010:680.
[110] ibid [14] (emphasis added).
[111] See also Kaila (n 29) 312.
[112] The *Dassonville* formula equally seemed to have no limits: 'All trading rules enacted by Member States which are capable of hindering, directly or indirectly, actually or potentially, intra-Community trade are to be considered as measures having an effect equivalent to quantitative restrictions.' Case 8/74 *Dassonville* [1974] EU:C:1974:82 [5].

*ERT*. This could have the consequence of expanding the influence of the Charter beyond the mandate of both Article 51(1) of the Charter and Article 6(1) TEU.[113] Nevertheless, the political situation surrounding the Charter did not warrant the justification present in *Dassonville*: that of the lack of the necessary consensus in the Council in the course of creating the internal market and the ensuing need for measures of negative integration by the Court of Justice.[114] A further look at the relevant case law will reveal whether the Court of Justice indeed intended for Article 51(1) of the Charter to follow the *Dassonville* trajectory.

In *NS*,[115] the Court of Justice was asked 'whether the decision adopted by a Member State [ ... ] to examine a claim for asylum which is not its responsibility [ ... ] falls within the scope of European Union law'.[116] The choice to decide on the asylum application is within the discretion of the Member State when it is not responsible for the claim according to the Dublin Regulation.[117] However, once this discretion is exercised, it has the effect of bringing Member State action within the scope of the relevant regulation and under the scrutiny of the Court of Justice as regards the Charter.[118]

It appeared that Article 51(1) of the Charter will not be used in a *Dassonville*-ian fashion when the Court in *Iida* cross-referred to the previously mentioned decision in *Annibaldi*:

> [To] determine whether the German [decision] falls within the implementation of European Union law within the meaning of Article 51 of the Charter, it must be ascertained among other things whether national legislation [ ... ] is intended to implement a provision of European Union law, what the character of that legislation is, and whether it pursues objectives other than those covered by European Union law, even if it is capable of indirectly affecting that law, and also whether there are specific rules of European Union law on the matter or capable of affecting it [ ... ].[119]

113 The second sentence of art 6(1) TEU states that '[the] provisions of the Charter shall not extend in any way the competences of the Union as defined in the Treaties.'

114 See eg K Alter and S Meunier-Aitsahalia, 'Judicial Politics in the European Community: European Integration and the Pathbreaking *Cassis de Dijon* Decision' (1994) 26(4) *Comparative Political Studies* 535, 536; F W Scharpf, 'The Asymmetry of European Integration, or Why the EU Cannot Be a "Social Market Economy"' (2010) 8 *Socio-Economic Review* 211, 223; C Barnard, *The Substantive Law of the EU: The Four Freedoms* (OUP 2016) 75.

115 Joined Cases C-411/10 and C-493/10 *NS* [2011] EU:C:2011:865.

116 ibid [55].

117 Council Regulation (EC) No 343/2003 of 18 February 2003 establishing the criteria and mechanisms for determining the Member State responsible for examining an asylum application lodged in one of the Member States by a third-country national [2003] OJ L50/1.

118 Joined Cases C-411/10 and C-493/10 *NS* (n 115) [68]–[69].

119 Case C-40/11 *Iida* [2012] EU:C:2012:691 [79].

However, this more detailed account of the conditions to be met for the Charter to apply has not been referred to in *Fransson*.[120] Mr Fransson was subject to criminal and administrative proceedings for tax fraud, parts of which pertained to VAT, which is the income of the Union. Advocate General Cruz Villalón suggested to the Court to reject the reference as inadmissible.[121] Having presented the discrepancies between the case law and the Explanations relating to the Charter, Advocate General Cruz Villalón proposed the following interpretation of Article 51(1) of the Charter:

> To my mind, on a proper interpretation of the basic constitutional structure of the compound comprising the Union and the Member States, which has been described as the 'European Verfassungsverbund', it is, as a rule, for the Member States themselves, in the context of their own constitutional order and the international obligations which they have entered into, to review acts of their public authorities.
>
> However, that rule is accompanied by an exception [ ... ] where national public authorities are implementing Union law, to use the wording of the Charter. In my opinion, the perception of the dialectical relationship between the two scenarios in terms of rule and exception continues to be justified today.[122]

The proposal of the Advocate General is rather narrow as it revolves around the notion of 'implementation', rather than the 'any connection' terminology used by the Court of Justice in *Estov*.[123] Cruz Villalón added that fundamental rights review of Member State action must be 'explained by reference to a specific interest of the Union in ensuring that [it] accords with the interpretation of the fundamental rights by the Union.'[124] He concluded that there is no such direct interest of the Union. A completely opposite view was proposed by Advocate General Kokott a year earlier in *Bonda*, arguing that:

> [For] the purposes of the obligation to comply with the fundamental rights of the European Union when imposing penalties in respect of infringements of European Union law, it cannot make a difference whether the Member State's measure [ ... ] was adopted explicitly when implementing European Union law or whether it already existed. In both cases it serves to implement Union law.[125]

[120] Case C-617/10 *Fransson* [2013] EU:C:2013:105.

[121] Opinion of Advocate General Cruz Villalón in Case C-617/10 *Fransson* [2012] EU:C:2012:340 [5].

[122] ibid [35]–[36].

[123] Order C-339/10 *Estov* (n 109) [14].

[124] Opinion of Advocate General Cruz Villalón in Case C-617/10 *Fransson* (n 121) [40]. The proposal could have sat well with the more specific guidance the Court of Justice mentioned in Case C-40/11 *Iida* (n 119). See also Editorial Comments, '*Ultra Vires*: Has the *Bundesverfassungsgericht* Shown its Teeth?' (2013) 50(4) *Common Market Law Review* 925, 926.

[125] Opinion of Advocate General Kokott in Case C-489/10 *Bonda* [2011] EU:C:2011:845 [20]. An even broader proposal was put forward in the Opinion of Advocate General Sharpston in Case C-34/

The Court of Justice's conclusion in *Fransson* sidelined the proposal of Advocate General Cruz Villalón and reasoned closer to the proposal of Advocate General Kokott:

> Since the fundamental rights guaranteed by the Charter must [ . . . ] be complied with where national legislation falls within the scope of European Union law, situations cannot exist which are covered in that way by European Union law without those fundamental rights being applicable. The applicability of European Union law entails applicability of the fundamental rights guaranteed by the Charter.[126]

The Court thus essentially concluded that 'implementing Union law' overlaps with 'the scope of Union law' and both are to be read as 'applicability of Union law'. Reading the Court's reasoning jointly with the previous case law, it results in a wide interpretation of the notion of implementation, as was the case in *Kücükdeveci*, *Estov*, and *NS*.[127] Commenting on this expansion, Interviewee 1 stated that from the standpoint of determining the limits of the scope of EU law, the decision in *Kücükdeveci* is far more controversial (or in their words, 'borderline') than the one in *Fransson*. The private nature of the dispute and the decision on the relevant standard of review (the Framework Directive[128] or primary EU law) were contentious points that could have led to the inadmissibility of the reference.

After *Fransson*, the Court of Justice further addressed the same question in *Siragusa*,[129] this time connecting it to the more specific reasoning from *Iida*. This enabled the Court of Justice to carry out a substantive analysis of the connection between national and EU law and establish whether the national measure in question would result in the level of protection of fundamental rights differing among Member States to the extent of undermining the 'unity, primacy and effectiveness of EU law'.[130] If the Court of Justice continues the *Annibaldi-Iida-Siragusa* trend,[131]

09 *Ruiz Zambrano* [2010] EU:C:2010:560 [163]: 'It seems to me that, in the long run, the clearest rule would be one that made the availability of EU fundamental rights protection dependent neither on whether a Treaty provision was directly applicable nor on whether secondary legislation had been enacted, but rather on the existence and scope of a material EU competence.'

[126] Case C-617/10 *Fransson* (n 120) [21].

[127] See also J Snell, 'Fundamental Rights Review of National Measures: Nothing New under the Charter?' (2015) 21(2) *European Public Law* 285, 293. For a proposal for a clearer demarcation of the scope of the Charter see D Sarmiento, 'Who's Afraid of the Charter? The Court of Justice, National Courts and the New Framework of Fundamental Rights Protection in Europe' (2013) 50(5) *Common Market Law Review* 1267; X Groussot, L Pech, and G T Petursson, 'The Scope of Application of EU Fundamental Rights on Member States' Action: In Search of Certainty in EU Adjudication' (2011) Eric Stein Working Paper 1/2011 https://csesp.files.wordpress.com/2015/05/eswp-2011-01-groussot.pdf.

[128] Council Directive 2000/78/EC of 27 November 2000 establishing a general framework for equal treatment in employment and occupation [2000] OJ L303/16.

[129] Case C-206/13 *Siragusa* [2014] EU:C:2014:126.

[130] Case C-206/13 *Siragusa* (n 129) [32]. See also Snell (n 127) 296.

[131] Confirmed as 'settled case law' by the Court of Justice in Case C-198/13 *Hernández* [2014] EU:C:2014:2055 [37]. See also M Dougan, 'Judicial Review of Member State Action under the General

it is unlikely that Article 51(1) of the Charter will follow the *Dassonville* approach. Moreover, unlike the scope of general principles, which stretches all the way to horizontal situations (*Mangold*)[132] and the exclusive competences of Member States (*Maruko*),[133] the Charter appears to have a narrower scope, constrained by Article 6(1) TEU and Article 51(1) of the Charter.[134]

The power relations between the Court of Justice and the constitutional court further clarified the leverage on behalf of the Court of Justice inasmuch as it is now established that fundamental rights review will be carried out in relation to all national measures in the scope of EU law, regardless of whether the measure is implementing, derogating from, or is connected to EU law in some other way (in accordance with *Estov*, *Kücükdeveci*, *NS* and *Fransson*).[135] The importance of the rebuttable presumption from *Solange II* and *Granital* has accordingly been diminished. From the perspective of the Court of Justice, however, the presumption remains influential only for situations outside the scope of EU law. One remaining reservation of a disproportionate intrusion of the Court of Justice into the traditionally exclusive realm for constitutional courts is *Iida*,[136] requiring the Court of Justice to more specifically justify undertaking the review.

The relationship between ordinary national courts and the Court of Justice, in relation to the review of both EU and national measures when in the scope of EU law, remains one of cooperation. Ordinary national courts will be bound by the jurisprudence of the Court of Justice despite the possible contrary interpretation provided by their constitutional court. In that sense, the remaining influence of the constitutional court towards ordinary national courts is that it continues to be the undisputed final authority in fundamental rights protection solely for cases outside the scope of EU law.[137]

Principles and the Charter: Defining the "Scope of Union Law"' (2015) 52(5) *Common Market Law Review* 1201, 1230.

[132] In relation to the principle of non-discrimination on grounds of age.

[133] In relation to the principle of non-discrimination generally.

[134] Dougan mentions the decision of the Court in Case C-476/11 *HK Danmark* [2013] EU:C:2013:590 [31], which points to the horizontal application of the Charter. In my view, however, the case deals with the prohibition of discrimination on grounds of age and corresponds to the content of the same general principle from *Mangold*, which does not lead to an automatic conclusion as to the horizontal applicability of the Charter. Dougan (n 131) 1203.

[135] Weatherill reads the consequence of *Fransson*, and more generally the case law on citizenship, as the Court's assertion of 'a general jurisdiction in matters of human rights when they arise on the territory of the EU, even in cases when the matter appears to be internal to a single Member State'. S Weatherill (n 82) 211.

[136] And the subsequent case law confirming these conditions. See n 131.

[137] For example see Case C-617/10 *Fransson* (n 120) [48]:

> It follows that [EU] law precludes a judicial practice which makes the obligation for a national court to disapply any provision contrary to a fundamental right guaranteed by the Charter conditional upon that infringement being clear from the text of the Charter or the case law relating to it, since it withholds from the national court the power to assess fully, with [ . . . ] the cooperation of the Court of Justice, whether that provision is compatible with the Charter.

### 3.3 External Actors

While the relationship between the Court of Justice and external actors is not within the scope of the present book, I will briefly address the Court's findings aiming to delineate its position towards external actors in relation to fundamental rights protection. The aim of such an exercise is to sketch the influence this has had on the status of fundamental rights review and consequently on the courts under analysis.

The applicants in *Kadi*[138] sought to annul an EU regulation implementing the counter-terrorism UN Security Council Resolution, according to which all their funds and other financial resources in the EU were frozen. The basis for the appellants claims before the Court of Justice relied on a *Solange* claim of the EU: so long as the UN do not provide for an independent judicial fundamental rights review, the Union courts should make sure the implementing measures are fundamental rights compliant.[139]

Accordingly, the Court stated that the Community was bound to ensure the minimum of fundamental rights protection in its implementation of the UN Security Council Resolution.[140] The Community is based on the rule of law and any measure incompatible with the protection of fundamental rights is not acceptable.[141] Furthering the *Solange* logic, it concluded that the review mechanisms in the UN system are inadequate and thus cannot prevent the Court of Justice to ensure fundamental rights protection by way of reviewing the implementing regulation.[142]

The inspiration, or at least a strong resemblance to the different limits that national constitutional courts have placed on the principle of primacy is hard to miss when reading the Court of Justice positioning EU law vis-à-vis the acts of the UN,

138 Joined Cases C-402/05 P and C-415/05 P *Kadi and Al Barakaat International Foundation* [2008] EU:C:2008:461. For a more general commentary of the international law aspects of the case see G de Búrca, 'The European Court of Justice and the International Legal Order after *Kadi*' (2010) 51(1) *Harvard International Law Journal* 1; D Halberstam and E Stein, 'The United Nations, the European Union, and the King of Sweden: Economic Sanctions and Individual Rights in a Plural Legal World' (2009) 46(1) *Common Market Law Review* 13. For a more fundamental rights driven approach see T Isiksel, 'Fundamental Rights in the EU after *Kadi and Al Barakaat*' (2010) 16(5) *European Law Journal* 551.

139 Joined Cases C-402/05 P and C-415/05 P *Kadi and Al Barakaat International Foundation* (n 138) [256].

140 ibid [279].

141 ibid [281], [284]. For an analysis of the constitutional core of the EU, and consequently its constitutional identity see D Sarmiento, 'The EU's Constitutional Core' in A Saiz Arnaiz and C Alcoberro Llivina (eds), *National Constitutional Identity and European Integration* (Intersentia 2013).

142 ibid [320]–[326]. Note here that the Court of Justice is using the same method as some national constitutional courts, by focusing its review on implementing measures rather than the decision emanating from another legal order. See eg German Bundesverfassungsgericht Case 2 BvR 2236/04 *EAW Constitutionality* Decision of 18 July 2005, where the Bundesverfassungsgericht declined to rule on the constitutionality of the EAW, but assessed the national implementing measure. With thanks to Richard O. Melanzana for a fruitful discussion on this point.

but also other actors in the international law arena more generally.[143] The rights-based claim to ultimate authority was at the source of constitutional pluralism (initiated by *Frontini* and *Solange I*), and it continues to provide a substantive basis for such claims.[144]

Defending its position may have been more straightforward for the Court of Justice against the UN, given its apparent lack of fundamental rights protection mechanisms. The Court of Justice was able to resort to the dualist rhetoric in *Kadi* and use the ECHR as a shield[145] to establish its own reputation in fundamental rights protection. Yet, the Court turned the same argument into a sword in relation to a possible ECHR accession.

The Court of Justice set out the constitutional[146] matrix of the EU,[147] underlining its distinctive nature which needs to be reflected and taken into account in the ECHR accession agreement. In this sense, the EU treaties 'unlike ordinary international treaties established a new legal order'[148] which has 'its own constitutional framework and founding principles, a particularly sophisticated institutional structure, and a full set of legal rules to ensure its operation'.[149] The emphasis on the 'constitutional' is there for two important reasons: it extends the sovereignty vocabulary to the EU and underlines the EU's own capacity in fundamental rights protection.

Ultimately, the Court found that the accession to the ECHR is contrary to the specific features of the EU and its Treaties.[150] As Halberstam points out, the decision of the Court of Justice is no surprise.[151] It has previously made similar assertions concerning the accession to the ECHR,[152] the original EEA agreement,[153] and, most recently, the UN in *Kadi*. The fundamental rights protection record of the EU is satisfactory in the view of the Court of Justice and does not invoke the need to accede formally to the ECHR.[154]

[143] See also Isiksel (n 138) 559–60.

[144] W T Eijsbouts and L Besselink, '"The Law of Laws": Overcoming Pluralism' (2008) 4(3) *European Constitutional Law Review* 395, 397–98.

[145] Joined Cases C-402/05 P and C-415/05 P *Kadi and Al Barakaat International Foundation* (n 138) [283].

[146] The constitutional vocabulary is particularly present, obviating the Court's intention to place the EU's distinctiveness and autonomy at the centre of the argument.

[147] Opinion 2/13 [2014] EU:C:2014:2454 [154]–[174].

[148] ibid [157].

[149] ibid [158].

[150] For a more detailed analysis see D Halberstam, '"It's the Autonomy, Stupid!" A Modest Defense of *Opinion 2/13* on EU Accession to the ECHR, and the Way Forward' (2015) 16(1) *German Law Journal* 105. For critical accounts see S Douglas-Scott, 'Autonomy and Fundamental Rights: The ECJ's Opinion 2/13 on Accession of the EU to the ECHR' (2016) 1 *Europarättslig tidskrift (Swedish European Law Journal)* 29 https://papers.ssrn.com/sol3/papers.cfm?abstract_id=2752133; T Isiksel, 'European Exceptionalism and the EU's Accession to the ECHR' (2016) 27(3) *European Journal of International Law* 565.

[151] Halberstam (n 150) 111.

[152] Opinion 2/94 [1996] EU:C:1996:140.

[153] Opinion 1/91 [1991] EU:C:1991:490. For analysis of the case see also ch 5, s 4.

[154] Isiksel (n 150) 566.

Is the conclusion of the Court of Justice solely an expression of hubris or is it rooted in a plausible argument of a possible dismantling of the EU's constitutional set-up? Let us reverse the situation and consider a national constitutional court deciding on the constitutionality of accession to a polity which might distort their constitutional set-up and ultimately influence national sovereignty. For purposes of illustration, let us imagine this polity is one which displaces the position of constitutional courts in the national judicial hierarchy and grants all national courts the power of judicial review. If such a distortion would threaten the constitutional core of the state in question, the decision of the constitutional court may well be to require the amendment of the constitution or a renegotiation of the accession treaty to accommodate these concerns. I consider it the analogous right of the Court of Justice to require the Commission to renegotiate the accession agreement so as to keep in line with the mandate of Article 6(2) TEU.

The two decisions have indirect influence on the system of constitutional pluralism. Building upon the discussion on the existence of sovereignty on the behalf of the EU, it was concluded that substantively, late sovereignty[155] and constitutionalism overlap. According to such a construct, it was concluded that the Court of Justice developed a self-referential normative constitutional order, resulting in a plausible claim to ultimate authority,[156] overlapping in the same geographical space with that of the Member States and their courts tasked with upholding national constitutions. What *Kadi* and Opinion 2/13 add to this construct is an emphasis on the entrenchment of fundamental rights protection, materially one of the essential elements of a constitutional system.[157]

[155] Understood as the claim to ultimate authority and constitutional representation in a post-national context. N Walker, 'Late Sovereignty in the European Union' in N Walker (ed), *Sovereignty in Transition* (Hart Publishing 2003) 19.

[156] In his reply to Halberstam (n 150), Komárek stated: 'Structurally, the ECJ seems to understand autonomy in a similar way as national constitutional courts conceive of sovereignty: EU law should reign supreme in its jurisdiction and any encroachment by another authority must be put under the ECJ's check.' For him, the EU's claim to ultimate authority is inherently limited due to the lack of political legitimacy, as opposed to that of the Member States. Conversely, and agreeing with de Búrca, I find that the claim to ultimate authority by the Court of Justice (and the EU) is rooted in not only the autonomy of the EU's constitutional order, but also in its independence and non-derivativeness. Thus, if we genuinely believe there is any such thing as sovereignty beyond the state, subjecting it to identical conditions as state sovereignty (namely popular representation) would be a *contradictio in adiecto*. See J Komárek, 'It's a Stupid Autonomy . . .' *Verfassungsblog* (14 March 2015) http://verfassungsblog.de/its-a-stupid-autonomy-2/; G de Búrca, 'Sovereignty and the Supremacy Doctrine of the European Court of Justice' in N Walker (ed), *Sovereignty in Transition* (Hart Publishing 2003) 453.

[157] J Shaw, 'Process and Constitutional Discourse in the European Union' (2000) 27 *Journal of Law & Society* 4, 16; A Stone Sweet, 'The Structure of Constitutional Pluralism: Review of Nico Krisch, *Beyond Constitutionalism: The Pluralist Structure of Post-National Law*' (2013) 11(2) *International Journal of Constitutional Law* 491, 493.

## 4 The Common Perspective after the Charter

Having addressed the expansions in the jurisdiction of the Court of Justice in fundamental rights review, the aim of this section is to analyse responses from the national level and the ensuing judicial interactions that took place, ultimately determining the relationship between the EU's and the national constitutional standard of fundamental rights protection. The appropriate standard of fundamental rights protection is determined by Article 53 of the Charter:

> Nothing in this Charter shall be interpreted as restricting or adversely affecting human rights and fundamental freedoms as recognised, in their respective fields of application, by Union law and international law and by international agreements to which the Union, the Community or all the Member States are party, including the European Convention for the Protection of Human Rights and Fundamental Freedoms, and by the Member States' constitutions.

The wording of the provision suggests it functions as a minimum standard clause, similar to the operation of the ECHR in national law.[158] However, as the case law analysis to follow will demonstrate, fundamental rights protection set by EU law may only be surpassed if this does not hamper the effectiveness and uniform application of EU law. In what follows, I will look at the Area of Freedom, Security and Justice (AFSJ) and the developments concerning the Data Retention Directive, analysing both the EU and national jurisprudence of the courts under analysis in a chronological fashion, with the aim of a clear presentation of the constitutional conflict and the manner of its resolution through the constitutional pluralism framework. Another reason warranting a joint analysis lies in the specificities of the post-Lisbon context: as Besselink explains, the power of EU institutions in fundamental rights protection 'intrude into areas previously within the constitutional autonomy of Member States in a more invasive manner than could have been imagined in the early days of EU fundamental rights protection'.[159] Thus, reactions from the national level deserve attention beyond the *Solange II*/*Granital* accommodation of the initial constitutional conflict in fundamental rights protection.

[158] Sarmiento (n 127) 1287–88.

[159] L Besselink, 'The Protection of Fundamental Rights Post-Lisbon: The Interaction between the EU Charter of Fundamental Rights, the European Convention on Human Rights (ECHR) and National Constitutions' (FIDE General Report 2012) 22 www.fide2012.eu/index.php?doc_id=94.

## 4.1 The Area of Freedom, Security and Justice

The tension between fundamental rights protection and the principle of mutual trust in the former third pillar[160] became obvious with the enactment of the European Arrest Warrant (EAW) Framework Decision,[161] which contradicted the wide-spread constitutional prohibition of extraditing Member States' own nationals.[162] The second source of tensions between the principle of mutual trust and fundamental rights protection is the application of the EU's asylum legislation, specifically connected to the process of determining the Member State responsible for processing the asylum application.[163]

The Lisbon Treaty did away with the previous pillar structure and the differences between EU and EC law, where primacy was originally applicable solely in relation to the latter.[164] The Court of Justice gained full jurisdiction to interpret and review those measures pursuant to Article 19(1) TEU and the *Foto-Frost* jurisprudence.[165] The newly gained jurisdiction is to be exercised keeping in mind Article 67(1) TFEU: 'The Union shall constitute an area of freedom, security and justice with respect for fundamental rights and the different legal systems and traditions of the Member States.' However, the bulk of the criticism directed to Opinion 2/13 of the Court revolved around the impression that the principle of mutual trust was elevated above fundamental rights protection,[166] contrary to the main tenets

[160] Previously called Police and Judicial Cooperation in Criminal Matters.

[161] Council Framework Decision 2002/584/JHA of 13 June 2002 on the European arrest warrant and the surrender procedures between Member States [2002] OJ L190/1. It was further amended by Council Framework Decision 2009/299/JHA of 26 February 2009 amending Framework Decisions 2002/584/JHA, 2005/214/JHA, 2006/783/JHA, 2008/909/JHA and 2008/947/JHA, thereby enhancing the procedural rights of persons and fostering the application of the principle of mutual recognition to decisions rendered in the absence of the person concerned at the trial [2009] OJ L81/24. On its legislative history see O Pollicino, 'European Arrest Warrant and Constitutional Principles of the Member States: A Case Law-based Outline in the Attempt to Strike the Right Balance between Interacting Legal Systems' (2008) 9(10) *German Law Journal* 1313, 1316–23.

[162] J Komárek, 'European Constitutionalism and the European Arrest Warrant: In Search of the Limits of "Contrapunctual Principles"' (2007) 44(1) *Common Market Law Review* 9, 14. Another issue concerned the abolition of double criminality. A Hinarejos, 'The Lisbon Treaty Versus Standing Still: A View from the Third Pillar' (2009) 5(1) *European Constitutional Law Review* 99, 103. More generally see V Mitsilegas, 'The Constitutional Implications of Mutual Recognition in Criminal Matters in the EU' (2006) 43(5) *Common Market Law Review* 1277.

[163] P Eeckhout, 'Opinion 2/13 on EU Accession to the ECHR and Judicial Dialogue: Autonomy or Autarky' (2015) 38(1) *Fordham International Law Journal* 1, 14.

[164] For a more detailed analysis of the previous set-up and the changes introduced by the Lisbon Treaty see Hinarejos (n 162).

[165] Case 314/85 *Foto-Frost* [1987] EU:C:1987:452 [17]. The exception to this was Protocol No 36 to the Lisbon Treaty on transitional provisions [2008] OJ C115/322. Its art 10 stated that the existing measures from the former third pillar shall be subject to the previously set powers of the institutions for five years (unless repealed, annulled or amended in implementation of the Treaties according to art 9 of the Protocol), thus limiting the review powers of the Court of Justice until 2014.

[166] Eeckhout (n 163) 15; S Peers, 'The EU's Accession to the ECHR: The Dream Becomes a Nightmare' (2015) 16(1) *German Law Journal* 213, 221.

of Article 67(1) TFEU. Peers emphasized that the 'Treaty does not give priority to mutual trust over human rights—quite the opposite'.[167]

The constitutional conflict that emerged against this backdrop will therefore be at the centre of the following analysis. I will first address the national jurisprudence on the constitutionality of the EAW Framework Decision and the response of the Court of Justice. Second, I will explore the divergences in the standard of fundamental rights protection and how they are to be balanced against the principle of mutual trust both as regards the EAW and the Common European Asylum System.

### 4.1.1 The EAW Framework Decision

#### *4.1.1.1 Poland*

The approach of the Polish Trybunał Konstytucyjny to matters of European integration has been analysed in detail in Chapter 6[168] with regard to its claims to perform identity review of EU acts. By way of a brief introduction, it is worth recalling the *Accession Treaty* decision of the Trybunał Konstytucyjny, where it first set out the limits to the principle of primacy in relation to fundamental rights protection.[169] The Trybunał Konstytucyjny, in establishing the obligation of a Euro-friendly interpretation, positioned fundamental rights as its limit:

> The principle of interpreting domestic law in a manner 'sympathetic to European law', as formulated within the Constitutional Tribunal's jurisprudence, has its limits. [ … ] In particular, the norms of the Constitution within the field of individual rights and freedoms indicate a minimum and unsurpassable threshold which may not be lowered or questioned as a result of the introduction of Community provisions.[170]

The Trybunał Konstytucyjny will therefore perform fundamental rights review against EU law whenever it might jeopardize the minimum level of fundamental rights protection.[171]

The EAW Framework Decision was thus an opportunity for the Tribunal to apply its standard of review. The Regional Court of Gdańsk, being faced with the request to surrender a Polish citizen to the Netherlands, contrary to the constitutional prohibition of extradition of Polish nationals, referred a question of constitutionality to the Tribunal.[172] The initial analysis of the Trybunał Konstytucyjny

167 Peers (n 166) 221.

168 Section 2.2.1.

169 Polish Trybunał Konstytucyjny Case K 18/04 *Accession Treaty* Judgment of 11 May 2005 http://trybunal.gov.pl/fileadmin/content/omowienia/K_18_04_GB.pdf.

170 ibid [14].

171 Sadurski concludes that the intention of the Trybunał Konstytucyjny was to set a *Solange*-like limit to the primacy of EU law. W Sadurski, '"Solange, Chapter 3": Constitutional Courts in Central Europe: Democracy—European Union' (2008) 14(1) *European Law Journal* 1, 20.

172 Polish Trybunał Konstytucyjny Case P 1/05 *European Arrest Warrant* Judgment of 27 April 2005 http://trybunal.gov.pl/fileadmin/content/omowienia/P_1_05_full_GB.pdf. For the background

addressed the (then existing) differences between EC and EU law,[173] and demarcated the institutional power leverage of the Trybunał Konstytucyjny in relation to the jurisdiction of the Court of Justice.[174] The Tribunal then turned its attention to the limits of consistent interpretation as regards the third pillar,[175] specifically in relation to fundamental rights protection.

The Trybunał Konstytucyjny found that the right of a Polish citizen to be tried before a Polish court, the requirement of double criminality, and the prohibition of extradition of a Polish citizen for the purposes of serving imprisonment abroad are all instances of deteriorated rights protected by the Polish Constitution.[176] The introduction of EU citizenship cannot be corrosive to those constitutionally protected rights.[177] The tribunal thus concluded the relevant provision of the Criminal Code is unconstitutional and the constitutional prohibition of extraditing Polish nationals will therefore need to be amended.[178] With the aim of avoiding a breach of its obligations under EU law and the Accession Treaty, the Trybunał Konstytucyjny postponed the invalidation of the implementing provisions for eighteen months.[179]

#### *4.1.1.2 Germany*

The German jurisprudence has been analysed extensively throughout this book.[180] At this point it suffices to add the *Banana Market Regulation* decision[181] to the *Solange I* and *II* jurisprudence and its contribution towards fundamental rights review. The decision came after almost a decade-long process[182] initiated by the enactment of the Council Regulation regulating the market in bananas.[183] Three

of the case see D Leczykiewicz, '*Trybunał Konstytucyjny* (Polish Constitutional Tribunal), Judgment of 27 April 2005, No P 1/05, on the Constitutionality of the European Arrest Warrant National Implementation' (2006) 43(4) *Common Market Law Review* 1181.

173 Polish Trybunał Konstytucyjny Case *European Arrest Warrant* (n 172) [2.1].

174 The same advantage is present in the situation where courts with constitutional jurisdiction decide on the constitutionality of a Treaty amendment pending ratification.

175 The Court of Justice concluded on the existence of the obligation of consistent interpretation in the third pillar two months later. Case C-105/03 *Pupino* [2005] EU:C:2005:386 [43].

176 Polish Trybunał Konstytucyjny Case *European Arrest Warrant* (n 172) [3.6], [4.2].

177 ibid [4.3]. For a contrary view see the analysis of the Czech decision in s 4.1.1.4 below.

178 ibid [5].

179 ibid [5.2]. Komárek comments that, while the reasoning of the Trybunał Konstytucyjny is not entirely justified, the postponement of the effects of its decision falls into one of the welcomed methods of avoiding constitutional conflict. Komárek (n 162) 19.

180 The Bundesverfassungsgericht has placed limits on the principle of primacy in relation to competence monitoring (ch 5, s 6.1) and the preservation of German constitutional identity (ch 6, s 2.1).

181 German Bundesverfassungsgericht Case 2 BvL 1/97 *Banana Market Regulation* Order of 7 June 2000, https://www.bundesverfassungsgericht.de/SharedDocs/Entscheidungen/EN/2000/06/ls20000607_2bvl000197en.html.

182 For a more detailed analysis of the intricacies of the case see C U Schmid, 'All bark and no bite: notes on the Federal Constitutional Court's "Banana Decision"' (2001) 7(1) *European Law Journal* 95; Claes (n 28) 610–20.

183 Council Regulation 404/93 of 13 February 1993 on the common organization of the market in bananas [1993] OJ L47/1. Challenges against the Banana Regulation were brought before national constitutional courts, the Court of Justice, and the Dispute Settlement Body of the WTO. Schmid (n 182) 96. These procedures will not be analysed as they are of no relevance for the present discussion.

challenges before the Court of Justice[184] were unsuccessful, and the Administrative Court of Frankfurt-am-Main ultimately submitted a reference to the Bundesverfass ungsgericht.[185] In finding the reference inadmissible, the Bundesverfassungsgericht outlined its approach towards fundamental rights review of secondary EU law:

> [Constitutional] review under Article 100(1) GG which refer to rules that are part of secondary European Community law [is] only admissible if [its] grounds show in detail that the present evolution of law concerning the protection of fundamental rights in European Community law, especially in case law of the Court of Justice of the European Communities, does not generally ensure the protection of fundamental rights required unconditionally in the respective case.[186]

Reiterating its *Solange* and *Maastricht* jurisprudence, the conditions for activating fundamental rights review by the Bundesverfassungsgericht are as follows:

> The constitutional requirements are satisfied [...] if the rulings of the Court of Justice [...] generally ensure effective protection of fundamental rights as against the sovereign powers of the Communities which is to be regarded as substantially similar to the protection of fundamental rights required unconditionally by the Basic Law, and in so far as they generally safeguard the essential content of fundamental rights.[187]

The judgment was criticized for its leniency and lack of engagement with actual infringements of the fundamental rights at stake[188] and for abandoning its cooperative relationship with the Court of Justice in fundamental rights review as set out in the *Maastricht* judgment.[189] What can be concluded for the purposes of the present discussion is that the Bundesverfassungsgericht will apply self-restraint in fundamental rights review, reviewing only manifest structural violations[190] of fundamental rights.[191]

[184] Case C-280/93 *Germany v Council* [1994] EU:C:1994:367; Case C-466/93 *Atlanta* [1995] EU:C:1995:370; Case C-68/95 *T Port* [1996] EU:C:1996:452.

[185] This was the third instance that the Bundesverfassungsgericht was deciding on the same regulation. For more information see Claes (n 28) 616.

[186] German Bundesverfassungsgericht Case *Banana Market Regulation* (n 181) [31].

[187] ibid [38].

[188] Schmid (n 182) 100.

[189] ibid; M Aziz, 'Sovereignty Lost Sovereignty Regained: Some Reflections on the *Bundesverfassungsgericht*'s Bananas Judgment' (2002) 9(1) *Columbia Journal of European Law* 109, 124; D P Kommers and R A Miller, *The Constitutional Jurisprudence of the Federal Republic of Germany* (3rd edn, Duke University Press 2012) 340.

[190] I am intentionally using the *Honeywell* language in this context, which was equally criticized for its unattainable threshold. See the discussion in ch 5, s 6.1. For criticism directly concerning this similarity see C Möllers, 'German Federal Constitutional Court: Constitutional *Ultra Vires* Review of European Acts Only Under Exceptional Circumstances; Decision of 6 July 2010, 2 BvR 2661/06, *Honeywell*' (2011) 7(1) *European Constitutional Law Review* 161, 161.

[191] An argument that I have not come across in the literature is a connection between the German initiative and role in the process of creating the Charter of Fundamental Rights, which began in 1999

The Bundesverfassungsgericht was given the opportunity to test its standard of review in the constitutional challenge to the German implementation act of the EAW Framework Decision.[192] The case concerned an arrest warrant and the request for extradition to Spain of a German and Syrian national, for his alleged participation in the Al-Qaeda activities and money laundering, crimes punishable only in Spain at the time.[193] Unlike the Polish state of affairs, the German Basic Law had already been amended so as to allow extradition of German nationals to another EU Member State (or to an international court of justice) under the condition that the rule of law is observed.[194]

The first important point in the decision follows the logic of the Polish Trybunał Konstytucyjny in concluding that the first and the third pillar represent different legal orders, with primacy and direct effect not operating as regards the latter:

> In particular with a view to the principle of subsidiarity, (Article 23.1 of the Basic Law), the cooperation that is put into practice in the "Third Pillar" of the European Union in the shape of *limited mutual recognition*, which does not provide for a general harmonisation of the Member States' systems of criminal law, is a way of preserving national identity and statehood in a single European judicial area.[195]

The third pillar is consequently, given its intergovernmental features, subject to constitutional review by the Bundesverfassungsgericht.[196] Mutual recognition in this area is in the view of the Bundesverfassungsgericht limited. But this conclusion does not come without the small print. Only a month earlier, the Court of Justice decided in *Pupino*[197] that the obligation of consistent interpretation operates in the

during the German Presidency and the more restrained approach of the Bundesverfassungsgericht a year later. After all, the lack of a binding catalogue of fundamental rights at the EU level was one of the main criticisms directed to the EU in the *Solange I* decision. In that sense, we may read the approach of the Bundesverfassungsgericht in the *Banana Market Regulation* decision as one of endorsing a satisfactory progress that European integration has made in the area of fundamental rights protection. As mentioned in ch 3, s 3 and ch 4, s 2, the pluralist constellation presupposes a dynamic development of the law through a constructive discussion across the jurisprudence of constitutional conflict (the auto-correct function of constitutional pluralism). Fundamental rights protection is but one example (the scope of application of general principles is yet to develop into another; see ch 5, s 6.3 on this point). On the more detailed analysis of the role of Germany in the creation of the Charter see de Búrca (n 96).

[192] German Bundesverfassungsgericht Case 2 BvR 2236/04 *European Arrest Warrant* Decision of 18 July 2005 http://www.bundesverfassungsgericht.de/SharedDocs/Entscheidungen/EN/2005/07/rs20050718_2bvr223604en.html.

[193] Kommers and Miller (n 189) 341.

[194] German Basic Law, art 16(2).

[195] German Bundesverfassungsgericht Case *European Arrest Warrant* (n 192) [78] (emphasis added).

[196] ibid [33], [83].

[197] Case C-105/03 *Pupino* (n 175) [43].

third pillar as well. The Bundesverfassungsgericht was most certainly aware of it, as the Dissenting Opinion of Judge Gerhardt made a case for its application. The majority, however, omitted any reference to *Pupino*, finding that the requirements of legal certainty and clarity run counter to any interpretation beyond the textual one.[198]

A final addition is due concerning the most recent instance of fundamental rights review by the Bundesverfassungsgericht: one where the German court deals with the right to be forgotten and openly disapplies the Basic Law in favour of the EU Charter.[199] This, according to the Bundesverfassungsgericht, is due to the fact that the right to be forgotten is a matter fully harmonized in Union law.[200] The judgment emphasizes that the Basic Law may be disapplied depending on the context of the case, where the validity or effectiveness of Union law is not in question, but merely its application.[201]

In following its established pluralist approach to the relationship between the Basic Law and EU constitutional law, the decision acknowledged that the two systems of fundamental rights protection are different in their validity, and the reservations from the earlier case law described still remain.[202] Keeping in mind the need for a uniform application of harmonized Union law, the Bundesverfassungsgericht will monitor the application of the Charter by national courts.[203] The German court summarized the status of fundamental rights protection in the EU, which is of use to finalize the analysis of the German approach:

> Today, the Union's fundamental rights are also part of the protection of fundamental rights that is to be enforced vis-à-vis the German state. In accordance with Article 51.1 of the Basic Law, they are applicable at the national level and constitute a functional equivalent to the fundamental rights of the Basic Law. Embedded in an elaborated catalogue of fundamental rights, they have a function largely identical to that of the German fundamental rights for law under the Basic Law in terms of their content and normative claim for Union law and its interpretation today.[204]

[198] For criticism on this point see A Hinarejos, '*Bundesverfassungsgericht* (German Constitutional Court), Decision of 18 July 2005 (2 BvR 2236/04) on the German European Arrest Warrant Law' (2006) 43(2) *Common Market Law Review* 583, 587–89.

[199] German Bundesverfassungsgericht Case 1 BvR 276/17 *Right to Be Forgotten II* Decision of 6 November 2019 [42].

[200] ibid.

[201] ibid [52].

[202] The standards of the Basic Law remain 'dormant' according to the Bundesverfassungsgericht so long as the EU level of protection is sufficiently effective. ibid [42], [46]–[47].

[203] ibid [66].

[204] ibid [59].

#### *4.1.1.3 Cyprus*

The Cypriot Ανώτατο Δικαστήριο also had the opportunity to rule on the constitutionality of the national act implementing the EAW Framework Decision.[205] By way of introduction, upon its accession to the EU, the Cypriot Constitution was amended and EU law was accorded supremacy over all sources of national law, including the Constitution.[206] However, the Constitution only allows extradition of non-Cypriot nationals and the Regional Court of Limassol accordingly rejected the execution of an EAW against a Cypriot national.[207] Having cited, among others, the Polish and German decisions, the Supreme Court found that the EAW Framework Decision, as a measure of the third pillar, does not have direct effect. It did, unlike the Bundesverfassungsgericht, consider the developments brought about by *Pupino*, but it concluded that the EAW Law could not be interpreted consistently with the EAW Framework Decision without resulting in an unconstitutional interpretation.[208] Leczykiewicz concluded that the lack of a possible consistent interpretation of the implementing act with the Constitution (although it is aligned with the EU act it implements) results in the limitation of primacy and direct effect for EU acts contrary to the Cypriot Constitution.[209]

Such a conclusion counters the constitutional provision granting all European Union sourced law (EC and EU) an all-purpose supremacy over the national constitution. As Tsadiras explains, the Supreme Court should have been clearer in determining the legal status of the third pillar in Cypriot law.[210] The consequence of this reasoning was a constitutional amendment which then explicitly also included the second and third pillars in the definition of supremacy of EC and EU law over the entirety of the Cypriot legal system.[211]

#### *4.1.1.4 Czech Republic*

The challenge to the EAW implementing act in the Czech Republic was put forward during the legislative procedure by a group of Parliamentarians, based again on the prohibition of extraditing own nationals and the abandonment of double

[205] Cypriot Ανώτατο Δικαστήριο Case 294/2005 *Attorney General of the Republic v Konstantinou* Judgment of 7 November 2005.

[206] National Report: The Supreme Court of Cyprus (2014) 1; art 1A of the Constitution.

[207] The application for surrender was made against the Cypriot national who was also a UK national. However, previous case law of the Supreme Court confirmed the prohibition in the Constitution applied regardless of dual nationality of the person concerned. Cypriot Ανώτατο Δικαστήριο Case *European Arrest Warrant Law* (n 205), summary. See also A Tsadiras, 'Cyprus Supreme Court (Ανώτατο Δικαστήριο Κύπρου), Judgment of 7 November 2005 (Civil Appeal no. 294/2005) on the Cypriot European Arrest Warrant Law' (2007) 44(5) *Common Market Law Review* 1515.

[208] Cypriot Ανώτατο Δικαστήριο Case *Attorney General of the Republic v Konstantinou* (n 205) [24]. Tsadiras (n 207) 1518.

[209] D Leczykiewicz, 'Constitutional Conflicts and the Third Pillar' (2008) 33(2) *European Law Review* 230, 236.

[210] Tsadiras (n 207) 1524. He even hints that the Supreme Court did not properly understand the difference between EU and EC law (at 1528).

[211] ibid 1527.

criminality.[212] The Ústavní Soud first referred to the status of the principle of primacy in the Czech Republic:

> In its judgment no. Pl. ÚS 50/04 of 8 March 2006,[213] the Constitutional Court refused to recognize the ECJ doctrine insofar as it claims absolute primacy of EC law. It stated that the delegation of a part of the powers of national organs upon organs of the EU may persist only so long as these powers are exercised by organs of the EU in a manner that is compatible with the preservation of the foundations of state sovereignty of the Czech Republic, and in a manner which does not threaten the very essence of the substantive law-based state. Understandably that, unless such an exceptional and highly unlikely eventuality comes to pass, the Constitutional Court, guided by the above-mentioned ECJ doctrine, will not review individual norms of Community law for their consistency with the Czech constitutional order.[214]

In line with the vocabulary analysis in Chapter 3, the principle of primacy will only be put into question in an exceptional, highly unlikely situation that the essence of the Czech constitutional order is put into question. The Ústavní Soud then analysed the legal nature of acts enacted in the third pillar, but not without taking into account the obligation of consistent interpretation established by *Pupino*.[215] However, without submitting a preliminary reference to the Court of Justice on the matter,[216] the Ústavní Soud found that status of primacy in the third pillar is not conclusively determined.[217] This did not prevent the Ústavní Soud from reviewing the implementing act and finding that a consistent interpretation is possible.[218] The acceptance of the obligation of consistent interpretation is in line with self-restraint and mutual accommodation driving the interactions in the pluralist European judicial space. After an extensive analysis of the status of fundamental rights protection granted by the EAW Framework Decisions, and taking into account safeguards in the EAW Framework Decision[219] and in the Czech implementing act,[220] the Ústavní Soud found the latter constitutional.

[212] Czech Ústavní Soud Case Pl. ÚS 66/04 *European Arrest Warrant* Judgment of 3 May 2006 http://www.usoud.cz/en/decisions/20060503-pl-us-6604-european-arrest-warrant-1/.

[213] The Ústavní Soud quotes its *Sugar Quotas III* decision. See ch 5, s 6.2 for a more detailed analysis of the case.

[214] Czech Ústavní Soud Case *European Arrest Warrant* (n 212) [53].

[215] ibid [56]–[58].

[216] This was not done since the Belgian Cour d'Arbitrage already submitted a preliminary reference concerning the validity of the EAW Framework Decision. ibid [60]. Leczykiewicz argues that this enabled the Ústavní Soud to use broader criteria for review than what would be the case had the principle of primacy conclusively applied to the third pillar. Leczykiewicz (n 209) 238.

[217] Czech Ústavní Soud Case *European Arrest Warrant* (n 212) [59].

[218] ibid [60], [83].

[219] Recital 10 of the EAW Framework Decision states its implementation may be suspended if a Member State commits a serious and persistent breach of art 6(1), determined by the Council through the rule of law mechanism in art 7 TEU.

[220] Czech Ústavní Soud Case *European Arrest Warrant* (n 212) [88].

### *4.1.1.5 Belgium and the Court of Justice's Response*

The Belgian Cour d'Arbitrage (today's Cour Constitutionnelle), faced with the challenge of constitutionality of the EAW Framework Decision, submitted a preliminary reference to the Court of Justice.[221] By way of introduction, it should be mentioned that the Belgian court has jurisdiction to perform fundamental rights review and it has assumed it also in relation to external sources of law, including primary and secondary EU law.[222]

The Court of Justice was thus given the perfect opportunity to contribute to the discussion on the EAW Framework Decision taking place in the European judicial space. The basis for the constitutionality challenge in Belgium was grounded in the abandonment of double criminality for a certain list of offences when committed in the Member State issuing the EAW, resulting in the breach of the principles of equality and legal certainty.[223] In essence, then, the Court of Justice was to give its view on the compliance of abandoning double criminality with fundamental rights the EU claims to safeguard.

In fact, the reference provided a perfect opportunity for the Court of Justice to carry out its fundamental rights review, on which it insisted throughout the decades of development of EU law. As Advocate General Ruiz-Jarabo Colomer put it:

> Accordingly, the Court must break its silence and recognise the authority of the Charter of Fundamental Rights as an interpretative tool at the forefront of the protection of the fundamental rights which are part of the heritage of the Member States. That undertaking must be approached with caution and vigour alike, in the full belief that, while the protection of fundamental rights is an essential part of the Community pillar, it is equally indispensable in the context of the third pillar, which, owing to the nature of its subject-matter, is capable of affecting the very heart of individual freedom, the foundation of the other freedoms.

[221] Belgian Cour d'Arbitrage Case 124/2005 *Advocaten voor de Wereld* Judgment of 13 July 2005 (reference) http://www.const-court.be/cgi/arrets_popup.php?lang=en&ArrestID=1993; Case C-303/05 *Advocaten voor de Wereld* [2007] EU:C:2007:26.

[222] Belgian Cour d'Arbitrage Case 136/2004 *Town and Country Planning* Judgment of 22 July 2004 http://www.const-court.be/cgi/judgments_popup.php?lang=en&ArrestID=1789. The Belgian court has declared the precedence of the Belgian Constitution in Case 29/1991 Judgment of 16 October 1991. An explicit definition of the relationship between the Belgian Constitution and EU secondary law has not yet been established by the Belgian court. Furthermore, equality and non-discrimination are envisaged in arts 10 and 11 of the Belgian Constitution and are the necessary link to trigger the Belgian court's jurisdiction for constitutional review. Since 2003, it is also able to perform fundamental rights review. M Bossuyt and W Verrijdt, 'The Full Effect of EU Law and of Constitutional Review in Belgium and France after the *Melki* Judgment' (2011) 7(3) *European Constitutional Law Review* 355, 358–59, 364.

[223] Belgian Cour d'Arbitrage Case *Advocaten voor de Wereld* (n 221) summary. See also Leczykiewicz (n 209) 231. The second challenge to the EAW Framework Decision disputed the use of the framework decision, as the EAW Framework Decision was going beyond mere 'approximation of laws and regulations'. This point will not be addressed in the analysis.

> In that way it might be possible to avoid repeating past misunderstandings with national courts which have been reticent about the capacity of the Community institutions to protect fundamental rights.[224]

After conducting an abstract and concrete analysis of the status of equality and legal certainty, Advocate General Ruiz-Jarabo Colomer concluded that the EAW Framework Decision is valid. The Court of Justice did not match the Advocate General's nuanced analysis, but started from the premise that the definition of offences for which the requirement of double criminality has been lifted is a matter of national law of the issuing Member State:

> [The] definition of those offences and of the penalties applicable continue to be matters determined by the law of the issuing Member State, which, as is, moreover, stated in Article 1(3) of the Framework Decision, must respect fundamental rights and fundamental legal principles as enshrined in Article 6 EU, and, consequently, the principle of the legality of criminal offences and penalties.[225]

The *non sequitur* is striking. For the Court of Justice, the validity of the EAW Framework Decision depends on the Member States' respect for fundamental rights.[226] The conclusion regarding double criminality is equally scant[227] in argumentation. The principle of equality is not put into question: different treatment of different offences is objectively justified because they are different. Or, in the Court's own words:

> Consequently, even if one were to assume that the situation of persons suspected of having committed offences featuring on the list set out in Article 2(2) of the Framework Decision or convicted of having committed such offences is comparable to the situation of persons suspected of having committed, or convicted of having committed, offences other than those listed in that provision, the distinction is, in any event, objectively justified.[228]

To make a short story shorter still, the EAW Framework Decision is valid.[229] The Court of Justice regrettably offered no analysis of the fundamental rights at issue, their possible infringement, or a possible justification.[230]

[224] Opinion of Advocate General Ruiz-Jarabo Colomer in Case C-303/05 *Advocaten voor de Wereld* [2006] EU:C:2006:552 [79]–[80].

[225] Case C-303/05 *Advocaten voor de Wereld* (n 221) [53].

[226] ibid [54]. Leczykiewicz (n 209) 240.

[227] E Cloots, 'Germs of Pluralist Judicial Adjudication: *Advocaten Voor De Wereld* and Other References from the Belgian Constitutional Court' (2010) 47(3) *Common Market Law Review* 645, 660.

[228] Case C-303/05 *Advocaten voor de Wereld* (n 221) [58].

[229] ibid [61].

[230] Cloots (n 227) 659–60.

The Cour d'Arbitrage accepted the decision of the Court of Justice and found the EAW Framework Decision in line with the principles of equality and legal certainty. It replicated the relevant analysis of the Court of Justice into its decision and found a material overlap between the protected rights and principles at issue. Consequently, the interpretation of the EAW Framework Decision was applied *mutatis mutandis* to the implementing act.[231]

#### *4.1.1.6 Consequences in Judicial Power Relations*

National decisions on the constitutionality of the EAW share two main similarities worth further examination. First, as they all deal with a measure of the third pillar, national courts have assumed jurisdiction to review it, concluding that primacy and direct effect are not applicable. The Court of Justice issued its decision in *Pupino* after the Polish decision had been handed down, but before the remainder of the analysed decisions.

The power relations at this point in time favour national constitutional adjudicators, albeit not absolutely. In this respect, the constitutional court has leverage over the Court of Justice in terms of the legal status of third pillar acts, similarly to the position of Treaty revisions pending national ratification. However, it is necessary to take into account *Pupino* and the limit of the obligation of consistent interpretation for the constitutional court. At this point in time, however, *Pupino* has not proven itself effective in the national constitutional review of the EAW Framework Decision, save for the Czech Ústavní Soud. Accordingly, constitutional courts still retain authority over ordinary national courts, given the legal status of the third pillar and the constitutional status of fundamental rights protection. Ordinary national courts are bound by *Pupino* up to the point where an EU-consistent interpretation would be *contra legem*. Equally, there is little basis for ordinary national courts to decide contrary to the interpretation mandated by the constitutional court.[232]

The second similarity the judgments share is a more general reluctance to subscribe to the principle of mutual trust. Mutual trust, which should be one of the foundations of the third pillar, was mentioned by the Trybunał Konstytucyjny only when addressing the need to carry out the legislative and constitutional amendment as soon as possible, due to the benefits of the Framework Decision:

> Effectiveness in combating [ ... ] crime depends to a large degree on the development of more advanced forms of cooperation between the Member States of

[231] Belgian Cour d'Arbitrage Case *Advocaten voor de Wereld* (n 221) [B.16]. See also T Vandamme, 'Prochain Arrêt: La Belgique! Explaining Recent Preliminary References of the Belgian Constitutional Court' (2008) 4 *European Constitutional Law Review* 127, 141.

[232] Note that at this point the Court of Justice had not yet delivered its judgments in *Melki and Abdeli*, *Cartesio*, and *Križan*, which caused further deterioration in the authority of constitutional courts over ordinary national courts, as described in the Introduction.

> the EU than the traditional extradition procedure. This is possible thanks to the high level of mutual confidence between legal systems, built on the basis of principles of political systems assuring the protection of fundamental human rights and liberties.[233]

The German decision talks about the *limited* mutual confidence in the third pillar. Conversely, and most certainly more convincing, Judge Gerhardt issued a Dissenting Opinion arguing for the application of *Pupino* and the importance of mutual trust:

> Pursuant to Article 6.3 of the Treaty on European Union, the Union shall also respect the national identities of its Member States. Already this implies the Member States' duty to mutual respect. In [ . . . ] *Pupino*, the Court of Justice [ . . . ] has emphasised that the principle of the Member States' loyal cooperation in the area of police and judicial cooperation in criminal matters also, and particularly, applies as regards the implementation of Framework Decisions [ . . . ]. Precisely for the sake of the effectiveness of this legal instrument, the European Judicial Community cannot support individual Member States' resorting to criminal sanctions in an imbalanced and one-sided manner by means of extraditions to them.[234]

The passage is instructive for understanding the relationship between national identity and mutual respect among Member States. In other words, insisting on the respect for national identity brings not only benefits, but also responsibilities. For the Bundesverfassungsgericht, however, the obligation of consistent interpretation cannot put into question constitutional fundamental rights protection.[235] While the values of Article 6(1) TEU mentioned by Judge Gerhardt were found to be a basis for mutual confidence by the majority,[236] the Bundesverfassungsgericht did not make a conclusion according to which it would apply automatically as regards fundamental rights associated with criminal procedure and extradition—after all, Article 6(1) TEU is no Basic Law.[237] Rather, the Bundesverfassungsgericht avoided the conflict by placing an obligation on the legislator to make use of all the available options set out in the EAW Framework Decision.

Similarly, the constitutional conflict between the EU and the Polish Constitution was avoided through a procedural avenue, by postponing the effects of the decision. However, the normative goal for the Polish Trybunał Konstytucyjny should

233 Komárek (n 162) 17–19.

234 German Bundesverfassungsgericht Case *European Arrest Warrant* Dissenting Opinion of Judge Gerhardt (n 192) [189].

235 German Bundesverfassungsgericht Case *European Arrest Warrant* (n 192) [119].

236 ibid [80].

237 Komárek (n 162) 25.

be balancing the supremacy of the Constitution with the principle of mutual trust between Member States. If constitutionally protected rights and freedoms are the 'unsurpassable threshold', the Tribunal should look for a solution according to which they are substantively protected.

It is unclear why, as Komárek points out in relation to the Polish decision, the trust in fundamental rights protection in other Member States was not sufficient to find that the essence of the constitutionally protected right was preserved. At this point, a clash was avoided in all Member States in one way or another through the operation of the self-imposed obligation to avoid conflict. Yet, the normative promise of constitutional pluralism requires the participants of the European judicial space to exhibit mutual respect towards their counterparts without any clear expression of superiority. The management of co-existing claims to ultimate authority in the same geographical space requires not only procedural conflict prevention, but should also be led by value pluralism, which is particularly important in fundamental rights protection, regardless of the institution ultimately upholding it. As Eijsbouts and Besselink put it:

> A judge or another public authority may qualify the validity, in his own jurisdiction, of a rule of more general circumscription than his own and binding on him. He shall do so not by mere reference to the autonomy or the supremacy of his own legal order, nor by reference to a legal hierarchy. He shall do so by reference to fundamental substantive norms valid in the wider circumscription also, or by putting forward such substantive norms that he holds to be applicable also there.[238]

Furthermore, the decision of the Court of Justice leaves a general impression of an opportunity missed more clearly to articulate its vision of fundamental rights review, the relationship to national constitutional standards of fundamental rights protection, and the role of mutual trust in this exercise. Despite the conclusion on the direct dependence of the EAW Framework Decision's validity on the Member States' fundamental rights protection, the Court of Justice mentioned constitutional traditions common to the Member States only in passing in the introductory sections of the judgment. It likewise passed on the chance to engage with the substance of the rights at issue from the perspective of the Charter, nor did it compare it to ECHR standards.

A fully pluralist approach would be, as Cloots argues, a more active engagement with the national standard of fundamental rights protection, a detailed reasoning,

[238] Eijsbouts and Besselink (n 144) 397. Similarly, Kumm's principle of best fit relies on normative ideals shared by the national and EU level as the aim. M Kumm, 'The Jurisprudence of Constitutional Conflict: Constitutional Supremacy in Europe before and after the Constitutional Treaty' (2005) 11(3) *European Law Journal* 262, 286.

and, most importantly, a high standard of protection.[239] Ultimately, a more detailed engagement with Member States' constitutional traditions would result in the Court of Justice acting as a platform for enhancing mutual trust in the standard of fundamental rights protection. In the words of Interviewee 1, the constitution of the EU in a material sense is based on and prolongs the constitutional traditions of Member States and the role of the Court of Justice is to 'accommodate the constitutional provisions in the substantive sense, and give them a coherent and unified meaning throughout the Union'. I argue this is not what we have seen in *Advocaten voor de Wereld*.

The Czech decision is an exception, as it uses the concept of EU citizenship to justify the imposition of obligations on Czech citizens, alongside the obvious benefits of free movement. It also concludes that there is no reason for doubting that fundamental rights protection standards in other Member States are not of an equal quality as in the Czech Republic.[240] Similarly, Alegre and Leaf provide an analysis of judicial decisions taken in France and the United Kingdom which set out a more accommodating approach than the Polish and German decisions.[241] In those countries, the courts have elaborated upon the importance of mutual trust and the contributions of the ECHR in safeguarding fundamental rights protection throughout the Member States to a generally satisfactory level.[242]

A final remark is to be made on heterarchy in the pluralist constellation. All the analysed decisions (save for the Court of Justice) have, to a greater or lesser extent, made cross-references to findings of other constitutional courts and their constitutional traditions.[243] This is in line with the view of the European judicial space as a cooperative one, where the participating courts are equal counterparts. According to Maduro, this contributes to the creation of a 'coherent and integrated European legal order'.[244] It thus remains regrettable that only the Czech Ústavní Soud applied this respect not only institutionally, but also in relation to the standard of fundamental rights protection in constitutional orders of other Member States. Maduro's idea of universalizability should be taken with a grain of salt, however: universalizability reeks of monism, as he places the EU legal order as the normative ideal for achieving coherence and integration of the European legal order.[245] The argument

[239] Cloots (n 227) 670.

[240] Czech Ústavní Soud Case *European Arrest Warrant* (n 212) [71], [86].

[241] A Alegre and M Leaf, 'Mutual Recognition in European Judicial Cooperation: A Step Too Far Too Soon? Case Study—the European Arrest Warrant' (2004) 10(2) *European Law Journal* 200, 210–13.

[242] For example, the United Kingdom High Court stated that '[it] is not, however, to be readily assumed or inferred that another state, particularly a fellow member of the Council of Europe represented on the European Court of Human Rights, will deny an accused person a fair trial'. United Kingdom High Court Case *Rachid Ramda* [2002] EWHC 1278 (Admin) [10].

[243] In the same vein see Komárek (n 162) 31–32.

[244] M P Maduro, 'Contrapunctual Law: Europe's Constitutional Pluralism in Action' in Walker (n 155) 501, 529.

[245] See also Komárek (n 162) 33, who addresses it from the aspect of its inability to provide for a conflict resolution method.

of this chapter is rather achieving a result which at different times accommodates either national or EU level of fundamental rights protection. Most certainly, this can only be achieved by adopting a dynamic understanding of law, regarding it as process rather than as a static matter of fact.

### 4.1.2 Balancing Fundamental Rights Protection and the Principle of Mutual Trust Post-Lisbon

The meagre reasoning of the Court of Justice in *Advocaten voor de Wereld* in fact sits well with its more general inactivity in fundamental rights review. As de Búrca reports, the role of the Court of Justice as a fundamental rights adjudicator has only seen a significant rise after the entry into force of the Charter.[246] Nevertheless, even after this point, the Court of Justice seemed reluctant to apply a more rigorous review of fundamental rights protection against EU measures.[247] Decisions in which the Court annulled a piece of EU legislation based on fundamental rights violations can easily be counted on the fingers of one hand.[248] As Weatherill points out, the assertion of fundamental rights protection is rarely followed by a finding of a violation, as the Court of Justice will most often defer to the legislative choices made by EU institutions.[249]

By contrast, as explained in Section 1, the activity of national courts with constitutional jurisdiction revolves around fundamental rights protection. After the initial judicial interactions concerning the validity of the EAW Framework Decision, I will now turn to further developments that took place after the Lisbon Treaty came into force. As is well-known, the pillar structure disappeared and EC and EU law merged in terms of their legal status.[250] The analysis will focus on the development of the relationship between mutual trust and fundamental rights protection and will include developments in the Dublin System[251] and further interactions concerning the application of the EAW Framework Decision.

The decision of the Court of Justice in *NS*[252] has already been mentioned in the context of the interpretation of the scope of application of the Charter. And while the Court found that the Charter is applicable, it was faced with the question

[246] G de Búrca, 'After the EU Charter of Fundamental Rights: the Court of Justice as a Human Rights Adjudicator?' (2013) 20(2) *Maastricht Journal of European and Comparative Law* 168, 170.

[247] Weatherill (n 82) 149.

[248] See s 4.2.2 below.

[249] Weatherill (n 82) 149, 152.

[250] See n 165.

[251] Council Regulation (EC) of 18 February 2003 establishing the criteria and mechanisms for determining the Member State responsible for examining an asylum application lodged in one of the Member States by a third-country national [2003] OJ L50/1 (Dublin II Regulation); repealed and replaced by Regulation (EU) No 604/2013 of the European Parliament and of the Council of 26 June 2013 establishing the criteria and mechanisms for determining the Member State responsible for examining an application for international protection lodged in one of the Member States by a third-country national or a stateless person [2013] OJ L180/13 (Dublin III Regulation).

[252] Joined Cases C-411/10 and C-493/10 *NS* (n 115).

whether the Member State processing the application may return the asylum seeker to the country of first entry deemed to be a safe country, if there are doubts that the person concerned will be subject to inhumane and degrading treatment. Greece (alongside Belgium) has already been found by the European Court of Human Rights (ECtHR) to be in violation of Article 3 ECHR, due to the unfair asylum procedure and detention, as well as humiliating and degrading living conditions.[253]

The Court of Justice placed a great emphasis on mutual trust between Member States in handling asylum claims, based on the presumption that all Member States are complying with the Charter, the Geneva Convention,[254] and the ECHR.[255] Such a presumption may only be rebutted if there are 'systemic flaws in the asylum procedure and reception conditions for asylum applicants in the Member State responsible, resulting in inhuman or degrading treatment [ ... ] of asylum seekers transferred to the territory of that Member State'.[256]

The result of such an approach is that the Member State handling the request must ascertain the existence of systemic deficiencies in the asylum request procedure of responsible Member State. The ECtHR, however, requires a more individualized investigation of the circumstances in every case being handled.[257] For the Court of Justice, the mutual trust that underlies the Common European Asylum System (and the AFSJ more generally) warrants the approach in *NS*.

Commenting on this discrepancy, the United Kingdom Court of Appeal found that: '[the] decision of the [CJEU] in the NS case [ ... ] has set a threshold in Dublin II and cognate return cases which exists nowhere else in refugee law'.[258] The United Kingdom Supreme Court further added:

> Violation of article 3 [ECHR] does not require [ ... ] that the complained of conditions said to constitute inhuman or degrading conditions are the product of systemic shortcomings. It is self-evident that a violation of article 3 rights is not intrinsically dependent on the failure of a system. [ ... ] And it means that those who would suffer breach of their article 3 rights other than as a result of a systemic deficiency in the procedure and reception conditions provided for the asylum seeker will be unable to avail of those rights in order to prevent their enforced return to a listed country where such violation would occur. That this

[253] European Court of Human Rights Case *MSS v Belgium and Greece* ECHR 2011-I. For a more detailed analysis of the case see M den Heijer, 'Joined Cases C-411 & 493/10, N.S. v. Secretary of State for the Home Department and M.E. and Others v. Refugee Applications Commissioner, Minister for Justice, Equality and Law Reform, Judgment of the Court (Grand Chamber) of 21 December 2011, nyr' (2012) 49(5) *Common Market Law Review* 1735.

[254] Convention Relating to the Status of Refugees [1951] 189 UNTS 137.

[255] Joined Cases C-411/10 and C-493/10 *NS* (n 115) [79]–[80], [83]. The presumption was further developed into the definition of mutual trust in the European Union. See Opinion 2/13 (n 147) [191].

[256] Joined Cases C-411/10 and C-493/10 *NS* (n 115) [86].

[257] European Court of Human Rights Case *MSS v Belgium and Greece* (n 253) [293].

[258] United Kingdom Court of Appeal Case *R (on the application of EM (Eritrea)) v Secretary of State for the Home Department* [2012] EWCA Civ 1336 [94].

should be the result of the decision of CJEU in the NS case would be, as I have said, remarkable.[259]

The approach was equally criticized in academia.[260] Nevertheless, the Court of Justice persisted. In *Abdullahi*,[261] it confirmed the presumption of fundamental rights compliance by Member States participating in the Common European Asylum System, the ensuing principle of mutual trust, and the right of the asylum seeker to invoke the systemic (rather than individual) deficiencies in the responsible Member State against the decision of removal.[262] The justification of this jurisprudence was expanded upon in Opinion 2/13, where the Court of Justice provided an analysis of the specificities of the AFSJ to defend the inconsistencies with the ECHR jurisprudence on the same matter.[263] Ultimately, mutual trust was given 'fundamental importance in EU law, given that it allows an area without internal borders to be created and maintained'.[264]

Against this backdrop, two courts with constitutional jurisdiction submitted references to the Court of Justice in an attempt to clarify the relationship between constitutional and EU standards of fundamental rights protection. The first such instance is the reference submitted by the Spanish Tribunal Constitucional in relation to the EAW, the execution of which contradicted the constitutional protection from prison sentencing *in absentia*.[265]

The Tribunal Constitucional thus asked the Court of Justice if the constitutional protection of the right to fair trial, specifically in relation to the trial *in absentia*, can be taken into account by the judicial authority tasked with deciding on the execution of an EAW.[266] As Torres Pérez explains, the Spanish level of protection is higher than that of the EAW Framework Decision and the ECHR (which share the same level of protection).[267] The tension between levels of protection goes to

[259] United Kingdom Supreme Court Case *EM v Secretary of State for the Home Department* [2014] UKSC 12 [42].

[260] See den Heijer (n 253) 1747; Halberstam (n 150) 127–30.

[261] Case C-394/12 *Abdullahi* [2013] EU:C:2013:813.

[262] ibid [52], [53], and [60], respectively.

[263] Opinion 2/13 (n 147) [191]. See also D Swoboda, 'The Self-perception of the European Court of Justice and Its Neglect of the Defense Perspective in Its Preliminary Rulings on Judicial Cooperation in Criminal Matters: A Small Note on a Fundamental Misunderstanding' (2015) 7–8 *Zeitschrift für Internationale Strafrechtsdogmatik* 361, 371.

[264] Opinion 2/13 (n 147) [191].

[265] The case has already been analysed in ch 6, s 2.2.3, from the perspective of identity review. The analysis here will therefore be confined to fundamental rights protection aspects of the case. It should also be added that in the meantime the EAW Framework Decision had been amended in 2009 (see n 161). In that respect, the relevant art 5(1), providing reasons for refusing to execute an EAW, was clarified by the new art 4a(1). See also A Torres Pérez, 'Constitutional Dialogue on the European Arrest Warrant: The Spanish Constitutional Court Knocking on Luxembourg's Door' (2012) 8(1) *European Constitutional Law Review* 105, 110–11.

[266] As Torres Pérez reports, the Court of Justice once avoided answering the question of whether the executing judicial authority is allowed to refuse the execution of an EAW if 'there are valid grounds for believing that its execution would have the effect of infringing the fundamental rights of the person concerned' in Case C-306/09 *IB* [2010] EU:C:2010:626. Torres Pérez (n 265) 112.

[267] Torres Pérez (n 265) 114.

the heart of constitutional conflict in fundamental rights protection and its relationship to mutual trust between Member States. If Spain can refuse to execute the EAW due to its higher level of protection not shared by the issuing Member State, mutual trust does not exist and the uniform application of the EAW throughout the Union is put into question. In connection to the first question, the Spanish court asked if Article 53 of the Charter allowed a Member State to provide for a higher level of protection than the level granted by EU law. In other words, are higher national standards of fundamental rights protection a limit to primacy of EU law?[268]

The Court of Justice expectedly upheld the level of fundamental rights protection of the EAW Framework Decision and dismissed the possibility of interpreting it so as to allow a Member State to apply its own fundamental rights protection standards and jeopardize its uniform application.[269] More importantly, in relation to Article 53 of the Charter, the Court found that:

> [Allowing] a Member State to avail itself of Article 53 of the Charter to make the surrender of a person convicted *in absentia* conditional upon the conviction being open to review in the issuing Member State, a possibility not provided for under Framework Decision 2009/299, in order to avoid an adverse effect on the right to a fair trial and the rights of the defence guaranteed by the constitution of the executing Member State, by casting doubt on the uniformity of the standard of protection of fundamental rights as defined in that framework decision, would undermine the principles of mutual trust and recognition which that decision purports to uphold and would, therefore, compromise the efficacy of that framework decision.[270]

Read together with a strong assertion as regards the scope of the Charter from *Fransson*, issued on the same day, the Court of Justice seems determined to reaffirm its commitment to fundamental rights protection. Yet, this commitment cannot be regarded in isolation of the remainder of EU law, where mutual trust plays a prominent role. As explained in Chapter 6, the Tribunal Constitucional accepted the interpretation of the Court of Justice, with the caveat that it will adhere to the principle of primacy up to the point where it clashes with Spanish constitutional identity.

The first preliminary reference of the French Conseil Constitutionnel[271] also concerned the EAW Framework Decision.[272] More specifically, the Conseil

[268] The Tribunal Constitucional usefully proposed three possible interpretations to this question. For further analysis see Torrez Pérez (n 265) 116–17; N de Boer, 'Addressing Rights Divergences under the Charter: *Melloni*. Case C-399/11, *Stefano Melloni v. Ministerio Fiscal*, Judgment of the Court (Grand Chamber) of 26 February 2013, nyr' (2013) 50(4) *Common Market Law Review* 1083, 1087.

[269] Case C-399/11 *Melloni* [2013] EU:C:2013:107 [46], [54].

[270] ibid [63].

[271] French Conseil Constitutionnel Case 2013-314P QPC *Mr Jeremy F* Decision of 4 April 2013 http://www.conseil-constitutionnel.fr/conseil-constitutionnel/francais/les-decisions/acces-par-date/decisions-depuis-1959/2013/2013-314p-qpc/decision-n-2013-314p-qpc-du-4-avril-2013.136588.html.

[272] For more information on the powers of the Conseil Constitutionnel see Introduction, s 3.2. On how its position affects its approach to the preliminary reference procedure; and its lack of reference to

Constitutionnel had before itself conflicting demands: the possibility in the EAW Framework Decision for the speciality rule[273] to be lifted without the right to appeal on the one hand and the constitutionally protected right to an effective judicial remedy on the other. This time around, the Court of Justice paid heed to the importance of the constitutionally protected right at stake:

> [A]rticle 1(3) of the Framework Decision expressly states that the decision is not to have the effect of modifying the obligation to respect fundamental rights and fundamental legal principles as enshrined in Article 6 EU, an obligation which moreover concerns all the Member States, in particular both the issuing and the executing Member States.[274]

It then carried out the analysis of effective judicial protection, its status in the ECHR, the Charter, and national constitutional law.[275] Ultimately, the Conseil Constitutionnel was able to provide for an appeal suspending the execution of the EAW in cases where the speciality rule is to be lifted, save for the requirement that the entire procedure is concluded within the time limits prescribed by the EAW Framework Decision.[276] The decision was praised as a demonstration of the 'maximum level of protection of human rights'[277] and the Conseil Constitutionnel accordingly annulled the implementing provision which previously excluded the right to appeal.[278]

The final national decision to be mentioned was handed down by the Bundesverfassungsgericht in the execution of the EAW, concerning the protection of the principle of individual guilt in opposition to the execution of the EAW based on a trial *in absentia*.[279] The Düsseldorf Higher Regional Court allowed the extradition of a person sentenced *in absentia* in line with the EAW Framework Decision, who then submitted a constitutional complaint. Although the threshold for fundamental rights review from its *Banana Market Regulation* decision had not been

constitutional identity in the submitted reference see F-X Millet, 'How Much Lenience for How Much Cooperation? On the First Preliminary Reference of the French Constitutional Council to the Court of Justice' (2014) 51(1) *Common Market Law Review* 195, 197–200, 204–205. For an analysis of the jurisprudence of the Conseil Constitutionnel in the area of identity review see ch 6, s 2.2.2.

[273] Article 27 of the EAW Framework Decision provides that 'a person surrendered may not be prosecuted, sentenced or otherwise deprived of his or her liberty for an offence committed prior to his or her surrender other than that for which he or she was surrendered'.

[274] Case C-168/13 PPU *Jeremy F* [2013] EU:C:2013:358 [40].

[275] ibid [43], [47], and [48]–[53], respectively.

[276] ibid [75].

[277] Millet (n 272) 210.

[278] French Conseil Constitutionnel Case 2013-314 QPC *Mr Jeremy F (II)* Decision of 14 June 2013 http://www.conseil-constitutionnel.fr/conseil-constitutionnel/root/bank/pdf/conseil-constitutionnel-140221.pdf.

[279] For the analysis of the identity review aspects of the case see ch 6, s 2.1.

met, the Bundesverfassungsgericht found that when the fundamental right in question is part of human dignity, which is part of the German constitutional identity, it will nevertheless carry out the review.[280] The Bundesverfassungsgericht found that the right to a fair trial was breached and quashed the decision of the Higher Regional Court, without submitting a preliminary reference to the Court of Justice.[281]

The Bundesverfassungsgericht engaged with the decision of the Court of Justice in *Melloni* and the limits it imposed on the refusal to execute an EAW in the name of effectiveness, uniformity and primacy of EU law. It moreover mentioned the exhaustive character of the EAW Framework Decision in respect of exceptions to the execution of the EAW concerning trials *in absentia*.[282] It concluded, nevertheless, that 'the principle of mutual trust that governs extraditions within Europe is limited by human dignity guaranteed under Art. 1 sec. 1 [of the Basic Law]'.[283]

The Court of Justice thus had to elaborate further upon the principle of mutual trust and its possible limits. In *Aranyosi and Căldăraru*[284] the Higher Regional Court in Bremen asked if the execution of an EAW is required, despite solid evidence pointing to the conclusion that fundamental rights of the person concerned protected by Article 6 TEU will be breached by the issuing Member State. The Court's decision in *Abdullahi* was firmly of the view that only systemic deficiencies will suffice to invoke the breach of inhumane and degrading treatment. The Court, however, appears to have softened its approach: 'limitations of the principles of mutual recognition and mutual trust between Member States can be made "in exceptional circumstances" '[285] and:

> [Where] the judicial authority of the executing Member State is in possession of evidence of a real risk of inhuman or degrading treatment of individuals detained in the issuing Member State, having regard to the standard of protection of fundamental rights guaranteed by EU law and, in particular, by Article 4 of the Charter [ . . . ] that judicial authority is bound to assess the existence of that risk when it is called upon to decide on the surrender to the authorities of the issuing Member State of the individual sought by a European arrest warrant.[286]

[280] German Bundesverfassungsgericht Case 2 BvR 2735/14 *Mr R.* Order of 15 December 2015 [34] http://www.bundesverfassungsgericht.de/SharedDocs/Pressemitteilungen/EN/2016/bvg16-004.html.

[281] Interestingly, Lenaerts concluded that the Bundesverfassungsgericht 'endorsed the level of fundamental rights protection provided for by the EAW Framework Decision as interpreted by the ECJ in *Melloni*'. K Lenaerts, 'La Vie après l'Avis: Exploring the Principle of Mutual (Yet Not Blind) Trust' (2017) 54(3) *Common Market Law Review* 805, 819.

[282] German Bundesverfassungsgericht Case *Mr R* (n 280) [79]–[82].

[283] ibid [83]. For a more detailed analysis see J Nowag, 'EU Law, Constitutional Identity, and Human Dignity: A Toxic Mix? Bundesverfassungsgericht: *Mr R* 2 BvR 2735/14, *Mr R v. Order of the Oberlandesgericht Düsseldorf*, Order of the Bundesverfassungsgericht (Second Senate) of 15 December 2015, DE:BVerfG:2015:rs20151215.2bvr273514' (2016) 53(5) *Common Market Law Review* 1441.

[284] Joined Cases C-404/15 PPU and C-659/15 PPU *Aranyosi and Căldăraru* [2016] EU:C:2016:198.

[285] ibid [82].

[286] ibid [88].

If a real risk is established, the national court must ascertain if this risk will manifest itself in relation to the person concerned.[287] Thus, although mutual trust is not blind trust,[288] an additional effort must be made by the relevant national authority to establish the breach of rights protected by Article 6 TEU by the issuing Member State in the individual case at hand.[289]

## 4.2 Data Retention

Constitutional conflict in fundamental rights protection eventually brings us to the area of the right to respect for private and family life from Article 7 and the right to data protection set out in Article 8 of the Charter.[290] The enactment of the Data Retention Directive[291] in 2006 resulted in a series of constitutional challenges on the national level, some of which arrived to the Court of Justice through the preliminary reference procedure. In that respect, the area of data retention offers an almost natural laboratory for exploring the descriptive and normative features of constitutional pluralism, where it was possible to observe a constructive back and forth resulting in the invalidation of the Data Retention Directive due to its deficient standards of fundamental rights protection.

The Data Retention Directive saw the light of day in response to an increasing threat posed by terrorist attacks across Europe.[292] It imposed an obligation on service providers to retain telecommunication data available for access to competent national authorities, in order for the latter to combat 'serious crime'.[293] The data to be retained excluded the communication content and was confined to traffic,

[287] ibid [92].

[288] G Anagnostaras, 'Mutual Confidence Is Not Blind Trust! Fundamental Rights Protection and the Execution of the European Arrest Warrant: *Aranyosi and Caldararu*' (2016) 53(6) *Common Market Law Review* 1675, 1683; Lenaerts (n 281) 821.

[289] By analogy, the Court of Justice relaxed its approach to finding a breach of art 3 ECHR in determining the Member State responsible for handling the asylum claim in Case C-63/15 *Ghezelbash* [2016] EU:C:2016:409 [34]–[46], distinguishing it from *Abdullahi* based on the amendment in the Dublin III Regulation.

[290] A separate discussion in literature developed concerning the relationship between art 7 and art 8 of the Charter. This will not be the subject of the present analysis. For further information see O Lynskey, 'Article 8: The Right to Data Protection' in Bobek and Adams-Prassl (n 1).

[291] Directive 2006/24/EC of the European Parliament and of the Council of 15 March 2006 on the retention of data generated or processed in connection with the provision of publicly available electronic communications services or of public communications networks and amending Directive 2002/58/EC (Data Retention Directive) OJ L105/54. It amended the Directive 2002/58/EC of the European Parliament and of the Council of 12 July 2002 concerning the processing of personal data and the protection of privacy in the electronic communications sector (Directive on privacy and electronic communications) [2002] OJ L201/37.

[292] A Vedaschi and V Lubello, 'Data Retention and Its Implications for the Fundamental Right to Privacy' (2015) 20 *Tilburg Law Review* 14, 18; B Grabowska-Moroz, 'Data Retention in the European Union' in M Zubik, J Podkowik, and R Rybski (eds), *European Constitutional Courts towards Data Retention Laws* (Springer 2020) 3.

[293] Serious crime is to be defined by each Member State in national law. See Data Retention Directive, art 1(1).

location and data necessary to identify the user.[294] The manner and procedure related to access itself was left to Member State discretion and excluded from the scope of the Directive, subject to the principles of proportionality and necessity.[295] The duration of retention was equally left for Member States to specify within the span of six months to two years.[296]

After its enactment, the Directive's legal basis was challenged by Ireland, arguing that the 'centre of gravity' test of the Directive's harmonization efforts is not the internal market but rather the fight against crime.[297] The Court excluded from its analysis a possible effect of the Directive on fundamental rights[298] and, recalling its *Tobacco Advertising* decision, concluded that so long as the directive aims to address disparities between national rules that affect the internal market,[299] this legal basis can be used.[300] The Data Retention Directive thus survived the competence challenge and was later directly or indirectly subject to a number of judicial proceedings on the national and EU levels.

This section will thus chronologically map the judicial interactions that led to the ultimate invalidation of the Directive in respect of its level of fundamental rights protection, allowing a nuanced look into the functioning of constructive constitutional conflict and the operation of the auto-correct function. I will start by presenting the national decisions after the enactment of the Directive, outlining the main issues that national constitutional courts found with the legislation implementing the Directive. Following this, I will reflect upon the decision of the Court of Justice in *Digital Rights Ireland* which marks the first pronouncement of invalidity, arguing that the Court has engaged with the substance of Member States' constitutional approaches to the rights to private and family life and data protection. This caused different reactions on the national level aiming to incorporate the Court's decision, which will be discussed from the perspective of the principle of primacy and the manner in which national courts approached it. National implementing legislation caused further doubts concerning the generalized manner of data retention for public security purposes and the Court of Justice again addressed the Directive's shortcomings in *Tele2 and Watson*. I will

[294] Data Retention Directive, art 1(2).

[295] ibid art 4. On the resulting internal inconsistencies of the Directive see C Markou, 'The Cyprus and Other EU Court Rulings on Data Retention: The Directive as a Privacy Bomb' (2012) 28 *Computer Law & Security Review* 468.

[296] Data Retention Directive, art 8.

[297] Case C-301/06 *Ireland v Parliament and Council* [2009] EU:C:2009:68 [30].

[298] ibid [57].

[299] ibid [84]–[85]. The approach of the Court falls squarely into its '*Tobacco Advertising* as a drafting guide' logic put forward by S Weatherill, 'The Limits of Legislative Harmonization Ten Years after *Tobacco Advertising*: How the Court's Case Law Has Become a "Drafting Guide"' (2011) 12(3) *German Law Journal* 827, analysed in ch 5, s 5.

[300] Case C-301/06 *Ireland v Parliament and Council* (n 297) [63].

finally reflect upon the consequences this has had for judicial power relations and heterarchy.

### 4.2.1 Data Retention before National Courts

Across the case studies in this book one can conclude that national courts rarely take it upon themselves to review sources of EU law directly,[301] but most commonly focus on the implementing measures in their national legal order. The Data Retention Directive is a textbook example of this practice. For the most part, national courts either did not make reference to the Data Retention Directive, or if they did, they still reviewed the implementing legislation rather than the Directive itself. As a result, the constitutional conflict materialized itself not in questioning the validity of the EU source of law, but rather in pointing out the demands it poses on national legislation in relation to constitutional levels of data protection across Member States. The constructiveness of this conflict thus arguably resulted in demanding a change of approach on the EU level that develops through mutual feedback with national constitutional orders.

The first legal challenge on the national level concerning data retention was decided in 2008 by the Bulgarian Supreme Administrative Court.[302] The court analysed the implementing legislation in respect of the right to privacy protected by the Bulgarian Constitution, as well as by the ECHR, without referring to the Data Retention Directive. The review resulted in the annulment of the challenged implementing provision which regulates access to the retained data, as the provision provides no limits that would safeguard the right to privacy. The manner of access is a matter that the Directive leaves to Member States to regulate, which could be a possible reason for the lack of reference to it.[303]

The next national judgment dealing with data retention was decided in 2009 by the Romanian Constitutional Court.[304] It sparked considerable scholarly interest[305] given its finding that data retention as regulated in the Data Retention Directive goes against the right to privacy and family life, without making a reference to the Directive.[306] However, the court did mention the e-Privacy Directive

301 Germany and Poland, as was visible in relation to *ultra vires* and identity review, at times reserved the power to review directly the EU law source. As regards *ultra vires* review see ch 5, s 6.1 for Germany. Identity review is analysed in ch 6, s 2.1 for Germany and s 2.2.1 for Poland.

302 Bulgarian Supreme Administrative Court Decision No 13627 of 11 December 2008.

303 E Kosta, 'The Way to Luxemburg: National Court Decisions on the Compatibility of the Data Retention Directive with the Rights to Privacy and Data Protection' (2013) 10(3) *SCRIPTed* 339, 346.

304 Romanian Curtea Constituţională Decision No 1258 of 8 October 2009. Unofficial translation available at https://www.statewatch.org/media/documents/news/2009/nov/romania-court-data-ret.pdf.

305 Kosta (n 303) 349; C C Murphy, 'Romanian Constitutional Court, Decision No 1258 of 8 October 2009' (2010) 47 *Common Market Law Review* 933, 939; O Lynskey, 'The Data Retention Directive is Incompatible with the Rights to Privacy and Data Protection and Is Invalid in its Entirety: *Digital Rights Ireland*' (2014) 51 *Common Market Law Review* 1789, 1792.

306 The Constitutional Court simply stated that the Directive grants discretion to the Member States on how to implement it. Romanian Curtea Constituţională Decision No 1258 (n 304) 4.

as the EU-relevant source protecting the right to private and family life, although the Data Retention Directive explicitly amends it.[307] The relevance of the judgment thus mainly lies in matters left unsaid: if data retention breaches the right to private and family life, can Romania ever implement any EU-sourced legislation that detracts from it? In other words, the relationship between primacy of EU law and the constitutional level of fundamental rights protection was not addressed and the Constitutional Court resorted to reliance on ECtHR jurisprudence to justify its findings on the problematic nature of data retention.[308]

Up next is the decision of the German Bundesverfassungsgericht from 2010,[309] following the 'largest mass constitutional complaint in the history'[310] of Germany. As a result, the Bundesverfassungsgericht invalidated the national implementing legislation of the Directive. A closer look at the reasoning reveals self-restraint in respect of reviewing EU law directly, but also a parallel expansion of its jurisdiction[311] as regards the scope of application of the Basic Law.

The Bundesverfassungsgericht reflected on the possibility of submitting a preliminary reference to the Court of Justice, as well as the relevant object of review. Recalling its *Solange* and *Banana Market Regulation* jurisprudence,[312] it reiterated it will not review EU law against fundamental rights so long as the EU generally safeguards the essential content of fundamental rights when those are substantially similar to those unconditionally protected by the Basic Law.[313] Taking into account that only the Basic Law is involved as the standard of review of the national implementing legislation, it also concluded that a preliminary reference to the Court of Justice is not necessary given that the validity of the directive is not being questioned.[314]

Importantly, the court justified the sole applicability of the Basic Law by the broad discretion that the Directive left to German authorities to implement it in compliance with the Basic Law. The court found that by not questioning the validity of the Directive, primacy of EU law is taken out of the equation and does not influence the review.[315] Albers explains that the unprecedented political pressure prevented the Bundesverfassungsgericht from engaging in a years-long procedure that a preliminary reference procedure entails.[316] Despite reserving for itself the

[307] Lynskey (n 305) 1791.
[308] Murphy (n 305) 940.
[309] German Bundesverfassungsgericht Case 1 BvR 256/08 *Data Retention* Judgment of 2 March 2010 <https://www.bundesverfassungsgericht.de/SharedDocs/Entscheidungen/EN/2010/03/rs20100302_1bvr025608en.html>.
[310] M Albers, 'Data Retention in Germany' in M Zubik, J Podkowik, and R Rybski (eds), *European Constitutional Courts towards Data Retention Laws* (Springer 2020) 118.
[311] ibid 122.
[312] See ss 2.3 and 4.1.1.2 above.
[313] German Bundesverfassungsgericht Case *Data Retention* (n 309) [181].
[314] ibid [183].
[315] ibid [186].
[316] Albers (n 310) 122.

review of the implementing legislation, it did not decide that the Basic Law outright prohibits data retention, but confined itself to finding the legislation in question disproportionate.[317] This allowed for a possible subsequent review to take place at the EU level and amendments to be made accordingly.

The decision of the Cypriot Supreme Court from February 2011[318] additionally contributed to this discussion, in particular given that the Constitution itself in Article 1A provides that none of its provisions can impede laws and regulations necessary for implementing the obligations for Cyprus stemming from EU law.[319] At first glance, one might conclude that in Cyprus, EU law has supremacy, rather than primacy.[320] This provision directly prevents a situation in which fundamental rights as protected in the Constitution would have any effect on the implementation of EU law obligations, such as those in the Data Retention Directive. It should also be mentioned that the Supreme Court did not conduct judicial review of the implementing legislation, but rather needed to decide on orders issued by lower courts authorizing the access to the retained data.[321]

To keep within the limits of Article 1A in according a proper place for EU law, the Supreme Court referred to the Court of Justice in *Ireland v Parliament and Council* to confirm that issues of access are outside the scope of the Directive.[322] But is access really outside the scope of the directive (as also stated by the Bulgarian court), or should it not be that the Directive affords the Member States broad discretion (as argued by the German, the Romanian, and, as will be seen below, the Czech court)? The Court of Justice admittedly used the expression 'do not govern'[323] which would support the Bulgarian and Cypriot interpretation. The Directive itself is not explicit in this regard and lends itself to different interpretations.[324] However, it is precisely this omission to impose limits to access that was later touted by the Court of Justice as one of the reasons why the Directive breached the fundamental

317 German Bundesverfassungsgericht Case *Data Retention* (n 309) [213].

318 Cyprus Supreme Court in Civil Applications 65/2009, 78/2009, 82/2009 and 15/2010-22/2010 of 1 February 2011.

319 See also discussion on the constitutional amendment as regards the merging of the former three pillars in s 4.1.1.3 above.

320 Even at a first glance, one might reply that it is by the authority of the Constitution that EU law was given precedence within the areas transferred to the EU, thus preventing a conclusion on a straightforward supremacy with an autonomous source of validity. This, however, brings the analysis to the famous omnipotence paradox: Can God, if omnipotent, create an immovable stone? Earlier in this book, the discussion on sovereignty claims on the part of the EU and the Member States attempted to show that the answer to the paradox is in the negative, as all sites of constitutional authority retain their right to the ultimate say. See ch 3, s 1.

321 Markou (n 295) 472.

322 ibid.

323 Case C-301/06 *Ireland v Parliament and Council* (n 297) [80].

324 According to art 1(1) of the Directive, the purpose of retention is 'to ensure that the data are available for the purpose of the investigation, detection and prosecution of serious crime, as defined by each Member State in its national law'. In addition, recital 25 of the Directive states: 'This Directive is without prejudice to the power of Member States to adopt legislative measures concerning the right of access to, and use of, data by national authorities, as designated by them.'

right to respect for private and family life and data protection and was thus invalidated.[325] The difference is of crucial relevance, given the discussion above on the applicability of EU law and the Charter in areas where Member States are given discretion. According to the Court of Justice in *NS*, once Member States exercise the discretion provided by EU law, they are within the scope of EU law and bound by the Charter.[326] In this scenario, the Supreme Court would arguably still remain within the scope of Article 1A of the Constitution and would have to conclude that all matters resulting from the existence of the Data Retention Directive automatically receive the seal of constitutionality.

Yet, the Supreme Court chose the less thorny road of excluding access from the scope of EU law, demonstrating thus that even a formal EU law superiority clause in the Constitution is not immune to legal acrobatics. The Supreme Court then conducted an analysis of compliance of the above mentioned access court orders with the right to secrecy of communication from Article 17 of the Constitution, found a breach and ordered they be annulled.[327]

The last national decision before the Court of Justice had its say in *Digital Rights Ireland* was taken by the Czech Constitutional Court in 2011.[328] The applicants sought from the court a submission of a preliminary reference to the Court of Justice on the interpretation of the Data Retention Directive. The Czech court, similarly to its German counterpart, decided a reference was not necessary due to the wide discretion provided by the Directive, allowing for constitutionally compliant implementation.[329] The court also underlined it has no competence to interpret EU law, but rather remains confined to reviewing the constitutionality of the implementing legislation.[330] This division of tasks between the EU and national judiciary aligns with the pluralist framework: the Court of Justice claims the ultimate right to interpret EU law and the national constitutional court the right to interpret the national constitution. These may well clash in substance (according to the Directive's requirements, as opposed to constitutional requirements) regardless of the different legal frameworks within which they operate.

After annulling the contested provision of national implementing measures due to their disproportionate infringement of the right to private and family life, the Czech court questioned the general usefulness of data retention and its collection by private operators obiter dictum.[331] While again not attacking the Directive directly, the Czech court came closest to the approach of its Romanian counterpart in

[325] Joined Cases C-293/12 and C-594/12 *Digital Rights Ireland* [2014] EU:C:2014:238 [60]–[61].

[326] See s 3.2.

[327] Markou (n 295) 472.

[328] Czech Ústavní Soud Case Pl. ÚS 24/10 *Data Retention* Decision of 22 March 2011 https://www.usoud.cz/fileadmin/user_upload/ustavni_soud_www/Decisions/pdf/Pl%20US%2024-10.pdf.

[329] ibid [25].

[330] ibid.

[331] ibid [55]–[57].

criticizing the basic premises of data retention as a tool to address the prevention and investigation of new forms of crimes in respect of its efficiency and trade-offs.

The judicial power relations at this point in time favour national constitutional adjudicators, albeit not absolutely. In this respect, constitutional courts have a leverage over the Court of Justice given that they all reviewed national implementing legislation and could apply constitutional, rather than EU, standards. Regardless of whether they characterized the regulation of access to retained data as outside the scope of the Directive or as an exercise of the wide discretion accorded by it, no national court considered that a preliminary reference, and by extension the interpretation of EU law, is necessary. However, taking into account that the Data Retention Directive is the shared reason why any of the legislation was under review in the first place, constitutional courts must remain within the limit placed by the obligation of consistent EU-friendly interpretation. This can be evidenced by the avoidance of review of the Directive itself, given the division of tasks between the Court of Justice and national courts under Article 19(1) TEU and *Foto-Frost*. Accordingly, the constitutional court retains significant power over ordinary national courts, given the constitutional status of fundamental rights protection and the finding that the legislation is outside the scope of the Directive. The Cypriot example is particularly instructive as the Supreme Court dealt directly with the orders issued by a lower national court in its application of the legislation implementing EU law. Ordinary national courts have not submitted preliminary references to challenge the findings of their constitutional courts and their interpretations of fundamental rights that have been found outside the scope of the Directive.

### 4.2.2 *Digital Rights Ireland*

The Data Retention Directive continued making judicial waves across the EU. The Commission led successful infringement proceedings for non-implementation against Greece,[332] Ireland,[333] Sweden,[334] and Austria.[335] The analysis in the previous section showed that, for the most part, national courts managed to avoid directly questioning the compliance of the Directive with constitutional fundamental rights protection by instead focusing on the implementing legislation where the Directive grants discretion to the Member States. But is it really that all these Member States just happened to implement the Directive in the constitutionally 'wrong' way?[336] It became obvious that there was something wrong with the Directive itself, regardless of how reluctant the national courts were to say it. Thus,

[332] Case C-211/09 *Commission v Greece* [2009] EU:C:2009:737.
[333] Case C-202/09 *Commission v Ireland* [2009] EU:C:2009:736.
[334] Case C-185/09 *Commission v Sweden* [2010] EU:C:2010:59.
[335] Case C-189/09 *Commission v Austria* [2010] EU:C:2010:455.
[336] P Molek, 'Czech Constitutional Court Unconstitutionality of the Czech Implementation of the Data Retention Directive; Decision of 22 March 2011, Pl. .S 24/10' (2012) 8 *European Constitutional Law Review* 338, 351.

with the increasing inevitability that constitutionally protected rights as well as Charter rights will be breached by complying with the Directive,[337] the question of its validity ultimately reached the Court of Justice via preliminary references from Ireland and Austria. The widespread nature of national challenges to the system of data retention could not escape the attention of the Court of Justice: in line with the principle of sincere cooperation based on mutual respect, there was a need to acknowledge the fundamental rights issues that the Directive created for national constitutional courts.[338]

Both the Irish and the Austrian reference questioned the compliance of the general system of data retention with Articles 7 (right to respect for private and family life), Article 8 (data protection), and Article 11 of the Charter (freedom of expression). The Irish court asked the Court of Justice to assess the proportionality of the Directive under Article 5(4) TEU (relating to the exercise of competence by the Union), whereas the Austrian court inquired whether proportionality under Article 52(1) of the Charter (concerning rights' limitations) is breached. The references included other questions, such as, for example, whether the national court should assess the validity of a directive in respect of the Charter in relation to the principle of sincere cooperation from Article 4(3) TEU.[339] The two courts also engaged in a preliminary analysis of the Directive's influence on fundamental rights, with the Austrian Constitutional Court finding serious concerns in respect of the proportionality of the retention period, the lack of a specific reason to retain data and the possibility of abuse.[340]

The Austrian court also raised an interesting point concerning the level of protection in the Charter, as opposed to possibly higher national standards. It agreed with the Court of Justice in *Melloni* that a single constitutional provision should not displace the Charter's standard of protection. However, the situation changes where the higher standard can be found in constitutions of numerous Member States (I will term this a 'collective *Melloni*' situation), thus amounting to common constitutional traditions that should serve as an interpretative guide to Charter rights according to Article 52(4) of the Charter.[341] Taking up this point would indeed mean that Member States can, through their shared constitutional developments, change and arguably improve the interpretation of fundamental rights in the Charter, without the principle of primacy or the uniform interpretation of EU

[337] Austrian Verfassungsgerichtshof Decision in Cases G 47/12-11, G 59/12-10, G 62,70,71/12-11 of 28 November 2012 [3.2] https://www.vfgh.gv.at/downloads/vorabentscheidungsvorlagen/Vorlage_VRDspeicherung_G_47-12_EN_4.4.2017.pdf.

[338] Lynskey (n 305) 1789, 1801.

[339] Reference for a preliminary ruling from High Court of Ireland made on 11 June 2012 in Case C-293/12 https://curia.europa.eu/juris/document/document.jsf?text=&docid=125859&pageIndex=0&doclang=en&mode=req&dir=&occ=first&part=1&cid=11972563.

[340] Austrian Verfassungsgerichtshof Decision in Cases G 47/12-11, G 59/12-10, G 62,70,71/12-11 (n 337) [4.2]–[4.5].

[341] ibid [5.2].

law being put into question. In that sense, the Data Retention Directive and its life before national courts could be seen as a manifestation of constructive constitutional conflict where national courts across Member States contributed to the development of the EU's own standard of protection of fundamental rights.

However, the Court of Justice skipped the opportunity to delve into the nuances of this question and focused solely on addressing the compatibility of the Directive with Articles 7 and 8 of the Charter.[342] The Court made no mention of common constitutional traditions of Member States or the possibility of distinguishing between an individual and a collective *Melloni* situation, which would in my view remain within the letter of the Charter while significantly opening up a substance-based dialogue concerning fundamental rights,[343] thus assuaging some of the concerns that arose in the aftermath of *Melloni*.[344] Yet, some have found this narrow approach of the Court to reflect precisely the awareness of the above analysed national procedures by reinforcing directly the Charter itself as the relevant standard for invalidating the Directive.[345] There is merit to this approach of the Court. By acknowledging the high standard of the right to private and family life and data protection, the Court is in fact using the Charter to harmonize the different approaches taken by national courts and prevent a similar situation from occurring in respect of future legislation in this area. This has another important benefit: it instils confidence on behalf of national courts that the Court will police legislative activities of EU institutions for their compliance with fundamental rights.

This tendency can also be seen from the Court's approach to proportionality. As mentioned above, the two national courts inquired about two different proportionality standards, one concerning the exercise of competence and the other Charter derogations. The Court of Justice, arguably also not to contradict its own decision in *Ireland v Parliament and Council* concerning the correct legal basis of the Directive being the pursuit of an internal market objective under Article 114 TFEU, focused only on proportionality as a Charter derogation from its Article 52(1)[346] and did not even mention Article 5(4) TEU. This also allowed the Court to conduct the proportionality test only in relation to its secondary objective (prevention,

[342] Joined Cases C-293/12 and C-594/12 *Digital Rights Ireland* (n 325) [31]. On this well-established practice of simplifying national questions see U Šadl and A Wallerman, '"The Referring Court Asks, in Essence": Is Reformulation of Preliminary Questions by the Court of Justice A Decision Writing Fixture or a Decision-making Approach?' (2019) 25 *European Law Journal* 416.

[343] Arguably, the attempt of the Austrian court was to start a comparative analysis of data protection across Member States, although admittedly it refrained from doing so explicitly and only summarily referred to a few other Member States' constitutions. Austrian Verfassungsgerichtshof Decision in Cases G 47/12-11, G 59/12-10, G 62,70,71/12-11 (n 337) [5.2].

[344] See s 4.1.2 above.

[345] Lynskey (n 305) 1800–801.

[346] Advocate General Cruz Villalón specifically addressed this conundrum and concluded that the Court in *Ireland v Parliament and Council* ruled only on the choice of the legal basis, but not on its proportionate use. See Opinion of Advocate General Cruz Villalón in Joined Cases C-293/12 and C-594/12 *Digital Rights Ireland* [2013] EU:C:2013:845 [88].

investigation, detection and prosecution of serious crime)[347] and avoid the discussion concerning the relationship between primary and secondary objectives of EU legislation.[348] As mentioned above, while the Court concluded that rules on access to data are outside the scope of the Directive in *Ireland v Parliament and Council*, here this lack of substantive and procedural conditions for access to retained data by competent national authorities amounted to a fundamental rights deficiency. Thus, the dilemma of the Cypriot Supreme Court described above could also have been interpreted by considering that the Directive left too wide a discretion to the Member States,[349] still subjecting them to the Charter. Indeed, here the Court immediately applied the Charter to the Directive. Taking into account the lack of limits on the retention of data, including time periods and lack of judicial control, the Court concluded that Articles 7 and 8 of the Charter were disproportionately breached and annulled the Directive *ab initio*.[350]

This decision provides two important lessons for constitutional pluralism. First, it demonstrates with impressive clarity the interwoven nature of the EU's constitutional structure that operates through mutual feedback between the national and EU level. The contributions of different levels of authority interact through the operation of sincere cooperation and mutual respect, as outlined in Chapter 3. Let me clarify: some national courts focused on national implementing legislation and attempted to provide an EU-friendly interpretation. Specifically, they showed that a constitutionally compliant implementation of the Directive is possible within the discretion it leaves to the Member States, rather than questioning the validity of the Directive. In other Member States, instead of focusing exclusively on the implementing legislation, courts have submitted a preliminary reference to the Court of Justice to provide it with an opportunity to address the wide-spread concerns that the Directive created in the area of fundamental rights. In other words, through the principle of sincere cooperation, the Austrian and Irish courts made it possible for the Court of Justice to incorporate the feedback from the national level. The Court of Justice has accepted this possibility, demonstrating an implicit acknowledgement of national constitutional concerns.[351]

The second lesson is substantive in nature and provides further insight into the operation of the normative side of constitutional pluralism. As explained in Chapter 3, the EU's constitutional law, broadly understood, progresses through permanent contestation between the national and the EU level through

[347] Joined Cases C-293/12 and C-594/12 *Digital Rights Ireland* (n 325) [41].

[348] Unlike the Advocate General, who nevertheless concluded that the proportionality analysis under art 52(1) of the Charter should ultimately determine the validity of the Directive. Opinion of Advocate General Cruz Villalón in Joined Cases C-293/12 and C-594/12 *Digital Rights Ireland* (n 346) [89]–[105]. See also Lynskey (n 305) 1802.

[349] See also I Cameron, 'Balancing Data Protection and Law Enforcement Needs: *Tele2 Sverige and Watson*' (2017) 54 *Common Market Law Review* 1467, 1470.

[350] Joined Cases C-293/12 and C-594/12 *Digital Rights Ireland* (n 325) [71].

[351] Vedaschi and Lubello (n 292) 25.

constructive constitutional conflict, so long as such conflict stays within the confines of reasonable disagreement in the interpretation of values in Article 2 TEU. In this instance of judicial interactions and contestation from the national level, the Court of Justice was able to provide further insight into the meaning of Articles 7 and 8 of the Charter by developing an EU-wide standard. This ensured that judicial interactions having taken place due to the Data Retention Directive caused permanent changes in EU's interpretation of Articles 7 and 8 of the Charter.[352]

With the Data Retention Directive dead, it was now for the national courts to incorporate this new legal situation into their constitutional orders. Constitutional courts in Austria,[353] Slovenia,[354] Romania,[355] Poland,[356] Bulgaria,[357] Slovakia,[358] Belgium,[359] and Portugal[360] have as a result all annulled national implementing legislation. Interestingly, only in 2019 did the Czech Constitutional Court find that the national implementing legislation is constitutional.[361] It is particularly striking that the Czech court grounded this finding in stating that the annulment of the Directive created legislative space for the Member States.[362] It did so despite referring to the Court of Justice in *Tele2 and Watson* (according to which data retention nevertheless falls in the scope of the e-Privacy Directive), by finding there is still insufficient consensus on the EU level for a replacement of the Data Retention Directive.[363]

The last remark again invites us to look at the changes in judicial power relations. The Court of Justice acquired a certain amount of leverage over constitutional courts inasmuch as it is now established that the Data Retention Directive was subject to the requirements of the Charter and was thus taken out of the scope of fundamental rights review under national constitutions. The doubt encountered

[352] See also Lynskey (n 305) 1804.

[353] Austrian Verfassungsgerichtshof Decision in Cases G 47/2012-49, G 59/2012-38, G 62/2012-46, G 70/2012-40, G 71/2012-36 of 27 June 2014 https://www.vfgh.gv.at/downloads/vorabentscheidungsvorlagen/vds_schriftliche_entscheidung.pdf.

[354] Slovenian Constitutional Court Case No U-I-65/13 Decision of 3 July 2014 https://www.us-rs.si/decision/?lang=en&q=2006%2F24&df=&dt=&af=&at=&vd=&vo=&vv=&vs=&ui=&va=&page=1&sort=&order=&id=111602.

[355] Romanian Constitutional Court Case No 440 Decision of 8 July 2014 http://legislatie.just.ro/Public/DetaliiDocumentAfis/161081.

[356] Polish Constitutional Tribunal Case K 23/11 Decision of 30 July 2014 https://trybunal.gov.pl/en/hearings/judgments/art/8821-okreslenie-katalogu-zbieranych-informacji-o-jednostce-za-pomoca-srodkow-technicznych-w-dzialani.

[357] Bulgarian Constitutional Court Case No 8/2014 Decision of 12 March 2015 http://www.constcourt.bg/bg/Acts/GetHtmlContent/00025810-e1fb-4f7d-bced-a09c85bab51e.

[358] Slovak Constitutional Court Case No PL. ÚS 10/2014 Decision of 29 April 2015 https://www.ustavnysud.sk/documents/10182/71853347/PL_10_2014.pdf/55803f09-7020-41a4-a671-819fa297160d.

[359] Belgian Constitutional Court Case No 84/2015 Decision of 11 June 2015 https://www.fricore.eu/system/files/cconstbelgique_11juin15.pdf.

[360] Portuguese Constitutional Court Case No 403/2015 Decision of 27 August 2015 https://dre.pt/pesquisa/-/search/125515884/details/maximized.

[361] Czech Constitutional Court Case Pl. ÚS 45/17 Decision of 14 May 2019 https://www.usoud.cz/fileadmin/user_upload/ustavni_soud_www/Decisions/pdf/Pl-45-17_1_en.pdf.

[362] ibid [55].

[363] ibid [74].

prior to *Digital Rights Ireland* on whether access conditions are outside the scope of the Directive or within the discretion accorded by it is resolved in favour of the latter, meaning that the Charter, under *NS*, became the relevant standard of review. The rebuttable presumption from *Solange II* and *Granital* has accordingly been sidelined given that the Court of Justice undertook the relevant fundamental rights review. From the perspective of the Court of Justice, however, the presumption remains influential only for situations outside the scope of EU law, which is now arguably the area of data retention, given that it has not been replaced by new EU legislation.[364]

Ordinary national courts remain in a relationship of coordination with the Court of Justice in relation to the interpretation of the rights to respect for private and family life and data protection, despite the possibly differing standards provided by constitutional courts prior to *Digital Rights Ireland*. In that sense, the constitutional court continues to be the undisputed final authority in fundamental rights protection solely for cases outside the scope of EU law.

### 4.2.3 Data Retention after the Annulment of the Directive

What happens in a situation when the national legislation continues to regulate the matter of data retention and what is the relevance of the Court's findings in *Digital Rights Ireland* in this context? In other words, is the regulation of data retention an implementation of EU law[365] or in any other way within its scope, so as to invite the application of the Charter in accordance with *Fransson*? The short answer is yes. A longer answer is contained in the Court of Justice's decision in *Tele2 Sverige and Watson*.[366]

This question reached the Court by way of two preliminary references, from Sweden and the United Kingdom respectively. With the Data Retention Directive gone, the two Member States were not among the above analysed group where constitutional and supreme courts annulled the implementing legislation. Rather, a data retention obligation still remained valid and the two courts asked the Court of Justice whether the findings from *Digital Rights Ireland* represent applicable limits to the national regulation of data retention. For the purposes of bringing this situation within the scope of EU law in the first place, the Swedish court also asked whether data retention falls in the scope of Article 15(1) of the e-Privacy Directive,[367] which allows for an exception to the secrecy of electronic communications.

364 Note that this will change after the *Tele 2 and Watson* decision of the Court of Justice to be discussed in the next section, as data retention will be further discussed in the context of Directive 2002/58/EC (n 291), save for the Czech Constitutional Court who remained at the stance that there is legislative space for Member States in this area.

365 This point was also explicitly raised by the United Kingdom Court of Appeal in the Watson preliminary reference to the Court of Justice. United Kingdom Court of Appeal Case *Watson* [2015] EWCA Civ 1185 [103].

366 Joined Cases C-203/15 and C-698/15 *Tele2 and Watson* [2016] EU:C:2016:970.

367 Directive 2002/58/EC (n 291).

The question whether national regulation falls in the scope of the Directive is an interesting continuation of the above discussion concerning the discretion of Member States to regulate access to retained data under the Data Retention Directive. Given that the court concluded in *Digital Rights Ireland* that the Directive lacked more detailed rules of access, it is of little surprise that it equally found that the subject matter of data retention falls in the scope of Article 15(1) of the e-Privacy Directive, given that it expressly provides for an exception to the overall aims of the Directive and authorizes Member States to regulate it.[368] This approach goes beyond the 'implementation of EU law' as the limit to the scope of the Charter,[369] but follows the *Fransson* approach of the Charter applying to areas 'covered by EU law'.[370]

Now that the Court established that data retention generally pertains to EU law, it was easy to conclude that the reasons for invalidating the Data Retention Directive constitute binding conditions for any future regulation of data retention on the national level.[371] The Court of Justice took a rather detailed approach in outlining what sort of data retention might in principle be strictly necessary for fighting serious crime, referring to *Digital Rights Ireland* again by analogy.[372] Importantly, the Court stressed that any such retention must be solely for the purpose of fighting serious crime, be subject to prior review by a court or an independent administrative authority, and be retained within the EU.[373] Yet, as of September 2017, not a single Member State made any legislative changes to address the novelties of *Tele2 and Watson* and only 40 per cent of Member States made some effort to incorporate *Digital Rights Ireland*.[374]

The UK Court of Appeal's Lord Lloyd-Jones reaction to the preliminary ruling may summarize well why the interpretation of data retention in the EU was far from resolved: 'I regret to say that the task now facing this court is far from easy in view of the fact that the preliminary ruling from the CJEU is lacking in clarity.'[375] The UK, French, and Belgian courts pursued further preliminary references to push the Court of Justice in expanding the possible justifications for data retention, such as terrorist threats or the protection of minors, decided in *Privacy International* and *Quadrature du Net*.[376]

[368] Joined Cases C-203/15 and C-698/15 *Tele2 Sverige and Watson* (n 366) [72]–[76].

[369] X Tracol, 'The Judgment of the Grand Chamber Dated 21 December 2016 in the Two Joint Tele2 Sverige and Watson Cases: The Need for a Harmonised Legal Framework on the Retention of Data at EU Level' (2017) 33 *Computer Law & Security Review* 541, 545.

[370] Case C-617/10 *Fransson* (n 120) [21].

[371] Joined Cases C-203/15 and C-698/15 *Tele2 Sverige and Watson* (n 366) [92].

[372] ibid [108]–[112].

[373] ibid [125].

[374] Privacy International, 'National Data Retention Laws since the CJEU's Tele-2/Watson Judgment: A Concerning State of Play for the Right to Privacy in Europe' (2017) 12, 14 https://privacyinternational.org/sites/default/files/2017-12/Data%20Retention_2017.pdf.

[375] United Kingdom Court of Appeal Case *Watson* [2018] EWCA Civ 70 [7].

[376] Case C-623/17 *Privacy International* [2020] EU:C:2020:790; Joined Cases C-511/18, C-512/18 and C-520/18 *Quadrature du Net* [2020] EU:C:2020:791. Both decisions were delivered on the same day.

Indiscriminate and general retention of data remains prohibited under EU law. However, the Court of Justice expanded on possible reasons for retention, by granting special status to national security, in comparison to other public policy interests listed in Article 15(1) of the e-Privacy Directive.[377] What is more, the Court found national security so compelling that it concluded that even indiscriminate data retention can be considered concretely connected to the existence of a serious threat.[378] Such retention needs to be subject to effective review as introduced in *Tele2 and Watson*. Beyond national security, other aims are not considered important enough to warrant indiscriminate retention, but must be confined to the *Tele2 and Watson* test of strict necessity.[379] Overall, the Court of Justice prioritized fundamental rights protection in the Charter over national security that arguably remains within exclusive Member State competence under Article 4(2) TEU.[380] The same approach was applied by the Court in respect of access to data in the conduct of criminal proceedings.[381]

A consequence of this approach may be a further EU-caused intra-state layering[382] between the judicial and the executive branch, visible from the follow-up decision of the French Conseil d'État in *Quadrature du Net*.[383] The French court rejected the request of the Prime Minister to conduct an *ultra vires* review of the Court of Justice's decision and the division of competences between the EU and its Member States.[384] However, it also straightforwardly applied the connection between indiscriminate retention and national security to confirm the validity of the national law, restricting itself to invalidating portions of the law that do not provide for regular review of the existing threat.[385] In that respect, the Court of Justice's decision in *Quadrature du Net* may be seen as a concession to the Member States and their national security concerns that are not yet comprehensively enough addressed at the EU level.[386] At the same time, the Court's insistence on judicial control of state surveillance measures can be seen as a reinforcement of judicial

377 Joined Cases C-511/18, C-512/18 and C-520/18 *Quadrature du Net* (n 376) [136].

378 ibid [137].

379 ibid [141]. M Zalnieriurte, 'A Struggle for Competence: National Security, Surveillance and the Scope of EU Law at the Court of Justice of European Union' (2022) 85(1) *Modern Law Review* 198, 207.

380 Zalnieriurte (n 379) 16.

381 Case C-746/18 *Prokuratuur* [2021] EU:C:2021:152. Three more preliminary references are currently pending before the Court of Justice: Case C-793/19 *SpaceNet* (reference from the German Supreme Administrative Court); Case C-794/19 *Telekom Deutschland* (reference from the German Supreme Administrative Court); Case C-140/20 *Commissioner of the Garda Síochána and Others* (reference from the Irish Supreme Court); Case C-334/21 *Criminal proceedings against GB, RH* (reference from the Italian second instance court). Zalnieriurte (n 379) 18.

382 Weiler (n 8) 27.

383 French Conseil d'État Decision No 393099 *Quadrature du Net* of 21 April 2021 https://www.conseil-etat.fr/fr/arianeweb/CE/decision/2021-04-21/393099. For identity review aspects of the case see ch 6, s 2.2.2.

384 ibid [8].

385 ibid [35], [46].

386 Zalnieriurte (n 379) 21.

cooperation in the EU, where national courts form part of the EU's multilevel judiciary, rather than part of the homogeneous Member State fabric.

## 5 Conclusion

'When it comes to protecting fundamental rights, the Court of Justice seeks to define the EU constitutional space without denying that EU law influences, *and is influenced by*, the legal orders that surround it.'[387] The view of the Court of Justice, thus, cannot develop in isolation from the national constitutional jurisprudence on the same matter. Accordingly, mutual trust cannot develop only in the Luxembourg bubble and we have in fact seen how incrementalism and constitutional dialogue function in the system of constitutional pluralism.

Lenaerts connects the principle of mutual trust to the equality of Member States enshrined in Article 4(2) TEU.[388] In his view, when equality of Member States is read together with their shared endorsement of the values in Article 2 TEU, mutual trust is a necessary result and 'a constitutional principle that pervades the entire ASFJ'.[389] However, mutual trust is not limitless. Chapter 6 addressed the role of the national identity clause in Article 4(2) TEU, which enshrines the justified limits to the application of EU law in a Member State through the public policy gateway, in accordance with the principle of proportionality.[390] Equally, mutual trust reaches its limit when its functioning becomes harmful to fundamental rights protection,[391] where the public policy is again used to safeguard these concerns. In both situations, the Court of Justice applies the proportionality test and in a careful balancing exercise decides on the extent of deference to the national status of fundamental rights protection.[392] On the national level, when the case is pending before the constitutional court, it applies a EU-friendly interpretation driven by mutual respect and the self-imposed obligation of restraint. There is no single ultimate arbiter for every situation. Rather, we can see the existence of a heterarchical constellation grounded in mutual respect and self-restraint. That is constitutional pluralism at its best.

The jurisprudence in the area of data retention equally portrays the enmeshed relationship between EU and national constitutional law and their mutual influence through permanent contestation and feedback. The Court of Justice was not able to disregard the position of constitutional courts faced with constitutionally

[387] Lenaerts (n 281) 807 (emphasis added).

[388] ibid 808–809.

[389] ibid 813. See also German Bundesverfassungsgericht Case *European Arrest Warrant* Dissenting Opinion of Judge Gerhardt (n 192) [189].

[390] See ch 6, s 3.1.

[391] Lenaerts (n 388) 823.

[392] As analysed in ch 3, s 4, all the interviewees at the Court of Justice confirmed they take particular care of national constitutional concerns when they are relevant for the case at hand.

problematic implementing legislation. As a result, the Charter itself was positioned as the champion of the right to respect private and family life and the right to data protection. In further interactions, the Court of Justice also could not remain indifferent to the need to protect national security and is incrementally expanding the options for national authorities to use data retention in a limited, Charter-compliant manner.

Judicial power relations are thus not influenced so much by the overlap of jurisdiction, but rather the appropriate standard of fundamental rights protection. In this respect, *Melloni* provides the ceiling for the application of national standards, with the aim of preserving the effectiveness and uniformity of EU law. Procedurally, however, the leverage favours constitutional courts, as the cases are more likely to reach them than the Court of Justice. Equally, the analysed case law suggests that national constitutional adjudicators will insist on a more detailed assessment of the individual circumstances of the case in relation to the status of fundamental rights protection,[393] as opposed to the focus on 'systemic deficiencies' by the Court of Justice, now enhanced as regards the right to an effective legal remedy (in accordance with *Jeremy F*) and inhumane and degrading treatment (in accordance with *Aranyosi and Căldăraru*). Thus, the Court of Justice and constitutional courts appear to be in complete balance of powers.

An analogous balance can be seen between the Court of Justice towards ordinary national courts, as they will be able to adhere to a high standard of fundamental rights protection, save for the exceptions incrementally and jointly developed by the Court of Justice and national constitutional adjudicators (as in data retention). *Melloni* in isolation would suggest that constitutionally protected rights are always to yield before the uniformity, effectiveness and primacy of EU law under the principle of mutual trust. Yet, the Court of Justice will at times defer to the national level of protection (*Jeremy F*), but only when given the opportunity by constitutional courts (unlike in *Mr R*). In other words, the Court of Justice has *Melloni* as its weapon of choice, while constitutional courts have sidestepping the preliminary reference procedure as theirs. It does not appear that any of the courts under analysis has so far abused the options available.

By contrast, the Bundesverfassungsgericht's approach is particularly instructive for heterarchy in constitutional pluralism. Specifically, while EU law more generally protects human dignity to a sufficient degree, it is only in exceptional cases, which do not undermine the validity of EU law, that the Basic Law will take precedence. In the same manner, the application of primacy that exceptionally disapplies a provision of the Basic Law does not render it invalid. Rather, the auto-correct function of constitutional pluralism balances out these respective claims to sovereignty, as they are both accommodated over time.

393 As was the case in *Mr R*.

In conclusion, the increased dependency of the Court of Justice on national courts, and in particular on courts with constitutional jurisdiction, is conducive to boosting mutual respect, self-restraint, and ultimately mutual accommodation—the features of the auto-correct function. In addition, the normative promise of constitutional pluralism goes beyond mere institutional conflict avoidance/resolution. In the area of fundamental rights review, the normative drive of pluralism strives to provide, following a careful balancing, the optimal level of fundamental rights protection.

# PART III
# CONCLUSIONS

# 8
# Judicial Triangles across Case Studies

> Thus we have on stage two men, each of whom knows nothing of what he believes the other knows, and to deceive each other reciprocally both speak in allusions, each of the two hoping (in vain) that the other holds the key to his puzzle.[1]

After first coming across the different instances of constitutional conflict in the European Union, I imagined the different courts' relationship precisely as the one between the two men Eco describes. To my mind, the courts under analysis were behaving in completely random and at times inexplicable ways: the Czech decision in *Landtová* seemed rushed, unnecessary, and poorly argued; the Spanish decision in *Melloni* overly submissive; and the Court of Justice's decision in *Mangold* mind-boggling and unconvincing. Then, the unusual suspect,[2] the Danish Højesteret, rejected the expansion of the general principles of EU law to horizontal situations in *Dansk Industri*. It seemed that all these courts were in vain attempting to deceive each other through various allusions of their approach to the principle of primacy, hoping it would result in an ultimate resolution of the puzzle: the constitutional matrix of the European Union. Yet, after years of examining the rich and vast jurisprudence of constitutional conflict, the situation now looks far less puzzling.

It has become clear that the courts under analysis do not share the ultimate rule of recognition, a *Grundnorm*, to which they all unconditionally adhere. They often do not even share the same methods of interpretation or the same degree of verbosity in presenting their views. Nevertheless, without a doubt they share the commitment to basic values contained in Article 2 TEU and ensure that in their work they carefully and respectfully carry out their tasks. More often than not, they all employ the same or similar vocabulary.

The main objective of this book was thus to determine the actual application of the principle of primacy of EU law by constitutional adjudicators in the European Union through a mutual feedback loop of contestation with the Court of Justice.

[1] U Eco, *The Island of the Day Before* (Vintage 1998) 399.

[2] See ch 5, s 6.3, where the analysis demonstrated that Danish courts more generally exhibit strong self-restraint in favour of the national parliament, and the Højesteret equally maintains a low profile as regards constitutional review.

*The Jurisprudence of Constitutional Conflict in the European Union*. Ana Bobić, Oxford University Press. © Ana Bobić 2022.
DOI: 10.1093/oso/9780192847034.003.0008

In so doing, I have relied upon the framework of constitutional pluralism, arguing it is both descriptively and normatively relevant for the web of relations in the European judicial space. Descriptively, it is characterized as a system in which we can observe a parallel operation of different constitutional sites claiming ultimate authority. These sites regularly engage in conflict, which is resolved incrementally through the auto-correct function, sustained in turn by the application of sincere cooperation and mutual respect. The actors in the system are in a relationship of heterarchy, as they continually change their ranking over time. Normatively, constitutional pluralism is comprised of a shared normative core codified in Article 2 TEU, representing the minimum requirements for Union membership. The emergence of constitutional conflict in this constellation is a regular and desirable feature of the system that promotes a dynamic development of law and puts in place checks and balances between different sites of constitutional authority. However, when constitutional conflict reaches such extremes that basic values from Article 2 TEU can no longer be respected even in their most minimalist interpretation and in addition lacks any trace of sincere cooperation and mutual respect, we are speaking of destructive conflict that can only be resolved jointly by political and legal means.

The analysis throughout this book has had the aim of corroborating the descriptive and normative side of constitutional pluralism, by looking at the way in which the principle of primacy works in the jurisprudence of the Court of Justice and national courts tasked with constitutional review. To this end, I have explored in detail the three areas of constitutional conflict—*ultra vires* review, identity review, and fundamental rights review—to provide further nuance in the analysis of the way the Court of Justice has expanded the self-referential system of the Treaties; the different limits that constitutional adjudicators have placed on the principle of primacy as a result; what possible solutions they envisage in the event of a constitutional conflict; and whether such solutions pertain to a constructive or destructive interpretation of the shared normative core codified in Article 2 TEU. In what follows, I will summarize the theoretical and the empirical findings of the book.

Descriptively, the theory of constitutional pluralism asserts that the European Union represents a political space with co-existing claims to sovereignty put forward by the Court of Justice and constitutional adjudicators of Member States. The question of the ultimate arbiter in the EU is not conclusively defined, meaning that the courts under analysis incrementally shift their positions over time in a heterarchical fashion. Without hierarchical superiority to hold the position of the final arbiter permanently and authoritatively, all courts take part in a mutual feedback through constructive contestation. In addition, in managing constitutional conflict, the participating courts are guided by mutual respect, the obligation of sincere cooperation, and a self-imposed obligation to avoid conflict. As the analysis in chapter 3 has shown, all the courts under analysis have put forward sovereignty claims, considering themselves to be ultimate arbiters in their respective jurisdictions. Equally, the Court of Justice has developed jurisprudence according to which it has made an analogous[3] claim to sovereignty by continually expanding the self-referential system of the Treaties.

Equally, all the courts under analysis have employed the vocabulary of mutual respect and self-restraint as principles guiding the management and resolution of constitutional conflict. Constitutional conflict materializes itself through incremental and permanent contestation and accommodation of opposing claims to sovereignty (the auto-correct function) that result in a coherent interpretation and application of Union law, but never without sidelining conferral as its defining principle. In *ultra vires* review, not only have Member States announced they will police the transfer of competences from the national to the EU level, but they have also found individual decisions of the Court of Justice outside the Treaty mandate. Yet, in all those cases, the finding was based on previously established standards of competence control, the Court of Justice was first involved through the preliminary reference procedure, and *ultra vires* review was an option available only to courts performing constitutional review, rather than ordinary courts.

In identity review, constitutional adjudicators on the national level are consistently re-emphasizing their prerogative to protect the constitutional core (the Portuguese and Italian constitutional courts have both recently included the constitutional identity discourse into their jurisprudence, whereas the Belgian Cour Constitutionnelle introduced constitutional core limits to the operation of the principle of primacy). Identity review on the EU level showed that the Court of Justice deferred to the national level to define the content of their specific constitutional values with wide discretion, and confined its role to ensuring a common denominator for the protection of such values through the proportionality test. This area of review has shown that, without the application of sincere cooperation and mutual respect, constitutional courts under the control of the executive can stretch constitutional identity beyond recognition and descend into destructive conflict. The usefulness of the auto-correct function in accommodating constitutional conflict stops here: judicial interactions in destructive conflict only legitimize the captured courts' decisions, while allowing them free reign to malform the rule of law according to the needs of authoritative tendencies of executive. Rather, destructive conflict demands joint political and legal action at both EU and national levels, top-down but also bottom-up, in order to sustain and further the cooperative nature of the EU's constitution, grounded heavily in individual rights enforcement.

Finally, in fundamental rights review, constitutional adjudicators on the national level enforced substantive limits to the principle of primacy grounded in a satisfactory level of fundamental rights protection. The Court of Justice has reacted by subscribing to the imperative of fundamental rights protection at the EU

[3] Albeit qualitatively not the same, or in the words of Walker, incommensurate. See the discussion in ch 3, s 1.

level. Through the incremental development of jurisprudence, and despite occasionally descending into constructive conflicts (for example, concerning the EAW Framework Decision and the Data Retention Directive), the landscape of fundamental rights protection has improved considerably due to the jurisprudence of constitutional conflict (for example, the Court of Justice's decisions in *Aranyosi and Căldăraru* and *CK*, as well as the annulment of the Data Retention Directive).

In all three areas of review, we can conclusively state that a heterarchical constellation is more conducive to cooperation, mutual respect, and the will to avoid conflict. The role of national constitutional adjudicators is to keep the Court of Justice in check and control its jurisprudence in a constructive manner. Conflict resolution should be guided and resolved through mutual negotiation, learning, open dialogue, and cross-examination. Ultimately, there is no single ultimate arbiter for every situation nor should there be one. Rather, we can see the existence of a heterarchical constellation—the potential of all the courts involved for being ranked in a number of different ways at different times—grounded in mutual respect and self-restraint. Even in destructive conflict, a hierarchical imposition of solutions sourced exclusively on the EU level results in further resistance by the national level to respect the rule of law. However, a heterarchical approach endorses the constitutional claim on the national level by promoting a cooperative solution to rule of law issues. For example, it would be impossible for the Court of Justice to expand the self-referential system of the Treaties concerning judicial independence had ordinary national courts in countries such as Poland and Romania not submitted numerous preliminary references to defend themselves from rule of law backsliding. In order for constitutional conflict to remain conducive to constructive contestation and feedback between EU and national courts, the relationship between them needs to remain heterarchical. I will thus now turn to the analysis of how power relations changed across time and area of review in the judicial triangle.

Heterarchy is defined as a relationship of elements to one another when they are unranked or they possess the ability to be ranked in a number of different ways. In practice, this means that we cannot ascribe ultimate superiority neither to the national nor the EU claim to ultimate authority. Rather, both levels of constitutional authority possess the potential of prevailing in single points of conflict, whereas incrementally we are able to see a balance of these claims through the application of mutual respect and sincere cooperation. This ultimately means there are no predetermined winners and losers, but rather, different courts will have the final say at different times.

As will become visible throughout the analysis of different constellations of the judicial triangle, heterarchy pervades the power relations between the courts under analysis. The different judicial triangles placed alongside each other will enable us to see power relations changing over time as if they were in a flipbook animation. It will become vividly clear that there is no balanced triangle, as power relations are always skewed at individual points of conflict. The auto-correct function of constitutional pluralism instead shows us that, when regarded in the aggregate, the triangles demonstrate a balance.

## 1 *Ultra Vires* Review

First, *ultra vires* review addresses the structural view of the relationship between the EU and the national level, and may be seen as a representation of the underlying struggle in the relationship between the Court of Justice and national courts with constitutional jurisdiction. This struggle is sourced in the contradiction between the principle of conferral and the exclusive power of the Court of Justice to interpret EU law (under Article 19 TEU) joined by extension with the power to annul EU law (following *Foto-Frost*). *Ultra vires* review is also content-neutral, as it can result in both more and less integration. National case law has demonstrated that the Court of Justice does not operate in a vacuum: its expansive interpretations of the self-referential system of the Treaties are constructively contested by national courts. The judicial triangle in Figure 8.1 thus looks at the power relations after the introduction of primacy and direct effect by the Court of Justice.

Direct effect and primacy can be seen as the original expansion by the Court of Justice of the self-referential system of the Treaties, one to trigger all future constitutional conflicts to arise. This is so given the consequences that individual judicial enforcement had for national judiciaries. In that sense, the thick arrow 1 demonstrates the newly established relationship between the Court of Justice and ordinary national courts, who are able to bypass constitutional courts through the use of the preliminary reference procedure and their respect of direct effect of EU law. The weaker arrow 2 shows us the resulting reduced influence of constitutional courts, in particular taking into account the wide-reaching finding of

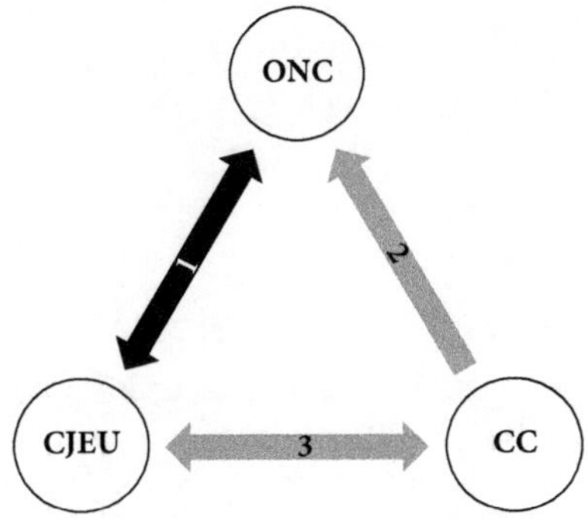


**Figure 8.1** Power relations in the judicial triangle after *Van Gend en Loos*, *Costa v ENEL*, and *Internationale Handelsgesellschaft*

*Internationale Handelsgesellschaft* that every and any provision of national (constitutional) law is to yield before EU law. Constitutional review remains influential up to the point where a matter is regulated by EU law. The Court of Justice's new relationship with ordinary national courts placed it in interpretative competition with the constitutional court and we can conclude that at this point in time, the power relations are imbalanced to the benefit of the Court of Justice.

The situation shifted in favour of constitutional courts (both vis-à-vis ordinary national courts and the Court of Justice) in cases that concern pending Treaty amendments, as shown in Figure 8.2.

The thicker of the two arrows (arrow 3) represents the leverage of constitutional adjudicators. With respect to cases concerning Treaty amendments pending ratification, they are the only ones empowered to determine the constitutional limits to integration. This makes the mandate of the Court of Justice conditional upon the acceptance of the proposed Treaty change by the constitutional court. Nevertheless, as the analysis of the case law has shown, national constitutional courts demonstrated awareness of the need for the respect of the principle of sincere cooperation and mutual respect, and none of them have yet taken advantage of their privileged position in this context (illustrated by the white arrow 3). Secondly, the relationship between constitutional adjudicators and ordinary national courts in situations of constitutional review of Treaty amendments is one of classic hierarchy, without the imbalance introduced by the preliminary reference procedure (arrow 2). Finally, ordinary national courts are still in the relationship of cooperation with the Court of Justice as regards the *acquis communautaire* (arrow 1), but this relationship is weakened by the hypothetical possibility that the constitutional court rejects the Treaty amendment or imposes qualifications on the existing EU law obligations for ordinary national courts. The leverage in this constellation shifts to the benefit of the constitutional court.

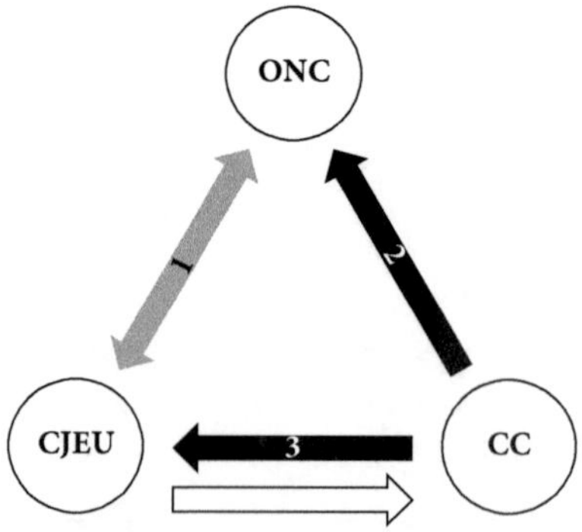


**Figure 8.2** Power relations in the judicial triangle in the context of a Treaty amendment pending ratification

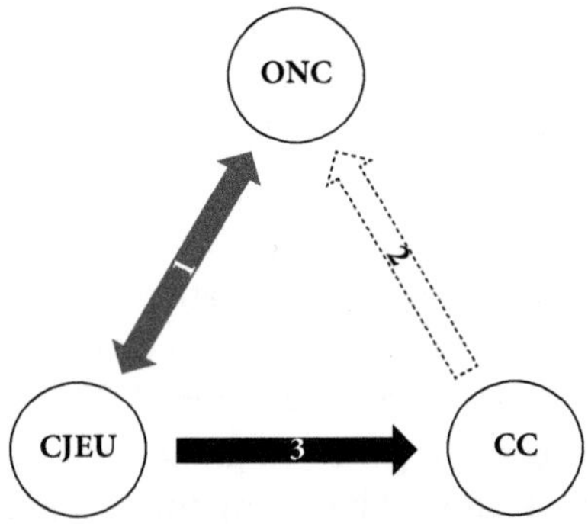


**Figure 8.3** Power relations in the judicial triangle after *Mangold* and *Maruko*

The power balance, however, shifted back to the Court of Justice after its decision on expanding the applicability of the general principle of non-discrimination based on age to horizontal situations in *Mangold* and the general principle of non-discrimination to areas of exclusive Member State competence in *Maruko*. These are depicted in Figure 8.3.

Ordinary national courts are bound to apply the general principle of non-discrimination on grounds of age to vertical and horizontal situations alike, so long as the situation is within the scope of EU law. In systems of majoritarian democracy such as Denmark and the United Kingdom, this extension is exacerbated by the strong position of the parliament that is expected to step in through authoritative legislative action, rather than the supreme court (as it later transpired in Denmark). Yet, so long as this does not take place, ordinary national courts are more likely to abide by the requirements of EU law. In systems of constitutional democracy, the distance of ordinary national courts from the influence of constitutional courts is stretched further through the application of the general principle of non-discrimination to areas of exclusive Member State competence. This is so given that non-discrimination cases usually involve a fundamental rights breach where constitutional courts were previously an undisputed final authority, and as was visible in *Dansk Industri*, countervailing constitutional principles were in this jurisprudence of the Court of Justice not taken into account.

The relationship between the constitutional court and the Court of Justice in this particular triangle favours the latter, due to the expansion of the self-referential system of the Treaties that further extends into the jurisdiction of constitutional courts. The same power constellation can be applied to the later expansions of the Court of Justice concerning the general applicability of rule of law and judicial independence. Constitutional courts have in that context acquired additional obligations stemming from EU law. However, given that these latter expansions align with EU membership criteria, it is to be assumed that this expansion will have little practical significance unless conditions of judicial independence and the rule of law are reduced to a problematic level amounting to destructive constitutional conflict.

The Court of Justice has gained similar leverage to that depicted in Figure 8.3 as a consequence of finding an infringement of EU law when the last instance court did not submit a preliminary reference (in *Commission v France*). In situations of constructive constitutional conflict, an obligation to submit a preliminary reference most commonly means that both levels of judiciary can take part in the interpretation of the common content of the EU constitution. The enforcement of this obligation through infringement proceedings, however, needs to be used with utmost care to prevent the creation of hierarchy among the courts claiming ultimate authority in the same political space.

The next triangle (Figure 8.4) is instructive of the dynamic and heterarchical nature of power relations in the EU's judicial space. Constitutional courts introduced their standards of *ultra vires* review and Danish and German courts applied them to decisions of the Court of Justice.

The analysed case law demonstrated that national courts with constitutional jurisdiction have not fully accepted the Court of Justice's case law on general principles and monetary policy. Hence, the black arrow (arrow 3) represents not only a theoretical power of *ultra vires* review, which is an indication of power leverage in itself, but also the position of the ultimate arbiter on behalf of those constitutional adjudicators that have found individual decisions of the Court of Justice outside the Treaty mandate. In line with the vocabulary analysis in chapter 3, however, this power is not absolute, hence the second arrow 3. National courts will perform *ultra vires* review only in exceptional circumstances and will reach their conclusion in line with the principle of sincere cooperation (by always submitting a preliminary reference to the Court of Justice first), EU-friendly interpretation, and the will to avoid conflict if possible: all restraining elements of national constitutional jurisprudence in line with the auto-correct function of constitutional pluralism.

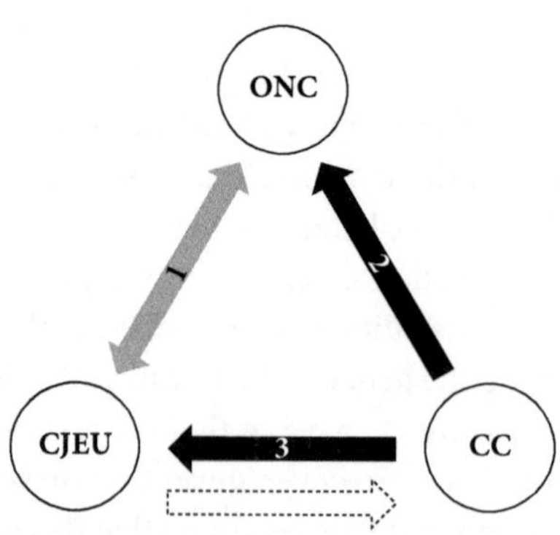


**Figure 8.4** Power relations in the judicial triangle after *Dansk Industri* and *Weiss II*

Ordinary national courts remain in the relationship of cooperation with the Court of Justice through the preliminary reference procedure (arrow 1), although it remains to be seen if this relationship will be influenced by the *ultra vires* decisions of constitutional/supreme courts. Expectations for the future diverge slightly depending on the national constitutional setting, as in systems of majoritarian democracies we can expect deference towards the parliament rather than the supreme court. The opposite is true in constitutional democracies, where the constitutional court retains the power of constitutional review of parliamentary acts. Finally, constitutional adjudicators have strengthened their position in relation to ordinary national courts (arrow 2), by placing limits on the operation of the principle of primacy in cases of competence conflicts and assuming exclusive jurisdiction to conduct such review.

*Ultra vires* review has brought about one final power constellation (Figure 8.5) that manifests itself in a situation of destructive conflict, such as we have seen in Poland and Romania.

In response to the Court of Justice's expansions of rule of law and judicial independence obligations regardless of the applicability of EU law in a specific case, the Polish Supreme Court declared a decision of the Court of Justice void without submitting a preliminary reference or even setting out the standard for its review. In a similar manner, the Romanian Constitutional Court stated that primacy of EU law does not apply to any act that passed muster of constitutional review. Here, both national courts refused to apply any of the interpretative tools that form part of the auto-correct function and enable judicial accommodation of constructive conflict. This removed the link between the Court of Justice and the constitutional court in question.

To defend themselves against independence attacks carried out by the executive and supported by constitutional courts, ordinary national courts have taken it upon themselves to protect their position by submitting numerous preliminary

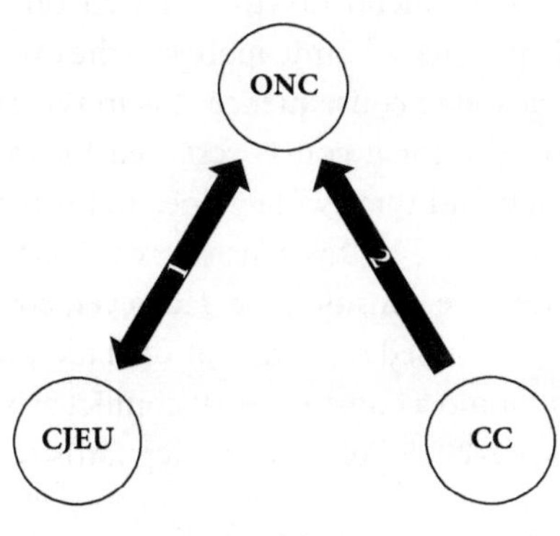


**Figure 8.5** Power relations in a situation of destructive constitutional conflict in *ultra vires* review

references to the Court of Justice, which in turn strengthened their cooperative relationship, visible by arrow 1. However, the disciplinary tools against ordinary judges made available to constitutional courts by the executive equally reinforced arrow 2. The lack of arrow 3 depicts the inability of the auto-correct function to resolve destructive conflicts through judicial accommodation, as there is no sincere cooperation and mutual respect between the constitutional court and the Court of Justice. As reiterated numerous times throughout this book, such situations demand collective political and legal action both at the EU and national level.

## 2 Identity Review

The jurisprudence of identity review demonstrated in essence two different approaches. First, constitutional courts maintained a view that constitutional identity does not necessarily correspond to national identity protected by Article 4(2) TEU, but is rather found in provisions with stronger constitutional entrenchment that cannot be influenced by the primacy of EU law. The second line of interpretation (by the Court of Justice and some constitutional courts) offers a congruent understanding of Article 4(2) TEU, according to which the concept of fundamental political and constitutional structures also encompasses core constitutional values of Member States.

The analysis of judicial triangles in identity review will thus start with the power relations that result from the first interpretation of constitutional identity. We have seen this materialize in decisions of constitutional courts in Germany and Poland (pre-2015) when reviewing a Treaty amendment pending ratification[4] and in the review of EU secondary legislation and implementing legislation. Figure 8.6 depicts power relations in a situation where constitutional courts review secondary EU law and national implementing legislation against constitutional identity.

While constitutional adjudicators carry out a review of valid EU acts, they appear reluctant to find them unconstitutional based on constitutional identity. A conclusion that an identity-based limit applies to the exercise of EU competence carries permanent and absolute consequences (as in the case of Germany for example). In addition, constitutional courts reserved for themselves the power of identity review when they find that EU law does not provide for equivalent protection (for example in France). In this sense, arrow 3 is black because powers of constitutional adjudicators are considerable. However, constitutional courts have not applied limits to EU law based on constitutional identity, but have introduced reconciliatory methods should a constitutional conflict arise in the area of identity review (for example, in pre-2015 Poland) or safeguards such as first submitting a

[4] See Figure 8.2 above for the analysis of power relations in this situation.

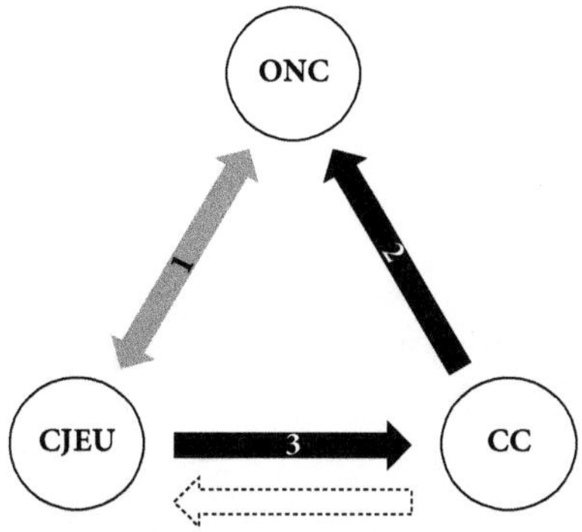


**Figure 8.6** Power relations in the judicial triangle in the context of constitutional identity review

preliminary reference (for example in Italy or Portugal). Thus, constitutional courts tend to practice self-restraint and defer to the exclusive jurisdiction of the Court of Justice to interpret and annul EU legislation, hence the second white arrow 3.

The Court of Justice is (per *Foto-Frost*) the exclusive institution which may invalidate an EU act, thus retaining influence on ordinary national courts (arrow 1). Yet, the same arrow is two-directional, illustrating the dependency of the Court of Justice on national courts to submit a preliminary reference concerning the validity of an EU act. Finally, arrow 2 depicts the power of constitutional adjudicators to mandate constitutional review and interpretation upon ordinary national courts and an obligation for the latter to seek review from the constitutional court rather than the Court of Justice (as in Italy, for example).

The next triangle focuses on power relations that result from the Court of Justice's case law concerning Article 4(2) TEU (Figure 8.7).

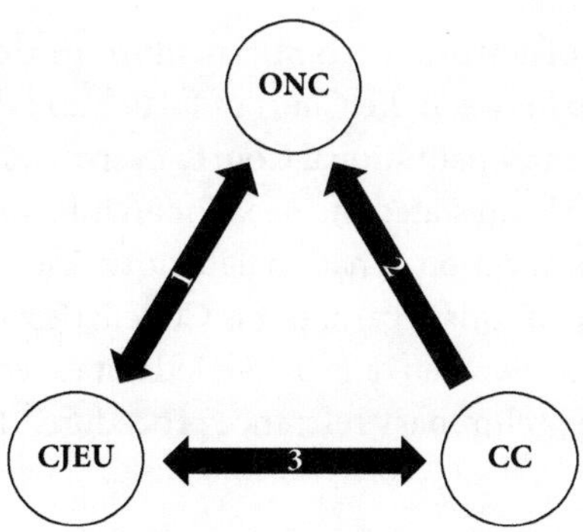


**Figure 8.7** Power relations in the judicial triangle as regards the Court of Justice's interpretation of Article 4(2) TEU

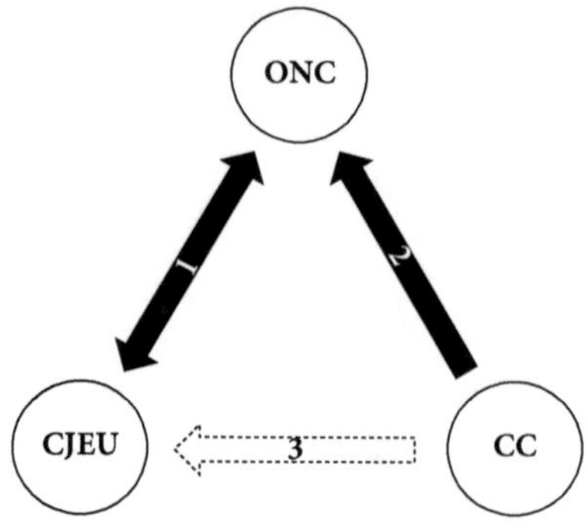


**Figure 8.8** Power relations in a situation of a potentially destructive constitutional conflict in identity review

This situation demonstrates an almost complete balance of powers between the constitutional court and the Court of Justice. Arrow 3 represents the division of tasks in the interpretation of Article 4(2) TEU, according to which the national constitutional adjudicator defines the national value, while the Court of Justice applies the proportionality test as to the limits within which this value can be protected. In essence, their relationship is cooperative and is in addition supported by the role of ordinary national courts who most commonly submit a preliminary reference where the interpretation of Article 4(2) TEU is triggered (arrow 1). Finally, arrow 2 depicts the power of constitutional adjudicators to mandate constitutional interpretation and review upon ordinary national courts, but only to the limit of the principle of proportionality as interpreted by the Court of Justice (as was the case in *Coman*).

The final judicial triangle (Figure 8.8) again brings us to a potential destructive constitutional conflict in the area of identity review, as we have seen in the Hungarian open-ended interpretation of constitutional identity concerning the refugee allocation scheme.

Unlike in a situation of destructive conflict in *ultra vires* review, there is still a possibility of a relationship between the Court of Justice and the constitutional court, given that the Hungarian Constitutional Court nevertheless connected identity review to Article 4(2) TEU and stated the need for an informal cooperation with the Court of Justice in the protection of national identity. The Hungarian court also referred to mutual respect in this regard. In his Concurring Opinion, Judge Dienes-Oehm added that such review can only be carried out exceptionally, and if need be, after making use of the preliminary reference procedure.[5] Furthermore, the Court

[5] Concurring Opinion of Judge Dienes-Oehm in Hungarian Magyarország Alkotmánybírósága Judgment No 22/2016 *Refugee Allocation Scheme* of 5 December 2016 https://hunconcourt.hu/uploads/sites/3/2017/11/en_22_2016-1.pdf [76], [82].

of Justice maintains influence in cooperation with the Commission through the use of the infringement procedure.[6]

Both the constitutional court and the Court of Justice maintain a strong influence on ordinary national courts: the Court of Justice through the preliminary reference procedure[7] and the constitutional court by the authority of the national constitution and the resulting judicial hierarchy (arrows 1 and 2, respectively). In this respect, this conflict still holds the potential of judicial accommodation through mutual respect and sincere cooperation.

## 3 Fundamental Rights Review

The normative argument of constitutional pluralism is most visible in fundamental rights review, where Article 2 TEU and the Charter represent the shared values that both Member States and the EU are striving to protect. The normative strength of fundamental rights review in the pluralist constellation also stems from the high degree of contestation from the national level that pushed the progress on the EU level. Power relations have as a result changed considerably over time, with the first judicial triangle depicting the state of play at the very beginning of European integration (Figure 8.9).

The power relations among the courts under analysis are balanced as both the Court of Justice and national constitutional courts have their respective spheres of authority. Arrow 3 thus represents a lack of overlap in jurisdiction to perform the fundamental rights review, meaning that each of the courts retains influence

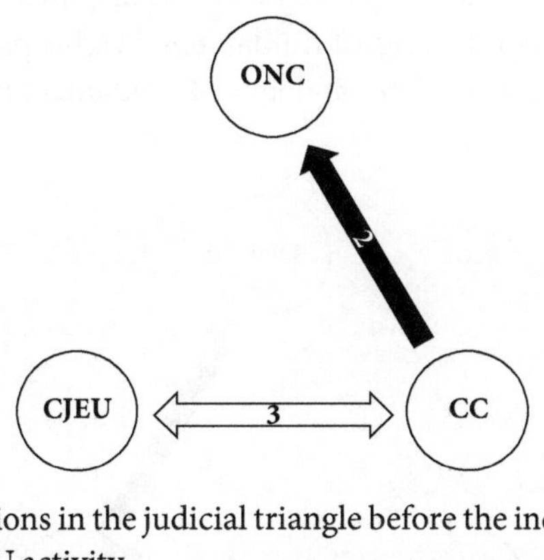


**Figure 8.9** Power relations in the judicial triangle before the inclusion of fundamental rights in the scope of EU activity

[6] See eg Case C-808/18 *Commission v Hungary* [2020] EU:C:2020:1029.

[7] See eg Joined Cases C-924/19 PPU and C-925/19 PPU *FMS, FNZ, SA, SA Junior* [2020] EU:C:2020:367.

in their sphere of competence. The constitutional court is at the top of the national judicial hierarchy, and their constitutional fundamental rights protection is at this point in time not affected by the principle of primacy of EU law. The constitutional court remains an undisputed final authority over ordinary national courts in the area of fundamental rights, hence arrow 2 is pointing in only one direction. The Court of Justice's authority towards ordinary national courts when it comes to fundamental rights protection does not yet exist, hence there is no arrow between them.

This original position has changed after the decisions of the German and Italian constitutional courts in *Solange I* and *Frontini* as depicted in Figure 8.10.

The power leverage in this period favours constitutional courts. Arrow 3 illustrates the power of the constitutional court to review EU legislation against the constitutional standard of fundamental rights protection, given that the EU standard is at this point in time not considered to provide equivalent protection. Nevertheless, given that the Court of Justice in *Stauder* decided that EU action must comply with fundamental rights that form part of general principles of EU law, the second arrow 3 depicts the commitment of the Court of Justice to ensure that fundamental rights are not breached by EU action.

The relationship between ordinary national courts and the Court of Justice changed insofar as the former, in submitting a preliminary reference, are to follow the findings of the Court of Justice concerning fundamental rights (arrow 1). This arrow is however dashed, given that the ordinary national court would be obliged to follow the constitutional court should it find that an EU measure violates the constitutional standard of fundamental rights protection (illustrated in turn by arrow 2). The position of the constitutional court is accordingly strengthened in relation to ordinary national courts, as it is the undisputed final authority over ordinary national courts in the area of fundamental rights protection, since the EU does not (yet) have an appropriate catalogue of fundamental rights.

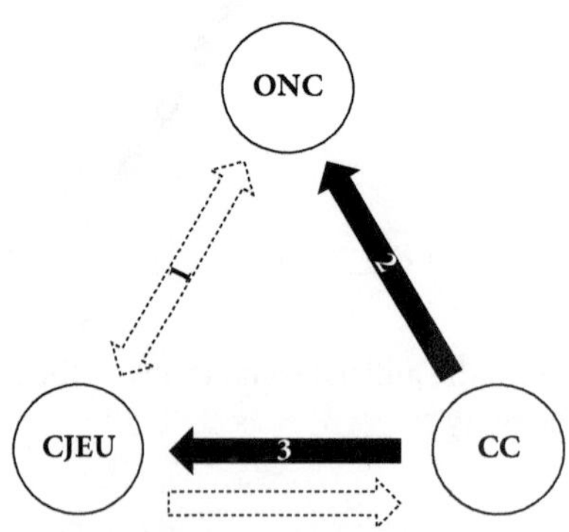


**Figure 8.10** Power relations in the judicial triangle after *Stauder*, *Solange I*, and *Frontini*

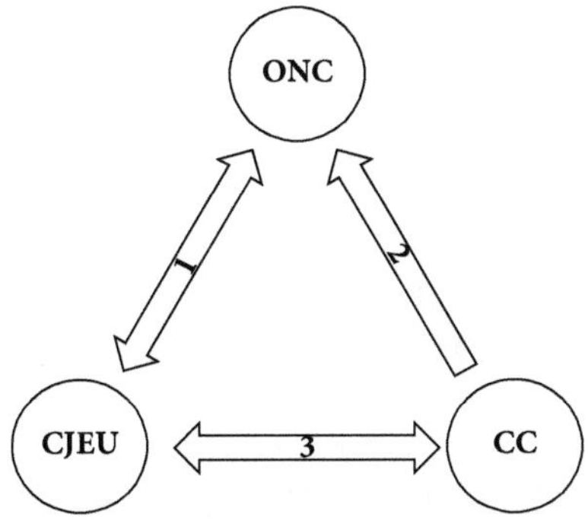


**Figure 8.11** Power relations in the judicial triangle after *Nold, Solange II*, and *Granital*

As we have seen in Chapter 7, contestation from the national level concerning the appropriate fundamental rights catalogue at the EU level prompted the Court of Justice to revisit its approach. In *Nold*, common constitutional traditions of Member States were flagged as the inspiration for determining the level of fundamental rights protection that the Court of Justice will protect. In response, the German and Italian courts (in *Solange II* and *Granital* respectively) reversed the rebuttable presumption from *Solange I* and *Frontini*, by placing trust in the Court of Justice to ensure fundamental rights protection in EU action, retaining the right to review it only exceptionally. The ensuing power relations are illustrated in Figure 8.11.

The judicial power relations at this point in time are entirely in balance. This balance is however sourced in a different legal structure, as the spheres of jurisdiction of the Court of Justice and constitutional courts now overlap. Nevertheless, the relationship between their opposing claims to fundamental rights review is heterarchical, as the jurisprudence on both levels leaves open the possibility of such review under specific circumstances. For the Court of Justice, this is a situation when EU law allegedly breaches fundamental rights. For constitutional courts, this is the situation when the standard of fundamental rights protection on the EU level sinks below the constitutional level of protection.

Arrow 1 depicts the relationship of cooperation of ordinary national courts with the Court of Justice, which will only be put in question if the presumption established by *Solange II* and *Granital* is rebutted. Otherwise their relationship is cooperative and sustained by the preliminary reference procedure. The constitutional court remains the undisputed final authority for ordinary national courts in fundamental rights review of national law (arrow 2). Finally, the constitutional court will exhibit self-restraint in matters of EU law, according to the presumption, whereas the Court of Justice will safeguard the standard of fundamental rights protection in line with the standard of national constitutions (arrow 3).

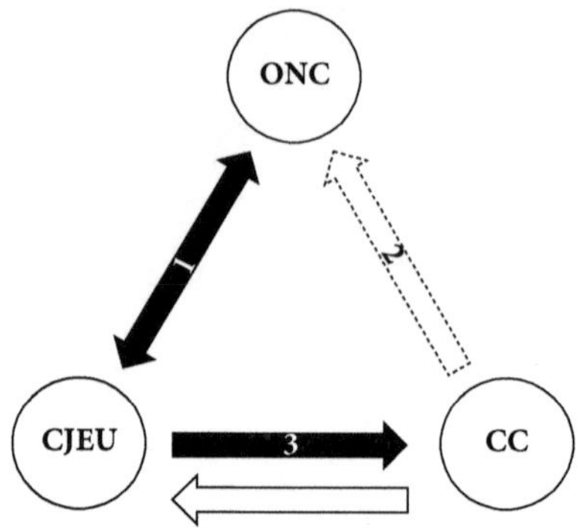


**Figure 8.12** Power relations in the judicial triangle after *Wachauf* and *ERT*

In an expansion of the self-referential system of the Treaties, the Court of Justice subsequently introduced fundamental rights review of national measures when they implement (*Wachauf*) or derogate (*ERT*) from EU law obligations. This shifted the power relations in the judicial triangle, as in Figure 8.12.

As seen from the thick arrows in the triangle (1 and 3), the leverage in this triangle is on the side of the Court of Justice. First, it has the advantage in relation to constitutional courts (black arrow 3) thanks to the presumption of compliance with constitutional protection of fundamental rights, per *Solange II* and *Granital*. Secondly, it now also has the advantage of reviewing national measures implementing or derogating from EU law that may have not been questioned for their constitutionality on the national level. This results in a more influential relationship towards ordinary national courts, as they will be bound by the fundamental rights review of national measures carried out by the Court of Justice.

Constitutional courts remain firmly influential towards their ordinary national courts solely in situations of constitutional review of measures that fall outside the scope of EU law, which results in an additional decrease of their authority in the national judicial hierarchy (arrow 2). Yet, the existence of the rebuttable presumption from *Solange II* and *Granital* maintained some influence of constitutional courts towards the Court of Justice (white arrow 3). Finally, the power of the Court of Justice to review national measures has increased the overlap of its jurisdiction with that of national courts performing constitutional review. Constitutional pluralism presupposes such an overlap, whereas in line with the definition of heterarchy, now it was the Court of Justice that had the upper hand. Having established the catalogue of fundamental rights (per *Nold*), and the scope of fundamental rights review of both EU and national measures in the scope of EU law (per *Internationale Handelsgesellschaft*, *Wachauf*, and *ERT*), the Court of Justice holds most influence in the judicial triangle at this point in time.

This power constellation changed with the national review of the European Arrest Warrant Framework Decision, originally enacted in the former third pillar

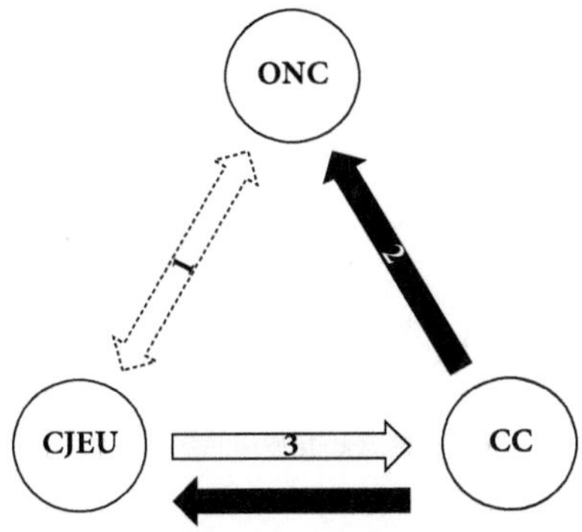


**Figure 8.13** Power relations in the judicial triangle after national EAW decisions

where direct effect and primacy did not apply prior to the entry into force of the Lisbon Treaty. Constitutional courts accordingly regained leverage in the judicial triangle by reviewing the EAW Framework Decision against constitutionally protected fundamental rights (Figure 8.13).

The power relations in this judicial triangle favour national constitutional adjudicators, albeit not absolutely. In this respect, arrow 3 is comprised of a black arrow, depicting the leverage of the constitutional court over the Court of Justice in terms of the legal status of third pillar acts, similarly to the position of Treaty revisions pending national ratification. However, taking into account *Pupino,* the white arrow 3 represents the limit placed by the obligation of consistent interpretation for the constitutional court. At this point in time, however, *Pupino* has not proven itself effective in the national constitutional review of the EAW Framework Decision, save for a mention by the Czech *Ústavní Soud.* Arrow 2 represents the analogous authority of the constitutional court towards ordinary national courts, given the legal status of the third pillar and the constitutional status of fundamental rights protection. Arrow 1 thus signifies the weakest relationship, as ordinary national courts are bound by *Pupino* up to the point where an EU-consistent interpretation would be *contra legem.* Equally, there is little basis for ordinary national courts to decide contrary to the interpretation mandated by the constitutional court.

The introduction of the Charter of Fundamental Rights and its entry into force alongside the Lisbon Treaty created new questions concerning the limits of the self-referential system of the Treaties: when does the Charter apply and where are its limits? The Court of Justice used this opportunity to provide a generous interpretation of Article 51(1) of the Charter determining its scope of application, strengthening further its position in the judicial triangle (Figure 8.14).

The leverage on behalf of the Court of Justice (black arrow 3) rests on the case law establishing that fundamental rights review will be carried out in relation to all national measures in the scope of EU law, regardless of whether the measure is

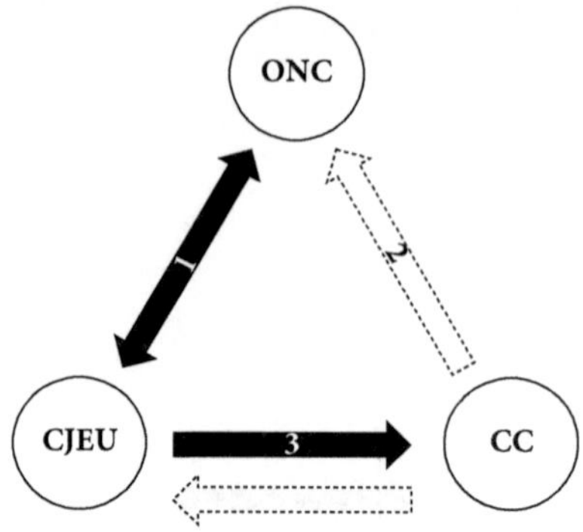


**Figure 8.14** Power relations in the judicial triangle after *Fransson* and *Siragusa*

implementing, derogating from, or is connected to EU law in some other way (per *Estov*, *Kücükdeveci*, *NS*, and *Fransson*). The importance of the rebuttable presumption from *Solange II* and *Granital* has accordingly been diminished (dashed arrow 3). From the perspective of the Court of Justice, however, the presumption remains influential only for situations outside the scope of EU law. One remaining reservation of a disproportionate intrusion of the Court of Justice into the traditionally exclusive realm for constitutional courts is *Iida*, requiring the Court of Justice more specifically to justify undertaking the review.

Arrow 1 represents the relationship of coordination between ordinary national courts and the Court of Justice, in relation to the review of both EU and national measures when in the scope of EU law. Ordinary national courts will be bound by the jurisprudence of the Court of Justice despite a possible contrary interpretation provided by their constitutional court. In that sense, Arrow 2 depicts the remaining influence of the constitutional court towards ordinary national courts, as it continues to be the undisputed final authority in fundamental rights protection for cases outside the scope of EU law.

Judicial interactions concerning the Data Retention Directive demonstrated the power of mutual contestation and feedback between the national and EU level in promoting the normative core of EU's constitution broadly understood. After the enactment of the Directive, a number of national constitutional courts took issue with implementing legislation and the position of the right to privacy and family life as well as data protection. Power relations resulting from this contestation are presented in Figure 8.15.

The power relations in this judicial triangle favour national constitutional adjudicators, albeit not absolutely. In this respect, arrow 3 is comprised of a black arrow, depicting the leverage of the constitutional courts over the Court of Justice given that they all reviewed national implementing legislation and could apply constitutional, rather than EU, fundamental rights standards. Regardless of whether they

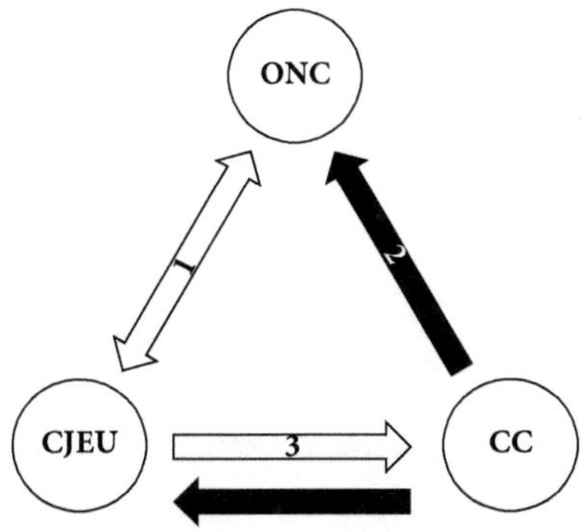


**Figure 8.15** Power relations in the judicial triangle after national constitutional courts' annulment of legislation implementing the Data Retention Directive

characterized the regulation of access to retained data as outside the scope of the Directive or as an exercise of the wide discretion accorded by it, no national court considered that a preliminary reference, and by extension the interpretation of EU law, is necessary. However, taking into account that the Data Retention Directive is the shared reason why any of the legislation was under review in the first place, the white arrow 3 represents the limit placed by the obligation of consistent EU-friendly interpretation for the constitutional court. This can be evidenced by the avoidance of review of the Directive itself, given the division of tasks between the Court of Justice and national courts under Article 19(1) TEU and the decision in *Foto-Frost*. Arrow 2 represents the analogous authority of the constitutional court towards ordinary national courts, given the constitutional status of fundamental rights protection and the finding that the legislation is outside the scope of the Directive. Arrow 1 thus signifies the weakest relationship, as ordinary national courts did not submit preliminary references to challenge the findings of their constitutional courts and their interpretations of fundamental rights that have been found outside the scope of the Directive.

Ultimately, the Austrian Constitutional Court and the Irish Supreme Court submitted preliminary references concerning the compliance of the Directive itself with the Charter. The Court of Justice thus regained a degree of leverage in the judicial triangle (Figure 8.16).

The Court of Justice's influence over constitutional courts (black arrow 3) is increased inasmuch as it is now established that the Data Retention Directive was subject to the requirements of the Charter and is thus taken out of the scope of fundamental rights review under national constitutions. The doubt encountered prior to *Digital Rights Ireland* on whether access conditions are outside the scope of the Directive or within the discretion accorded by it is resolved in favour of the latter, meaning that the Charter, under *NS*, becomes the relevant standard of review. The

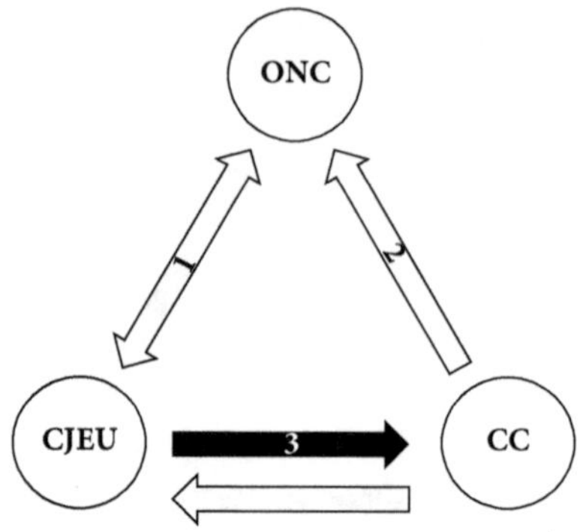


**Figure 8.16** Power relations in the judicial triangle after *Digital Rights Ireland*

rebuttable presumption from *Solange II* and *Granital* has accordingly been sidelined given that the Court of Justice undertook the relevant fundamental rights review. From the perspective of the Court of Justice, however, the presumption remains influential only for situations outside the scope of EU law, which is now arguably the area of data retention, given that it has not been replaced by new EU legislation (hence the white arrow 3).

Arrow 1 represents the relationship of coordination between ordinary national courts and the Court of Justice, in relation to the interpretation of the rights to private and family life and data protection, despite the possible differing standards provided by constitutional courts prior to *Digital Rights Ireland*. In that sense, Arrow 2 depicts the remaining influence of the constitutional court towards ordinary national courts, as it continues to be the undisputed final authority in fundamental rights protection solely for cases outside the scope of EU law, which is, based on subsequent findings in *Tele2/Watson* and *La Quadrature du Net*, limited to areas of national security.

The final judicial triangle will address the power relations in situations where national constitutional courts protect national security and the rights of the accused in the criminal procedure (Figure 8.17).

The power relations are at this point in time not influenced so much by the overlap of jurisdiction, but rather the appropriate standard of fundamental rights protection. In this respect, *Melloni* provides the ceiling for the application of national standards, for the purpose of preserving the effectiveness and uniformity of EU law. Procedurally, however, the leverage favours constitutional courts, as the cases are more likely to reach them than the Court of Justice (arrow 3). Equally, the analysed case law suggests that national constitutional adjudicators will insist on a more detailed assessment of the individual circumstances of the case in relation to the status of fundamental rights protection (as in *Mr R*), as opposed to the focus on 'systemic deficiencies' by the Court of Justice, now enhanced as regards the right to

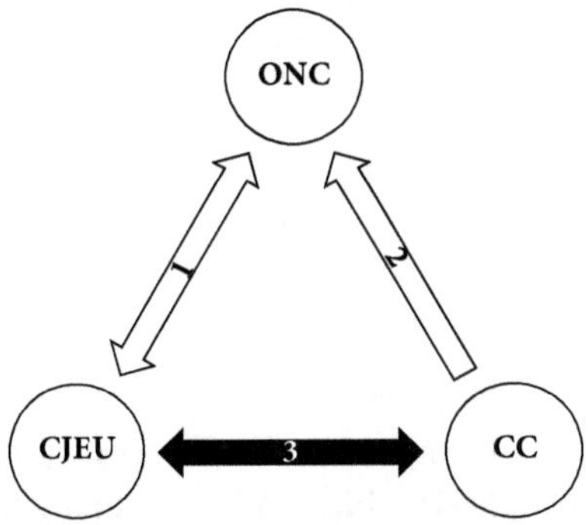


**Figure 8.17** Power relations in the judicial triangle *Jeremy F*, *Mr R*, and *La Quadrature du Net* (Conseil d'État)

an effective legal remedy (per *Jeremy F*) and inhumane and degrading treatment (per *Aranyosi and Căldăraru*). Thus, the Court of Justice and constitutional courts appear to be in complete balance of powers. Arrows 1 and 2 are illustrating the analogous balance towards ordinary national courts, as they will be able to adhere to a high standard of fundamental rights protection, save for the exceptions incrementally and jointly developed by the Court of Justice and national constitutional adjudicators. *Melloni* in isolation would suggest that constitutionally protected rights are always to yield before the uniformity, effectiveness, and primacy of EU law under the principle of mutual trust. Yet, the Court of Justice will at times defer to the national level of protection (*Jeremy F*), but only when given the opportunity by constitutional courts (unlike in *Mr R*). In other words, the Court of Justice has *Melloni* as its weapon of choice, while constitutional courts have sidestepping the preliminary reference procedure as theirs.

# 9
# Three Lessons and a Warning

The metamorphosing nature of power relations in the European judicial space provides valuable lessons about the nature of the EU's constitution and the central role that constitutional conflict plays within it. Were we to flip through the illustrations of all the triangles presented and analysed, what would emerge is an animation of power leverage permanently shifting between the Court of Justice and national courts performing constitutional review. We were also able to see the ways in which judicial triangles sustain the descriptive and normative premises of constitutional pluralism in accounting for heterarchy, the auto-correct function, as well as constructive and destructive contestations in judicial interactions. What I would like to do in this final chapter of the book is to summarize three lessons and a warning ensuing from the jurisprudence of constitutional conflict in the EU.

The first lesson is nuance. Power relations in the judicial triangle shift not only between actors, but also over time and across areas of review. Not only is it impossible to define the final arbiter, but more importantly, analyses of individual instances of constitutional conflict necessarily miss the ability to address this question in the first place. Many a conflict analysed in this book has in isolation been the subject of gargantuan academic commentary, with wide-reaching conclusions about the EU's constitution and its future. Individual instances of conflict, when analysed in isolation, do have the benefit of helping us understand specific areas of EU or national law. However, every constitutional conflict necessarily forms part of an elaborate embroidery of the pluralist EU constitution. Consequently, it must always be read taking into account the before and after (incrementalism), the procedural and institutional context, other interactions in the relevant area of law and head of review, to name a few considerations.

The same lesson applies to assessing the constructive nature of the conflict in question. Numerous examples of contestation from the national level have often been conflated into one problematic development threatening the EU's constitution, regardless of whether they influenced the Court of Justice to improve its jurisprudence, impose higher standards upon EU institutions or served merely as a way for a national court to find a way out of complying with an EU obligation. The analysis in this book has instead showed that the constructiveness of national contestation and the mutual feedback loop it produces and reproduces depends on a number of factors without a one size fits all approach. In the same vein, the characterization of a constitutional conflict as destructive is to be used wisely and with caution, once there is absolutely no link connecting the Court of Justice and the

*The Jurisprudence of Constitutional Conflict in the European Union*. Ana Bobić, Oxford University Press. © Ana Bobić 2022.
DOI: 10.1093/oso/9780192847034.003.0009

constitutional court in question. This link manifests itself in numerous interpretative or procedural options described throughout this book that allow for at least a minimalist interpretation of values in Article 2 TEU and exhibit sincere cooperation and mutual respect.

The second lesson is interconnectedness. No site of constitutional authority in the EU stands alone in a vacuum. Instead, what we have seen across the three areas of review is a permanent enmeshment of national and EU constitutional content, resulting from the cross-fertilization through judicial contestation and interactions. Thus, the shared values in Article 2 TEU are not the exclusive ownership of any single site of constitutional authority. What is decided by one necessarily impacts the others, be it through cross-referencing, the use of the preliminary reference procedure, or indirect interactions where the same substance is the subject of interpretation.

This tells us something about constructive and destructive conflicts. More specifically, as we have seen in judicial triangles above, when destructive conflicts occur, the link between the inherently interconnected national and EU level of constitutionalism is broken, displayed by the lack of mutual trust and sincere cooperation between the constitutional court and the Court of Justice. Under such conditions, there is no possibility for a mutual feedback loop of contestation nor a possibility for a back and forth between the different sites of constitutional authority to take place. So the gravest danger of destructive conflicts lies precisely in their tendency to break with the tradition of enmeshment, allowing the constitutional court in question to escape the minimum requirements of Article 2 TEU (also representing EU membership criteria) and roam freely without the checks and balances provided by the heterarchical character of contestation.

The third lesson is delicateness. Yes, the courts under analysis in this book often disagree. At first glance, it might seem these disagreements disparage well-established constitutional principles (for example primacy or fundamental rights protected by national constitutions) and must be wiped off the face of the EU's constitutional landscape. Yet, the way these disagreements have been playing out in practice tells us that they form a delicate equilibrium, built incrementally over a long period of time, which allows them to remain predominantly constructive.

In fact, when an actor in a constitutional conflict does not carefully balance the delicate relationship between the relevant push and pull factors (to name a few: sincere cooperation, EU-friendly interpretation, the use of the preliminary reference procedure, the relevance of the national identity clause), nuance and interconnectedness is lost. Heterarchy is rejected, the auto-correct function is not able to accommodate the conflict in question, and we are entering the realm of destructive conflict.

The warning that I should like to end this book with is always to maintain a level-headed approach that does not blow individual points of conflict out of proportions. Contestation of the shared constitutional fabric of the EU is here to stay, so long as a future Treaty amendment does not introduce a hierarchical multilevel structure between the EU and its Member States. As academics, we may agree or disagree about to the need and desirability for such an amendment to take place. Yet, given the unlikeliness of such a development in the foreseeable future, the three lessons described above should guide our understanding and analysis: the nuanced, interconnected, and delicate nature of constitutional conflict in the European Union.

# Bibliography


Albers M, 'Data Retention in Germany' in M Zubik, J Podkowik, and R Rybski (eds), *European Constitutional Courts towards Data Retention Laws* (Springer 2020)

Alegre A and Leaf M, 'Mutual Recognition in European Judicial Cooperation: A Step Too Far Too Soon? Case Study—the European Arrest Warrant' (2004) 10(2) *European Law Journal* 200

Almeida Ribeiro G, 'Judicial Review of Legislation in Portugal: A Brief Genealogy' in F Biagi, J O Frosini, and J Mazzone (eds), *Constitutional History: Comparative Perspectives* (Brill 2020)

Alston P (ed), *The EU and Human Rights* (OUP 1999)

Alston P and Weiler J H, 'An "Ever Closer Union" in Need of a Human Rights Policy' (1998) 9 *European Journal of International Law* 658

Alter K, 'Explaining National Court Acceptance of European Court Jurisprudence: A Critical Evaluation of Theories of Legal Integration' in A-M Slaughter, A Stone Sweet, and J H H Weiler (eds), *European Court and National Courts: Doctrine and Jurisprudence. Legal Change in its Social Context* (Hart Publishing 1998)

Alter K, *Establishing the Supremacy of European Law: The Making of an International Rule of Law in Europe* (OUP 2003)

Alter K and Meunier-Aitsahalia S, 'Judicial Politics in the European Community. European Integration and the Pathbreaking *Cassis de Dijon* Decision' (1994) 26(4) *Comparative Political Studies* 535

Amalfitano C and Pollicino O, 'Two Courts, Two Languages? The Taricco Saga Ends on a Worrying Note' *Verfassungsblog* (5 June 2018) https://verfassungsblog.de/two-courts-two-languages-the-taricco-saga-ends-on-a-worrying-note/

Amaral M L and Pereira R A, 'The Portuguese Constitutional Court' in A von Bogdandy, P Huber, and C Grabenwater (eds), *The Max Planck Handbooks in European Public Law: Volume III: Constitutional Adjudication: Institutions* (OUP 2020)

Anagnostaras G, 'Activation of the *Ultra Vires* Review: The *Slovak Pensions* Judgment of the Czech Constitutional Court' (2013) 14(7) *German Law Journal* 959

Anagnostaras G, 'Mutual Confidence is Not Blind Trust! Fundamental Rights Protection and the Execution of the European Arrest Warrant: *Aranyosi and Caldararu*' (2016) 53(6) *Common Market Law Review* 1675

Arena A, 'Exercise of EU Competences and Pre-emption of Member States' Powers in the internal and the External Sphere: Towards "Grand Unification"?' (2016) 35(1) *Yearbook of European Law* 28

Avbelj M, 'The EU and the Many Faces of Legal Pluralism' (2006) 2 *Croatian Yearbook of European Law and Policy* 377

Avbelj M and Komárek J, 'Symposium: Four Visions of Constitutional Pluralism (Symposium Transcript)' (2008) 2(1) *European Journal of Legal Studies* 325

Avbelj M and Komárek J (eds), *Constitutional Pluralism in the European Union and Beyond* (Hart Publishing 2012)

Aziz M, 'Sovereignty Lost Sovereignty Regained: Some Reflections on the *Bundesverfassungsgericht*'s Bananas Judgment' (2002) 9(1) *Columbia Journal of European Law* 109
Aziz M, 'Sovereignty *Über Alles*: (Re)configuring the German Legal Order' in N Walker (ed), *Sovereignty in Transition* (Hart Publishing 2003)
Bache I and Flinders M (eds), *Multi-Level Governance* (OUP 2004)
Bańkowski Z and Christodoulidis E, 'The European Union as an Essentially Contested Project' (1998) 4(4) *European Law Journal* 341
Barber N, 'Legal Pluralism in the European Union' (2006) 12(3) *European Law Journal* 306
Barceló III J J, 'ECJ Review of Member State Measures for Compliance with Fundamental Rights' (2009) Cornell Law School Legal Studies Research Paper No 10-001
Barnard C, *The Substantive Law of the EU: The Four Freedoms* (OUP 2016)
Bast J, 'Don't Act beyond Your Powers: The Perils and Pitfalls of the German Constitutional Court's *Ultra Vires* Review' (2014) 15(2) *German Law Journal* 167
Baquero Cruz J, 'The Legacy of the Maastricht-Urteil and the Pluralist Movement' (2008) 14 *European Law Journal* 389
Beck G, 'The Lisbon Judgment of the German Constitutional Court, the Primacy of EU Law and the Problem of *Kompetenz-Kompetenz*: a Conflict between Right and Right in Which There Is No *Praetor*' (2011) 17(4) *European Law Journal* 470
Belling V, 'Supranational Fundamental Rights or Primacy of Sovereignty? Legal Effects of the So-called Opt-out from the EU Charter of Fundamental Rights' (2012) 18(2) *European Law Journal* 251
Besselink L, 'National and Constitutional Identity before and after Lisbon' (2010) 6(3) *Utrecht Law Review* 36
Besselink L, 'The Protection of Fundamental Rights Post-Lisbon: The Interaction between the EU Charter of Fundamental Rights, the European Convention on Human Rights (ECHR) and National Constitutions' FIDE General Report (2012)
Biagi F, *European Constitutional Courts and Transitions to Democracy* (CUP 2020)
Birkenkötter H, 'International Law as a Common Language across Spheres of Authority?' (2020) 9(2) *Global Constitutionalism* 318
Bobek M, *Comparative Reasoning in European Supreme Courts* (OUP 2013)
Bobek M, '*Landtová, Holubec*, and the Problem of an Uncooperative Court: Implications for the Preliminary Ruling Procedure' (2014) 10 *European Constitutional Law Review* 54
Bobek M and Adams-Prassl J (eds), *The EU Charter of Fundamental Rights in the Member States* (Hart Publishing 2020)
Bobić A, 'A Dynamic Analysis of Judicial Behaviour: The Auto-correct Function of Constitutional Pluralism' in M Derlén and J Lindholm (eds), *The Court of Justice of the European Union. Multidisciplinary Perspectives* (Hart Publishing 2017)
Bobić A, 'Developments in the EU-German Judicial Love Story: The Right to Be Forgotten II' (2020) 21(S1) *German Law Journal* 31
Bobić A, 'Constructive Versus Destructive Conflict: Taking Stock of the Recent Constitutional Jurisprudence in the EU' (2020) 22 *Cambridge Yearbook of European Legal Studies* 60
Bobić A and Dawson M, 'Making Sense of the "Incomprehensible": The PSPP Judgment of the German Federal Constitutional Court' (2020) 57(6) *Common Market Law Review* 1953
de Boer N, 'Addressing Rights Divergences under the Charter: Melloni' (2013) 50(4) *Common Market Law Review* 1083

von Bogdandy A, 'The European Union as a Human Rights organization? Human Rights at the Core of the European Union' (2000) 37(6) *Common Market Law Review* 1307

von Bogdandy A, 'Pluralism, Direct Effect, and the Ultimate Say: On the Relationship between International and Domestic Constitutional Law' (2008) 6 *International Journal of Constitutional Law* 397

von Bogdandy A, 'Ways to Frame the European Rule of Law: *Rechtsgemeinschaft*, Trust, Revolution, and Kantian Peace' (2018) 14 *European Constitutional Law Review* 675

von Bogdandy A, 'Principles of a Systemic Deficiencies Doctrine: How to Protect Checks and Balances in the Member States' (2020) 57 *Common Market Law Review* 705

von Bogdandy A and others, 'Reverse *Solange*: Protecting the Essence of Fundamental Rights against EU Member States' (2012) 49(2) *Common Market Law Review* 489

von Bogdandy A and Ioannidis M, 'Systemic Deficiency in the Rule of Law: what it Is, What Has Been Done, what Can Be Done' (2014) 51 *Common Market Law Review* 59

von Bogdandy A and Schill S, 'Overcoming Absolute Primacy: Respect for National Identity under the Lisbon Treaty' (2011) 48 *Common Market Law Review* 1417

Bonelli M, 'The Taricco Saga and the Consolidation of Judicial Dialogue in the European Union' (2018) 25(3) *Maastricht Journal of European and Comparative Law* 357

Bonelli M and Claes M, 'Judicial Serendipity: How Portuguese Judges Came to the Rescue of the Polish Judiciary ECJ 27 February 2018, Case C-64/16, *Associação Sindical dos Juízes Portugueses*' (2018) 14 *European Constitutional Law Review* 622

Bossuyt M and Verrijdt W, 'The Full Effect of EU Law and of Constitutional Review in Belgium and France after the *Melki* Judgment' (2011) 7(3) *European Constitutional Law Review* 355

van den Brink M, 'Is the Reasoning in "Coman" as Good as the Result?' *Verfassungsblog* (10 June 2018) https://verfassungsblog.de/is-the-reasoning-in-coman-as-good-as-the-result/

de Brito Gião Hanek R and Gallo D, *Constitutional Change through Euro Crisis Law: Report of Portugal* (2017)

Broberg M, 'National Courts of Last Instance Failing to Make a Preliminary Reference: The (Possible) Consequences Flowing Therefrom' (2016) 22(2) *European Public Law* 243

Bryde B-O, 'The ECJ's Fundamental Rights Jurisprudence: A Milestone in Transnational Constitutionalism' in M P Maduro and L Azoulai (eds), *The Past and Future of EU Law. The Classics of EU Law Revisited on the 50th Anniversary of the Rome Treaty* (Hart Publishing 2010)

Brzezinski M F and Garlicki L, 'Judicial Review in Post-Communist Poland: The Emergence of a Rechtsstaat?' (1995) 31 *Stanford Journal of International Law* 13

Buchanan A, *Justice, Legitimacy, and Self-Determination: Moral Foundations for International Law* (OUP 2004)

de Búrca G, 'Reappraising Subsidiarity's Significance after Amsterdam' (1999) Harvard Jean Monnet Working Paper 7/99

de Búrca G, 'The Drafting of the European Union Charter of Fundamental Rights' (2001) 26(2) *European Law Review* 126, 130

de Búrca G, 'Sovereignty and the Supremacy Doctrine of the European Court of Justice' in N Walker (ed), *Sovereignty in Transition* (Hart Publishing 2003)

de Búrca G, 'The European Court of Justice and the International Legal Order after *Kadi*' (2010) 51(1) *Harvard International Law Journal* 1

de Búrca G, 'The Road Not Taken: The European Union as a Global Human Rights Actor' (2011) 105 *American Journal of International Law* 649 de Búrca G, 'After the EU Charter of Fundamental Rights: The Court of Justice as a Human Rights Adjudicator?' (2013) 20(2) *Maastricht Journal of European and Comparative Law* 168

Burley A-M and Mattli W, 'Europe before the Court: A Political Theory of Legal Integration' (1993) 47 *International Organization* 41

Calliess C, 'The Future of the Eurozone and the Role of the German Federal Constitutional Court' (2012) 31(1) *Yearbook of European Law* 402

Cameron I, 'Balancing Data Protection and Law Enforcement Needs: *Tele2 Sverige and Watson*' (2017) 54 *Common Market Law Review* 1467

Canotilho M, Violante T, and Lanceiro R, 'Austerity Measures under Judicial Scrutiny: The Portuguese Constitutional Case-law' (2015) 11 *European Constitutional Law Review* 155

Carcassonne G, 'Case Note: *Conseil Constitutionnel* on the European Constitutional Treaty: Decision of 19 November 2004, 2004–505 DC' (2005) 1(2) *European Constitutional Law Review* 293

Carp R, 'The Struggle for the Rule of Law in Romania as an EU Member State: The Role of the Cooperation and Verification Mechanism' (2014) 10(1) *Utrecht Law Review* 1

Cartabia M, 'The Italian Constitutional Court and the Relationship between the Italian Legal System and the European Union' in A-M Slaughter, A Stone Sweet, and J H H Weiler (eds), *European Court and National Courts: Doctrine and Jurisprudence. Legal Change in Its Social Context* (Hart Publishing 1998)

Cartabia M, 'The Legacy of Sovereignty in Italian Constitutional Debate' in N Walker (ed), *Sovereignty in Transition* (Hart Publishing 2003)

Cartabia M, 'Taking Dialogue Seriously: The Renewed Need for a Judicial Dialogue at the Time of Constitutional Activism in the European Union' (2007) Jean Monnet Working Paper 12/07 https://jeanmonnetprograMorg/wp-content/uploads/2014/12/071201.pdf

Cartabia M, 'Europe and Rights: Taking Dialogue Seriously' (2009) 5 *European Constitutional Law Review* 5

Castillo-Ortiz P, 'The Illiberal Abuse of Constitutional Courts in Europe' (2019) 15 *European Constitutional Law Review* 48

Chandler D, 'New Rights for Old: Cosmopolitan Citizenship and the Critique of State Sovereignty' (2003) 51 *Political Studies* 332

Chowdhury N and Wessel R, 'Conceptualising Multilevel Regulation in the EU: A Legal Translation of Multilevel Governance?' (2012) 18 *European Law Journal* 335

Christiansen T and Reh C, *Constitutionalizing the European Union* (Macmillan International 2009)

Claes M, 'Constitutionalizing Europe at Its Source: The 'European Clauses' in the National Constitutions: Evolution and Typology' (2005) 24(1) *Yearbook of European Law* 81

Claes M, *The National Courts' Mandate in the European Constitution* (Hart Publishing 2006)

Claes M, 'Luxembourg, Here We Come? Constitutional Courts and the Preliminary Reference Procedure' (2015) 16(6) *German Law Journal* 1331

Claes M and Reestman J-H, 'The Protection of National Constitutional Identity and the Limits of European Integration at the Occasion of the *Gauweiler* Case' (2015) 16(4) *German Law Journal* 917

Claes M and de Visser M, 'Are You Networked Yet? On Dialogues in European Judicial Networks' (2012) 8(2) *Utrecht Law Review* 100

Cloots E, 'Germs of Pluralist Adjudication: *Advocaten Voor de Wereld* and Other References from the Belgian Constitutional Court' (2010) 47(3) *Common Market Law Review* 645

Cloots E, *National Identity in EU Law* (OUP 2015)

Cloots E, 'Cruz Villalón's "Gauweiler" Opinion: Lost in Platitudes' *Verfassungsblog* (15 January 2015) http://www.verfassungsblog.de/en/cruz-villalons-gauweiler-opinion-lost-platitudes/#.Va16HF9Viko

Coppel J and O'Neill A, 'The European Court of Justice: Taking Rights Seriously?' (1992) 12(2) *Legal Studies* 227

Craig P, 'Competence: Clarity, Conferral, Containment and Consideration' (2004) 29(3) *European Law Review* 323

Craig P and de Búrca G, *EU Law. Text, Cases and Materials* (OUP 6th Ed 2015)

Crumley C L, 'Heterarchy and the Analysis of Complex Societies' (1995) 6 *Archaeological Papers of the American Anthropological Association* 1

Davies G, 'Interpretative Pluralism and the Constitutionalisation of the EU Legal Order' in M Dawson and M Jachtenfuchs (eds), *Autonomy without Collapse in a Better European Union* (OUP forthcoming 2022)

Dawson M and Bobić A, 'Quantitative Easing at the Court of Justice – Doing whatever It Takes to Save the Euro: *Weiss and Others*' (2019) 56(4) *Common Market Law Review* 1005

Dehousse R, *The European Court of Justice: The Politics of Judicial Integration* (Macmillan St Martin's Press 1998)

Dehousse R, 'Beyond Representative Democracy: Constitutionalism in a Polycentric Polity' in J H H Weiler and M Wind (eds), *European Constitutionalism Beyond the State* (CUP 2003)

Dougan M, 'When Worlds Collide! Competing Visions of the Relationship between Direct Effect and Supremacy' (2007) 44 *Common Market Law Review* 931

Dougan M, 'Judicial Review of Member State Action under the General Principles and the Charter: Defining the "scope of Union Law"' (2015) 52(5) *Common Market Law Review* 1201

Douglas-Scott S, 'Autonomy and Fundamental Rights: The ECJ's Opinion 2/13 on Accession of the EU to the ECHR' (2016) 1 *Europarättslig tidskrift (Swedish European Law Journal)*

Dupré C, 'Human Dignity in Europe: A Foundational Constitutional Principle' (2013) 19(2) *European Public Law* 319

Eckert A E., 'Peoples and Persons: Moral Standing, Power, and the Equality of States' (2006) 50 *International Studies Quarterly* 841

Eco U, *The Island of the Day Before* (Vintage 1998)

Editorial Comment, 'The Scope of Application of General Principles of Union Law: An Ever Expanding Union?' (2010) 47 *Common Market Law Review* 1589

Editorial Comments, '*Ultra Vires*: Has the *Bundesverfassungsgericht* Shown Its Teeth?' (2013) 50(4) *Common Market Law Review* 925

Editorial Comments, 'Not Mastering the Treaties: The German Federal Constitutional Court's PSPP Judgment' (2020) 57 *Common Market Law Review* 965

Eeckhout P, 'The EU Charter of Fundamental Rights and the Federal question' (2002) 39(5) *Common Market Law Review* 945

Eeckhout P, 'Opinion 2/13 on EU Accession to the ECHR and Judicial Dialogue: Autonomy or Autarky' (2015) 38(1) *Fordham International Law Journal* 1

Eisenhut D, 'Delimitation of EU-competences under the First and Second Pillar: A View between ECOWAS and the Treaty of Lisbon' (2009) 10 *German Law Journal* 585

Ejisbouts W T and Besselink L, '"The Law of Laws" – Overcoming Pluralism' (2008) 4(3) *European Constitutional Law Review* 395

Elliott M, 'The Supreme Court's Judgment in *Miller*: In Search of a Constitutional Principle' (2017) 76(2) *Cambridge Law Journal* 257

Engel A, 'Delimiting Competences in the EU: CFSP Versus AFSJ Legal Bases' (2015) 21(1) *European Public Law* 47

Eriksson A, 'European Court of Justice: Broadening the Scope of European Nondiscrimination Law' (2009) 7(4) *International Journal of Constitutional Law* 731

Everson M, 'An Exercise in Legal Honesty: Rewriting the Court of Justice and the Bundesverfassungsgericht' (2015) 21(4) *European Law Journal* 474

Fabbrini F, *Fundamental Rights in Europe: Challenges and Transformations in Comparative Perspective* (OUP 2014)

Fabbrini F, 'After the *OMT* Case: The Supremacy of EU Law as the Guarantee of the Equality of the Member States' (2015) 16(4) *German Law Journal* 1003

Fabbrini F, 'The European Court of Justice, the European Central Bank and the Supremacy of European Law: Introduction' (2016) 23 *Maastricht Journal of European and Comparative Law* 1

Fabbrini F and Maduro M P, 'Supranational Constitutional Courts' (2017) iCourts Working Paper Series 98/2017

Fabbrini F and Pollicino O, 'Constitutional Identity in Italy: Institutional Disagreements at a Time of Political Change' in C Calliess and G van der Schyff (eds), *Constitutional Identity in a Europe of Multilevel Constitutionalism* (CUP 2019)

di Federico G, 'Joined Cases 58 and 59/13, C-58/13 and C-59/13 *Angelo Alberto Torresi and Pierfrancesco Torresi v. Consiglio dell'Ordine degli Avvocati di Macerata*, Judgment of the Court (Grand Chamber) of 17 July 2014' (2015) 21(3) *European Public Law* 481

Fennelly N, 'Pillar Talk: Fundamental Rights Protection in the European Union' (2008) 8(1) *Judicial Studies Institute Journal* 95

Ferreres Comella V, 'The European Model of Constitutional Review of Legislation: Toward Decentralization?'(2004) 3(2) *International Journal of Constitutional Law* 461

Fichera M, 'Solidarity, Heterarchy, and Political Morality' (2020) 2 *Jus Cogens* 301

Flynn T, *The Triangular Constitution: Constitutional Pluralism in Ireland, the EU and the ECHR* (Hart Publishing 2019)

Fontanelli F, Martinico G, and Carrozza P (eds), *Shaping Rule of Law through Dialogue: International and Supranational Experiences*, (Europa Law Publishing 2009)

Goldmann M, 'Constitutional Pluralism as Mutually Assured Discretion: The Court of Justice, the German Federal Constitutional Court, and the ECB' (2016) 23(1) *Maastricht Journal of European and Comparative Law* 119

Gaja G, 'Constitutional Court (Italy), Decision No 170 of 8 June 1984, S.p.a. Granital v. Amministrazione delle Finanze dello Stato' (1984) 21(4) *Common Market Law Review* 756

Garlicki L, 'The Experience of the Polish Constitutional Court' in W Sadurski (ed), *Constitutional Justice, East and West. Democratic Legitimacy and Constitutional Courts in Post-Communist Europe in a Comparative Perspective* (Kluwer Law International 2002)

Garlicki L, 'Constitutional Court and Politics. The Polish Crisis' in C Landfried (ed), *Judicial Power. How Constitutional Courts Affect Political Transformations* (CUP 2019)

Grabowska-Moroz B, 'Data Retention in the European Union' in M Zubik, J Podkowik, and R Rybski (eds), *European Constitutional Courts towards Data Retention Laws* (Springer 2020)

Grainger M-P, 'The Future of Europe: Judicial Interference and Preferences' (2005) 3 *Comparative European Politics* 155

Griffiths J, 'What Is Legal Pluralism?' (1986) 24 *Journal of Legal Pluralism and Unofficial Law* 1

Grimm D, 'A Long Time Coming' (2020) 21 *German Law Journal* 944

Groussot X, Pech L, and Petursson G T, 'The Scope of Application of EU Fundamental Rights on Member States' Action: In Search of Certainty in EU Adjudication' (2011) Eric Stein Working Paper 1/2011

Guarnieri C and Piana D, 'Bringing the outside Inside: Macro and Micro Factors to Put the Dialogue among the Highest Courts into Its Rights Context' (2012) 8 *Utrecht Law Review* 139

Guastaferro B, 'Beyond the Exceptionalism of Constitutional Conflicts: The Ordinary Functions of the Identity Clause' (2012) Jean Monnet Working Paper 01/12

Hailbronner M, *Traditions and Transformations. The Rise of German Constitutionalism* (OUP 2015)

Halberstam D, 'Constitutional Heterarchy: The Centrality of Conflict in the European Union and the United States' in J L Dunoff and J P Trachtman (eds), *Ruling the World? Constitutionalism, International Law, and Global Governance* (CUP 2009)

Halberstam D, '"It's the Autonomy, Stupid!": A Modest Defense of *Opinion 2/13* on EU Accession to the ECHR, and the way Forward' (2015) 16(1) *German Law Journal* 105

Halberstam D and Möllers C, 'The German Constitutional Court Says "Ja zu Deutschland!"' (2009) 10(8) *German Law Journal* 1241

Halberstam D and Stein E, 'The United Nations, the European Union, and the King of Sweden: Economic Sanctions and Individual Rights in a Plural Legal World' (2009) 46(1) *Common Market Law Review* 13

Harck S and Olsen H P, 'Decision Concerning the Maastricht Treaty. 1998 Ugeskrift for Retsvaesen, H 800' (1999) 93(1) *The American Journal of International Law* 209

Hart H L A, *The Concept of Law* (2nd edn, OUP 1994)

den Heijer M, 'Joined Cases C-411 & 493/10, NS v. Secretary of State for the Home Department and ME and Others v. Refugee Applications Commissioner, Minister for Justice, Equality and Law Reform, Judgment of the Court (Grand Chamber) of 21 December 2011, nyr' (2012) 49(5) *Common Market Law Review* 1735

Helfer L and Slaughter A-M, 'Toward a Theory of Effective Supranational Adjudication' (1997) 107 *Yale Law Journal* 273

Henckaerts J-M, 'The Protection of Human Rights in the European Union: overview and Bibliography' (1994) 22 *International Journal of Legal Information* 228

Higgins R, *Problems and Process. International Law and How We Use It* (Clarendon Press 1995)

Hinarejos A, '*Bundesverfassungsgericht* (German Constitutional Court), Decision of 18 July 2005 (2 BvR 2236/04) on the German European Arrest Warrant Law' (2006) 43(2) *Common Market Law Review* 583

Hinarejos A, 'The Lisbon Treaty Versus Standing Still: A View from the Third Pillar' (2009) 5(1) *European Constitutional Law Review* 99

Hofmann A, 'Is the Commission Levelling the Playing Field? Rights Enforcement in the European Union', (2018) 40(6) *Journal of European Integration* 737

Hooghe L and Marks G, 'Unraveling the Central State, But How? Types of Multi-Level Governance' (2003) 97 *American Political Science Review* 233

Huber P M, 'The Federal Constitutional Court and European Integration' (2015) 21(1) *European Public Law* 83

Iglesias Sánchez S, 'The Court and the Charter: The Impact of the Entry into Force of the Lisbon Treaty on the ECJ's Approach to Fundamental Rights' (2012) 49(5) *Common Market Law Review* 1565

Isiksel T, 'Fundamental Rights in the EU after *Kadi and Al Barakaat*' (2010) 16(5) *European Law Journal* 551

Isiksel T, 'European Exceptionalism and the EU's Accession to the ECHR' (2016) 27(3) *European Journal of International Law* 565

Jacobs F G, 'Human Rights in the European Union: The Role of the Court of Justice' (2001) 26(4) *European Law Review* 331

Jacobs F G, 'Judicial Dialogue and the Cross-fertilization of Legal Systems: The European Court of Justice' (2003) 38 *Texas International Law Journal* 547

Joerges C, 'Pereat Iustitia, Fiat Mundus. What Is Left of the European Economic Constitution after the *Gauweiler* Litigation?' (2016) 23(1) *Maastricht Journal of European and Comparative Law* 99

Kaila H, 'The Scope of Application of the Charter of Fundamental Rights of the European Union in the Member States' in P Cardonell, A Rosas, and N Wahl (eds), *Constitutionalising the EU Judicial System: Essays in Honour of Pernilla Lindh* (Hart Publishing 2012)

Kaiser A-B, '"It Isn't true that England Is the Moon": Comparative Constitutional Law as a Means of Constitutional Interpretation by the Courts?' (2017) 18(2) *German Law Journal* 294

Kaltsa A, 'The Review of Constitutionality of Laws in Greece' (1998) 4(3) *European Public Law* 292

Kavanagh A, *Constitutional Review under the Human Rights Act* (CUP 2009)

Kelemen D, 'The Structure and Dynamics of EU Federalism' (2003) 36(1–2) *Comparative Political Studies* 184

Kelemen D, 'On the Unsustainability of Constitutional Pluralism: European Supremacy and the Survival of the Eurozone' (2016) 23(1) *Maastricht Journal of European and Comparative Law* 136

Kelemen D and Pech L, 'The Uses and Abuses of Constitutional Pluralism: Undermining the Rule of Law in the Name of Constitutional Identity in Hungary and Poland' (2019) 21 *Cambridge Yearbook of European Legal Studies* 59

Kelsen H, 'Judicial Review of Legislation. A Comparative Study of the Austrian and the American Constitution' (1942) 4 *The Journal of Politics* 183

Klinge S, 'Dialogue or Disobedience between the European Court of Justice and the Danish Constitutional Court? The Danish Supreme Court Challenges the Mangold-principle' *EU Law Analysis Blog* (13 December 2016) http://eulawanalysis.blogspot.nl/2016/12/dialogue-or-disobedience-between.html

Kochenov D (ed), *EU Citizenship and Federalism: The Role of Rights* (CUP 2017)

Kokott J, 'Report on Germany' in A-M Slaughter, A Stone Sweet, and J H H Weiler (eds), *The European Court and National Courts, Doctrine and Jurisprudence: Legal Change in Its Social Context* (Hart Publishing 1998)

Komárek J, 'European Constitutionalism and the European Arrest Warrant: In Search of the Limits of "Contrapunctual Principles"' (2007) 44(1) *Common Market Law Review* 9

Komárek J, 'Institutional Dimension of Constitutional Pluralism' (2010) Eric Stein Working Paper 3/2010 https://csesp.files.wordpress.com/2015/05/eswp-2010-03-komarek.pdf

Komárek J, 'Czech Constitutional Court Playing with Matches: The Czech Constitutional Court Declares a Judgment of the Court of Justice of the EU *Ultra Vires*; Judgment of 31 January 2012, Pl. ÚS 5/12, *Slovak Pensions XVII*' (2012) 8 *European Constitutional Law Review* 323

Komárek J, 'The Place of Constitutional Courts in the EU' (2013) 9(3) *European Constitutional Law Review* 420

Komárek J, 'It's a Stupid Autonomy ...' *Verfassungsblog* (14 March 2015) http://verfassungsblog.de/its-a-stupid-autonomy-2/

Komárek J and Editors, 'The Czech Constitutional Court's Second Decision on the Lisbon Treaty of 3 November 2009' (2009) 5(3) *European Constitutional Law Review* 345

Kommers D P, 'The Federal Constitutional Court in the German Political System' (1994) 26(4) *Comparative Political Studies* 470

Kommers D P and Miller R A, *The Constitutional Jurisprudence of the Federal Republic of Germany* (3rd edn, Duke University Press 2012)

Konstantinides T, 'Drawing the Line between Circumvention and Gap-Filling: An Exploration of the Conceptual Limits of the Treaty's Flexibility Clause' (2012) 31(1) *Yearbook of European Law* 227

Kosta E, 'The Way to Luxemburg: National Court Decisions on the Compatibility of the Data Retention Directive with the Rights to Privacy and Data Protection' (2013) 10(3) *SCRIPTed* 339

Krisch N, 'Who Is Afraid of Radical Pluralism? Legal Order and Political Stability in the Postnational Space' (2011) 24(4) *Ratio Juris* 386

Krisch N, *Beyond Constitutionalism: The Pluralist Structure of Postnational Law* (OUP 2013)

Kühling J, 'Fundamental Rights' in A von Bogdandy and J Bast (eds), *Principles of European Constitutional Law* (Hart Publishing 2006)

Kumm M, 'Who Is the Final Arbiter of Constitutionality in Europe: Three Conceptions of the Relationship between the German Federal Constitutional Court and the European Court of Justice' (1999) 36 *Common Market Law Review* 351

Kumm M, 'The Jurisprudence of Constitutional Conflict: Constitutional Supremacy in Europe before and after the Constitutional Treaty' (2005) 11(3) *European Law Journal* 262

Kumm M, 'The Cosmopolitan turn in Constitutionalism: An Integrated Conception of Public Law' (2013) 20(2) *Indiana Journal of Global Legal Studies* 605

Kumm M, 'Rebel without a Good Cause: Karlsruhe's Misguided Attempt to Draw the CJEU into a Game of "chicken" and what the CJEU Might Do about It' (2014) 15(2) *German Law Journal* 203

Lacatus C and Sedelmeier U, 'Does Monitoring without Enforcement Make a Difference? The European Union and Anti-corruption Policies in Bulgaria and Romania after accession' (2020) 27(8) *JEPP* 1236

Ladenburger C, 'Protection of Fundamental Rights Post-Lisbon: the Interaction between the Charter of Fundamental Rights, the European Convention of Human Rights and National Constitutions' FIDE Institutional Report (2012)

Lawrence J C, 'Constitutional Pluralism's Unspoken Normative Core' (2019) 21 *Cambridge Yearbook of European Legal Studies* 24

Laws J, 'Constitutional Guarantees' (2008) 29(1) *Statute Law Review* 1

Leczykiewicz D, '*Trybunał Konstytucyjny* (Polish Constitutional Tribunal), Judgment of 27 April 2005, No P 1/05, on the Constitutionality of the European Arrest Warrant National Implementation' (2006) 43(4) *Common Market Law Review* 1181

Leczykiewicz D, 'Constitutional Conflicts and the third Pillar' (2008) 33(2) *European Law Review* 230

Leczykiewicz D, 'The "national Identity Clause" in the EU Treaty: A Blow to Supremacy of Union Law?' (UK Constitutional Law Association Blog 12 June 2012) http://ukconstitutionallaw.org/2012/06/21/dorota-leczykiewicz-the-national-identity-clause-in-the-eu-treaty-a-blow-to-supremacy-of-union-law/

Lenaerts K, 'Constitutionalism and the Many Faces of Federalism' (1990) 38(2) *American Journal of Comparative Law* 205

Lenaerts K, 'The Rule of Law and the Coherence of the Judicial System of the European Union' (2007) 44 *Common Market Law Review* 1625

Lenaerts K, 'Federalism and the Rule of Law: Perspectives from the European Court of Justice' (2010) 13 *Fordham International Law Journal* 1338

Lenaerts K, 'The Court of Justice of the European Union and the Protection of Fundamental Rights' (2011) 31 *Polish Yearbook of International Law* 79

Lenaerts K, 'EU Values and Constitutional Pluralism: The EU System of Fundamental Rights Protection' (2014) 34 *Polish Yearbook of International Law* 135

Lenaerts K, 'The Court's outer and Inner Selves: Exploring the External and Internal Legitimacy of the Court of Justice' in M Adams, H de Waele, J Meeusen, and G Straetmans (eds), *Judging Europe's Judges. The Legitimacy of the Case Law of the European Court of Justice* (Hart Publishing 2015)

Lenaerts K, 'La Vie Après l'Avis: Exploring the Principle of Mutual (yet Not Blind) trust' (2017) 54(3) *Common Market Law Review* 805

Lenaerts K and Gutiérez-Fons J A, 'The Constitutional Allocation of Powers and General Principles of EU Law' (2010) 47(6) *Common Market Law Review* 1629

Lenaerts K, Wójcik A, 'Judges Should Be Fully Insulated from any Sort of Pressure' *Verfassungsblog* (30 January 2020) https://verfassungsblog.de/judges-should-be-fully-insulated-from-any-sort-of-pressure/

Lindahl H, 'Sovereignty and Representation in the European Union' N Walker (ed), *Sovereignty in Transition* (Hart Publishing 2003)

Lindblom P H, 'The Role of Supreme Courts in Scandinavia' (2000) 39 *Scandinavian Studies in Law* 325

Lindeboom J, 'Is the Primacy of EU Law Based on the Equality of the Member States? A Comment on the CJEU's Press Release Following the PSPP Judgment' (2020) 21(8) *German Law Journal* 1649

Lord Goldsmith, 'A Charter of Rights, Freedoms and Principles' (2001) 38(5) *Common Market Law Review* 1205

Loughlin M, 'Constitutional Pluralism: An oxymoron?' (2014) 3(1) *Global Constitutionalism* 9

Luebbe-Wolff G, 'Who Has the Last Word? National and Transnational Courts: Conflict and Cooperation' (2011) 30(1) *Yearbook of European Law* 86

Lynskey O, 'The Data Retention Directive Is Incompatible with the Rights to Privacy and Data Protection and Is Invalid in Its Entirety: *Digital Rights Ireland*' (2014) 51 *Common Market Law Review* 1789

Lynskey O, 'Article 8: The Right to Data Protection' in M Bobek and J Adams-Prassl (eds), *The EU Charter of Fundamental Rights in the Member States* (Hart Publishing 2020)

MacCormick N, 'The Maastricht Urteil: Sovereignty Now' (1995) 1 *European Law Journal* 259

MacCormick N, 'Risking Constitutional Collision in Europe?' (1998) 18(3) *OJLS* 517

MacCormick N, *Questioning Sovereignty: Law, State and Nation in the European Commonwealth* (OUP 1999)

Madsen M R, Olsen H P and Šadl U, 'Legal Disintegration? The Ruling of the Danish Supreme Court in AJOS' *Verfassungsblog* (30 January 2017) http://verfassungsblog.de/legal-disintegration-the-ruling-of-the-danish-supreme-court-in-ajos/

Madsen M R, Olsen H P, and Šadl U, 'Competing Supremacies and Clashing Institutional Rationalities: The Danish Supreme Court's Decision in the *Ajos* Case and the National Limits of Judicial Cooperation' (2017) 23(1–2) *European Law Journal* 140

Maduro M P, *We the Court. The European Court of Justice and the European Economic Constitution* (Hart Publishing 1998)

Maduro M P, 'Contrapunctual Law: Europe's Constitutional Pluralism in Action' in N Walker (ed), *Sovereignty in Transition* (Hart Publishing 2003)

Maduro M P, 'Europe and the Constitution: what If this Is as Good as It Gets?' in J H H Weiler and M Wind (eds), *European Constitutionalism Beyond the State* (CUP 2003)

Maduro M P, 'Three Claims of Constitutional Pluralism' in M Avbelj and J Komárek (eds), *Constitutional Pluralism in the European Union and Beyond* (Hart Publishing 2012)

Malleson K, 'The Evolving Role of the Supreme Court' (2011) *Public Law* 754

Mancano L, 'Judicial Harmonisation through Autonomous Concepts of European Union Law: The Example of the European Arrest Warrant Framework Decision' (2018) 43(1) *European Law Review* 69

Mancini F, 'The Making of a Constitution for Europe' (1989) 26(4) *Common Market Law Review* 595

Markou C, 'The Cyprus and other EU Court Rulings on Data Retention: The Directive as a Privacy Bomb' (2012) 28 *Computer Law & Security Review* 468

Martinico G, 'Judging in the Multilevel Legal Order: Exploring the techniques of "hidden Dialogue" ' (2010) 21 *King's College Law Journal* 257

Martinico G, 'Multiple Loyalties and Dual Preliminarity: The Pains of Being a Judge in a Multilevel Legal Order' (2012) 10(3) *International Journal of Constitutional Law* 871

Martinico G and Pollicino O, 'Between Constitutional tolerance and Judicial Activism: The Specificity of European Judicial Law' (2008) 10(1) *European Journal of Law Reform* 97

Martinico G and Pollicino O, *The Interaction between Europe's Legal Systems. Judicial Dialogue and the Creation of Supranational Laws* (Edward Elgar 2012)

Mattli W and Slaughter A-M, 'Revisiting the European Court of Justice' (1998) 52 *International Organization* 177

Mayer F, 'The European Constitution and the Courts Adjudicating European Constitutional Law in a Multilevel System' (2003) Jean Monnet Working Paper 9/03

Mazák J and Moser K M, 'Adjudication by Reference to General Principles of EU Law: A Second Look at the *Mangold* Case Law' M Adams, H de Waele, J Meeusen, and G Straetmans (eds), *Judging Europe's Judges. The Legitimacy of the Case Law of the European Court of Justice* (Hart Publishing 2015)

Michaels R, 'Global Legal Pluralism' (2009) 5 *Annual Review of Law and Social Science* 243

Millet F-X, 'How Much Lenience for How Much Cooperation? On the First Preliminary Reference of the French Constitutional Council to the Court of Justice' (2014) 51 *Common Market Law Review* 195

Mitsilegas V, 'The Constitutional Implications of Mutual Recognition in Criminal Matters in the EU' (2006) 43(5) *Common Market Law Review* 1277

de Mol M, '*Kücükdeveci: Mangold* Revisited: Horizontal Direct Effect of a General Principle of EU Law' (2010) 6 *European Constitutional Law Review* 293

de Mol M, 'The Novel Approach of the CJEU on the Horizontal Direct Effect of the EU Principle of Non-discrimination: (Unbridled) Expansionism of EU Law?' (2011) 18(1–2) *Maastricht Journal of European and Comparative Law* 109

Molek P, 'Czech Constitutional Court Unconstitutionality of the Czech Implementation of the Data Retention Directive; Decision of 22 March 2011, Pl. .S 24/10' (2012) 8 *European Constitutional Law Review* 338

Möllers C, 'German Federal Constitutional Court: Constitutional U*ltra Vires* Review of European Acts only under Exceptional Circumstances; Decision of 6 July 2010, 2 BvR 2661/06, *Honeywell*' (2011) 7(1) *European Constitutional Law Review* 161

Murkens J E K, '"We Want Our Identity Back": The Revival of National Sovereignty in the German Federal Constitutional Court's Decision on the Lisbon Treaty' (2010) 25 *Public Law* 530

Murphy C C, 'Romanian Constitutional Court, Decision No 1258 of 8 October 2009' (2010) 47 *Common Market Law Review* 933

Nicolaïdis K, 'Germany as Europe: How the Constitutional Court Unwittingly Embraced EU Demoi-cracy. A Comment on Franz Mayer' (2011) 9(3–4) *International Journal of Constitutional Law* 786

Norberg S, '20 Years on: Some Reflections on the European Economic Area Judicial Mechanism' in P Cardonnel, A Rosas, and N Wahl (eds), *Constitutionalising the EU Judicial System: Essays in Honour of Pernilla Lindh* (Hart Publishing 2012)

Nowag J, 'EU Law, Constitutional Identity, and Human Dignity: A toxic Mix? Bundesverfassungsgericht: *Mr R* 2 BvR 2735/14, *Mr R v. Order of the Oberlandesgericht Düsseldorf*, Order of the Bundesverfassungsgericht (Second Senate) of 15 December 2015, DE:BVerfG:2015:rs20151215.2bvr273514' (2016) 53(5) *Common Market Law Review* 1441

Olsen H P, 'The Danish Supreme Court's Decision on the Constitutionality of Denmark's Ratification of the Lisbon Treaty' (2013) 50 *Common Market Law Review* 1489

Pech L, 'The Rule of Law as a Constitutional Principle of the European Union' (2009) Jean Monnet Working Paper 04/09

Pech L and Scheppele K L, 'Illiberalism Within: Rule of Law Backsliding in the EU' (2017) 19 *Cambridge Yearbook of European Legal Studies* 3

Pech L and Kochenov D, 'Respect for the Rule of Law in the Case Law of the European Court of Justice: A Casebook overview of key Judgments Since the *Portuguese Judges* Case' SIEPS Report 2021 (forthcoming) https://www.sieps.se/globalassets/publikationer/2021/sieps-2021_3-eng-web.pdf?

Peers S, 'The EU's Accession to the ECHR: The Dream Becomes a Nightmare' (2015) 16(1) *German Law Journal* 213

Pernice I, 'Introduction: Achievements and Challenges – The European Union, Its Constitutional Courts and the Perspectives after Lisbon' in J M Beneyto and I Pernice (eds), *Europe's Constitutional Challenges in the Light of the Recent Case Law of National Constitutional Courts – Lisbon and Beyond* (Nomos 2011)

Pernice I, 'Motor or Brake for European Policies? Germany's New Role in the EU after the Lisbon-Judgment of Its Federal Constitutional Court' in J M Beneyto and I Pernice (eds), *Europe's Constitutional Challenges in the Light of the Recent Case Law of National Constitutional Courts – Lisbon and Beyond* (Nomos 2011)

Pernice I, 'Multilevel Constitutionalism and the Crisis of Democracy in Europe' (2015) 11(3) *European Constitutional Law Review* 541

Pescatore P, 'The Doctrine of "direct Effect": An Infant Disease of Community Law' (2015) 40(2) *European Law Review* 135 (an Update from the original article that appeared in (1983) 8 *European Law Review* 155)

Piccirilli G, 'The 'Taricco Saga': The Italian Constitutional Court Continues Its European Journey' (2018) 14 *European Constitutional Law Review* 814

Pollicino O, 'European Arrest Warrant and Constitutional Principles of the Member States: a Case Law-based outline in the Attempt to Strike the Right Balance between Interacting Legal Systems' (2008) 9(10) *German Law Journal* 1313

Priban J, 'Asking the Sovereignty question in Global Legal Pluralism: from "weak" Jurisprudence to "strong" Socio-legal theories of Constitutional Power operations' (2015) 28(1) *Ratio Juris* 31

Priban J, 'The Semantics of Constitutional Sovereignty in Post-sovereign "new" Europe: A Case Study of the Czech Constitutional Court's Jurisprudence' (2015) 13(1) *International Journal of Constitutional Law* 180

Rauchegger C, 'National Constitutional Rights and the Primacy of EU Law: MAS' (2018) 55(5) *Common Market Law Review* 1521

Rasmussen H, *On Law and Policy in the European Court of Justice: A Comparative Study in Judicial Policymaking* (M Nijhoff 1986)

Rasmussen H, 'Denmark's Maastricht Ratification Case: Some Serious questions about Constitutionality' (1998) 21(1) *Journal of European Integration* 1

Ratner S R, *The Thin Justice of International Law* (OUP 2015)

Reestman J-H, 'The Franco-German Constitutional Divide' (2009) 5(3) *European Constitutional Law Review* 374

Rehling Larsen S, *The Constitutional Theory of the Federation and the European Union* (OUP 2021)

Repasi R, 'Karlsruhe, Again: The Interim-interim Relief of the German Constitutional Court Regarding Next Generation EU' (EU Law Live 29 March 2021) https://eulawlive.com/analysis-karlsruhe-again-the-interim-interim-relief-of-the-german-constitutional-court-regarding-next-generation-eu-by-rene-repasi/

Rodin S, 'Back to Square one: The Past, the Present and the Future of the *Simmenthal* Mandate' in J M Beneyto and I Pernice (eds), *Europe's Constitutional Challenges in the Light of the Recent Case Law of National Constitutional Courts: Lisbon and Beyond* (Nomos 2011)

Rodin S, 'National Identity and Market Freedoms after the Treaty of Lisbon' (2011) 7 *Croatian Yearbook of European Law and Policy* 11

Rodin S, 'Dumb and No More Here', Presented on the Conference: Central and Eastern European Judges Under the EU Influence: The Transformative Power of Europe Revisited on the 10th Anniversary of the Enlargement, 12–13 May 2014, European University Institute, Florence, Italy

Rossi L S, 'The Principle of Equality Among Member States of the European Union' in L S Rossi and F Casolari (eds), *The Principle of Equality in EU Law* (Springer 2017)

Rytter J E and Wind M, 'In Need of Juristocracy? The Silence of Denmark in the Development of European Legal Norms' (2011) 9(2) *International Journal of Constitutional Law* 470

Šadl U and Wallerman A, "The Referring Court Asks, in Essence': Is Reformulation of Preliminary questions by the Court of Justice a Decision writing Fixture or a Decision-making Approach?' (2019) 25 *European Law Journal* 416

Sadurski W, '"Solange, Chapter 3": Constitutional Courts in Central Europe: Democracy—European Union' (2008) 14(1) *European Law Journal* 1

Sarmiento D, 'Who's Afraid of the Charter? The Court of Justice, National Courts and the New Framework of Fundamental Rights Protection in Europe' (2013) 50(5) *Common Market Law Review* 1267

Sarmiento D, 'The EU's Constitutional Core' in A Saiz Arnaiz and C Alcoberro Llivina (eds), *National Constitutional Identity and European Integration* (Intersentia 2013)

Sarmiento D, 'The *OMT* Case and the Demise of the Pluralist Movement' (Despite Our Difference Blog 21 September 2015) https://despiteourdifferencesblog.wordpress.com/2015/09/21/the-omt-case-and-the-demise-of-the-pluralist-movement/

Sarmiento D, 'The Luxembourg "Double Look": The Advocate General's Opinion and the Judgment in the *Gauweiler* Case' (2016) 23(1) *Maastricht Journal of European and Comparative Law* 40

Sciarra S and Nicastro G, 'A New Conversation: Preliminary References from the Italian Constitutional Court' (2016) 23 *Maastricht Journal of European and Comparative Law* 195

Scharpf F W, 'The Asymmetry of European Integration, or why the EU Cannot Be a "social Market Economy"' (2010) 8 *Socio-Economic Review* 211

Schilling T, 'The Autonomy of the Community Legal Order: An Analysis of Possible Foundations' (1996) 37(2) *Harvard International Law Journal* 389

Schimmelfennig F, 'Competition and Community: Constitutional Courts, Rhetorical Action, and the Institutionalisation of Human Rights in the European Union' (2006) 13(8) *JEPP* 1247

Schmid C U, 'All Bark and No Bite: Notes on the Federal Constitutional Court's "Banana Decision"' (2001) 7(1) *European Law Journal* 95

Schmidt S K, *The European Court of Justice and the Policy Process: The Shadow of Case Law* (OUP 2018)

Schneider K, 'Gauging "Ultra-Vires": The Good Parts' (2020) 21 *German Law Journal* 968

Scholtes J, 'Abusing Constitutional Identity' (2021) 22 *German Law Journal* 534

van der Schyff G, 'Constitutional Review by the Judiciary in the Netherlands: A Bridge too Far?' (2010) 11 *German Law Journal* 175

van der Schyff G, 'The Constitutional Relationship between the European Union and Its Member States: The Role of National Identity in Article 4(2) TEU' (2012) 37(5) *European Law Review* 563

van der Schyff G, 'Member States of the European Union, Constitutions, and Identity' in C Calliess and G van der Schyff (eds), *Constitutional Identity in a Europe of Multilevel Constitutionalism* (CUP 2019)

Selejan-Gutan B, 'A Tale of Primacy Part II: The Romanian Constitutional Court on a Slippery Slope' *Verfassungsblog* (18 June 2021) https://verfassungsblog.de/a-tale-of-primacy-part-ii/

Shaw J, 'Process and Constitutional Discourse in the European Union' (2000) 27 *Journal of Law & Society* 4

Simon S, 'Direct Cooperation Has Begun: Some Remarks on the Judgment of the ECJ on the OMT Decision of the ECB in Response to the German Federal Constitutional Court's First Request for a Preliminary Ruling' (2015) 16(4) *German Law Journal* 1025

Slapin J B, 'How European Union Membership Can Undermine the Rule of Law in Emerging Democracies' (2015) 38(3) *West European Politics* 627

Śledzińska-Simon A and Ziółkowski M, 'Constitutional Identity in Poland. Is the Emperor Putting On the Old Clothes of Sovereignty?' in C Calliess and G van der Schyff (eds), *Constitutional Identity in a Europe of Multilevel Constitutionalism* (CUP 2019)

Snell J, 'Fundamental Rights Review of National Measures: Nothing New under the Charter?' (2015) 21(2) *European Public Law* 285

de Sousa Santos B, *Towards a New Legal Common Sense* (Butterworths 2002)

Spieker L D, 'Framing and Managing Constitutional Identity Conflicts: How to Stabilize the Modus Vivendi between the Court of Justice and National Constitutional Courts' (2020) 57(2) *Common Market Law Review* 361

Stein E, 'Lawyers, Judges, and the Making of a Transnational Constitution' (1981) 75(1) *American Journal of International Law* 1

Stone Sweet A, 'A Cosmopolitan Legal Order: Constitutional Pluralism and Rights Adjudication in Europe' (2012) 1(1) *Global Constitutionalism* 53

Stone Sweet A, 'The Structure of Constitutional Pluralism: Review of Nico Krisch, *Beyond Constitutionalism: The Pluralist Structure of Post-National Law*' (2013) 11(2) *International Journal of Constitutional Law* 491

Swoboda D, 'The Self-perception of the European Court of Justice and Its Neglect of the Defense Perspective in Its Preliminary Rulings on Judicial Cooperation in Criminal Matters. A Small Note on a Fundamental Misunderstanding' (2015) 7–8 *Zeitschrift für Internationale Strafrechtsdogmatik* 361

Tadeusz Koncewicz T, 'Of Institutions, Democracy, Constitutional Self-defence and the Rule of Law: The Judgments of the Polish Constitutional Tribunal in Cases K 34/15, K 35/ 15 and Beyond' (2016) 53(6) *Common Market Law Review* 1753

Tănăsescu E S, 'The Independence of Justice as Proxy for the Rule of Law in the EU Case Study – Romania' (2021) 3(1) *Nuovi Autoritarismi e Democrazie: Diritto, Istituzioni e Società* 103

Tavares Lanceiro R, '"The Portuguese Constitutional Court Judgment 422/2020: A 'Solange' Moment?"' (EU Law Live 24 July 2020) https://eulawlive.com/op-ed-the-portuguese-constitutional-court-judgment-422-2020-a-solange-moment-by-rui-tavares-lanceiro/#:~:text=Primacy%20and%20the%20Portuguese%20Constitution&text=This%20provision%20expressly%20allows%20the,basis%20for%20primacy%20in%20Portugal.

Temple Lang J, 'The Duties of National Courts under Community Constitutional Law' (1997) 22 *European Law Review* 3

Teubner G, 'The Two Faces of Janus: Rethinking Legal Pluralism' (1992) 5 *Cardozo Law Review* 1443

Theil S, 'What Red Lines, If Any, Do the Lisbon Judgments of European Constitutional Courts Draw for Future EU Integration?' (2014) 15(4) *German Law Journal* 599 M R S

Thym D, 'In the Name of the Sovereign Statehood: A Critical Introduction to the Lisbon Judgment of the German Constitutional Court' (2009) 46 *Common Market Law Review* 1795

Thym D, 'From Ultra-vires-control to Constitutional Identity Review: The Lisbon Judgment of the German Constitutional Court' in J M Beneyto and I Pernice (eds), *Europe's Constitutional Challenges in the Light of the Recent Case Law of National Constitutional Courts – Lisbon and Beyond* (Nomos, 2011)

Thym D, 'Separation Versus Fusion—or: How to Accommodate National Autonomy and the Charter? Diverging Visions of the German Constitutional Court and the European Court of Justice' (2013) 9(3) *European Constitutional Law Review* 391

Tobler C and Waaldijk K, 'Case C-267/06, *Tadao Maruko v. Versorgungsanstalt der deutschen Bühnen*, Judgment of the Grand Chamber of the Court of Justice of 1 April 2008, Not Yet Reported' (2009) 46 *Common Market Law Review* 723

Torres Pérez A, *Conflicts of Rights in the European Union. A Theory of Supranational Adjudication* (OUP 2009)

Torres Pérez A, 'Constitutional Dialogue on the European Arrest Warrant: The Spanish Constitutional Court knocking on Luxembourg's Door' (2012) 8(1) *European Constitutional Law Review* 105

Tracol X, 'The Judgment of the Grand Chamber Dated 21 December 2016 in the Two Joint Tele2 Sverige and Watson Cases: The Need for a Harmonised Legal Framework on the Retention of Data at EU Level' (2017) 33 *Computer Law & Security Review* 541

Tridimas T, 'Knocking on Heaven's Door: Fragmentation, Efficiency and Defiance in the Preliminary Reference Procedure' (2003) 40(1) *Common Market Law Review* 9

Tridimas T, 'Constitutional Review of Member State Action: The Virtues and Vices of an Incomplete Jurisdiction' (2011) 9(3–4) *International Journal of Constitutional Law* 737

Tridimas T and Xanthoulis N, 'A Legal Analysis of the Gauweiler Case. Between Monetary Policy and Constitutional Conflict' (2016) 23(1) *Maastricht Journal of European and Comparative Law* 17

Tsadiras A, 'Cyprus Supreme Court (Ανώτατο Δικαστήριο Κύπρου), Judgment of 7 November 2005 (Civil Appeal no 294/2005) on the Cypriot European Arrest Warrant Law' (2007) 44(5) *Common Market Law Review* 1515

Tuori K, *European Constitutionalism* (CUP 2015)

Turmo A, 'A Dialogue of Unequals: The European Court of Justice Reasserts National Courts' Obligations under Article 267(3) TFEU' (2019) 15 *European Constitutional Law Review* 340

Tushnet M, 'Policy Distortion and Democratic Debilitation: Comparative Illumination of the Countermajoritarian Difficulty' (1995) 94(2) *Michigan Law Review* 245

Twining W, *Globalization & Legal Theory* (Butterworths 2000)

Urrutia I, 'Approach of the European Court of Justice on Accommodation of the European Language Diversity in the Internal Market: Overcoming Language Barriers or Fostering Linguistic Diversity?' (2012) 18(2) *Columbia Journal of European Law* 243

Usher J, 'Case C-376/98, Germany v. European Parliament and Council (tobacco Advertising). Judgment of the Full Court of 5 October 2000, [2000] ECR I-8419' (2001) 38(6) *Common Market Law Review* 1519

Vandamme T, 'Prochain Arrêt: La Belgique! Explaining Recent Preliminary References of the Belgian Constitutional Court' (2008) 4 *European Constitutional Law Review* 127

Vedaschi A and Lubello V, 'Data Retention and Its Implications for the Fundamental Right to Privacy' (2015) 20 *Tilburg Law Review* 14

de Visser M, *Constitutional Review in Europe. A Comparative Analysis* (Hart Publishing 2014)

Voss R, 'The National Perception of the Court of First Instance and the European Court of Justice' (1993) 30(6) *Common Market Law Review* 1119

Voßkuhle A, 'Multilevel Cooperation of the European Constitutional Courts: Der Europäische Verfassungsgerichtsverbund' (2010) 6(2) *European Constitutional Law Review* 175

Vranes E, 'German Constitutional Foundations of, and Limitations to, EU Integration: A Systematic Analysis' (2013) 14(1) *German Law Journal* 75

de Waele H, 'The Role of the European Court of Justice in the Integration Process: A Contemporary and Normative Assessment' (2010) 6 *Hanse Law Review* 3

Walker N, 'The Idea of Constitutional Pluralism' (2002) 65(3) *MLR* 317

Walker N, 'Late Sovereignty in the European Union' in N Walker (ed), *Sovereignty in Transition* (Hart Publishing 2003)

Walker N, 'European Constitutionalism in the State Constitutional Tradition' (2006) 59 *Current Legal Problems* 51

Walker N, 'Reconciling MacCormick: Constitutional Pluralism and the Unity of Practical Reason' (2011) 24(4) *Ratio Juris* 369

Walker N, 'Constitutional Pluralism Revisited' (2016) 22(3) *European Law Journal* 333

Weatherill S, *Law and Integration in the European Union* (OUP 1995)

Weatherill S, 'Competence Creep and Competence Control' (2004) 23(1) *Yearbook of European Law* 1

Weatherill S, 'The Limits of Legislative Harmonization Ten Years after Tobacco Advertising: How the Court's Case Law Has Become a "Drafting Guide"' (2011) 12(3) *German Law Journal* 827

Weatherill S, *Law and Values in the European Union* (OUP 2016)

Weiler J H H, 'Journey to an Unknown Destination: A Retrospective and Prospective of the European Court of Justice in the Arena of Political Integration' (1993) 31(4) *Journal of Common Market Studies* 417

Weiler J H H, 'A Quiet Revolution: The European Court of Justice and Its Interlocutors' (1994) 26(4) *Comparative Political Studies* 510

Weiler J H H, 'Does Europe Need a Constitution? Demos, Telos and the German Maastricht Decision' (1995) 1(3) *European Law Journal* 219

Weiler J H H, 'The Reform of European Constitutionalism' (1997) 35 *Journal of Common Market Studies* 95, 106.

Weiler J H H, *The Constitution of Europe. "Do the New Clothes have an Emperor?" and other Essays on European Integration* (CUP 1999)

Weiler J H H, 'Prologue: Global and Pluralist Constitutionalism: Some Doubts' in G de Búrca and J H H Weiler (eds), *The Worlds of European Constitutionalism* (CUP 2012)

Weiler J H H and Lockhart N J S, '"Taking Rights Seriously" Seriously: The European Court and Its Fundamental Rights Jurisprudence – Part I' (1995) 32(1) *Common Market Law Review* 51

Wendel M, 'Lisbon before the Courts: a Comparative Perspective' (2011) 7 *European Constitutional Law Review* 96

Wendel M, 'Judicial Restraint and the Return to Openness: The Decision of the German Federal Constitutional Court on the ESM and the Fiscal Treaty of 12 September 2012' (2013) 14 *German Law Journal* 21

Wendel M, 'Paradoxes of Ultra-Vires Review: A Critical Review of the PSPP Decision and Its Initial Reception' (2020) 21 *German Law Journal* 979

Wiener A and Diez T (eds), *European Integration Theory* (2nd edn, OUP 2009)

de Witte B, 'The Lisbon Treaty and National Constitutions: More or Less Europeanisation?' in C Closa (ed), *The Lisbon Treaty and National Constitutions: Europeanisation and Democratic Implications* (Oslo Centre for European Studies 2009)

de Witte B, 'Internal Market Law and National Language Policies' in K Purnhagen and P Rott (eds), *Varieties of European Economic Law and Regulation:* Liber Amicorum *for Hans Micklitz* (Springer 2014)

Yein Ng G, 'Judicialisation and the End of Parliamentary Supremacy: Shifting Paradigms in the Protection of the Rule of Law and Human Rights in the UK, France and the Netherlands' (2014) 3 *Global Journal of Comparative Law* 50

Zalnieriurte M, 'A Struggle for Competence: National Security, Surveillance and the Scope of EU Law at the Court of Justice of European Union' (2022) 85(1) *MLR* 198, 207

van Zeben J and Bobić A, *Polycentricity in the European Union* (CUP 2019)

Ziller A, 'National Constitutional Concepts in the New Constitution for Europe' (2005) 1(2) *European Constitutional Law Review* 247

# Index

*For the benefit of digital users, indexed terms that span two pages (e.g., 52–53) may, on occasion, appear on only one of those pages.*

Tables and figures are indicated by *t* and *f* following the page number